DEPRESSION, EMOTION AND THE SELF

Philosophical and Interdisciplinary Perspectives

Edited by

Matthew Ratcliffe and Achim Stephan

imprint-academic.com

Published in the UK by
Imprint Academic Ltd, PO Box 200, Exeter EX5 5YX, UK

Distributed in the USA by
Ingram Book Company,
One Ingram Blvd., La Vergne, TN 37086, USA

ISBN 9781845407489

A CIP catalogue record for this book is available from the
British Library and US Library of Congress

This volume was originally published as a special issue of the
Journal of Consciousness Studies, **20** (7–8).

Cover image by Beth J. Ross.

Contents

Part III: Body & Culture

Part IV: Phenomenological and Neurobiological Perspectives

Matthew Ratcliffe, Achim Stephan and Somogy Varga

Introduction

First-person accounts of depression almost always emphasize the extent to which depression departs from what is — for most of us — 'everyday experience'. It is often described as akin to inhabiting a different world, a suffocating, alien realm that is isolated from the rest of social reality. On the basis of a very substantial body of testimony, it seems that depression is not simply a matter of certain unpleasant emotions being heightened while other emotions are diminished. The phenomenological changes that the depressed person undergoes are somehow more profound than that. They involve a qualitative shift in the overall structure of experience, encompassing self, agency, the body, temporal experience, interpersonal relations, and the sense of being rooted in a world. Many sufferers add that this shift or some aspect of it is indescribable, ineffable, and that the various metaphors they appeal to are ultimately inadequate to the task. Furthermore, some state that an inability to communicate the experience of depression exacerbates the sense of alienation that is already so central to it. When we turn to diagnostic manuals, matters are no clearer; skeletal descriptions of the various symptoms that are together sufficient for one or another diagnosis do nothing to further illuminate the kinds of phenomenological change that patients struggle to describe.

Hence an aim of this volume is to draw upon work in philosophy and other disciplines in order to cast light upon poorly understood experiences that are associated (but, most likely, not exclusively associated) with depression. 'Depression', construed broadly, is consistent with a range of diagnoses. However, most of our contributors emphasize kinds of experience that would be compatible with a DSM-IV or DSM-5 diagnosis of 'major depression'. A further aim of the book is to draw upon the phenomenology of depression in order to better understand the structure of experience more generally. By contrasting the phenomenology of depression with 'everyday' experience, we can draw attention to and attempt to describe aspects of the latter that might otherwise be overlooked. It is also our hope that this kind of enquiry will have some kind of practical application. In so far as failure to understand depression experiences can itself exacerbate them or at least hinder therapy, the results of phenomenological studies have the potential to inform clinical work. Furthermore, an increased understanding of what it is like to experience depression may benefit those who live or work with people who suffer from depression.

The principal focus of the volume is upon moods, feelings, and emotions, although that focus is far from exclusive. The theme of 'depression, emotion, and the self' intersects with a wide range of topics, including selfhood, motivation, the body, intersubjectivity, and world-experience. Furthermore, most contributors emphasize kinds of affective state that are generally neglected by discussions of mood and emotion in philosophy and the sciences. First-person reports of depression often describe a kind of all-enveloping affective change that permeates every aspect of experience. Hence, unlike many accounts of emotional states, the chapters in this collection tend not to concern themselves principally with intentional states that have specific contents. 'Affect', in the sense that is central to depression, is inextricable from experiences of self, belonging to a world, and being with other people. Another prominent theme of the volume is interdisciplinarity; contributors share the view that, in order to understand the nature of emotional experience in depression, one needs to draw upon and bring together work in a range of disciplines.

The chapters are grouped into four sections. The first three pieces are all concerned with 'self and agency'. **Svenaeus** investigates the relationship between selfhood and depression. He offers a phenomenological analysis that focuses upon the body's capacity to engage in different patterns of resonance or 'attunement' to the world. Svenaeus argues that, while boredom, anxiety, and grief are to be described as ways of 'being-in-the-world', depression is characterized by a deficiency of bodily resonance that alienates the self from the world. **Slaby, Paskaleva and Stephan** then defend a broadly enactive approach to understanding emotions, which resists the common view according to which emotions are mental states that can be characterized in isolation from agency and action. They apply this approach to the affective aspects of depression. Drawing upon patient reports, they interpret affective changes in depression as something like a 'mirror image' of human affectivity, where the core impairment

involves an altered sense of agency. Their discussion is comple-
mented by the work of **Benson, Gibson and Brand**, who draw upon
an empirical investigation of 'suicidal feelings' in individuals suffering from psychiatric illness. Rather than describing these feelings in
cognitive terms (as suicidal ideations), the authors identify them as
'existential feelings', feelings that constitute an all-enveloping back-
drop to experience of self, world, and other people. Benson, Gibson
and Brand invoke a complex concept of agency that takes into account
the embodied and (socio-culturally) embedded nature of our affective
lives. Drawing on this, they argue that, in 'suicidal feelings', experience of the self as agent is disrupted in several ways.

The next four chapters all address the comparative phenomenology
of depression. They explore the similarities and differences between
experiences associated with depression and other psychiatric diagnoses, as well as addressing whether such differences should be
regarded as superficial or profound. **Radden** considers those moods
that are distinctive of depressive and manic states, and offers an
account of their relationship with more cognitive states. It is often
maintained that schizophrenia-spectrum disorders involve disruptions in pre-reflective self-experience and that this makes them distinctive. However, Radden argues that affective or mood disorders
also involve disruption of the self, albeit on a different level, hinder-
ing self-integration. This is because moods in depression and mania
are inflexible, resistant to change, and thus interfere with first-person
evaluation of their effects on judgment and response. Moreover, they
tend to impede certain types of self-knowledge and give rise to
epistemic deficits, thus reducing the capacity for agency. Two chapters by **Sass and Pienkos** follow. Their first chapter addresses some
apparent similarities between experiences of self in schizophrenia and
in affective disorders like melancholia and mania, which might seem
to blur the phenomenological boundaries between them. These,
according to Sass and Pienkos, in fact hide more profound differences. Drawing upon findings obtained with the EASE (a research
tool for phenomenological psychopathology used to study experiential changes in five domains of selfhood), they argue that the most
basic sense of self — the 'minimal self' — remains intact in affective
disorders, while it is disrupted in schizophrenia. In a second chapter,
Sass and Pienkos continue their investigation into the comparative
phenomenology of schizophrenia, melancholia, and mania, but shift
the focus from self-experience to world-experience. They supply a
comparative study of subtle similarities and differences in anomalous

perceptions of the world, relating to experiences of space and objects, events and time, and general atmosphere. While some degree of 'alienation' from the world is a common theme, Sass and Pienkos argue that there is a distinctive 'uncanniness' to schizophrenic experience. Then, **Stanghellini and Rosfort** turn to the emotional dimensions characteristic of borderline depression, in contrast to melancholic depression. Borderline individuals frequently experience intense emotional fluctuations and disproportionate emotional reactions, associated with lack of a stable sense of self-identity. Stanghellini and Rosfort argue that these complex emotional characteristics are attributable to trait-like dysphoric moods that lack intentional structure and that simultaneously involve a sense of fragmentation and of vitality (hence a 'desperate vitality').

The next four chapters turn to the theme of 'body and culture'. **Carel** draws attention to a tacit, non-rational, and ordinarily pre-reflective sense of certainty, which is anchored in our bodily, animal nature and shapes much of our everyday experience. She goes on to investigate a pervasive feeling of 'bodily doubt' that replaces the experience of certainty in many instances of somatic and psychiatric illness, resulting in profound phenomenological changes. **Ratcliffe, Broome, Smith and Bowden** also emphasize the extent to which depression experiences are 'bodily'. They draw upon patient reports that describe a wide range of bodily symptoms. In addition, they stress the extent to which somatic illness, like depression, involves more than just 'bodily' experience. Turning to the inflammation theory of depression, Ratcliffe, Broome, Smith and Bowden argue that some experiences of major depression are phenomenologically indistinguishable from some experiences of somatic illnesses such as influenza. However, they add that matters are complicated by the considerable heterogeneity of what goes by the name 'depression'. In the chapter that follows, **Fuchs** relates bodily experience in depression to the theme of cultural difference. He considers anthropological findings indicating that, in certain non-western cultures, affective disorders are construed as bodily, interpersonal, or even atmospheric processes. He also relates these anthropological findings to complementary work in phenomenological psychopathology, and analyses depression as a disorder that characteristically involves an affective and bodily 'detunement'. Following this, **Csordas** considers some interview data relating the experiences of adolescent psychiatric inpatients. Guided by phenomenological anthropology, his examination of empirical material focuses on subtle themes that characterize patients' talk about their illnesses. Csordas's method seeks to disclose aspects of the concrete 'experiential immediacy' of the affliction, while remaining sensitive to the fact that 'depression' may refer to a diagnosis or a feeling, and also function as a discursive token.

The three chapters that make up the final section touch on some of the issues already raised but are also explicitly concerned with the relationship between phenomenological and neurobiological perspectives. **Gerrans and Scherer** appeal to Multicomponential Appraisal Theory (MAT), and also to the concept of 'existential feeling', in order to explain the relationship between the neurobiology of depression and its phenomenology, while at the same time accounting for the efficacy of selective serotonin re-uptake inhibitors (SSRIs). They connect MAT with existential feelings by arguing that the latter arise as effects of shifts in appraisal patterns. Next, **Gaebler, Lamke, Daniels and Walter** focus more specifically upon an experience that is common to depersonalization disorder (DPD) and to some types of depression. In order to characterize it, they formulate an account of 'phenomenal depth', arguing that both DPD and depression involve reduced phenomenal depth, something that permeates experience of self, body, and world. Then they relate their account of depth to neurocognitive studies, and conclude by addressing the neurobiological basis of phenomenal depth. Finally, **Buchheim, Viviani and Walter** investigate the relationship between deficient attachment patterns, which are often traceable to negative life events in childhood, and depression. They consider empirical studies that link both borderline personality disorder and major depression to 'disorganized' attachment. They also show how successful therapy for depression can be associated with changed attachment patterns, which are correlated with altered patterns of activation in specific brains areas.

This volume arose out of the Anglo-German project, 'Emotional Experience in Depression: A Philosophical Study' (2009–12), in which most of the contributors were involved. We are very grateful to the UK Arts and Humanities Research Council (AHRC) and to the Deutsche Forschungsgemeinschaft(DFG) for supporting the project.

Fredrik Svenaeus

Depression and the Self
Bodily Resonance and Attuned Being-in-the-World

1. Introduction

That the suffering of depression has an impact on selfhood may seem like a rather self-evident claim. Every severe and/or chronic illness has a deep reaching impact on the identity of its bearer (Kleinman, 1988b), and depression is surely no exception in this regard (Karp, 1996). To a large extent, for psychiatry, as John Sadler notes, 'the phenomenological foreground *is* the self, the psyche, even, perhaps, the whole person' (Sadler, 2004, p. 165). Also, considering the tradition of psychoanalysis in which depression has often been thought to be dependent on an early abandonment suffered by the depressed person, a loss that has been turned into grief and self-hate, the claim that depression affects the self does not appear novel or exciting (Freud, 1957). Nevertheless, considering the diagnostic and biological turn in psychiatry and the present distrust put in psychoanalytic aetiology, I find it important to reconsider the ways in which depression and selfhood form interdependent phenomena.

The idea behind this chapter is to pursue a phenomenology of depression in order to determine in what way depression depends on personality traits and may affect selfhood in changing the experiences of the depressed person. To understand the structure of human experience I think we need to acknowledge that experience is always embodied and world-dependent, but also an ongoing creative effort of bringing meaning into the world by way of intentionality, and phenomenology allows us to do this in a sustained way. Psychiatry is a mixed discipline, and phenomenology, in my view, offers a kind of neutral ground on which it is possible to relate and connect the many different approaches to mental disorders that we find in the field.

My phenomenological attempt to investigate in what ways depression and self hang together does not proceed from any specific empirical investigation made by myself or others, instead it is primarily a philosophical attempt to analyse the question from a conceptual perspective. The first-person perspective will in this attempt be used as the pivotal point of analysis to which I will try to bring thoughts developed by phenomenological philosophers — Martin Heidegger and Thomas Fuchs — as well as accounts and results reported by empirical researchers investigating depression.

2. Diagnostic Psychiatry and the Self

In the introduction to DSM-IV-TR we find the following claim:

> A common misconception is that a classification of mental disorders classifies people, when actually what are being classified are disorders that people have. For this reason, the text of DSM-IV (as did the text of DSM-III-R) avoids the use of such expressions as 'a schizophrenic' or 'an alcoholic' and instead uses the more accurate but admittedly more cumbersome, 'an individual with Schizophrenia' or 'an individual with Alcohol Dependence'. (DSM-IV-TR, 2000, p. xxxi)

If this were true, there would probably be no point in investigating how different mental disorders, such as depression, are self-dependent in the double sense of being affected by and affecting personality traits. But the claim found in the introduction to the DSM is obviously not true, at least not if self and personality are interpreted in an everyday sense. Many diagnoses in the DSM are established by checking symptoms and behaviours that are very clearly related to issues of selfhood and personality. And, as many critiques of the new diagnostic psychiatry have pointed out, most diagnoses in the manual do *not* rest on the identification of disorders in the sense of something simply *had* by the individual, which it would be possible to detect without judgments about *who* she is (her life history) (Horwitz and Wakefield, 2007). The interpretation of life-world matters is a necessary part of psychiatry to a much larger extent than in the somatic medicine of diseases, a field which the authors of the DSM, in the quote above, are clearly trying to gain credibility from by way of analogy.

Now, while the authors of the DSM want to claim that the concept of disorder with which they are working — 'a clinically significant behavioural or psychological syndrome or pattern that occurs in an individual and that is associated with present distress (e.g., a painful symptom) or disability (i.e., impairment in one or more important areas of functioning) or with a significantly increased risk of suffering death, pain, disability, or an important loss of freedom' (DSM-IV-TR, 2000, xxxi) — is *categorical* in nature, a study of the different diagnoses in the manual clearly brings out that the way in which disorders are approached is instead *dimensional* in nature: the disorders overlap by degrees with unwanted or despised, yet still normal, experiences and behaviours of people which are to a large extent personality dependent.

In the case of depression, the suspicion that there is an overlap between disorder and personality traits is also made strong by the history of melancholy, the concept which preceded depression in identifying individuals suffering from an overwhelming sadness (Radden, 2000). Ironically, the term melancholy disappeared from the vocabulary of psychiatry around the year 1900, only to be rehabilitated by contemporary psychiatry. It is used in the DSM-IV-TR to describe a specified subtype of depression characterized by deep, persistent boredom (DSM-IV-TR, 2000, p. 419). In twentieth-century psychiatry, this form of depression has been qualified by many different adjectives — 'endogenous', 'vital', 'biological' — all contaminated, however, by aetiological hypotheses, which has made the designations unsuitable for DSM classification. Even more important in this context is the reappearance of the old notion of 'dysthymia' in the DSM, a notion similar to melancholia in its denotation of a certain temperament or personality type (*ibid.*, p. 376).

While the concept of melancholy in all its historical mentions and uses is clearly not the same thing as depression — melancholy is in fact far from a uniform concept, since it expresses rather different problems and positions during different historical epochs — the hypothesis of certain temperament traits being central to the development of melancholy raises the suspicion that such traits may be central to the suffering of depression, too. Considering more recent hypotheses on selfhood and depression, serotonin is sometimes considered to be the modern black bile of depression (affecting the feeling of self-esteem as well as depression). However, brain scientists are far from a position in which they would be able to examine in what ways the biology of depression affects the self, and vice versa, since they have too little knowledge of the neurophysiology of the self and the pathology of depression to be able to research this in any detailed way. Nevertheless, the physiology of feelings appear to be central to both things (see Damasio, 1999), and this finding of brain physiology, as we will see, squares well with the phenomenology of depression.

3. Depression:
Disease of the Brain or Illness of the Self?

The psychiatrist Peter Kramer claimed in his bestseller *Listening to Prozac* (1994) that the new antidepressants (SSRIs) effect self-changes. However, in his later book, *Against Depression* (2005), he makes a 180-degree U-turn and tries to convince us that depression is really nothing other than a biological disease, which has very little to do with questions of selfhood. The arguments he gives are, however, far from convincing. Kramer, in the same way as the authors of the DSM, seems to accept the idea that mental disorders are categorical in nature. This, in combination with the idea that depression is really nothing else than a biological dysfunction of the brain, fosters the conclusion that the depressed brain simply houses a healthy self, which might be prevented from full expression, or perhaps be injured by the disease of depression but not fundamentally altered by it.

The disease model of depression, however, does not capture the way in which depression shows up as a creature *invading* the self and taking control over it, an account found in most reports given by depressed people (also the ones found in Kramer's two books). Depression in this way is much more of an illness than a disease, it shows up on the same phenomenological level of experience as the self when it makes itself known. Nor does the disease model capture the way in which depression, as a more or less chronic illness, ultimately, for good or bad, is acknowledged by the sufferer as something belonging to her identity. To illustrate this, I will now quote two typical accounts given by people suffering from depression from a book by David Karp — *Speaking of Sadness: Depression, Disconnection, and the Meanings of Illness*:

> Depression is an insidious vacuum that crawls into your brain and pushes your mind out of the way. It is the complete absence of rational thought. It is freezing cold, with a dangerous, horrifying, terrifying fog wafting throughout whatever is left of your mind... Depression steals away whoever you were, prevents you from seeing who you might someday be, and replaces your life with a black hole. Like a sweater eaten by moths, nothing is left of the original, only fragments that hinted at greater capacities, greater abilities, greater potentials now gone. (Karp, 1996, pp. 23–4)

Depression in this way not only appears to be a disease that makes it harder for the person to get on with the life she enjoyed before depression hit her (as in the case of diabetes or arthritis), it appears to be an illness of the self itself (Jack, 1991). And, since depression as a more or less chronic illness (the depressive episodes most often recur) so thoroughly changes the identity of the person, the illness has to be lived with and integrated in the life story of the sufferer:

> I have a feeling of unpredictability and lack of control over something that has a life of its own [and] that contradicts my feeling of mastery. And I know that now. I've had this experience for so long that I am going to be up and that I am going to be down and I suppose it makes it a little bit easier. I mean, I know that it's going to happen. It is out of my control and therefore I shouldn't feel so dreadful when it does happen because it's just part of the rhythm of my life I suppose. (Karp, 1996, pp. 124–5)

If depression is not (only) a disease of the brain, what is it then really? Judging from the DSM the distinguishing characteristic of the disorder(s) is the presence of what is called 'a major depressive episode' (DSM-IV-TR, 2000, p. 356). This condition is thought to be present if a depressed mood (sadness, emptiness) and a loss of interest or pleasure have been present most of the day, nearly every day, for at least two weeks, and if, in addition to this, at least three of the following seven criteria have also been fulfilled during this period: significant weight change; insomnia or hypersomnia; psychomotor agitation or retardation; fatigue or loss of energy; feelings of worthlessness or excessive or inappropriate guilt; diminished ability to think or concentrate; and recurrent thoughts of death. These symptoms must also have resulted in 'clinically significant distress or impairment in social, occupational, or other important areas of functioning', and they should not have been directly caused by medication or bereavement.

Although depression, according to the DSM, does not include anxiety as a necessary ingredient of the disorder in question, it appears that people presently diagnosed with depression often have anxiety problems. Diagnostic tests for depression often include anxiety and anxiousness as parts of establishing if depression is present and how severe it is, and the most frequent treatments for depression are drugs that are also used to treat anxiety disorders (SSRIs) (Svenaeus, 2007; 2008). I will therefore include the issue of anxiety in my discussion of the phenomenology of depression below. Even if not every sufferer of depression will have anxiety attacks in the manner specified in the DSM (2000, p. 432), the presence of similar experiences, as well as the anxiousness and doubt about being able to do different things, appear to be typical of depression, especially in its milder forms (see many of the examples in Karp, 1996, and references in Solomon, 2001, p. 65). Symptoms such as psychomotor agitation or retardation, on the other hand, appear to be rare in most cases of depression presently diagnosed, and in diagnostic tests for depression, such as

MADRAS, it has, indeed, been replaced by anxiety as a diagnostic criterion (Svenaeus, 2008, p. 30).

Even if contemporary diagnostic psychiatry does not present us with any final definition or explanation of what depression is (and this is hardly surprising given the explicit aim of the DSM to stay clear of any aetiological hypotheses) or with any idea of how the different symptoms hang together (and this is perhaps worse, since it tends to isolate the different symptoms instead of linking them to a personal history of the sufferer), the list of criteria presented in the DSM provides good clues and starting points for phenomenological analysis: central to the diagnostic scheme of depression is the presence of painful *feelings* and of problems involving altered *embodiment* and estranged *engagement* with the *world*. The concepts of self and self-change, as I will try to show, are relevant to all three phenomena. Feelings have the power of overwhelming, plaguing, and deadening the self in a way that can feel like a parasitic overtaking.

4. Feelings and Being-in-the-World

The feelings that are characteristic of depression according to the overview above appear to be *boredom*, *sadness*, and *anxiety*. In his first major work *Being and Time*, originally published in 1927 (1986), and in the lecture course *The Fundamental Concepts of Metaphysics*, taught 1929–30 (1983), the phenomenologist Martin Heidegger offers extensive and in-depth analysis of the moods of anxiety and boredom respectively. In the two books, the two phenomena — anxiety and boredom — are assigned central, and in many ways parallel, places and functions. In later works, Heidegger also deals with the phenomenon of sadness (Haar, 1992).

What is particularly interesting with Heidegger's analyses is that he makes lucid that some feelings (moods) are *world constitutive* phenomena. Moods *open up* a world to human beings in which things *matter* to them in different ways. It is common in contemporary philosophy of feelings to make a distinction between sensations, emotions, and moods. Sensations have a distinct place in the body (pain), emotions have an object and are based upon beliefs (love or hate), whereas moods are not bodily and also lack a distinct object, they rather colour the way everything appears to the self (joy or sadness). This schematization has its roots in Aristotle and has been further developed in slightly different ways in the tradition of analytical philosophy (Goldie, 2000). What is central to the distinctions is that certain feelings — emotions — have a cognitive content: feelings are not merely passions, which lead the rational agent astray in his search for knowledge, feelings are indeed forms of knowledge in themselves.

Note, however, that this merely holds for emotions in this type of philosophy — in which an object of the feeling is involved — whereas in the case of sensations and moods the cognitive content is much harder to pinpoint and therefore tends to fall out of the analysis. This might appear adequate in the case of sensations, in which the possible cognitive content is very meagre in contrast to the content of emotions; for example that my finger hurts in contrast to the emotion of envy towards a certain person, a feeling that includes quite elaborate beliefs about the state of the world and the way I would like it to be. When it comes to moods, however, the lack of a distinct object of the mood in question seems to have forced the classic analysis in the wrong direction. Moods are, for sure, not something that contain thoughts in the same way that emotions do, but they are nevertheless determining which kinds of thoughts I will be able to develop by providing the general access to the way *all* things will appear to me. Moods, also, as Matthew Ratcliffe has recently pointed out, are, far from being devoid of bodily sensation, embodied in their very essence (Ratcliffe, 2008a). To feel anxiety, for instance, is a profoundly bodily experience, as any sufferer from a panic attack will know. Ratcliffe prefers 'existential feelings' to the label of moods in his book, but his central point is that these are bodily feelings and ways of finding oneself in the world at the same time, and not accidentally so. This link between moods and embodiment will be central to my attempt to understand the relationship between depression and selfhood in this chapter.

Feelings, especially in the form of moods, in Heidegger's phenomenology, are basic to our being-in-the-world, since they open up the world as meaningful, as having significance. They are the basic strata of what Heidegger refers to as *facticity*, our being thrown into the world prior to having made any thoughts or choices about it. We find ourselves *there*, always already busy with different things that matter to us, and this 'mattering to' rests on an *attunement*, a mood-quality which the being-in-the-world always already has (Heidegger, 1986, pp. 134ff; 1983, pp. 99ff). Every activity is attuned in a way that brings out its significance according to Heidegger. The different moods in question need not be powerful or directly paid attention to, but they are *there* as the constitutive ground of our being placed in the meaning pattern of the world. We do, indeed, not choose the moods we find ourselves to live in; the moods in question overwhelm us and cannot easily be changed.

Let us now come back to boredom, sadness, and anxiety. These are quite peculiar moods (or *Stimmungen* as the German language has it). What is special to these moods is that they do not only open but also *block* our possibilities to be in the world together with others. To Heidegger, such disturbing experiences as had in boredom, sadness, and anxiety carry important possibilities for phenomenological analysis itself. In these fundamental moods (*Grundstimmungen*) it becomes possible to catch sight of the very structure of the world and its meaningfulness in itself (Ferreira, 2002). No particular thing in the world matters anymore and therefore it becomes possible to address the meaning of the being-in-the-world *as such*. This situation brought about by the mood, according to Heidegger, is the possibility of an authentic, philosophically reflected life, which in contrast to the public anonymity of the 'they' (*das Man*) faces its finitude and accepts responsibility for its own choices (Heidegger, 1986, pp. 260ff).

I will not attempt to follow up on Heidegger's analysis of authenticity (*Eigentlichkeit*) and the 'they' here. His analysis is highly sophisticated and interesting, but also wanting in many ways which mainly have to do with Heidegger's treatment of intersubjectivity (Critchley and Schürmann, 2008). Instead I would like to focus upon some aspects of Heidegger's mood analysis that I think are fruitful for a phenomenology of depression and selfhood centred around the notion of alienation. Anxiety in *Being and Time*, and boredom in *The Fundamental Concepts of Metaphysics* are both characterized as *unhomelike* phenomena by Heidegger (1986, p. 189; 1983, p. 120). They make the settling, the being at home in the world, hard since the world resists meaningfulness. The world becomes alien, making us long for another place to be in. The key idea of authentic understanding in Heidegger is to develop this unhomelike-ness and home-longing to a kind of structural crescendo from which it is possible to make it productive for philosophical purposes. The problem from the point of view of psychiatry, however, seems to be that one might get stuck in these moods as destructive rather than productive life experiences. They can be so overwhelming that it becomes impossible to return to homelike-ness again. Unhomelike-ness might be a necessary part of life that can be rewarding in many ways, when it makes us see things in new and richer ways, but it needs to be balanced by homelike-ness if we are not to fall into a bottomless pit of darkness that makes us ill (Svenaeus, 2000, pp. 90ff).

Time is a key issue here; shorter periods of anxiety, boredom, and sadness might provide life with greater depth, whereas recurrent anxiety attacks and deep boredom and sadness that refuse to let go transform life in an unhomelike way which develops into pathology. It is important to realize, however, that such a focus on time, counting the hours, days, weeks, months, or even years of anxiety, boredom, and sadness, is not a phenomenologically developed understanding of time. The phenomenologist's interest is in *lived* time, time as our way of approaching the future from out of the past in the meaning-centred now. As the person suffering from depression will know, one second can pass in the blink of an eye or last for something which feels like an eternity. In anxiety the now is intensified, concentrated in a way that threatens to implode, whereas in boredom and sadness it is infinitely stretched out and inert. In both cases the now resists letting go of the person and forces her back upon herself by barring the flow of life which allows us to engage in matters of the world together with others. The feelings in question have a *lonesome* quality to them, and this is no doubt what fascinated Heidegger, as it has fascinated philosophers since the time of the Greeks. But, it is also in this non-chosen lonesomeness that the risk of pathology lies (Ratcliffe, 2008a, pp. 284ff).

5. Bodily Resonance and the Expressional Character of the World

Moods make a stepping out to the world of others possible by opening up a horizon of meaningfulness to live in. Consequently moods are not qualities of a self in contrast to the qualities of objects belonging to the world surrounding the self, but rather phenomena which *connect* the self to the world of others, making a being-*in*-the-world possible. I have stressed that moods are not chosen freely, but rather come to us as a basic predicament of being-in-the-world. This being the case, however, we seem to be presented by a basic problem in characterizing depression as *disorder* of mood, as a pathological phenomenon, in contrast to the boredom, sadness, and anxieties of everyday life. If moods are not qualities which essentially belong to the self, but rather a structure of being-in-the-world, how are we to understand the essential difference between being temporarily sad, bored, or anxious and being depressed? Why do some people 'get stuck' in these feelings in a way that transforms their being-in-the-world into a pathological condition of overwhelming unhomelike-ness, whereas others dwell in these moods more or less temporarily and are yet able to maintain a homelike being-in-the-world?

I would like to approach this question by making use of some concepts and distinctions developed by Thomas Fuchs in his study *Psychopathologie von Leib und Raum* (2000). Fuchs introduces the notion of '*leibliche Resonanz*' — bodily resonance — in explaining how the body 'picks up' moods in its way of connecting to the world of human projects. The lived body (*Leib*) is not only the central vehicle of our going outside ourselves to the world of others but it is so by its capability of being *affected* by the world in getting tuned. The lived body opens up a 'mood-space' — a '*Stimmungsraum*' — which our being-in-the-world can envelop, and it does so by acting as a kind of *resonance* box for moods, which are so to say still 'free-floating'; that is, which have not yet taken *hold* of the self. Fuchs views depression as a *loss* of bodily resonance, which makes the person no longer responsive to the call of the world and thus leads to being locked in (*ibid.*, pp. 104ff). The lived body is '*korporifiziert*' in depression, it is alienated as a stiffened, heavy thing, which no longer vibrates and opens up the mood-space necessary for a full-fledged, homelike being-in-the-world (*ibid.*, p. 102).

The obvious associations to music, which are present already in Heidegger's discussions of moods, and which are further strengthened by Fuchs' notion of bodily resonance, should not only be taken metaphorically, I believe, but rather as a reference to the most adequate vocabulary available in developing a phenomenology of depression. The closest we might come to describing what it means to be attuned is captured in the experience of how a piece of music sucks us into a pervasive mood, which colours our entire being-in-the-world. This is not to say that vision, smell, and touch are not part of the experience of becoming mooded; the attunement of human being-in-the-world rests on a bodily scheme in which the separate sense modalities have not yet been singled out, but work together in a primal unity (Gallagher, 2005).

Continuing Fuchs' analysis I would like to suggest that the lived body could become not only *devoid* of resonance, but also differently tuned in the sense of being more or less *sensitive* to different moods. In many cases of depression one might describe this as a being out of tune in the sense of only picking up the anxious, sad, and boring tune qualities of the world. This would allow us to elaborate on a spectrum stretching from a normal resonance of the lived body (the body being able to pick up a wide spectra of different moods) continuing over different kinds of sensitivities, preferences, and idiosyncrasies which might favour certain moods over others (different temperaments) to the cases which we would label pathologies (like depression) in the sense that the body is out of tune, or devoid of tune, as a tool of resonance.

But is it really correct to describe the body as a tool of resonance in the sense of picking up free-floating moods? Is not the mood to be understood as a *relation* between the self and the world, as an opening up of a space of meaning in which objects and other persons can be encountered? In what sense can moods be said to be present if somebody is not already experiencing them as sadness, joy, etc.? Fuchs' solution to this problem is to speak of 'atmospheres' rather than moods, when it comes to the features of the world that are not tied to the self but nevertheless have a particular tune to them (see also Schmitz, 1989). The world as something preceding our articulated interpretations, according to this phenomenological understanding, is not a senseless chaos, but rather a pattern of primordial 'expressional characteristics' (*Ausdruckscharaktere*) which allows for a lot of ambivalence and refinements, but still in a basic sense predetermines the ways we will connect to the world (Fuchs, 2000, p. 51).

It is important to not misunderstand this atmospheric influence on the lived body as a causal flux of sense data to be interpreted by the brain, if we want to stay true to the phenomenological mission of making sense of experience from a first-person perspective. Rather, the atmospheric influence should be viewed as the basic aspect of the world as a *constitutive* (not constituted) pattern of the self.

The standard phenomenological view on appearance (phenomenology as the science of that which shows itself: that is, appears, for the subject), starting out with Husserl, is that the self constitutes the world in its meaningfulness. From the first-person perspective the self and its different forms of experiences are not causal products of the physical stuff of reality; they are rather the necessary preconditions of the appearance of objects in the world in the first place. But this constitution of the world in its meaningfulness by the self cannot be the whole story of phenomenology. The physical set-up of the world around us in many ways determines what kind of objects it is possible to see, hear, smell, touch, and even fantasize about. The world is not only constituted by us, it also addresses us and affects us, it *draws* our attention in various ways, and this is exactly what Fuchs is getting at when he talks about 'atmospheres' and primordial 'expressional characteristics' of the world. That the world has an expressional characteristic means that it will draw our attention, and the most basic way of this to happen is precisely through a resonance of our bodies, which opens up a mood-space in which meaning can be developed through a being-in-the-world. Consequently the world is not only something constituted, it is also a *constituting* part of experience as something addressing us in an atmospheric way even before objects and other persons are clearly perceived and understood. If the lived body is unable to pick up these atmospheric traits we will have difficulties developing a rich, or even normal, being-in-the-word, and since the self attains its meaning and identity out of its being-in-the-world, it will suffer heavily from this basic deficiency of the lived body.

Connecting back to what I said about feelings and meaning above, the idea of a primal expressive pattern of the world could be viewed as a phenomenological attempt to rehabilitate not only moods but also sensations, to the realm of meaningfulness assigned to emotions, since it stresses the tune quality of the *body* as the most basic prerequisite of spotting appearances which underlie thought formation. In this context, the finding of a specific type of cells in the brain referred to as 'mirror neurons' should be mentioned (e.g. Ratcliffe, 2006). Such neurons make it possible for us to feel with others by mimicking their facial expressions and body postures before thinking anything about their predicaments. Maybe such neural structures are also set up to vibrate with expressional characteristics of the world that are not human bodies, but resemble them in various ways? Such scientific (third-person) investigations could support and be compatible with phenomenological (first-person) investigations of the moodedness of life.

6. The Unhomelike World of Depression

The lived body's position is the perspective from which the world can attain significance for a person. This position can be changed thanks to the body's mobility. Movement and perception are both sensorially and conceptually united (in kinaesthesis), as can be demonstrated by experiments in perception psychology (Gallagher, 2005). Perceiving is not the mind's window on the world; rather, it is a being-in, which establishes significance by way of moving and doing — making use of objects in establishing a world structure, as Heidegger shows in *Being and Time* when he introduces the notion of *tools* (*Zeuge*) in talking about the things of the world (1986, pp. 69ff). But the manipulation of concrete objects is just one aspect of human being-in-the-world. Our more complex capacities — to use language and create art, to think abstractly and develop theories, to form societies and write our history, and so on — enrich our world and endow it with a level of sophistication beyond simple tool use. Mental illness in its many forms is played out and attains significance in all these areas of selfhood; nevertheless, it has its roots in malfunctions of the lived body (Fuchs, 2002a).

Indeed, the phenomenological rendering of the lived body as an instrument of resonance seems to support the view that systematic alterations of the physiological organism (such as the inhibition, brought about by pharmaceuticals, of the reuptake of specific neuro-transmitters in the synapses of the brain) could alter the attunement of a person and thus the person's being-in-the-world as well (Svenaeus, 2007; 2009). The alien quality of depressed embodiment fits well with the idea of a disease process overwhelming the healthy organism. But, certainly, the qualities and contents of our being-in-the-world are not solely dependent upon what happens in our bodies — they are also dependent upon what happens in the world around us. Periods of depression are often triggered by specific events in the world — events that may or may not have something to do with the sufferer's personal history. Thus, the perspective of the lived body does not exclude the world, but rather points logically to it, and to the people who inhabit it.

A main characteristic of depression is the feeling of grief associated with guilt. The person suffering from depression seems to mourn the loss of somebody or something, and she often blames herself for this loss and for the feeling of worthlessness it has left behind. Grief can be described as a mood (sadness); but when, in the form of mourning, it is coupled to the loss of a specific object, it is an emotion. It seems, however, that most depressed people do not know what or whom they are missing or mourning; their grief becomes a mood-state, in the sense that it colours and determines their entire being-in-the-world in an unhomelike way.

In *Mourning and Melancholia*, written in 1915 (1957), Sigmund Freud seeks an explanation for the mourning and the feeling of guilt present in depression. As mentioned above, melancholia is the pre-modern term for depression and depressive personality traits. Freud's hypothesis in the essay is that the reason the melancholic (or depressed person) does not know what she is mourning is that the object of the feeling has been repressed and consequently made unconscious. Early in her life, the melancholic was abandoned by her mother, but this loss was too hard to bear, and it has therefore been repressed. The feelings of loss, desperation, and anger have instead been directed inwards, towards the melancholic herself, which explains the feelings of guilt and worthlessness.

There is, no doubt, something peculiar about the objectless grief and senseless self-blame of the depressive mood and depressive being-in-the-world that makes these states different from the sadness and self-criticism of everyday life. However, abstaining from evaluating the credibility of Freud's hypotheses, we should note that the unhomelike quality, outlined above, of moods being rooted in an embodiment that is out of tune can be said to be grounded in a primal loss made visible by the phenomenological analysis itself. The loss in question is not only a loss of the world, but also a loss of oneself, since it is only within the meaning patterns of being-*in*-the-world that one's identity can be established and one's life carried out. Here we have an explanation for the fact that the grief and guilt of depression fail to find 'normal' objects (that is, objects in the world) and are instead redirected towards the self. The grief of depression is a mood rather than an emotion since it suffuses the lonesome world of the melancholic in its entirety, and since it tends, owing to this lonesomeness, to reflect back on the melancholic herself.

7. Depression and the Self: Some Conclusions

Through the phenomenological analysis above, we have established that feelings like boredom, anxiety, and grief are constitutive of our being-in-the-world, but that they can also develop into pathologies such as depression. In the latter case, the self is no longer capable of engaging in a normal being-in-the-world, but is instead consigned to a painful, unrelenting unhomelike-ness. As we have seen, our being as worldly situated selves rests essentially on the attuned understanding of the body. The self is, according to Heidegger, open to the world; it is disclosed (*erschlossen*), in that it makes itself *at home* in the world (Heidegger, 1986, p. 54). This openness is a form of hospitality toward the world — a constant striving to find a place for new phenomena in the meaning pattern of the world, in order to make sense of them. Nevertheless, this openness and hospitality to the world, which is constitutive of the being of the self, resting on a bodily resonance, can be brought out of tune in various ways and depression is one example (or maybe, better, set of examples, considering the wide variety of attunement problems that are presently diagnosed as depression in the DSM).

Thus, the self is grounded in a bodily-attuned resonance, which makes transcendence to the world possible; but since the self *is* its being-in-the-world, it cannot be thought of as existing 'outside of' or 'prior to' this relation of being-in. If bodily resonance is too restricted, the formation of the self will not be possible; but, once established, what happens to the person in its being-in-the-world will alter bodily resonance in a variety of ways. Think about how falling in love, or being betrayed by the one you love, will change your attunement and thereby your entire way of responding to the call of the world. Antidepressants alter the concentrations of neurotransmitters in the synapses of the brain; therefore, their effects at the phenomenological, everyday level can be thought of in terms of alterations of bodily resonance — alterations that make new forms of transcendence to the world possible. It is likely that these effects are not limited to cases of depression; but because antidepressants modulate the peaks of boredom, grief, and anxiety, which profoundly affect our transcendence, their effects will be most striking in these cases (Svenaeus, 2008).

Recall the DSM-IV criteria for a depressive episode quoted above: the episode should cause 'clinically significant distress or impairment in social, occupational, or other important areas of functioning' (DSM-IV-TR, 2000, p. 356). This is a life-world matter, dependent upon how the person and people around her (including family, friends, and the doctor) interpret things, it is not a matter of any scientific judgment. In the domain of (psychiatric) illness, the question of when someone is suffering from a disorder such as depression is in the end always determined by such normative judgments (Svenaeus, 2008). It is important to point out that this domain of the normal is getting smaller by the day, not only because doctors and scientists are learning more about diseases and becoming more adept at treating them, but also because the companies that manufacture and sell pharmaceuticals have a clear interest in expanding the domain of the abnormal (Healy, 2004). It is not only the case that doctors treat a state of the body because it *is* a disease; the body state *becomes* a disease precisely by virtue of the fact that it can be treated (Elliott, 2003).

Depression, as I have pointed out, alienates the self from the world of others and also from the future as something providing a meaningful set of possibilities for the depressed person. The moods affecting the depressed person, as we saw in the quotes I gave above from the book by Karp (1996), can be so overwhelming that they are perceived as a different creature taking over the self. Metaphors that are often used by depressed persons (or rather by persons who have come out of depressive episodes and try to describe these to others) are drowning, suffocating, descending into a bottomless pit of darkness, being in a dark storm at sea, being imprisoned in a cage, or blinded by a grey fog (*ibid.*, pp. 28–9).

The effects of depression on selfhood do not stop with changing our ways of tuning into, or, rather, not being able to tune into the world of others. By the change of our basic self-feelings depression has effects throughout the whole domain of being-in-the-world, finally altering the narrative plot which is connected to our ways of creating purpose and meaning in life. Depression as a diagnostic category becomes integrated in the life plot as the person goes through being diagnosed, hospitalized, or prescribed medication by a doctor. To be diagnosed as depressed may offer new opportunities to understand and deal with the powerful negative feelings which one has felt oneself to be suffocated by. To view the depression as a disease affecting one's physiology, but basically not one's self, in the way Kramer does in the book I referred to above (2005), is a strategy which can be enacted in order to be able to live better with and fight the negative feelings of depression. It is a strategy which is often encouraged by doctors and which fits well with trying out different pharmacological interventions to change the mood profile of the depressed person.

But the strategy of reifying depression as a disease of the brain only also has disadvantages as a way of integrating depression in a person's life story. Although antidepressants help many people to a better life, they do not cure the illness, but rather help keeping it under control. For some people antidepressants do not help at all, or lead to the suffering of side effects of different sorts. And the analogy to diabetes often employed by psychiatrists such as Kramer tends to hide the fact that depression is an illness which is *constituted* by mood attack, rather than any chemical imbalance which we have been able to map out as the cause of the depressive moods. Depression is suffered *and identified* at the phenomenological level of experience and therefore the self-change brought about by it had better be integrated in the life story of the person by a set of self-reflections that takes feelings and their role in life seriously. Phenomenology can help facilitate such self-reflection, pointing not only to the destructive power of moods like boredom, anxiety, and sadness, but also to how such moods may be productive to persons and societies in providing more honest and reflected ways of life than the contemporary trend of positive thinking (Ehrenreich, 2009).

Jan Slaby, Asena Paskaleva
and Achim Stephan

Enactive Emotion and Impaired Agency in Depression

1. Introduction

Ideally, the philosophical illumination of central dimensions of human existence and descriptive work on core features of mental illness can inform and stimulate one another. Philosophy can devise careful phenomenological descriptions and develop concepts that capture recurring elements of experience and behaviour. The clinical observation of the characteristic features of mental illnesses (such as schizophrenia, depression, or mono-thematic delusions) can provide stunning evidence of possible alterations in, and breakdowns of, experience. These observations allow us to take stock of extreme cases that offer insights into the potential dissociation of dimensions of experience and behaviour that seem otherwise integrated or unitary and thereby delineate the spectrum of normal mental functioning — often in surprising, not previously thought-of ways.[1]

We will attempt such a mutual illumination in the fields of philosophy of emotion and the study of experiential changes undergone by sufferers from depression. First, we will sketch an approach to emotion that conceives of emotional processes as intimately tied up with agency. We gain much, or so we want to claim, by understanding emotional processes as specific modifications of our active engagements with the world, in response to significant events in the environment. Such an action-oriented view of emotion is more illuminating than the

---

[1] There is a lot of high quality philosophical work that has been done this way in recent years; see, for example, Fuchs (2003; 2005a); Radden (2003); Ratcliffe (2008a; 2009b); Sass (1992); Stanghellini (2004).

more common construals of emotions as mental states *separate* from action or behaviour. Second, we will argue that some of the central experiential changes reported by sufferers from depression likely result from an affliction of agency: from an awkward dysfunction or disability of active goal-pursuit that goes along with a profound sense of inability and even incapacity, virtually paralysing the depressed person. This conspicuous impairment leaves the depressed patient in a state in which her vital dynamics and her active striving are strangely arrested, a state of utter incapacity to do anything, a state that likely gives rise to feelings of being frozen in one's situation, unable to reach out or make contact with the world or with other people. We will assess evidence for this agency-related impairment by drawing on reports of characteristic experiences of depressive conditions — patients claiming to be disconnected from the world, unable to perform even routine acts, or that simple actions require immense amounts of physical and mental effort. By assessing these reports, we undertake to estimate in how far a broad range of characteristic experiential changes reported by depressed patients might result from such a fundamental affliction of agency.

Thus, in all, we have set ourselves a dual task. We explore the extent to which experiential changes in depression might be traced back to a deep-seated agency-related impairment. In addition, we hope to contribute to a much broader agenda: namely, to shifting the dominating conceptual and theoretical framework of current philosophy of emotion away from narrow forms of mentalism towards an agency-centred, enactive understanding of emotional phenomena.

2. Agency-Centred Accounts of Emotions — Forerunners

While it might seem obvious to the layperson that emotion is in no small degree a matter of being moved to pursue or avoid what comes in view as either good or bad, and thus in an important sense an active behavioural capacity, many current philosophical views of the matter tend to neglect (or at any rate, downplay) the active nature of emotion itself (see, for example, Döring, 2007; Goldie, 2000; Nussbaum, 2001; or Roberts, 2003). On these dominant views, emotions are seen as a special class of evaluative mental states intentionally directed at certain objects or events in the world. Even the opposing camps of cognitivists and feeling theorists seem to agree with regard to the relatively low importance of agency in emotion. Active pursuit, these views suggest, might be consequent upon an episode of emotion, not

constitutive of it.[2] Such pronounced mentalistic tendencies in philosophical emotion theory risk setting us on the wrong track. Emotions,
while indeed intentionally oriented towards events or objects in the
world appraised as either good or bad, are primarily matters of active
striving — various and variable forms of pursuing the good and of
avoiding (or otherwise 'opposing') the bad.[3] Hence, emotions belong
to the broader class of active world-orientation (engagement, goal-
oriented striving, activity) and not to the narrow category of passive
mental states (feeling, perception, thought, or mental image viewed as
predominantly passive mental occurrences). As already suggested by
the word *emotion* itself, emotions are bodies dynamically set in
motion, not minds in static states. What *is* mental about emotions is
bound up inextricably with the overall behavioural orientation of the
emoter — as opposed to a self-standing dimension of evaluative content. Importantly, this view entails an understanding of emotions
essentially as *processes*: many emotions unfold dynamically over
time — not as self-same 'states', but changing and developing according to a specific trajectory in which the agent's behaviour and experience is in dynamic, coordinated exchange with significant goings-on
in the environment.

A view along these lines is neither new, nor something that is utterly
radical or surprising. In the twentieth century, some authors in the phenomenological tradition have proposed action-oriented approaches to
emotion. The first name to mention in this regard is Heidegger. In *Being
and Time*, Heidegger (1927/1962) aligns, albeit in an unconventional
way, with the Aristotelian tradition by conceiving of human existence
as 'care': a concernful, affectively situated striving that unites emotional, active, and discursive elements to form an intimate interplay.
Emotions, as *Befindlichkeit*, are construed as a basic relatedness to
what matters in contexts of active goal-pursuit, dynamically situating
agents (both individually and collectively) in spaces of possibilities

---

[2] The situation is partly different in the field of psychology of emotion: especially Frijda but
also Scherer stress the importance of action tendencies as an essential component of emotional episodes (see, e.g. Frijda, 1986; Scherer, 2005).

[3] It is important to stress that we are not advocating a simplistic understanding of emotional
valence. Talk of 'good' and 'bad' in relation to the emotion's intentional directedness is a
convenient shorthand for talking about the evaluative character of emotions — obviously
an immensely complex matter. Emotional evaluations, regardless of whether they are
understood in an enactive or a cognitivist way, are highly differentiated and variable, the
spectrum of both the 'good' and the 'bad' is enormous, and our emotions are capable of
tracking very fine evaluative nuances. Also, we are not claiming that value properties are
simply 'out there' in the world, fully independent of our emotional repertoires. With
regard to both these points, we follow in outline the holistic account of emotional evaluation developed by Bennett Helm (see Helm, 2001).

(*cf. ibid.*).[4] In part inspired by Heidegger, Merleau-Ponty likewise argues for the intimate entanglement of conscious experience with agency. In particular, he foregrounds the *lived body* as the medium of all relatedness to the world, and the lived body's most important characteristic is precisely the fact that it manifests an agent's potentialities, embodying a practical world-orientation in the mode of 'I can' or 'I can't'. Affectivity figures prominently in this picture of 'action in consciousness': neither the lived body nor agency are thought to be in any way separable from a felt, qualitative dimension (*cf.* Merleau-Ponty 1942/1963).

For a particularly vivid phenomenological approach to action in emotion, consider finally Sartre's *Sketch for a Theory of the Emotions* (1939/1994). Sartre construes emotions as 'magical transformations of the world', often (but not always) in response to obstacles, problems, or hindrances encountered by a person in the course of her activities. To Sartre, emotions are embodied engagements, often employed strategically (not always consciously), acted out in response to unwanted or unexpected disruptions of activities. An emotion is like a theatre play, the emoter is 'performing a drama' geared to a specific environment, so that certain activities or stances become appropriate, which is a process that usually balances social expectations with the individual's own standards. Sartre's emotions are acted-out strategies of social action and interaction instead of passive experiential occurrences.[5]

These phenomenological approaches find a present-day echo in what is discussed under the label of enactivism (Varela, Thompson and Rosch, 1991; Noë, 2004; Thompson, 2007). Enactivists understand the mental in general as constitutively bound up with agency: intentional relatedness to the world is a matter of skilful activity; talk

---

[4]   Our reading of Heidegger takes seriously his repeated insistence on the inseparability of the three dimensions constitutive of care, affectivity (*Befindlichkeit*), understanding (*Verstehen*), and discourse (*Rede*). Thus, while affectivity 'on its own' might be seen as a predominantly passive capacity among the care-constitutents, it just does not exist in isolation. Affectivity can only be properly understood as constitutive of the essentially *active, practical* world-orientation of *Dasein*, to which it contributes decisively in providing a sense of situational relevance, inseparable, in the strongest sense of the word, from an active orientation towards possibilities (see §12 and especially §28 of *Being and Time*, 1927/1962).

[5]   Robert Solomon has followed closely in Sartre's footsteps, in so far as he spelled out and defended a theory of emotions as essentially active, deliberate strategies or strategic choices (see Solomon, 1976). More recently, Paul Griffiths has advocated an approach of emotional content as 'action-oriented representations' and of emotions in general as 'Machiavellian', i.e. evolved strategic responses to socially significant situations. As an evolutionary naturalist, Griffiths works within a rather different theoretical framework than Solomon (see Griffiths, 2004; Griffiths and Scarantino, 2009).

of mental content is either abandoned entirely (Hutto, 2005) or reconceived as a dynamical feature of active, skilful engagement with the world — this is what it means to say that intentional content is 'enacted' (Noë, 2004). Emotions are no exception: fundamentally, they come in view as an organism's active orientation towards and pursuit of salient value features in the environment (Colombetti, 2007; Colombetti and Thompson, 2008).[6]

Thus, we are certainly charting familiar territory. On the other hand, however, the narrower field of philosophy of emotion has been reluctant to subscribe to action-oriented accounts of their subject matter. Rather, emotional episodes have been likened to perceptual states (Döring, 2007), to cognitive states such as judgments (Nussbaum, 2001), to mental images or construals (Roberts, 2003), or to embodied appraisals combined with a Jamesian feeling dimension (Prinz, 2004), but not to actions or activities.[7] Candidate principles for securing the diachronic unity of complex, temporally extended emotional processes or chains of emotions have usually been discussed in mentalist or cognitivist terms, whereas action has not received comparable attention in this area of philosophy.[8]

3. Starting Point: The Body in (E)motion

The proper starting point of a philosophical investigation into the nature of emotion is the lived body. 'Lived' has to be taken literally: when not asleep or totally exhausted, the lived body is constantly active — either it is striving, pursuing what it needs or what the person aims at, or it is seeking to avoid what appears as harmful, repellent, or threatening. Other ways in which the lived body is active include

---

[6]   We cannot enter into the intricate debates about the details of the enactive approach; for an encompassing discussion of the notion that systematically analyses enaction, especially in comparison with related concepts such as embodiment, embeddedness, and extendedness, see Wilutzky, Walter and Stephan (2011, esp. pp. 307–14). Another valuable resource that puts particular emphasis on the social situatedness and interpersonal functions of emotions is Griffiths and Scarantino (2009).

[7]   One might say that these approaches are all in some way or other still committed to the classical 'sandwich model of the mind' (Hurley, 1998) that understands the mental as being a matter of clearly distinguishable inputs (perception), outputs (behaviour), and some central processing in between (thought or cognition). Emotions are usually either placed on the input side (as similar to perception), or identified with a form of central processing, either by being themselves a kind of cognition or by being placed alongside it as an extra level of spread on the infamous sandwich. The point is of course to abandon the whole model as it is fundamentally inadequate to capturing a creature's mindedness (see Thompson, 2007).

[8]   A clear exception to this trend is Ratcliffe (2008a), whose account of 'existential feelings' is much closer to Heidegger and Merleau-Ponty in its emphasis, within a broadly emotion-theoretic approach, upon the capacities and potentialities of the lived body.

various directed movements, states of readiness to act, or of being attentively focused. These basic modes of activity are always already affect-imbued: they develop from or otherwise relate to a baseline of felt responsiveness to what matters as worthy of pursuit or avoidance (*cf.* Helm, 2001; 2002). The lived body is always also a *feeling body* — a medium of evaluative world-orientation in the mode of pursuit or avoidance, and likewise a resonance field in which the successes or failures of one's active operations are registered immediately in the form of positive or negative feelings — feelings that modify one's activities from within, keeping them oriented towards their goals or within a zone of satisfaction (*cf.* Damasio, 1999; 2010; Prinz, 2004; Slaby, 2008; Ratcliffe, 2008a; Colombetti and Ratcliffe, 2012).[9]

From this basic embodied activity we can both look up — towards the embeddedness of individual agency in social practice and social structures — and look down, to the more basic bodily building blocks out of which sequences of goal-directed striving are constituted. These latter processes are patterns of directed, expressive movements characteristic of all animal life — what Daniel Stern has recently described as 'forms of vitality' (Stern, 2010). According to Stern, forms of vitality are the various expressive movement patterns that make up the basic processes of life and that fuse together movement, lived force, extension over time, the occupation of lived space, as well as basic directionality — the latter not yet in the form of explicit intentions, but often already oriented towards an end point, an anticipated goal-state implicit in the dynamic process. Vitality forms are the basic flow patterns of animal movement and the most fundamental ingredient of felt experience. Examples Stern gives include 'the force, speed, and flow of a gesture; the timing and stress of a spoken phrase or even a word; the way one breaks into a smile… the manner of shifting position in a chair; the time course of lifting the eyebrows when interested and the duration of their lift; the shift and flight of a gaze…' (*ibid.*, p. 6). What is important for our purposes is that Stern does not conceive of vitality forms as mere primitive movements without intentionality, but that he views them as natural Gestalts conjoining movement, time,

---

[9]   With this, we also have reconstructed the important sense in which emotions display an element of passivity, as has rightly been claimed by many authors working on 'the passions': the crucial point is that this affective responsiveness or receptivity is inextricable from active striving, as a guiding orientation intrinsic to this active dimension, concretely manifested as a varying sense of ability and possibility, sense of effort, a sense for potential obstacles and hindrances, and so on. It is important, however, not to overstate passivity and overlook the extent to which emotions are forms of engagement, initiative, and active positioning (with regard to this, we are very much in line with Sartre, and also with Robert Solomon's repeated insistence on the active nature of emotions; see Solomon, 1976).

force, space, *and intention* (*cf. ibid.*, pp. 6–8). Thus, forms of vitality are proto-actions in that they orient dynamic movement in a directional, pre-intentional way. Accordingly, vitality forms can become the building blocks of intentional activity.

Another, related point that is of considerable importance concerns the *interpersonal* character of these expressive bodily movement patterns. Stern's vitality forms are interpersonal from the start — they make up the currency of embodied interaction (*cf. ibid.*, pp. 106–9; see also Reddy, 2008). Accordingly, through their expressive lived bodies, human infants are from the outset placed and oriented in interpersonal, interactive space. The lived body is not in the first instance an individualized medium of agency and engagement, but a fundamental player in the pervasive game of social interaction — it is thus always already socially shaped and shared, influenced and infiltrated. In the same way, the world itself is from the outset a *shared* arena of significance; its intersubjective disclosedness takes precedence over any individualized realm that an adult person might idiosyncratically construe later in life. This fundamentally interpersonal character of the root dimension of affectivity — and likewise of the world itself as that which affective engagement always relates to — will become particularly relevant in our analysis of depressive experience presented below.

Approaching embodied activity from the other side, namely, that of its embeddedness within social structure and social practice, it becomes clear that much of the default mode of routine activity is spent by the adult person's being invested in projects or programmes of organized social action, often via enrolment in age-, status-, or occupation-related institutions (family, education, workplace, etc.). Much of our routine activity is in this way *socially* framed, prompted, and scaffolded (see Griffiths and Scarantino, 2009).

An important intermediate dimension between basic movement patterns and socially framed and organized action deserves more attention here. Besides clear-cut goal-oriented actions, much of a person's default activity — the constant baseline of activity that is present even when a person seemingly is not overtly engaged in a concrete doing — consists in conscious (or not so conscious) *social positioning*: these are the various ways we constantly orient ourselves towards, among, and with others in the various social situations that make up our lives. Here, very basic vitality forms and patterns of expressive movement directly link up with more sophisticated forms of social interaction, contributing to the complex fabric of organized interpersonal commerce in the life-world of civilized man. This pervasive positioning in and navigation through social space plays a particularly relevant role in the active process dynamics of emotion.

In line with all this, characteristic emotional episodes such as fear, anger, joy, sadness, shame, disappointment, pride, envy (and so on) can be described as the various modifications — and sometimes complications — of a basic process of active pursuit. As such, emotions are at any time embedded within social constellations of various sorts, aligned with the intentions, projects, and doings of others.

Let us consider a few examples. Fear is a reorientation of one's current pursuit in response to what is apprehended as dangerous — often in the form of a disruption of the previous behaviour and in a repositioning of oneself so as to avoid the threat. Anger is likewise an emphatic repositioning of oneself in response to an offence — with aggressive or confronting acts either openly directed at the person, group, or institution identified as the offender, or acted out symbolically in forms of expressive behaviour, or in the form of somewhat more self-related aggression or energetic withdrawal. Shame might seem at first sight to be a special case as it freezes us in a social situation, often leaving little 'to do' for us apart from characteristic shame behaviours (submissive gestures, avoiding the gaze of others, striving to disappear out of sight), but also here we find a strong orientation towards a repositioning of oneself in relation to others, to the witnesses of one's shameful deed or unfavourable characteristic. This repositioning, even if only a matter of posturing or gaze-direction, is clearly a mode of active striving. In joy, the process of goal-pursuit often has already reached its goal — in these cases, we rather find a tendency towards enhanced expression, sometimes including a symbolic 'taking possession' or attempted 'total consumption' of the object of one's joy (as described nicely by Sartre, 1939/1994, pp. 46–7). Sadness, on the other hand, is a harsh disruptor of activity, often a quite paralysing experience in which active pursuit is suspended almost entirely. In part depending on the severity of the loss suffered, the paralysis involved in sadness assumes different degrees of intensity, either remaining clearly circumscribed or overflowing into an all-enveloping passivity. Here, something resembling the phenomenal signature of depression as a clinical condition begins to shine through — the severely saddened person has temporally embarked upon the road into an encompassing passivity and incapacity that is characteristic of depressive experience.

4. Emotions and the Sense of Ability

One consequence of our action-oriented approach is that emotions are quite closely linked to an agent's *awareness of ability*. Emotions, as processes of active striving and engagement with the world, are intimately bound up with a sense of what we can do, what we are capable of, and what we can cope with or what we are able to 'take' more generally. More specifically, this affective sense of ability also differentiates between different degrees of effort necessary for performing specific tasks, or effort needed in countering opposition or resisting temptation. In this way, the emotion's intentionality might be glossed, with a nod to Merleau-Ponty, as an '*I can*'- or '*I can't*'-schema of relating to the world — a highly differentiated, embodied sense of capability (or its marked opposite, a specific sense of *in*ability or *in*capacity in relation to what confronts one, including a sense of particular resistances or partial breakdowns or slowing of one's activity).

Depending on this changeable background sense of ability, various individual emotions take shape and play out in their characteristic forms under varying circumstances (*cf.* Slaby, 2012). How I affectively engage with a situation is thus a function of my embodied sense of ability combined with the relevant features of the situation in as much as these are accessible to me. In this way, it is adequate to understand emotions as a complex *sense of possibility*: emotions disclose what a situation affords in terms of potential doings, and the specific efforts required in these doings, and potential happenings affecting me that I have to put up with or otherwise respond to adequately. These two aspects — *situational* (what is afforded by the environment) and *agentive* (what I can or cannot do) — are intimately linked to form a process of dynamic situation-access: an active, operative orientation towards the world.

5. Depression as an Impairment of Agency

Depending on this variable sense of ability and (potential or actual) agency, the world appears as a space of specific possibilities and as devoid of other possibilities, or as something remote and unreachable, or as a site of impending disaster, of threat and danger. This situatedness within varying spaces of possibilities is bodily felt, and these feelings are particularly pronounced when the possibilities change, such as when one is confronted by unexpected resistances or obstacles. These affective changes are especially striking and sustained in depressed patients, as will be illustrated in the sections to follow.[10]

We will draw mainly on material from an internet questionnaire study, which was conducted in 2011 as part of a research project on the experience of depression.[11] In addition, we provide quotations from published memoirs of depressive patients. The aim of the questionnaire is to provide a detailed description of what it is like to experience depression by posing questions particularly about different aspects of affective experience. Besides questions that request background information about the participants, such as age, gender, and specifics of psychiatric diagnoses, it mainly consists of questions dealing directly with personal experience in depression. These refer to experience of the world and others, of time, of one's body and one's abilities. The questionnaire obtained 147 complete responses, out of which 134 participants had a medical diagnosis of depression; two thirds of the respondents reported of being depressed at the time of writing. It also enquired about other psychiatric diagnoses, as depression has a high co-morbidity with a range of mental disorders; 88 participants indicated the absence of further psychiatric diagnoses.

6. Alienation from World and Other Persons

In a large number of cases, respondents to the Durham questionnaire talked about a profound sense of inability and incapacity, sometimes leaving them entirely unable to act, sometimes such that even simple actions posed enormous difficulties:[12]

---

[10] A detailed account of the experience of inability in mental disorder in general and depression in particular (and of pathological changes in caring) is the focus of Kerrin Jacobs' work (2011). Her model of depressives' existential situation includes a background and foreground dimension of possibility and ability and views the experience of inability in depression as rooted in changes in caring.

[11] The project, which was jointly funded by the AHRC (the UK's Arts and Humanities Research Council) and the DFG (the German Research Foundation), was run by researchers at Durham University, UK (http://philosophyofdepression.wordpress.com/), and the University of Osnabrück, Germany (http://www.animal-emotionale.de/eeid). The questionnaire was posted on the website of the mental health charity SANE. Respondents identified themselves as depressed and, in most cases, offered details of their diagnoses. They provided free text responses with no word limit. We have presented more extensive analyses of these published materials elsewhere, see Paskaleva (2011), Jacobs *et al.* (forthcoming). Helpful in organizing the wealth of autobiographical material has been a paper by Ratcliffe (2009b); see also the contributions in Clark (2008).

[12] In the following, when quoting from the questionnaire, we refer to the anonymous respondents by their corresponding number #, followed by a second number, referring to the items from the main section to which the specific answer belongs. In the quotations, irrelevant misspellings have been corrected. When introducing different responses throughout

> [Depression] makes me completely incapable of doing things. When I'm at my worst I can barely drag myself out of bed. My concentration is affected, I can't hold everyday conversations or complete everyday tasks. Even getting dressed feels like a challenge. (#292, Q5)
> I do nothing, won't even move from bed. (#341, Q5)

In this section, we explore the relationship between impaired agency and the loss of experiential access — access both to one's surroundings in general and to other people in particular. Could it be the case that a disturbance of agency prevents the depressed patient from 'making contact', so that both world and others come to seem remote, distant, inaccessible, and ultimately even alien and threatening?

Unlike our everyday experience of world and life as a matter of practical projects that we engage in, many respondents, and also Jeffrey Smith in his memoir, perceive the world and their life as highly inaccessible from a practical, active point of view:[13]

> There is the feeling that your life 'contracts' — you stop seeing it as an expansive project and it all zeroes in on feelings of despair and wanting to escape. (#61, Q8)
> ...when I was very young — 6 or less years old. The world seemed so large and full of possibilities... Now I feel that the world is small. (#130, Q8)

> Depression is a state of utter *being*: I could do nothing. Life had to be reduced to its most basic level... (Smith, 1999, p. 8)

The last passage even compares life in the state of depression to a state of '*utter being*' rather than an active engagement with various projects. These pronounced experiences likely extend to include other vital domains that are expressed in further affective phenomena characteristic of depression.

One of the domains affected is the depressed patient's interpersonal relatedness. In their incapacitated state, marked by a profound inability to interactively connect to other people, depressed patients come to feel removed, detached, and alienated from others. This might even reach the point that others might come to seem awkward, alien, proba-

---

this chapter, the respective questions will be indicated in a footnote. The responses to follow refer to item 5 of the questionnaire: 'How does depression affect your ability to perform routine tasks and other everyday activities?'

[13] The following responses all refer to item 8 of the questionnaire: 'In what ways, if any, does depression make you think differently about life compared to when you are not depressed?'

bly even hostile and dangerous, as in descriptions of 'social paranoia' expressed in passages like the following:[14]

> I feel like they are all out to get me, or they're in my way, dragging me down, or they are insensitive. There's always something wrong with them, and I can be quite abusive. (#130, Q3)

The material from the questionnaires indicates that there are strong negative feelings towards others, even one's closest ones. Patients often report being irritated by them, feeling paranoid and constantly judged by the others around them. One consequence of the depressive's inactive state seems to be strong feelings of guilt and worthlessness, which might be projected into other people in the form of negative feelings or ill will one assumes those others to harbour towards one.

> I think they find me weak. I feel a burden to them. (#186, Q3)
> Generally, I think they want both me and the depression to disappear so they can get on with their lives and address their own concerns. (#137, Q3)
> I feel like I'm being a burden and that they only put up with me because they feel they have to. (#107, Q3)
> Partner — I feel like he hates me, doesn't love me enough, like I'm a pain in the ass to live with. I feel like a burden. (#97, Q3)
> When I'm depressed I feel like my relationships are less stable and I trust others a lot less. I try to avoid people, as they seem angry and irritated at me, and like they don't want me around. **I feel like a burden to others** and don't want to cause anyone unnecessary distress. (#45, Q3, co-morbidity: eating disorder 2007, obsessive-compulsive disorder, borderline personality disorder, emphasis added)[15]

What is striking here is the recurring theme of feeling as being 'nothing but a burden' for one's friends and family, a feeling that might also result from the essential inability and incapacity to act meaningfully and contribute to social life as one normally does and as (one might anticipate) relevant others expect one to. In this way, the theme of being a burden to others might be the result of an initial implicit reflection upon one's incapacitated state.

In other characteristic passages, people, even one's closest ones, are described as strangers one cannot connect with:

---

[14] The answers to follow all refer to item 3 of the questionnaire: 'Do other people, including family and friends, seem different when you're depressed? If so, how?'

[15] For the purposes of this chapter we have focused on the respondents that indicated the presence of a medical diagnosis of depression. In some of these cases, respondents we quote from also indicated the presence of other psychiatric diagnoses. Whenever we refer to a participant who mentioned a co-morbidity, we provide information about their further psychiatric diagnoses.

> I spent an increasing amount of time alone. If I was with people, I felt as I were surrounded by strangers on a bus… I spent hours walking around campus at all times of day, encased in a loneliness as palpable armor, armed with an unreasoning hostility. (Thompson, 1995, p. 45)

In some cases, others can be experienced even as not being persons at all but instead 'shop dummies' (Plath, 1966, pp. 149–50).

This profound disconnectedness — 'yes they [other people] seem far away hard to relate to…' (#80, Q3) — likely is at the base of feelings of solitude and aloneness, as there no longer 'are' any others with which one *could* make contact or meaningfully 'be together'. This extremely awkward experience, we believe, might result from one's fundamental inability to engage in successful interactive connections to another person. The active exercise of one's communicative and interpersonal capacities — the coordination of gesture, posture, and gaze, the modulation of tone of voice, the ability to grab or engage the other's attention, the ability to empathize actively, and so on — obviously requires intact agency. The less one is able to act, the more impaired or slowed down one's embodied interactive capacities are, the less one will be able to actively 'be with' another person. The other will thus be practically unreachable, which might in turn let him or her appear remote, strange, or even potentially hostile as one has no way to probe the other's intentions or state of mind. This failure to connect, a marked decoupling from others, has been variously described as a potential core dimension of depressive experience, sometimes associated with a breakdown in bodily interaction or 'embodied intersubjectivity' (see, e.g. Fuchs, 2005a). It can go as far as preventing the patient from establishing or maintaining connection even with the people closest to him.

7. Disturbed Body Experience

Not surprisingly, there is a particularly close relation between the impairment of primordial agency and ability and the feelings that one has of one's own body. Once we understand the human body as an active and affectively responsive lived body, we see that there is no gap between our basic sense of agency and ability and our sense of the body. When the body, as part of a pathological process, ceases to operate smoothly as the medium of engagement with the world, it will increasingly turn into what feels like a mere object — a transformation that has been called 'corporealization' (by Fuchs, 2003; 2005a).[16]

---

[16] Fuchs describes this striking experiential change quite vividly in various places; one example: 'A leaden heaviness, constant exhaustion, and a sense of restriction and

In many depressed patients, the lived body seems to 'rigidify' and turn into something resistant:[17] 'tired and lethargic — too much effort needed to do the simple task of walking' (#308, Q4). The body is often described as '[t]ired, heavy, unresponsive...' (#21, Q4), 'leaden' (#137, Q4), '[a]s heavy as lead' (#26, Q4, co-morbidity: borderline personality disorder 2008), which turns it into something from which life has strangely receded, and thus into an obstacle — 'fat, ugly and pointless' (#200, Q4) — and hindrance to attempted engagements and activities — '...I can't drag it out of bed most of the time' (#26, Q4, co-morbidity: borderline personality disorder 2008).

In addition, or as a consequence, one's taken-for-granted relatedness to the world is altered completely as one no longer finds oneself within an everyday context of activity and amidst routinely encountered possibilities for action. Even routine tasks begin to require enormous efforts. The sense of ability is not entirely eroded, but modified dramatically, especially with regard to the estimate of effort necessary for each task:

> Everything feels 1000 times harder to do. To get out of bed, hold a cup of tea, it's all such an effort. (#14, Q4)
> Sometimes it felt impossible to live normally... Even getting out of bed was a struggle, and many times on the way to work I felt like simply curling into a ball and staying there. (#17, Q5)
> Things seem almost impossible... I used to eat a lot of ready meals or things that wouldn't take long to prepare, or I'd just snack, because cooking just felt too difficult. It was an effort to do things like have a shower and get dressed. (#22, Q5)

Some respondents relate their difficulties in performing routine tasks to the pointlessness of these tasks, given that their whole lives appear devoid of sense. This might again be the result of a process of reflection and self-interpretation consequent upon the primary experience of inability:

> When depressed your ability to perform routine tasks and activities become hindered. When life becomes pointless and your body seems to be on a permanent go slow normal routine goes out the window as the effort just seems too much and pointless. (#34, Q5, co-morbidity: anxiety disorder and borderline personality disorder)

---

tightening make the patient feel the bare materiality of his body that is otherwise hidden in the movement and performance of life... In serious cases a literal freezing and reification of the body ensues which is no longer capable of resonance with its environment' (Fuchs, 2001, p. 183).

[17] The responses to follow refer all to item 4 of the questionnaire: 'How does your body feel when you're depressed?'

The objectified, dysfunctional body might in this way cause a rift between person and world. This marks a fundamental alteration in emotional self-awareness. What results is bodily feelings of being trapped and unable to break free, feelings of being isolated from formerly meaningful surroundings. This might give rise to feelings of being encaged or imprisoned and of being unable to reach out to make contact with the world or other people:

> Sometimes I felt like some creature caught in a net, thrashing around and unable to get free. I didn't know what the net was, but I knew it was there; I didn't know what was standing between me and deep connections with other people, but that was there too. I felt it distinctly. It was a wall... I couldn't get around it, or over it. It was just there. (Thompson, 1996, p. 89)

As a further consequence, feelings of estrangement, of depersonalization, even of not being bodily existent at all might ensue — in all, a fundamental, encompassing sense of self-alienation.

8. Changes in Time Experience

Another dimension presumably resulting from the affective changes under discussion is the experience of time — depressives usually mention that 'time seems to drag. A day feels like a year' (#26, Q6).[18]

Depressed patients often complain about a radical disruption of everyday temporality.[19] Notably, the patient's orientation towards the future as a temporal dimension potentially different from the present seems profoundly distorted. Andrew Solomon provides a very detailed illustration of the altered sense of time as he experienced it during depressive episodes:

> When you are depressed, the past and the future are absorbed entirely by the present moment, as in the world of a three-year-old. You cannot remember a time when you felt better, at least not clearly; and you certainly cannot imagine a future time when you will feel better... depression is atemporal. Breakdowns leave you with no point of view. (Solomon, 2001, p. 55)

---

[18] The responses to follow refer all to item 6 of the questionnaire: 'When you are depressed, does time seem different to you? If so, how?'

[19] For more detailed analyses of the alterations in the experience of temporality in psychopathology in general and depression in particular see Fuchs (2001; 2005b; 2013a). Ratcliffe (2012a) likewise presents an insightful discussion of altered time experience in depression, partly responding to and diverging from Fuchs' account. Our own proposal has some overlap with these treatments, but tries out a different overall orientation, namely that of the primacy of impaired agency as a potential main source of altered temporality.

> Depression minutes are like dog years, based on some artificial notion
> of time. (*Ibid.*, pp. 53–4)

Solomon's observations are concordant with a significant number of
the questionnaire answers:

> Slooooooow. Time goes so slowly when I'm depressed. Painfully slow.
> Yet at the same time when I look at my past it seems to have passed me
> by without me noticing. (#14, Q6, co-morbidity: anxiety, possibly
> post-traumatic stress disorder)

Time can appear to stand still, as the very idea of a potential change of
the current state seems to be absent from experience. Again, it makes
sense to assume that a distortion of agency might lie at the root of this
pathological change, disabling the patient's sense of capability, their
sense of being able to effect a change in the world. Often, this is initially reflected in a kind of desynchronization between the experienced temporality of the depressed person and the temporality of
worldly affairs in her surroundings (*cf.* Fuchs, 2013a). The subjective
side of this mismatch seems to be closely tied to the patient's diminished ability to act, as described in the following passage:

> Time is immaterial to me during a depressional episode. I lose track of
> time. I wonder what I've done all day when the children suddenly burst
> through the door from school. Time has gone by, but I have done noth-
> ing, even to think one thought seems to have taken all day. Everything
> around me seems to carry on with routines and time scheduled activi-
> ties, it feels like I'm watching it all happen but am not part of it: as
> though I'm inside a bubble. My living becomes mechanical, based on
> necessities to be done. Children need to be fed. Plates need to be
> washed. School clothes need to be clean. Everything else in life is put on
> hold. (#117, Q6)

Besides this robot-like slowing of agency and disconnection from the
everyday temporality of their surroundings, some patients report even
more profound disruptions of time experience. Finding themselves
unable to act and thus unable to bring about any change in the world,
these depressed persons seem to lose their sense of the possibility and
likelihood of a change of the present state (both of the surrounding
world and of their own situation). Something like this is also illustrated by the following entries:

> I felt a genuine sense of being an incapable person and was tired of try-
> ing to put it right. Life seemed like a struggle, and admittedly one I did-
> n't always want to work at... I felt trapped, like nothing I did could
> make things better... (#21, Q8)
> You can't see far into the future so you can't see aspirations or dreams.
> Everything I ever wanted to do with my life before seemed impossible

now. I also would think that I would never get out, that I'd be depressed forever. (#22, Q8)

Being unable to act, and likewise unable to enter into meaningful contexts of activities (such as joining a team, feeling like being a part of a group such as a family that struggles for a common cause, having something at stake collectively, etc.) leaves one tied to the current state of affairs and thus to the present moment. The experienced present may in this way extend indefinitely and turn into what Heidegger has called *stehendes Jetzt* — a 'standing now', a total breakdown of existential temporality (*cf.* Heidegger, 1929–30/1995, pp. 123–6). Obviously, this arrested temporality has nothing to do with a blissful absorption in the present moment, but rather amounts to a total loss of what normally is the lived presence of undisrupted agency. Heidegger's 'standing now', as the phenomenal signature of profound boredom, is a wasteland of lost meaning, a desert of senseless existence that has totally transformed all of the temporal dimensions, past, present, and future (see also Slaby, 2010).[20]

In light of this it is not surprising that altered experience of time can give rise to violent feelings of dread and despair — feelings regularly reported by depressed persons:

> Time seems to run slower and hang when depressed. The word oppressive comes to mind and fear grows as to when and if any respite will come. (#231, Q6)

With respect to these emotions that in some instances contain an element of expectation or anticipation, it has to be noted that the patients have not always lost any sense of the future whatsoever. In some instances of depression, patients rather anticipate the future specifically in terms of impending disaster and doom, leading them to expect the future to bring only more pain and misfortune, or even outright catastrophe:

> You think negatively, feel under threat, like something bad will happen. (#312, Q8)
> I am paranoid and pessimistic, convinced something bad will happen to

---

[20] Note that we are not conflating the experience of depression with profound boredom (let alone profound boredom as analysed by Heidegger). We are merely noting a parallel in the specific modification of existential temporality between these two conditions: the experience of a loss of the lived present that affects the entire configuration of temporal experience. It may well be that boredom is still much closer to a kind of action readiness that is simply interrupted for a certain period of time, while in severe depression agency is eroded almost completely.

me or others. (#85, Q2)[21]
There are lots of threats in the world and they all seem to be about to happen, or be very likely they will happen. Loved ones are in danger. (#312, Q2)

This conspicuous negative framing of anticipated happenings might also be a result of distorted or diminished agency. Finding oneself unable to act amounts to a radically altered relationship to possible future events. These events will inevitably come in view as alien, as if having been installed or caused by strange outside forces, uncontrollable and thus potentially threatening. One feels delivered over to happenings that one has no say in.

I lose faith in myself and my ability to cope with life… There seemed to be no future, no possibility that I could ever be happy again or that life was worth living… (#160, Q8)

A fundamental sense of being incapable and powerless in general might amount to construing oneself as being at the mercy of distant, alien, and uncontrollable events (see also Wyllie, 2005; Ratcliffe, 2012a). Certainly, one could say much more about the intricate, and quite variable, alteration of lived time in depressive experience. While the evidence is surely not conclusive in favour of our thesis concerning the primacy of a loss of agency that would explain disturbances of existential temporality, we think there is enough material already to at least give this idea careful consideration in subsequent work.[22]

9. Conclusion

In sum, the condition of severe depression might in some respects come close to a kind of 'mirror image' of human affectivity — exactly *inverting* central features of an undisturbed capacity for emotion. Depression marks a profound distortion of a root dimension of our affective orientation towards the world. Describing its experiential profile and assessing the patient's self-reflections concerning their condition therefore might help us gain deeper insights into the complex structures constituting human affectivity in general. For exam-

---

[21] The responses to follow refer to item 2 of the questionnaire: 'Does the world look different to you when you are depressed? If so, how?'

[22] Thomas Fuchs' view of depression, centred on desychronization, corporealization, and a loss of 'conative drive' is in some points similar to our proposal (see Fuchs, 2001; 2005a; 2013a). The chief difference lies in our focus on the primacy of impaired agency while we view the other salient dimensions of depressive experience — distorted interpersonal attunement, disconnection from the world, corporealization, distorted experience of time — as being consequent upon that core affliction and its immediate experiential ramifications (such as a marked sense of incapacity, insecurity, anxiety, etc.).

ple, with regard to affective self-awareness — a crucial ingredient in what we have elsewhere called 'affective intentionality' (Slaby and Stephan, 2008) — depressive experience seems to confirm the suggestion that a basic form of self-awareness comes in view as a modification of a person's sense of ability and capacity, a sense that, in non-pathological cases, is not distinct from agency itself. In these default cases, it simply *is* a person's capacity to act, usually guided by a tacit, felt estimation of one's potentialities *vis-à-vis* the specific effort and the approximate time required in performing certain tasks, along with an estimation of potential resistances and obstacles one has to surmount in order to achieve one's goals.

However, in depression, the capacity to act is severely distorted, leaving the patient with an uncanny sense of inability and impossibility. The place of agency within the behavioural economy of the person is now occupied by a conspicuous experiential structure — a structure not present in cases of smooth and undisturbed behavioural engagement. This sense of incapacity and impossibility subsequently affects other key domains of experience, distorting the depressed person's relationship to the world in general, her situatedness among (and relationships to) other people, and also the patient's relationship to his or her lived body. Accordingly, the sense of incapacity expands into a general awareness of oneself as fundamentally and irredeemably defective and weak, and it thereby also gives rise to processes of self-reflection and partial rationalization that might in turn feed back into the basic experiential dimension.[23] This variable, partly reflective affective sense of inability encompasses all three temporal dimensions, present, past, and future — the latter one at least in so far as the patient is still capable of anticipating or imagining future states of affairs. Emotions such as guilt (i.e. feelings reflecting one's past incapacity and failures to act), feelings of passivity, incapacity, uselessness, isolation, and of imposing a burden upon others (i.e. feelings directed mostly at one's *present* inabilities), and anticipations of the future either in terms of stagnation, or in terms of misery, catastrophe,

---

[23] It would be worthwhile to follow this lead and assess more carefully the amount and role of self-reflection and rationalization within the experiential processes discussed in this chapter. It seems to us that patient reports, and even more so edited, polished reports from patient memoirs, often present an amalgamated mixture combining (more or less) direct expression of experience with the results of reflection upon and rationalization of those experiences, both *in statu nascendi* and afterwards when reporting or creating narratives about this episode of one's life. Attempts at disentangling these elements pose all sorts of difficulties — a methodological problem that pertains to phenomenological description in general. We cannot here address this intricate issue (but see Ratcliffe, 2008a, pp. 4–10; and 2009b, for helpful methodological considerations relevant to this problem).

doom (i.e. feelings anticipating future situations) — all of these might be the intelligible *results* of the basic condition of severely impaired agency. Overall and in general, this condition comprises feeling isolated, cut off from things and people, threatened and powerless, without hope and meaning in life, being burdensome for others, while these others also often appear as menacing, threatening, obnoxious. In this truly horrifying way, depression wreaks havoc to the very foundation of a person's existential perspective on the world, by paralysing or entirely eroding the patient's agency — modifying, suspending, or even destroying her practical point of view.

Acknowledgments

Our work on this chapter was made possible by a joint AHRC/DFG grant (STE 729/4-1). We wish to thank Matthew Ratcliffe and Philipp Wüschner for highly helpful comments and suggestions. We also thank the two anonymous referees for the *Journal of Consciousness Studies*, whose comments have helped us greatly in improving the manuscript.

Outi Benson, Susanne Gibson
and Sarah L. Brand

The Experience of Agency in the Feeling of Being Suicidal

1. Introduction

This chapter reports on an empirical exploration of 'suicidal feelings' among those who have experienced them at first hand. The focus of suicide research to date has been on suicidal ideation; in other words, thoughts rather than feelings. This is evidenced by the relatively high number of research articles referring to the former in their title, abstract, or keyword compared to the relative absence of references to the latter, and by a tendency to equivocate between the terms.[1] These tendencies are also evident in clinical literature, one obvious example of which is the omission of the term 'suicidal feelings' from the index of the 774-page *International Handbook of Suicide and Attempted Suicide* (Hawton and van Heeringen, 2000). It should therefore come as no surprise that clinical and research instruments developed for the purpose of measuring suicidality also tend to address aspects of suicidal thinking — beliefs, attitudes, and expectations — rather than feelings.[2] Thus well-known aspects of suicidal experience such as hopelessness, which common sense would construe as a feeling

---

[1] A search of three psychology databases for the ten-year period between May 2002 and April 2012 produced 29 articles with either 'suicidal affect', 'suicide affect', or 'suicidal feelings' in their abstract (databases PsycInfo, PsycArticles, PsycExtra; search date 2 November 2012). The same search for the terms 'suicidal ideation', 'suicide ideation', or 'suicidal thoughts' yielded 4,077 results. Only one of the 29 article abstracts appeared to treat suicidal feelings as in any way distinct from suicidal thoughts; in most there was an ambiguity about what was meant, and in six the use of the terms 'suicidal feelings' and 'suicidal ideation' was clearly equivocal.

[2] These include Paykel, Myers and Lindenthal's (1974) 'Suicidal Ladder', the 'Harkavy Asnis Suicide Scale' (Harkavy Friedman and Asnis, 1989a,b), and the 'Beck Hopelessness Scale' (Beck, 1986; Beck *et al.*, 1985; Beck, Brown and Steer, 1989).

accompanied by characteristic ways of thinking, have become operationalized as cognitive constructs.[3]

However, as we have discovered and will report on here, suicidal feelings are something quite different to suicidal thoughts. The force of this statement resides not in any general distinction between thoughts and feelings, but in the characteristics of the suicidal state. Importantly, suicidal thoughts alone (that is, without the presence of suicidal feelings) do not lead to suicidal acts. Further, they may precede and continue beyond the suicidal state: some of our participants reported finding thoughts about suicide that occur after suicidal feelings have passed little more than a curiosity. In addition, suicidal thoughts that are 'just a thought' can occur to people who are in no danger of ever becoming suicidal. It is true that some suicidal thoughts are like 'command thoughts' in schizophrenia (and conversely, some command thoughts in schizophrenia are suicidal thoughts), thus having a stronger and more immediate link with action than 'ordinary thoughts'. However, as we demonstrate below, the experience of resisting suicidal thoughts is part of the core of suicidal feelings.

Data for the study were collected using a questionnaire combined with in-depth interviews. The online questionnaire consisted of a modified, evidence-based measure of suicidality,[4] some demographic questions, and a qualitative section that asked the participant to describe their experience of suicidal feelings ('what is it like to feel suicidal?'). Further qualitative data were collected by means of email, telephone, and face-to-face interviews with a self-selected sub-sample of the survey participants. There were 124 participants in the online survey, 21 of whom continued to the interview stage. The study was granted NHS ethics approval. Table 1 shows basic participant characteristics.

---

[3] See Ratcliffe (2013a) for a clear and thorough elaboration of this matter.

[4] A modified version of the Harkavy Asnis Suicide Scale (Harkavy Friedman and Asnis, 1989a,b). Questions loading on the factor 'substance abuse' were removed from the scale, leaving the factors 'thoughts of suicide', 'thoughts of death', and 'suicidal plans and actions'. The following three questions were added: 'How long ago did you first experience suicidal feelings?', 'How long ago did you last experience suicidal feelings?', and 'Have you ever self-harmed without wanting to die by the act?'

Participant characteristics (N = 124)	
Gender	68.55% Female (n = 85)
	29.03% Male (n = 36)
	2.42% Not specified (n = 3)
Age	Range 16–67 years
	Mean 37.89 years
	SD 13.05
Diagnosis (self-reported)	81.45% Has diagnosis (n = 101)
	18.55% Does not have diagnosis (n = 23)
	50.81% Unipolar depression (n = 63)
	14.52% Anxiety disorder (n = 18)
	11.29% Borderline personality disorder (n = 14)
	8.06% Bipolar disorder (n = 10)
	7.26% Schizophrenia/Schizo-affective disorder (n = 9)
	3.23% Post-traumatic stress disorder (n = 4)
Suicidal & self-harming behaviour	66.13% At least one suicide attempt (n = 82)
	62.10% Self-harm without suicidal intent (n = 77)

The process of data collection and analysis followed the principles of grounded theory (Glaser and Strauss, 1967; Glaser, 1978; 1992; 2005). The grounded theory approach was chosen chiefly for its ability to let the participants' collective understanding steer the course of the research through a process of repeated cycles of data collection, analysis, and reformulation of research questions.

This grounded theory approach was combined with phenomenological philosophy, which was used to describe the subject matter of the study — the subjective experience of self, body, world, and others — and to sensitize the researchers to these broad areas of interest. The concepts presented in Section 3 of this chapter were developed from the data through the following procedures: first, all data were categorized by constant comparative analysis ('open coding'), in which units of meaning in the data are compared to each other and to emerging categories. Second, theoretical connections were sought between categories identified in open coding ('theoretical coding'). Third, one core category was identified, which in our view did much of the explanatory work, and this category became the subject of this chap-

ter. The analytic commentary offered in Section 4 is also led by the
data, in the sense that it uses extant literature only to refine and con-
textualize the theory in order to make best sense of the data. This literature includes but is not limited to works in phenomenology: the
grounded theory methodology conceptualizes the literature review as
a process to fit the needs of the emerging theory rather than something
that can be decided upon and to a large extent carried out prior to data
collection.

In this chapter we present an analysis of our data to show that there
is 'something it is like' to feel suicidal, that is, that there are sufficient
consistencies among our participants' experiences, and to describe the
central features of 'the feeling of being suicidal'. We then seek to
elaborate this further by suggesting that these are a function of a disruption of the experience of human agency.

2. The 'Feeling of Being Suicidal' —
Is There Such a Thing?

Our questioning yielded descriptions of loss, lack, or change in the
very core of the participants' experience of ordinary living, in the usually hidden, taken for granted aspects of it. In other words, as we
expected, by asking what it is like to *feel* suicidal, we learned about
what it is like to *be* suicidal.

> *I knew I was going to do it, really... it became more and*
> *more intense. [Towards the end I saw it as] inevitable. [Sui-*
> *cide] began to colour everything. It sort of was the back-*
> *ground, or the wallpaper, to every situation I had in my mind*
> *at that time.* (Male, 29, face-to-face interview)

Our participants described suicidal feelings as a bodily experience
that was also a restructuring of their experience of self, world, and
others. As it was explained to us, 'becoming suicidal' constitutes a
fundamental change in the person's experiential background such that
no thought, perception, or emotional response is left completely
unchanged. The feeling of being suicidal is therefore what Ratcliffe
(2005) calls an 'existential feeling', a way of finding yourself in the
world that provides the variable but always present structure to the
experiences of self and world.

It may come as a surprise that there are any striking similarities in
how people feel when they are suicidal, given the diversity of circumstances and psychiatric diagnoses that give rise to suicidal feelings,
and the differences in the characteristics of the people who experience

them. Men and women die by their own hand at all stages of life (Fincham *et al.*, 2011); childhood adversity, recent bereavement, and unemployment are all associated with increased suicide risk (Cole-King and Lepping, 2010); both mood disorders and psychotic disorders raise the likelihood of suicide for the person who experiences them (Harris and Barraclough, 1997). Our participants reflect this variety of risk factors.

Another notable, even counter-intuitive, feature of the feeling of being suicidal is that unlike any other existential feeling, such as feelings of homeliness, belonging, separation, unfamiliarity, and so on (examples from Ratcliffe, 2008a), it refers exclusively to a type of action (or so it seems).[5] In what follows, we question whether suicides should be considered actions in the ordinary sense, given the extent to which the experience of agency is disrupted when suicidal. Further, it would be misleading to say that the feeling of being suicidal has an action as a referent. Though it is an experience of being directed towards suicide, it isn't *about* suicide in the sense of having propositional content. If it were, it could not be called a background feeling in Ratcliffe's sense (*ibid.*). As we shall see, being towards suicide is a reorientation of the whole of one's existence rather than simply a wish to die by one's own hand. In fact, when suicidal, people as a rule do *not* wish to die. Mostly, what they are reorientated towards is bringing an intolerable mode of existence to an end. It is this mode of existence that we describe when we elaborate the feeling of being suicidal.

We will describe four aspects of the feeling of being suicidal (FBS 1–4) which seem to us at this stage of the study to be, to a degree, a part of the experience of anyone who seriously considers suicide. We do not of course suggest that everyone who feels suicidal feels the same way; rather, each individual experience is a unique and culturally informed combination of the in some ways quite diverse experiences that constitute the aspects discussed. The claim we make is that when someone becomes suicidal,

1. Their core assumptions of being an integrated self, ordinarily taken for granted, is problematized (FBS 1);
2. Reciprocal action between their self and world is disrupted (FBS 2);
3. Their 'mental resources' are becoming dangerously depleted (FBS 3);

and

4. The body comes to the foreground of experience (FBS 4).

---

[5] Thanks to Matthew Ratcliffe for pointing this out.

It is not possible to say from our data whether these experiences tend to take place in a particular order, nor whether any linear causal relations exist between the four aspects of the feeling of being suicidal. Indeed, they might be best understood as a web of interconnected experiences so that changes in one imply changes in all of the other three: this is something we consider further in elaborating our understanding of human agency.

As seen in Table 1, just over a half of our participants reported having a diagnosis of depression. Other diagnoses were also represented. As headline statements, FBS 1–4 could be taken to describe the phenomenology of almost any mental disorder. We therefore need to answer the question: 'is the feeling of being suicidal something different to the existential feelings associated with depression and other disorders?' In other words, is it more than just a thought of suicide being added to an existential predicament associated with mental disorder that has become intolerable? We hope that by the end of this chapter the reader is persuaded that, though the feeling of being suicidal is not distinct, independent, or in any way separable from the experiences one might have as part of depression, there is a difference between feeling suicidal and feeling depressed. What we suggest we've found, and intend to show below, is some common ground between several different mental disorders which amounts to those experiences having the content 'being directed towards suicide'.

Limitations

The 'feeling of being suicidal' as we present it here is not the full construct. In particular, explicit discussion of some of the better known aspects of suicidal experience such as hopelessness, anger, and shame/guilt is outside of the scope of this chapter, although all of these are present in our data. Further work is required to make the theoretical connections between FBS1–4 and these aspects of emotional experience in suicide.

The scope of this chapter is limited to suicidal feelings that arise in response to severe psychological stress or distress of some kind. In addition, the majority of the participants reported long-standing mental health problems and therefore there may be some instances of suicidal feelings that are not within the scope of the feeling of being suicidal as it is described here.

When interpreting the results it should also be taken into account that all participants were UK residents and the majority described themselves as belonging in the ethnic group 'White British'.

3. Aspects of the Feeling of Being Suicidal

FBS 1: The core assumption of being an integrated self,
ordinarily taken for granted, is problematized

Underlying ordinary experience is the assumption of an integrated self who is the subject of those experiences. It is a part of the feeling of being suicidal that this assumption is problematized. This can manifest as a loss or lack of consistency between the public or social self and the hidden suicidal self, which is actively concealed.

> *I keep coming back to the feeling that my life is 'fraudulent'... The thing that worries me most is what I feel I've become and am now (internally)... The majority of people who know me think I'm 'sorted'. It would worry them to know the inner me... This is why my life feels fraudulent — and as such, not really worth that much.* (Male, 40, questionnaire)

> *I can sit in a meeting at work, with... 'important people', doing my job, being respected for my opinion, needed for my advice, and thinking 'oh my god, what would happen if you knew that yesterday I was contemplating an overdose?'* (Female, 32, email interview)

> *From 19... until my breakdown at 30 I just thought, 'pull yourself together and get on with it', and never talked about... any of what I was feeling or what I was coping with.* (Female, 39, face-to-face interview)

Sometimes the experience of lost consistency is one of a loss of continuity between the past non-suicidal self and the present suicidal self.

> *The person I am 'normally' has gone and I am a fragmented human being with no hope, direction or future... Where have I gone and what is happening?* (Male, 50, questionnaire)

> *A total horror at what your life has become and a despair at ever getting back your old self.* (Female, 22, questionnaire)

Implicit or explicit in the loss of consistency of self is the impact on the experience of self as a moral self. In some cases the act of presenting a public self is experienced as fraudulent; then there is at the centre of one's experience of self a kind of moral failure. Any positive evaluations by others in support of the person's self-worth seem meaningless because — addressed to the public self — they miss their target, while negative evaluations are felt particularly keenly as they seem to reveal parts of the carefully hidden truth. Where there is a loss of continuity between past and present self, the values of the past self are no longer accessible as a guide to action and the values of the present suicidal self, such as they are, are at best precariously action-guiding.

Nevertheless, even where there is a loss of consistency of the self, actions are still experienced as self-authored — as arising from the self (O'Connor, 1995; Gallagher, 2000) — albeit that they might be experienced as inauthentic in some way. Although there is a question about *whom* the person is, there is still a clear sense of *what* one is: an individual, a person, a human being.

However, the disruption to the assumption of an integrated self can be experienced as a loss of coherence in the sense of self, such that the experience of self-authorship of actions is threatened or even absent. This can include a sometimes visceral sense of a battle being fought between distinct parts of the self, both of which are competing for control:

> *When I am feeling well, I have no awareness of any division of my self into parts. I just operate as a normal, functioning being. However, if I am very depressed/experiencing suicidal thoughts as a side effect of medication, I sometimes think the only way to solve my problems is to not be here any more. It is then that I seem to feel the dislocation. It feels like the thinker in me (perhaps this is my normal 'self') is quite sure that suicide is not a solution but that side of me is aware of something akin to another entity within me which is emitting thoughts of what it considers the easy solution — ending things.* (Female, 43, questionnaire)

> *Suicidal feelings (which I have far less often, thankfully) are quite different to [suicidal thoughts]... this is more like an overwhelming urge (like a craving almost) to die... [I] spent all of one day (whilst alone at home) holding on to window ledge, if I let go I would kill myself.* (Female, 50, questionnaire)

> *My mind wants to kill myself — but my body won't let me. Somehow I have developed a stronger survival instinct than I can account for.* (Female, 41, questionnaire)

Alternatively, it can be experienced as a detachment between different parts of the self. Actions become observed behaviour, separate from the observer, and proceed under their own momentum without being subjected to ongoing evaluation. They may be disowned or experienced as no longer under voluntary control.

> *I was running around the house shouting 'no no no' but mentally I felt completely separate from it... I felt like I was just playing the part of someone horribly distressed.* (Female, 23, questionnaire)

> *I felt that a glass box separated me from the person who was still out there functioning.* (Female, 61, questionnaire)

> *It's almost like being in a state of shock, maybe, or something, it's like, you're actually, your body's on automatic... The conscious thought processes have all gone because it's the subconscious [taking over]: 'Right, kill yourself, this is how.' And then it's the rest of the world's not there at all. There [are] no reasons behind it in that sense or anything like that... No thought, totally cold, emotionless. You know, and then that's when I feel more in danger... Because... once the thought processes have been removed then there's no subconscious fighting with [it] saying, this is just a thought and therefore we can get past it.* (Male, 43, face-to-face interview)

> *It was not myself who was engaging in such an act. I did not feel connected to myself, as if I was an automaton and suicide was the natural response.* (Female, 22, questionnaire)

FBS 2: Reciprocal action between self and world is disrupted

In the experiences described in FBS 2 the person is no longer integrated with her environment in the relationship of reciprocal action that is associated with ordinary living. Some participants report that the world's impact on the self appears diminished or distorted in some way; in most of these cases there is a feeling of physical distance having been introduced between the self and the world, though it sometimes has the character of anomalous perceptual experiences. For some, these combine in a single, almost paradoxical experience (see the first quote below). Others talk about their sense of inability to affect the world, which can be an experience of inefficacy, a failure or inability to act, but can also be experienced as being unable to make any impression on the world whatsoever; of leaving no footprints on the world, or marks on others' retinae.

> *The world is too noisy, voices sound too loud and physically you feel far away.* (Female, 46, questionnaire)

> *I feel very disconnected to the world, as if I'm floating, not quite there or visible to others.* (Male, 23, questionnaire)

Although there tended to be this division of directionality in the way this experience was reported, it seems that the same experience can be described either as a matter of being impacted by something, or as a matter of failure to act in some way:

> *When I have been suicidal, I have felt almost as though I have become impervious to any stimuli, be it other people, colours, tastes, etc. It feels very much as though I am separate from anything and anyone else — in other words, detached and unable to make connections with any other thing.* (Female, 43, email interview)

> *I want to reach out to the world, but it isn't there to reach out to… Nothing can get into or out of my psyche, I am emotionally isolated, on an island with sea all around and no chance of rescue.* (Male, 50, questionnaire)

FBS 2 is often described with the help of metaphors. The most prominent in our data were, first, being stuck inside a 'bubble', 'glass wall', 'glass box', or 'glass coffin', recollecting Plath's (1966) 'bell jar' metaphor, and second, a metaphor of light and colour; the world being described as engulfed in darkness or fog, or lacking its usual colour. The world is thus variously described as inaccessible to the self, or with changed meaning, in the sense of having lost or altered in its significance for the self.

> *It was like the world had been deserted I was in the world alone. Things were going on and stuff but I just felt like I was in a bubble. I couldn't talk to anyone.* (Female, 25, questionnaire)

> *It's like a mist clouding your vision, there's no more colour or happiness in the world and you can't really focus on anything because nothing matters.* (Female, 19, questionnaire)

Here 'the world' encompasses not only the physical environment but also the social one; the ailing reciprocality concerns equally one's relationship with other people. This is true of both experiences of inaccessibility ('glass wall') and of lost or changed meaning ('loss of colour'). Where others are referred to, it is almost exclusively in the context of a reference to the self; they may appear uncaring, hostile, manipulative, or hateful towards the suicidal person, or not within reach, or they are simply not experienced at all.

> *My daughter would tell me 'I love you mummy'. I'd think 'you manipulative little cow, don't try to stop me. Don't emotionally blackmail me'. She was three, and totally incapable of knowing how I was feeling, or doing anything of the sort. Now, 'I love yous' are 'I love yous'.* (Female, 32, email interview)

> *At the times I feel worst, I feel cold and removed from the world, as I don't matter to anybody, even my lovely daughter.* (Male, 50, questionnaire)

> *At this time all the endless thoughts I had had before about methods and reasons went away. My concern about hurting my family didn't enter my brain. I was only aware of myself.* (Female, 23, questionnaire)

FBS 3: Mental resources are felt to be dangerously depleted

An integral part of the feeling of being suicidal is a sense of overwhelming demand on one's mental resources deriving to a large extent from a felt need to control negative, including suicidal, thoughts and feelings. This demand can also be felt in the context of routine tasks that wouldn't typically require focused mental effort. Even normally fully automated tasks seem to draw on resources usually reserved for deliberate action.

> *It gets to a point where whatever I think is wrong... I can't stop the snowballing thoughts and I can't see a way out, which makes me feel suicidal and distressed, adding to the snowball.* (Female, 25, email interview)

> *I generally do not think about suicide for extended periods, but force myself to 'snap out of it'. Controlling this urge is mentally tiring, and ironically one of the things I would wish to escape via suicide.* (Male, 24, questionnaire)

> *[When they are effective, the crisis team] talk me through process of making a cup of tea as too complex for my head to work out at the time, remind me to breathe when even that's an effort.* (Female, 39, questionnaire)

I've tried so very, very, hard, months and months have gone by can't think straight any more my brain feels overloaded, exhausted so exhausted my body has got so weak. (Female, 54, questionnaire)

The mental exhaustion that goes along with the feeling of relentless demand can thus be felt as physical exhaustion, the depleted state becoming an embodied sense of effortfulness that imbues life and world. As such, escape becomes the only possibility for rest.

When I feel suicidal, it feels as though the process of being alive is too much of a struggle to continue with... I cannot see anything positive — my life seems like an uphill battle and I just want to escape so I can rest. (Female, 24, questionnaire)

FBS 4: The body comes to the foreground of experience

FBS 1–3 are all embodied experiences in the sense that they are experienced through the lived body and as such cannot be properly described without reference to it. However, the feeling of being suicidal can also be an experience *of* the body, so that the body comes to the fore in some way.

Thus the body can be experienced as a battle ground, or as a turbulent, fragile, or diseased source of discomfort and pain that is difficult to inhabit and that the person wants to escape from. It is a body under strain: put simply, too much is going on.

I physically shake while the battle goes on inside... I get very confused and can sit for hours battling with myself. (Female, 58, questionnaire)

A horrible physical pain in my stomach that is constant, a restlessness that makes me tense up all my muscles and writhe around, and an endless shortness of breath, is so bad that I am sure that I must be dying or that these feelings must be some signal that my life is about to end — because no one can possibly endure these feelings for any significant amount of time. (Female, 23, questionnaire)

Other experiences of the body are characterized by the lack or absence of some animating principle or feeling: the body is a heavy, unwieldy object, or corpse-like, numb, and hollow.

I have a physical ache in my head. It feels like it had drooped right down to my toes and its not going to rise. I feel physically and emotionally drained by this life. (Female, 21, questionnaire)

I either feel very agitated inside or, sometimes, as [if] I'm dead anyway and that I can feel nothing... If I feel numb and dead it feels as if I am an empty shell and not really alive anyway, so it wouldn't make a difference if I died. (Female, 55, questionnaire)

I felt very numb and closed off... At times it felt as if there was a hole in me and all my energy was just perpetually gushing out of me, leaving me this little shell of a person. (Female, 33, questionnaire)

4. Discussion

Our research concerns the *experience* of suicidal feelings, and so, in so far as we analyse this experience in terms of agency, what we are talking about first and foremost is the *experience* of agency, that is, the phenomenology of first-person agency (Bayne and Levy, 2006).[6] It is a notable feature of this experience that in one sense it just is our everyday experience of being human, and as such, it remains mostly in the background. Further, the concept of agency employed here is one in which, as human agents, our actions are guided both by our being embodied and embedded in an environment, and by our having a set of socially and culturally embedded goals and values that persist over time. We refer to these two aspects of agency as 'bodily agency' and 'normative agency', or 'bodily guidedness' and 'normative guidedness', and argue that in the feeling of being suicidal, both get into difficulty.[7]

To begin with normative agency, this depends upon persisting and more or less consistent goals and values that are partly constitutive of who one is, or takes oneself to be. These goals and values are in turn embedded in the social relations that both enable and require a shared and consistent account of the self (Hilton and Elder, 2007).

---

[6]   For discussions of the veridicality of the phenomenology of agency, see Bayne and Levy (2006) and Pacherie (2008).

[7]   For conceptions of self and agency built on a foundation of embodied, real-time engagement with the immediate environment, see for example Clark (1997), Hurley (1998), Stuart (2002), and Steward (2009). For conceptions of the agent as a socially and culturally embedded normative self, see MacIntyre (1999), Gallagher (2000), Hilton and Elder (2007), Westlund (2009), and Freeman (2011). For the significance of body in normative agency, see Giddens (1991).

Thus, while the values one lives by may alter over time, they are not usually subject to radical change. In FBS 1, the loss of consistency in the sense of a loss of continuity between past and present self is just such a change, so that the question of who I am cannot be taken for granted as a guide to action. In addition, to the extent that the present suicidal self does possess a set of coherent goals and values, they are action-guiding primarily in so far as they point towards the extinguishing of agency in death. Another way to put this is to say that while the narrative of any life is subject to interruption, for example because of illness, bereavement, or even good fortune, in most cases the narrative continues, albeit in a different direction and perhaps with an altered sense of self (Carel, 2008). For the suicidal self this appears impossible, since they are now someone with '*no hope, direction or future*' and the sense of an enduring self is diminished or even lost.

Likewise, the loss of consistency between public and hidden self is marked by a sharp division. The public self does not appear to be just one version or presentation of the self, as in ordinary experiences of multifaceted identity where some aspects of the personality remain hidden in particular contexts. It is a self that is unrelated to, and shares little with, the hidden suicidal self. Performing for others in one sense facilitates action, since it gives both a reason to act and a guide to action. However, actions lack meaning since they are neither guided by nor constitutive of the real self. There is a narrative, but one that is or may as well be happening to someone else, and that fails to sustain action beyond the need to perform in public.

> *You see people reacting to you, and life carrying on as normal. People laugh at jokes, make banal chit chat round the water cooler, and somehow you're part of that, but you're not. Because actually you're locked in this glass coffin, but have just enough air to not suffocate. You're an actor. People are responding to their expectations of you, and not the real you... [The feeling of watching your life happening to someone else] comes in the interpretation of everyone around you, who thinks that you're something that you're not.* (Female, 32, email interview)

> *When there was no pressure on me to perform my public role I could do nothing.* (Female, 61, questionnaire)

The loss of shared meaning and its impact on normative agency is further apparent in FBS 2, where reciprocality between self and other breaks down and the suicidal person becomes disembedded from their social and cultural environment. It is not just that one's own life lacks meaning: it is a struggle to understand, much less share, other people's attributions of meaning.

> *I do use the Samaritans from time to time and... you know when I sort of express this feeling [of lack of hope for change], I'm usually speaking to somebody who's sixty plus... saying, oh yeah, there's great things you can do... and I just don't see it.* (Female, 58, telephone interview)

> *I become confused by people talking about how they want to have children because I cannot find any reason why they think they are doing anyone any favours by bringing them into the world. At this stage my fantasies of suicide become more detailed as the idea of doing it seems more reasonable and less impulsive.* (Female, 23, questionnaire)

The loss of reciprocality between self and other in FBS 2 also impacts on normative agency in so far as the experience of caring for and being cared for by others is undermined. It is notable that the feeling of being suicidal does not preclude care for others: for many of our participants, a wish to avoid hurting loved ones acts as the final barrier to suicide. But this last vestige of normative guidedness away from suicide is vulnerable to attack from two directions: first, the idea that the self is of no use or, worse, a burden to others may mean that others become viewed as, despite some suffering, 'better off without me'. Second, loss of reciprocality in one's relationships with others may erode the belief that one's death *would* cause suffering, in so far as others are experienced as uncaring or even hostile. Sometimes others simply 'go off the radar' to the extent that the guiding value 'to not cause suffering' is annihilated.

> *I am scared of going out and seeing people in town as I feel that they look at me and can see that I am suicidal and they are laughing at me and urging me to just hurry up and kill myself and leave this planet.* (Female, 30, interview)

> *I do a mental check about how others would feel if I wasn't around any more. If [I] can give reasons why they would be better off or if I don't care how they would feel then I know that it is time to worry.* (Female, 37, questionnaire)

> *[The] awareness that there are people around you who care for you and would be devastated to lose you, becomes*

impossible to believe, or even acknowledge. It's not on the radar. (Female, 27, questionnaire)

The protective role of normative agency in suicide, then, seems to rely upon a basic sense of connectedness with others, in which the self is experienced both as a giver and receiver of care. In FBS 1 and in FBS 2 this is disrupted. It also depends on the agent's ability to translate her system of goals and values into action. The experience of chronic depletion of mental resources described in FBS 3 deprives the agent of that ability, and may in the long term erode the system of goals and values itself. This sense of depletion, described by the majority of participants, seems likely to be, at least to an extent, veridical. We see in the data numerous occasions where participants could be appropriately characterized as *trying* to do something. Many of these instances of trying relate to *mental action*, taken here to mean actively directing one's thought and attention, deliberately bringing up and subduing mental imagery, regulating emotional responses and suppressing emotional behaviours, acting against one's strongest desire, making decisions, and so on. For example, participants try, and fail, to control their thoughts, which are experienced as oppressing, obsessive, or too fast and numerous. They try, and fail, to regulate their emotions that are experienced as overwhelming. In addition, participants try to prevent their true feelings from manifesting in their behaviour, which is then experienced as inauthentic. They also try to inhibit suicidal action impulses, often experienced as a struggle between different selves or parts of self.

Changes to the way the immediate surroundings are experienced place additional demands on the person's mental resources. In some cases at least, the feeling of being suicidal implies a change in which aspects of the environment are salient: bridges, tall buildings, train tracks, packets of paracetamol, and knives stand out while everything else recedes to the background. The meaning of everyday objects also changes: a 'window to look out of' becomes a 'window to jump out of'. Ordinary environments thus become sources of constant distraction, where concentration on a task is continually disrupted by cues for suicidal thoughts and behaviour issuing from the person's surroundings. Each redirection of attention constitutes a mental action and consumes mental resources, depleting the resources available to the normative agent.

While normative guidedness is a constitutive part of what it is to be a human agent, much of what we do in daily life is pre-reflective, guided by cues from the environment and our bodies. This 'animal agency' (Steward, 2009) is at its strongest at times when our actions are guided less by who we are than by what we are, an organism that needs to find nourishment and avoid immediate physical danger. It is most pronounced when we, for example, eat while very hungry or leap out of the way of a fast moving car, and it recedes into the background when we ignore feelings of exhaustion and the sound of a dripping tap to work on a philosophical problem.

It is a feature of actions arising from bodily agency that they can be 'done without thinking'. For example, when turning off a tap that has been distracting you, it bears little on the success of the action whether you attend to what you are doing, or whether your mind is still churning over the problem and you execute the action without taking much notice of doing so. The action is not spared any thought, and thought is not required. However, some kind of minimal awareness does persist throughout the action so that if the tap suddenly falls apart and attention is drawn to the task there will be no difficulty determining what you were trying to do and why. It will not require deduction, and the justification for the action is already there. Even when performed in a way often described as 'automatic', our actions are intrinsically meaningful to us and have a sense of continuity about them that survives such qualitative shifts. In other words, the experience of bodily agency provides a steady background of meaning and continuity to our experiences of action.

In FBS 2 some of the accounts describe disruptions of bodily agency that are inseparable from a loss of feelings of a certain kind. A closer look at the 'glass wall' metaphor suggests just such an absence of an experience of agency; one that persists despite continued behavioural effects. That is, in the cultural context in which the study is situated, seeing is a metaphor for understanding ('I see' meaning 'I understand'). Thus a person behind glass knows about and can reflect on her surroundings. However, something is missing from the experience; a feeling or feelings that would bring a sense of reality to the experience and a sense of being present in the scene. Ratcliffe (2008b) argues that the kinds of feelings that are closely linked with the modality of touch involve a lack of differentiation between the body and objects in the world. Having them, we experience ourselves as part of the scene and the scene has, to us, a sense of reality attached to it. Having lost the feelings, on the other hand, we experience the opposite — the scene as detached from us and ourselves as not present.

To interpret the metaphor, then, it seems significant that a sheet of glass allows a person to both look without touching and to observe without acting on. Some less metaphorical expressions corroborate this analysis:

> *Things around me feel different. For example I can see and know that it is a lovely sunny day, but this is at a 'head' level. It's as if it's not real and I can't feel it. Everything seems to be detached and not real... I find it very hard to reach out to people. I just want to be left alone and don't want anything or anyone to bother me. I feel somehow stuck in this place and unable to do anything. It's also quite a physical feeling — that I somehow can't physically reach out to others.* (Female, 55, email interview)

The 'lack of light/lack of colour' metaphor described in FBS 2 is less obviously about acting and appears instead to relate more to the impact the scene is able to have on the person. However, the punch this state of being packs is all about acting: one's environment is no longer experienced as eliciting a bodily response, either in the sense of arousing feelings or in the sense of being drawn into action. To retain 'normal functioning', the impetus to move at all has to be manufactured within the confines of the self, and the resulting joyless, effortful actions fail to amount to living.

> *Living with depression is like living in black and white when everyone else is living in colour. You feel like you're just functioning, not living. Literally just functioning. And everything just seems twice as hard for no reason you can pinpoint.* (Female, 24, questionnaire)

In the absence of the kind of bodily agency just described, actions that would normally require a minimum of physical effort and no mental effort, such as boiling the kettle for tea, now seem to require both in abundance. Life as a whole is infected with a sense of effortfulness and death comes to mean rest.

The loss of bodily response is described further in FBS 4, where the disruption to bodily agency is an experience *of* the body: a body diseased, disintegrating and in pain, exhausted beyond recovery, or already lost (numb, hollow, 'not there'). Of late, it has been popular to focus on 'psychache' and associated escape theories of suicide, where suicide is seen as an escape from mental pain (Shneidman, 1996; Williams, 2001). Our data show the visceral nature of this experience. Our participants describe their suicidal state as one that requires an immediate response rather than a future-focused solution, a response capable of establishing a sense of balance that is at least analogous, and perhaps directly related to, homeostasis in the organism.

So far we have treated normative and bodily agency separately in order to elicit the structure of the experience of agency in suicidal feelings. However, the separation is artificial: bodily and normative guidedness are dimensions rather than distinct parts of human agency, both ontologically and phenomenologically. In everyday experience we mostly have a 'minimal' sense of agency with an 'immersed awareness' of our actions (Pacherie, 2008) and just get on with acting, non-reflectively, with neither aspect of agency brought to our awareness. We take our agency for granted, with specific experiences of agency appearing against this background. When the experience of agency does come to the fore, it is in the interplay between bodily and normative guidedness and the physical and social environment in which they are embedded. For example when deciding whether to walk or drive to the supermarket, an immediate desire to take the car, constituted by feelings of physical fatigue and the thought of having to carry home heavy bags along a busy road, may go counter to longer term socially embedded goals of minimizing your carbon footprint and keeping fit. In such a case having to draw on your 'strength of will' brings normative guidedness to the foreground, while at the same time you retain an awareness of the resistant bodily self, and perhaps also of the material and social context in which the conflict takes place. These everyday conflicts are part of what it is to experience oneself as an agent, and it is plausible that some amount of conflict is a part of this experience most of the time: there is often in the background a mild thirst or hunger, for example, or awareness of a duty to be fulfilled while satisfying these. These ordinary conflicts pose no threat to agency, or the self, being experienced in a unified way; indeed, the ongoing resolution of such conflicts may even contribute to the experience of a unified self.

However, our contention is that the conflicts experienced in the feeling of being suicidal are of a different order, affecting the core structure of the sense of self as bodily and normative agency become reified as distinct parts of the self. In FBS 1, we distinguished between the experience of a loss of consistency in the normative self, and the experience of a loss of coherence between the normative self and the bodily self. While in experiences of loss of consistency there is a problem with the sense of normative agency, nevertheless, the internal structure of agency is left intact. As we put it above, there is a question of who I am, but not what I am. In experiences of lost coherence, this internal structure has broken down so that there is a disruption of the interaction between normative and bodily agency. Where the experience is one of a battle between the two, the normative self is experienced as further weakening, or even disappearing in the face of the conflict. Where there is a sense of detachment between different parts of the self, and as the experience of actions being guided by long-term goals and values diminishes and bodily agency is disrupted, actions become devoid of the feelings of significance usually associated with them. What the person does seems 'mechanical' and 'not real' to the extent that he 'loses his humanity' (Male, 29, face-to-face interview).

This experience is also apparent in accounts of suicide attempts. One participant describes herself as being like 'an automaton' and the suicide attempt as being 'the natural response' (Female, 22, questionnaire). 'Cold, emotionless' action without conscious evaluative thought can also signal an approaching attempt (Male, 43, face-to-face interview). While the *decision* to die can be felt as the last spark of normative agency, a final flare before extinction, the act itself may still be 'automated'. Thus one participant distinguishes between the decision to die and the process of suicide, with the decision being 'the key to the completion of the act' (Female, 22, questionnaire). However, unlike skilled action such as driving the car without thinking about gear changes, which is also described as 'automatic', 'automatism' in this sense does not imply ease; it can be very difficult to kill oneself, with the coming apart of normative and bodily agency acting now as a barrier to suicide. Our participants talk about their bodies 'not letting them' do it (Female, 41, questionnaire) and refer to 'battling' again, this time with 'a life instinct' (Female, 22, questionnaire). This phenomenon needs further examination but stands at least to remind us that the 'lived body' is not just the emotional body but also the biological organism that has during the course of its life added to its self-protective reflexes (gagging when swallowing noxious fluids) many learned routines serving the same end (avoiding skin contact with sharp objects).[8]

For Heidegger (2001) there is an essential difference between human kind of being and nature's kind of being: 'I am surely not a sequence of processes. That is not human. For example, that an exam[9] takes place is not simply a process as, for instance, as when it is raining, but it is something historical, [occurring] in a human situation and within the history of a human life' (*ibid.*, p. 210). Some of our participants describe suicide as feeling like a part of the natural order, which

---

[8]   Thanks to Toby Newson for reminding us of the learned element.

[9]   Meaning a medical examination.

can mean either that the act of suicide shares something of the form of a process of nature, or that there is a sense of natural rightness about suicide, or both. Both of these ideas are expressed in the work of a writer with first-hand experience of suicidal feelings, with suicide finding an analogy in apoptosis, a programmed self-destruction of a diseased or useless cell (Humpston, 2011).[10] The analogy conveys a sense of a deterministic sequence following a contingent initiator, and thereby captures the phenomenology of a suicide attempt, which, once the decision is made, follows its course without being open to revision.

Further, when suicidal, all actions can have this process-like character. That is, acting in the world can *in general* feel like it does not take place within a human situation or locate itself within a history of a human life. The loss of situatedness was described in FBS 1 and FBS 2, where experiences of one's surroundings are no longer experiences of being implicitly guided to act. Historicity is compromised in the feeling of being suicidal wherever the experience of normative guidedness of actions diminishes. It is worth noting that the impact of this loss of temporal structure is evident in results from experimental psychology, which show that suicidal behaviour is associated with deficits in the ability to recall specific events in one's past and with a vagueness in future-oriented thinking that seems to mirror the memory deficit (Williams, 2001). The self-concept becomes a fixed point rather than a fluid work-in-progress and the sense of being able to draw on one's past to create a much improved future gives way to a blind hopelessness regarding the self and its possibilities for growth.

The relationship between the loss of self-worth that is implicitly and sometimes explicitly part of being suicidal and the experience of suicide as a process in the domain of nature suggests a further relationship between the experiences of 'psychache' demanding an immediate act to restore balance and the feeling that the self is bad, worthless, or diseased:

> *By rights I should be dead. How can my body sustain this? How can my mind sustain this?... I felt so intensely miserable that... I thought it was going to overwhelm me completely. And it didn't, you see. That was, it was letting me live... It's like an illness, a physical illness or a cancer that... doesn't kill you entirely, but leaves you in such a reduced... pitiless state, for the rest of your life... It doesn't kill you but it does something a lot worse. You know it keeps*

---

[10] See also Kean (2011).

you alive in this, this terrible, terrible condition. (Male, 29, face-to-face interview)

The intense misery can *feel* like a bodily disease capable of bringing death, which however does not come, and unfathomable as it is, the body goes on living. Yielding to a suicidal impulse can then be seen as a case of 'letting nature take its course'. This feeling, that one should 'by rights be dead' signals a loss of embodied self-worth and contributes, we argue, to the experience of suicide being a part of the natural order in the sense of natural rightness. Experiences of the body being somehow 'already dead' — empty, hollow, non-responsive, numb, 'not there' — make sense of suicide in the same way: as an act that restores coherence and equilibrium, returning things to the way they should be.

Conclusion

The feeling of being suicidal is an existential feeling in the sense that it involves changes to the core structures of experience that form the background for ordinary thinking, acting, and feeling. We have claimed that these changes can be cashed out in terms of anomalies in the experience of agency, in so far as that can be understood in terms of normative guidedness (the coming to bear on one's actions an understanding of the self) and bodily guidedness (the experience of being directed to act in virtue of being embodied and embedded in one's immediate environment). We have described the suicidal self as a self for whom agency is disrupted and depleted, and believe that such understanding forms the appropriate background for interpreting suicidal thoughts and intentions.

Acknowledgments

We thank all the participants, some of whom have shown long-standing commitment to the study, and our advisors both past and present. Thanks also to The James Wentworth-Stanley Memorial Fund for both financial assistance and moral support and to the BIG Lottery Fund Research Programme for the grant that has enabled us to continue work on the subject of suicide. We would also like to thank the two anonymous reviewers for their insightful and helpful comments.

Jennifer Radden

The Self and Its Moods in Depression and Mania

1. Introduction

On most accounts, the self is some sort of unifying principle or unified entity.[1] My particular interest, here as in past research, is the self's unity as it relates to mental health norms, and the way psychopathology can illuminate and allow us to better understand the normal, and normally unified and integrated, self.[2] A modest degree of integration is indicative of mental health, and the want of it (in the extreme self-fracture of dissociative states, for example) is appropriately seen as calling for some form of self-unifying treatment.

Whether or not separate disorders (or even separate symptoms, such as delusions) are natural kinds, as some have supposed, mental illness as a broader class is not — it is a category reflecting social goals and values. That suggests we ought explore how psychopathological states reveal the disunity of the disordered self (and expose aspects of the normally unified and integrated self) in a piecemeal way, one disorder cluster or category at a time. And the self, in turn, might be expected to be incomplete or dis-unified in more than one way. It is, arguably. And I take this to affirm, and call into play, several of the range of theoretical accounts of self-unity and integration currently entertained, both those at the pre-reflective level, and those affecting the reflective self. The deficiencies of pre-reflective *ipseity* identity in schizophrenic-spectrum disorders, for example, represent one kind of incomplete self.[3] They direct our attention to an aspect of normal self-unity that had until recently gone unremarked in

---

[1] Not of course on 'no self' theories, or the various descendents of Hume's account.

[2] Selves have admitted of divisions in a tradition that traces to Plato, so we are at most talking about the normal degree of division, not some absolute integration and oneness.

[3] See Sass, Parnas and Zahavi (2011), Parnas and Sass (2011), and Zahavi (2011).

discussions of self-identity, the *pre-reflective* consciousness of one-self as an embodied, unitary subject, sometimes known as the minimal or core self (Gallagher, 2011, p. 119). From the perspective of the *reflective* self, by contrast, impulse control disorders have been seen to exemplify incoherence between desires at odds with the normal, 'real', or 'deep' self (Frankfurt, 1971; Wolf, 1990).[4] And the divided consciousness and amnesic barriers of dissociative disorder indicate another way the pathological self can be seen to lack the degree of wholeness enjoyed by more normal selves. (See Braude, 1991; Radden, 1996; 2010.)

Beyond the light they may shed on theories of self, these ideas have some potential in accounting for the disorder status of psychiatric conditions that want for complete neurobiological explanations.[5] Included among these are the schizophrenias, impulse control and dissociative disorders, and disorders of mood.[6] In the case of mood disorders, whose biological origins are widely advertised, such non-biological explanations have been relatively sparse, and presumed more often than defended. Grounds for the presumption that depression and mania warrant disorder status seem to lie with their disabling effects on normal social functioning (depression is enervating; mania leads to recklessness; both conditions are linked to self-destructive acts), their deviation from other social norms (they are judged inappropriately intense, or mercurial) or, more recently, their link to cognitive biases exceeding the norm.[7] By identifying how the characteristic mood states (rather than other aspects) of depression and mania affect the self's integration, the present analysis might supplement these appeals to social norms of functionality, affective appropriateness, and bias.

Of the self in depression and mania, it must first be noted that the bipolarity of manic-depressive conditions will almost certainly interfere with their subjects' diachronic ('extended' or 'narrative')[8] unity.

---

[4] The kleptomaniac, Susan Wolf explains in her Frankfurtian account of the Real Self View, is alienated from her will because her will is not the result of her choice; her action does not spring from the real self with which she is to be properly identified (see Wolf, 1990, pp. 23–45).

[5] The completion of such explanation may be necessary yet not sufficient to warrant disorder status, but it would be a start.

[6] The ambitions of programmes of cognitive neuropsychiatry are of course to identify and blend into one unified theory both functional deficits and their neurobiological correlate (see Lloyd, 2011).

[7] For an important discussion of the basis for attributing mental disorder, and the inadequacies of normativism, see Graham (2010, Chapter 5).

[8] These terms seem to be used almost interchangeably in the literature.

To some extent so presumably do the disruptive and unwelcome episodes of most kinds of mental disorder. But taken apart from that extended perspective, and looked at more synchronically, neither unipolar nor bipolar affective states seem to leave their subjects lacking along any of the dimensions sketched above. At times depression and mania reach psychotic and delusional extremes, it is true, and they may then exhibit such lack of integration. But while serious, the run of the mill cases of depressive and manic mood states in which we are interested are non-psychotic, and appear to exhibit an intact minimal sense of self.[9] Moreover, the arrangement of their desires reflects the hierarchy found in (normal) Frankfurtian selves, and their conscious awareness is not riven with dissociative barriers. They are normally integrated selves in addition, we'll see, because of the characteristic 'mood congruence' they exhibit. Perhaps not surprisingly, given this, these states are sometimes indistinguishable from the more ordinary ones deemed normal and even appropriate responses to life's vicissitudes, such as the sadness we feel at the loss of a person we have loved, or the exhilaration felt when, for instance, we are blessed with great good fortune.[10]

And yet, the status of unipolar and bipolar depression and mania as disorders of mood is responsible for ways in which depressed and manic selves will likely be incomplete, or insufficiently integrated — due to a combination of the nature of moods in general, the particular moods to which the depressed and manic person is prone, and the motivational traits of depressed and manic frames of mind. Every human is subject to (even, Heidegger would insist, constituted by) moods. Yet a closer look at the extreme, pervasive, limited, and limiting moods, and respective apathy and satisfactions associated with depression and mania, suggests they will serve to hinder the self's integrative capabilities. In contrast to conditions that are not primarily mood-based (delusional, volitional, and behavioural disorders, for example), these mood-based affective disorders involve a distinctive impediment to the self-knowledge and integrity of their sufferers.

---

[9]   Estimates vary, but on one, psychotic features occur in 15% of depression and 58% of mania cases (Kempf, Hussain and Potash, 2005). Fundamental classificatory questions about such psychotic affective conditions remain unresolved, however, leaving the implications of these estimates unresolved. On some analyses psychotic affective disorders represent a subtype of affective illness, on others they are a separate schizoaffective disorder. For reviews, see Kendler (1991) and Kumazaki (2011).

[10]   For some of the problems to which this gives rise in the case of depression, see Horwitz and Wakefield (2007).

The beliefs associated with depression, particularly, have received extensive attention with the emergence of cognitive therapy.[11] But moods in general, and with them the moods of affective disorder in particular, have been relatively neglected, in philosophical and non-philosophical writing alike.[12,13] So the following discussion begins by distinguishing moods in general from the other affective states, or emotions, they often accompany. The complex and ambiguous relationship between these less and more cognitive, and seemingly less and more intentional, states is provided preliminary conceptual clarification using work by Goldie (2000) and Ratcliffe (2010a). Turning next to disordered moods, some respects in which the mood-disordered self is whole and integrated in contrast to the self with other kinds of disorder require acknowledgment; the patient suffering these disorders exhibits so-called mood congruence that seems to ensure a kind of personal integration. Nonetheless, I show, the moods that characterize those disorders can be expected to impede self-integration as it is explained by philosophers such as Richard Moran (2001).

Two further preliminaries are called for. First, while affective disorders sometimes reach psychotic proportions, the focus of the following discussion is states of depression and mania that are severe but non-psychotic, as we have seen, and the conclusions drawn here must not be supposed to extend beyond them. Second, I do not mean to suggest that these features of the moods of mania and depression exhaust the interesting phenomenological aspects of these conditions, or that mania and depression may not have as many phenomenological differences as similarities.[14] But this discussion is focused on the analogous ways aberrant moods might affect self-integration in each disorder.

---

[11] For a careful and thorough account of the beliefs involved in depression as they are the focus of cognitive therapy, see Biegler (2011).

[12] As one authority has put it, speaking of their neglect in relation to psychopathology: 'The recognition of the so-called "primary" disorders of mood has not led... to a refinement of the semiology of the experiences themselves. This has been impeded by the use of descriptive behavioral surrogates or by metapsychological accounts of affect as a form of energy... None of these developments has contributed to the clinical description of the mood disorders' (Berrios, 1985, p. 745).

[13] More generally, affective cognition, as distinct from emotional *feelings*, has been privileged by philosophers because of the role it plays in normative analyses. I am grateful to Catriona Mackenzie for drawing attention to this point.

[14] The depression sufferer's experience of time, for example, has been shown to be characteristically disordered (Fuchs, 2001; Ratcliffe, 2012a).

2. Moods and Emotions, Conceptual Distinctions

Moods are affections that are unbounded in their psychological effects, colouring and framing experience in its moment-by-moment totality. Their 'objects' have an elusive, indiscriminate generality that sets them apart from the objects of more directed and discrete affective states.[15] This much we know to be true of all moods, not merely those associated with disorder. The syndromes containing depressive sadness and manic exhilaration, respectively, are named for their characteristic moods that, as this suggests, touch *all* experience (they are classified as Mood Disorders). In depressive states, the world appears bleak, meaningless, and without consolation, blanketed with gloom; and the manic mood contains a sense of vitality and excitement matched by an external world that seems to brim with promise and possibility.

Depression and mania also involve many affective states with more exact cognitive content. Thus, typical responses found in depression include feeling sad (miserable, dispirited, listless, bored, dull, world-weary, without hope, oppressed, and disgusted with everything), but also, for instance, being inclined to disparaging self-assessments (I am worthless, incompetent, inadequate, sinful, guilty, and so on). And as well as exhilaration, excitement, an almost bodily sense of vitality and exuberance, and feeling 'on top of the world', typical manic states include believing in oneself to an extreme degree (I am a genius, the cleverest, most promising, most successful, important).[16] As these examples show, like most if not all normal affections, the affective states of depression and mania are loosely separable at the conceptual level into less and more cognitive or belief-based states. These elements interpenetrate: belief states emerge from, and seemingly give rise to, inchoate as well as more directed feelings; moreover from the perspective of the phenomenological whole, these characteristically discouraged attitudes and beliefs of depression, and positive ones of mania, are co-mingled with the feeling states. Although in varying mixes, depressive and manic states typically combine elements of each sort. Following a standard philosophical convention, the more belief-like of these states (the conviction that I am worthless, for example, or exceptional) are referred to here as *emotions* in contrast to

---

[15] Within psychology, these have sometimes been identified as 'free-floating emotions' and 'pure feelings', although they have received little attention. See Lambie and Marcel (2002, p. 224).

[16] These are at most a selection of states typifying depression and mania, and even granting that, the prevalence of so-called mixed-state syndromes that combine depressed and manic responses requires us to proceed with caution in drawing on these generalizations.

more amorphous and pervasive *moods* (a sense of disinterested list-lessness, for example, or feeling 'on top of the world').

The relationship between these two has been a source of philosophical disagreement.[17,18] Thus, when affects are analysed as intentional states, whose objects are what they are about or over, it is commonly said that emotions are about particulars, or particulars generalized, while moods are about nothing in particular or, alternatively, about the world as a whole. This is found in the influential appraisal theories of emotion.[19] (As the above examples of depressive listlessness and manic vitality suggest, moods seem to encompass, or at least accompany, bodily sensations, a point often confirmed in clinical description and memoirs.)[20] The categories of mood, feeling, and even emotion are loose and heterogeneous, not conducive to capture in tight analytic definition.[21] But we can at least say that on this account moods and emotions share intentional status; and each may involve phenomenal feelings, including but not limited to bodily sensations (whether such sensations are constituents, epiphenomenal, or causal antecedents is also a matter over which there is disagreement, although not one addressed here).[22]

It is widely accepted that phenomenal feelings somehow accompany many emotions. We speak of *feeling* sad, glad, or remorseful, for example, and of sad, glad, or remorseful feelings.[23,24] In a recent analysis, emotions are partially constituted by such feelings, which are intentional in being over or about the object of the emotion felt (Goldie, 2000). When feelings are part of emotions, they help define

---

[17] Because emotions are linked to social norms of appropriateness and conceptions of character, this matter has extensive implications for philosophical conceptions of the self, and a more complete analysis would better acknowledge these normative aspects of the contrast between moods and emotions. However, they are beyond the scope of the present discussion.

[18] It may even reflect two separate concepts of emotion — as feeling and cognitive state. See Deigh (2010).

[19] See Solomon (1993).

[20] See, for example, this observation about the experience of depression: 'My body became inert, heavy and burdensome. Every gesture was hard... My existence was pared away almost to nothing, except for the self-contempt that bruised my eye sockets and throat, that turned my stomach and made my tongue into some large, coarse creature in my mouth' (Shaw, 1997, pp. 2, 27).

[21] Emotions make up a varied class whose boundaries are not well fixed. See Rorty (1980).

[22] For discussion of these alternative positions, see Goldie (2010).

[23] 'Feeling' also has non-phenomenal uses, sometimes functioning as a synonym for 'judgment' or 'belief' (Nussbaum, 2001, p. 1).

[24] A compelling case for the importance and irreducibility of *psychic* feelings, as distinct from bodily-localized ones, is to be found in Stocker (1983).

the emotion and, at least in some cases, seem to be essential components.[25] Being in a state of fear, for example, is as intimately tied to the
feelings of apprehension it brings as it is to the thought of the danger
occasioning it.

Phenomenal feelings are also involved in depressed and manic
mood states. The phenomenology of depression and mania suggest
there is something (actually many things) it is like to feel depressed, or
manic. 'Feeling down', 'feeling high', 'feeling blue', 'feeling ebul-
lient', 'feeling miserable' — these descriptions have a breadth and
range that distinguish them from the more precisely directed emotions
to which their sufferers are prone. Although difficult to describe, the
feelings associated with depression and mania seem to be primary,
non-reducible *qualia*, directly accessible to their possessor through
introspection. Whether they can at the same time be said to be over or
about something, or everything, is one question calling for resolution
here, for it is often supposed that as phenomenal items, or *qualia*,
mental states are intransitive, and so non-intentional.[26]

That ordinary emotions are intentional needs little explanation or
support: we feel sad, or glad, over or about something particular, and
that something constitutes the intentional object of our emotion.[27] Not
all emotions may involve feelings.[28] But when they do, and the
intentionality of the feelings is at issue, several routes to attributing
some form of intentionality to feelings themselves can be identified.
In asking whether the phenomenal feelings that occur in, and seem to
partially constitute, mood states can be intentional, the ascription of
intentionality to the feelings attached to emotions, while different,
will provide us with initial landmarks.

First, it can be said that whatever intentional status is ascribed to
feelings comes by proxy only, through their association with the cognitive states they accompany. So on Goldie's analysis, introduced

[25] Goldie's is a view that runs contrary to Freud's, where feelings may come astray from to
the objects of the emotions with which they are associated. See Deigh (2010).

[26] For example: '...it is often taken for granted that, however significant, the phenomenal
character of an experience is neither *toward*, or *about*, anything. It could be claimed, therefore, that as a type of feeling, emotional feelings are states that denote nothing beyond
"how it is like" for a subject to experience them, thus barring the possibility of emotional
feelings having intentional objects' (Hatzimoysis, 2005, p. 107). See also Pacherie, speaking of feelings of agency as they are construed in a non-representational ('raw feels') analysis: 'Phenomenal feels are not about anything and have no satisfaction conditions; they
are simply present or absent' (Pacherie, 2011, p. 455).

[27] The 'aboutness' of emotion is customarily employed to indicate its intentional status.
Goldie prefers to speak of having a directedness towards an object (Goldie, 2000, p. 16).

[28] Many 'calmer' emotions, such as wistfulness, or equanimity, are not accompanied by any
discernable feelings at all (see Hume, 1978, p. 276).

above, phenomenal feelings may be intentional more or less fully and
directly: *bodily* feelings possess a sort of proxy intentionality bor-
rowed from the full intentionality of 'feeling towards', whereas *emotional* feelings are, as he says, 'essentially bound up with content —
with what the feeling is directed towards' (Goldie, 2000, p. 51).[29] An
alternative analysis can be traced to William James's famous identification of emotion with bodily feelings: for neo-Jamesians the objects
of the emotions are the felt bodily states that accompany, or occasion,
the emotional response.[30] On a final analysis, feelings are an expression or manifestation of the particular emotions of which they form a
part, and gain their intentionality this way. If our tears or other expressions are said to be over or about the object of our sadness, we can say
our feelings are intentional by regarding them as similarly expressive
(this is Deigh, 2010, pp. 38–9).

None of these analyses completely shows how we might account
for the intentionality of mood states in the absence of the cognitive
description that seems to pin down the feeling as a state within that
particular intentional frame — identifying it as a feeling of sadness,
say, rather than nostalgia, or grief, or despair. To respect such nuances
and yet to suppose we can distinguish between moods that are phenomenally similar seems to be to rely too much on our powers of
phenomenological discernment. The 'objects' of moods, as we noted
earlier, are different from those of emotions: our moods alight on them
— not exactly haphazardly, but insatiably, carelessly, and indiscrimi-
nately, as if any one will do as well as the next (in this respect, they
possess the sort of fungibility that we associate with money, any dollar
bill as good as the next).[31] To suggest that the mood states are over or
about such indiscriminate and unstable 'objects' seems to subvert the
aspect of intentionality by which its object usually serves to identify
and distinguish the mental state involved.

Intentional analyses of moods and of feelings have recently been
challenged directly: the intentional model, in terms of which moods
are over or about something even if something vague and general, is

---

[29] Feelings toward are characterized as subject to the will, based on evidence in the same way
as beliefs, and as possessing of a distinctive phenomenology (Goldie, 2000, pp. 50–83).

[30] The focus of the emotion is not, or not exhausted by, any bodily sensations, however. If I
am angry with my neighbours and it makes my blood boil, my emotion is about the neighbours, not, or not merely, the sensations of heat and turmoil I feel (I owe the example to
Anthony Hatzimoysis). So neo-Jamesians sometimes add to definitions in terms of bodily
perceptions *representations of properties of vital interest to their subjects* (see Prinz,
2004, pp. 52–78. For a critique of this account of representationalism see Hatzimoysis,
2005, and Deigh, 2010).

[31] I am grateful to Amélie Rorty for this analogy.

misleading, Matthew Ratcliffe (2008a) insists. Some moods are unlike (intentional) emotions in this respect, he argues: they '…do not incorporate any conceptual content'. This is because, as feelings, these moods are better seen as conditions for the possibility of intentional states, rather than themselves intentional states. 'Existential feeling', Ratcliffe asserts, describes the moods he is interested in, which are pre- rather than non-intentional, primordial, and sometimes so far *beneath* reflective awareness as to be 'phenomenologically inconspicuous'. Moods are described as '…a space of possibilities within which we experience, think and act… presupposed by conceptual judgements' (Ratcliffe, 2010a, p. 368).

Ratcliffe's analysis of moods as conditions of possibility suggests an analogy with dispositional states such as attitudes that may explain the quasi-objects of moods without fully attributing intentionality. Attitudes comprise a host of emotional responses to particular objects.[32] For example, if I harbour an attitude of distrust towards all Doberman dogs, the intentional object of the attitude is the general class of Dobermans. But this attitude is manifested in particular emotions of momentary fear, dislike, wariness, and so on, whose object is in each case particular experiences of encountering a given dog of that breed.[33] Some moods are passing and short-lived, and some emotions are enduring (on the model of the way the passions were understood in earlier eras).[34] So it is not merely their duration and stability that distinguish moods from any constitutive emotions, it is also their degree of generality. When moods are more enduring and even recalcitrant states, as they often are, they appear to be analysable in somewhat the same way as are attitudes. Thus, it might be said that a depressive mood involves not necessarily a longer-term but a more encompassing state that disposes me to have emotional responses to many, most, or even all the particular objects prompted by the passing parade of my thoughts and experiences — the way each experience of a particular Doberman prompts a separate and particular emotional response. (Sunk in a gloomy mood, I am discouraged about some particular personal failure, *as well as* the most recent economic news, *and* an unsatisfactory encounter with an employer, and so on.) By analysing moods into their constituent, intentional emotions, there may be a way to

---

[32] 'Attitude' can be used in a general way to cover any mental stance toward an object. Here, it means stable and enduring emotional dispositions or traits with cognitive elements.

[33] This is not to claim that emotions cannot be dispositional, they can. But they can also be occurrences, briefly felt, then gone.

[34] See Charland (2010) for an account of the change between the passions of past times, and today's emotions.

explain the apparent 'objects' of moods while preserving the division by which emotions alone are intentional.

It is undeniable that mood states, or at least those characterizing depression and mania, are redolent with more straightforwardly intentional emotional responses. Moods do not exactly *reduce* to the particular emotions to which they give rise, for as we saw, they involve phenomenal qualities over and above their manifestations as particular emotions.[35] Nonetheless their tendency to spawn a host of fully intentional states may explain the way (feature by feature, moment by moment) moods involve intentional descriptions of how the whole world is, creating, in the case of our mood disorders, generalized 'objects' of depression — the world as gloomy and hopeless — and mania — the world as full of promise and possibility. (Again, although it is not the focus of the present discussion, this loosely dispositional analysis bears on the way emotions are subject to appraisal as moods are often not. If, when, and to the extent that moods have given rise to particular emotions, those emotions may be apt for normative evaluation. So may the moods themselves, however, we shall see in Section 5, when they can be affected by their subject.)

3. The Personally Integrated Self

Before turning to the way its moodiness is likely to render the depressed and manic self incompletely integrated by contrast with more normal selves, it will be helpful to remember the respects in which these moody selves *are* normally integrated according to the terms of the theoretical accounts of self-integration noted above, and by contrast to some other kinds of disorder. Except when their condition has psychotic features, the minimal selves of those with mood disorders remain intact; similarly, they are normal Frankfurtian selves with respect to their desires; and their consciousness is not fractured by dissociation. We might distinguish these different accounts of integration by speaking of the *minimal* self-integration, *volitional* integration, and *consciousness* integration.

There is another respect in which the depression and mania sufferer enjoys a self that is integrated in the normal way: this we can call *personal* self-integration. The cognitive states associated with non-psychotic mood disorders are often marked by their *congruence* with the

---

[35] This is illustrated by Charlotte Perkins Gilman when, of her melancholia, she writes that '...a brain, of its own nature, gropes for reasons for its misery. Feeling the sensation fear, the mind suggests every possible calamity; the sensation shame — remorse — and one remembers every mistake and misdeeds of a lifetime...' (Gilman, 1935, p. 90).

mood they accompany.[36,37] Her suicidal preoccupations and self-neglect seem appropriate to the depressive despair and self-loathing expressed by the depression sufferer, just as the manic man's over-blown and grandiose delusions often nicely match his cheerful and sanguine expression and expansive behaviour. Incongruence between outer, more public responses and inner states as they are inferred (from verbal expressions, context, and so on) is typical of the 'inappropriate affect' deemed a symptom of schizophrenia-spectrum disorders, and of the so-called Mood Incongruent Psychotic Affective Illnesses (Kendler, 1991). But such incongruence is not characteristic of psychotic states in depressive or manic disorders, let alone of the non-psychotic kind discussed here. These are typically mood-congruent — matched in the case of depression by inertia, attitudes of indifference, and expressions of suffering, and by expansive gestures and cheerful insouciance in mania.[38] Whatever the qualities of depression and mania that indicate their disorder status, it does not seem to be a lack of integration at this personal level.

The category of mood congruency is a loose one, leaving its status as a clinical criterion unsatisfactory (Kumazaki, 2011).[39] Nonetheless, it is one that we seem to recognize as central to normal social interaction. Of course, we want to say, the person who feels sad acts and behaves sad, and may voice her sadness — if she never does, we suspect her of denial at best, hypocrisy and deceit at worst. So obvious is this aspect of the normally integrated self that we might be inclined to take it for granted.[40] Yet the normal self is intelligible to others in great

---

[36] The terms 'mood-congruent' and 'mood-incongruent' have changed little since their initial definition in the third edition of DSM in relation to whether the content of delusions or hallucinations was 'consistent with the predominant mood' and themes; examples of such themes for depression included 'themes of either personal inadequacy, guilt, disease, death, nihilism, or deserved punishment' (p. 215). See Spitzer *et al.* (2002), WHO (1993). For a useful review, and important conceptual clarification, see Kumazaki (2011).

[37] Arguably, mood congruence is what best distinguishes the condition known as Paranoid Disorder from paranoid schizophrenia. See Butler and Braff (1991), Radden (2007).

[38] It is this intelligibility and coherence that forms Jaspers' central distinction between delusion-like states, of which these would be some, and the incomprehensible cognitions that he deemed delusions proper; it also led him to say of the affective illnesses generally that they 'appear to us to be open to empathy and natural' (Jaspers, 1997, p. 578).

[39] Some of the imprecision attaching to this category and its implications for clinical work are discussed by Kumazaki, who concludes that although a finer definition is desirable to clarify differential diagnosis, the concept of mood congruence 'inevitably involves a certain degree of ambiguity and subjectivity' (Kumazaki, 2011, p. 327).

[40] It is not a coherence that is perfect, needless to say, any more than the self's unity is exact.

part due to this coherence and personal integration.[41] Without it, we would not be able to adopt the intentional stance that is our ordinary or folk-psychological way of approaching others — attributing beliefs and desires to comport with the responses we observe more directly.[42]

Studies on the cognitive processing of depression sufferers, but also moods more generally, seem to indicate that mood congruence is achieved through reasoning biases, and selective memory.[43] In this respect, mood congruence may be supposed to represent a form of deficiency, and we shall see later that when combined with other aspects of depressive and manic frames of mind, the limitations imposed by such mood congruence stand in the way of one sort of self-integration. But in spite of this evidence of abnormal or disturbed functioning, the resultant mood congruence apparently provides another, quite publicly important, kind of self-integration.

4. Depression, Mania, and the Self's Integrative Capabilities

The normal elements of self-knowledge and integration that are placed in jeopardy by mood disorder are to be found in accounts of reflective self-awareness and self-constitution associated with the so-called narrative ('diachronic', or 'extended') self.[44] These regularly rest on, and sometimes emphasize, the trait of reflective self-awareness, described by Harry Frankfurt as 'our peculiar knack of separating from the immediate content and flow of our own consciousness and introducing a sort of division within our minds [which]… puts in place an elementary reflexive structure… [enabling] us to focus our attention directly upon ourselves' (Frankfurt, 2006, p. 4).[45] This trait is presupposed in Richard Moran's discussion on the aspect of the

---

[41] Jaspers' insistence on the applicability of *verstehen*, here, makes the same point. We understand these states because of the way they can be formed into intelligible, coherent wholes.

[42] The 'intentional stance' has been defined as 'the strategy of prediction and explanation that attributes beliefs, desires, and other "intentional" states to systems — living and non-living — and predicts future behavior from what it would be rational for an agent to do, given those beliefs and desires' (Dennett, 1988, p. 495). See also Bolton and Hill (1996).

[43] See Matthews and MacLeod (2005), Gotlib *et al.* (2004), Joormann, Teachman and Gotlib (2009), van Wingen *et al.* (2010), Harris *et al.* (2010).

[44] Theories of narrative self differ over the self's ontology, the nature of and role of others in self construction, and so on, but I will not enter into those debates here. For a fair and careful review of these differences, see Schectman (2011).

[45] In their influential review of psychological work on consciousness, Lambie and Marcel mark this distinction by speaking of *second-order states of awareness* (Lambie and Marcel, 2002).

narrative self that is an active self-interpreter, a status that explains the authority accorded self-knowledge. And Moran's account will be used here to illustrate the kind of agency entailed in that, which is placed in jeopardy by moods.

Moran is concerned to avoid the mistaken idea that the (allegedly indubitable) self-knowledge required for a properly integrated self comes through a passive, inwardly-focused apprehension akin to the perception of outer-world objects. On this misleading, 'inner sense' view, we discover, and through introspection observe, the unity of our selves (or don't, as Hume famously pointed out). Instead, according to Moran, knowing my mental states often involves looking outward and assessing facts in the world, not looking inward: Moran's 'transparency' principle makes beliefs and attitudes not psychological facts about a person but commitments to states of affairs beyond the self — a normative demand that requires us to see as primary processes of deliberative reflection. And the active, deliberative aspects of the self's awareness explain our distinctively authoritative self-knowledge.

Our unity as selves comes, then, as the result of authorial action and reflective awareness. The aspect of Moran's thesis of importance to us is where he says the person himself '...plays a role in how he thinks and feels' through an introspective, interpretive process. We are 'self interpreting animals', he says, '...and... the exercise of this capacity plays a crucial role in *making us who we are*' (Moran, 2001, p. 59, emphasis added). In contrast to states of which we are passive recipients, beliefs and other attitudes are stances of the person involving agency and authority. The person is the responsible author of his beliefs and attitudes, and 'the question he asks himself about his belief or desire is normally answered by a *decision* rather than a *discovery*' (*ibid.*, p. 114, emphasis added).[46]

---

[46] Variants on the ideas explored here through Moran's analysis are to be found in Harry Frankfurt's ideas. For Frankfurt we act freely when what we do is what we want to do, and we will freely when what we want is what we want to want (Frankfurt, 2006, p. 15). Willing freely means that the self is at that time harmoniously integrated, and this process is also made possible by our ability to distance ourselves from our experiences and accept them, or not. The willing *acceptance* of attitudes, thoughts, and feelings transforms their status from mere items in our psychic history, Frankfurt asserts, to authentic expressions of ourselves. This takes time, and Frankfurt's is a more extended or diachronic self, constructed by going beyond merely wanting various things to coming to care about them, regard them as important, and loving them — when this love itself serves to integrate the self.

The exercise of self-interpretation depicted by Moran echoes processes described by Frankfurt as *supervisory*. The elementary reflexive structure enabling us to focus our attention directly upon ourselves, Frankfurt says, 'situates us to come up with a variety of supervisory desires, intentions, and interventions that pertain to the several constituents

In the reflexive exercise of self-interpretation depicted by Moran our states and experiences are the objects of mental *acts* of deliberation and decision. These are things that I *do*, not experiences I am subject to. And I cannot deliberate, or attend, without a fundamental sense of agency. A feeling of agency is *part of the experiential phenomenology of* my deliberating, attending, accepting, and so on.[47] The phenomenology of agency, hitherto rarely analysed, is thus of inescapable importance here. That phenomenology requires explication along at least three lines: the level at which the experience occurs *vis à vis* conscious or reflective awareness, the degree to which phenomenal feeling is involved, and the extent to which felt agency is tied to the fullest sense of public, bodily action.

5. The Phenomenology of Mental Agency

The agentic exercises and accompanying sense of agency emphasized by Moran take place as part of reflective self-awareness. By contrast, there is also said to be an experiental or phenomenal 'feeling of agency' that takes place at an implicit or first-order level; this is Vogeley and Gallagher's 'SoA' (Vogeley and Gallagher, 2011, p. 119). Presumably, the sense of agency (SoA) that occurs at the level of pre-reflective awareness will be a necessary or precondition of the capability exhibited in the more reflective exercise Moran describes. In addition, at the reflective level I am also able to form what have been described as 'agentive judgments' attributing agency to myself, such as 'I did it' (Bayne and Pacherie, 2007), complicating matters.[48] While related, these agentive judgments are distinct from the agentive experiences that seem to make possible, yet at the same time accompany or constitute part of, our active deliberations. Not only feelings of agency at both pre-reflective and reflective levels must be

and aspects of our conscious life' (*ibid.*, p. 4).

   In addition to the effect of moods on such self-reflective, supervisory states, states of severe depression may reflect a failure of the will essential to Frankfurt's account in other ways as well, it should be added, including the more obvious one that the depressed person is apathetic and passive, disinclined to will in any way.

[47] Vogeley and Gallagher apparently confirm this analysis, although their focus is on outward, rather than mental, actions. Attributions of agency ('I did it'), they say, 'involve the narrative self, although they *may normally be reports on, or based on, my actual pre-reflective experience of agency...*' (Vogeley and Gallagher, 2011, p. 119, emphasis added).

[48] Gallagher (2007) has contrasted first-order, phenomenal experience of agency and higher-order, reflective attribution, which corresponds to the distinction drawn by Bayne and Pacherie (2007) between agentive experiences and agentive judgments.

distinguished, then, but we must also separate each of those from reflective, non-phenomenal judgments about one's agency.

Recent analyses of the phenomenology of agency, whether as implicit or more reflective experience, have focused on a sense of agency accompanying corporeal action, things we do in the world. As Merleau-Ponty has persuasively insisted, this is the primordial source of agency and of our ideas about it (Merleau-Ponty, 1962). We acquire our sense of doing or agency from the experiences of embodied action (what we can call *actions proper*). Thus, what we know as deliberating, deciding, directing attention, judging, following a train of thought, recalling, and making a choice seem likely to be logically secondary, their feel shaped by metaphors derived from actions proper.[49]

Because of their focus on the agency of bodily actions, even those who acknowledge a sense of agency accompanying bodily actions may doubt whether such a sense of agency accompanies mental actions of these kinds.[50] Yet, however secondary and dependent, a parallel awareness of *doing* accompanies the group of states that are less public (deliberating, or acts of attention, for example) and is absent from others such as perceiving, or being in receipt of unbidden thoughts.[51] And these are differences among mental states that present themselves phenomenally. Bodily actions or actions proper are often placed in contrast to movements, when the contrast, which has phenomenological force, is that between say, jumping (an action) and being pushed (involving movement), and the *feel of doing* accompanies jumping, but not being pushed. Mental states allow of the same contrast: our mental actions such as deliberating and acts of attention seem to be akin to actions (jumping), not movements (being pushed). Moreover, these mental actions are also in sharp experiential contrast to more passive mental states such as being in receipt of unbidden thoughts, passions, impulses, or (sometimes) memories — states that lack a sense of agency in just the same way as being pushed. The intrusive memories that are deemed instances of psychopathology also illustrate, and rest on, this phenomenological contrast. Recalling an

---

[49] To say that these states are less public is not to deny that they will often have public, real-world effects, as theories of mental causation assert.

[50] The very presence of experiences of agency is apparently denied by some (for a review of such scepticism, see Bayne, 2008).

[51] As Bayne says, 'Although deliberation, decision-making, mental effort and the voluntary allocation of attention presumably involve movements in the head, *this is not how these states are experienced*' (Bayne, 2008, p. 185).

event is a mental action of which I am author; being subject to flash-backs is a distressing symptom *that feels quite different*.

In any moods, we find the antithesis of this kind of agency, and of the 'authorial' capacity that, as Moran (2001) says, 'makes us who we are'. First, we are usually passive recipients of moods, as powerless in our apprehension of them as we are of our perceptions or our unbid-den thoughts. Their comings and goings, try as we may to control them, are quixotic and often mysterious. Moods assail us, is the way Heidegger puts it. And although this may sometimes be true of more emotional feelings as well, it is notably characteristic of moods. Sec-ond, the pervasive and at the same time elusive qualities of moods seem to hold us in their thrall — preventing us from easily escaping them, and so imposing a kind of epistemic trap whereby we can rarely, or cannot without considerable difficulty and indirection, extricate ourselves from their influence. Again, some emotional feelings may exhibit these features also, although less commonly.[52]

While in varying degrees, these features apply to moods in general, not merely those of the person afflicted with mood disorder. And since we are all subject to moods, these two characteristics will not alone serve to distinguish mood disorder. So we will need to consider other differences of quality and quantity in the moods and frames of mind that beset the depression and mania sufferer.

Moods come intense or weak; steady or shifting; obdurate or easily dispelled; and they come with a particular range of what Ratcliffe calls existential possibilities. In each of these ways, too, both clinical lore and first-hand accounts suggest the moods of mood disorder exceed the norms, and so will work against self-integrating agency, depriving sufferers of the capabilities for self-integration described by Moran, I want presently to show. However, the more cognitive emotions also experienced in depression and mania do not share those limitations, and mood disorders, we must remember, typically comprise an inter-twined mix of more moody feelings and fully intentional states. To illustrate this contrast, it will be useful to begin with the more cogni-tive states involved (the self-denigrating assessment that 'I am worth-less' in depression or the inflated 'I am exceptional' of mania, for example); then we can proceed to why moods are deficient.

Cognitive states with propositional content can usually be objects of a distancing reflection, just as can all beliefs (as well as belief-like

---

[52] When a specific emotion is dispelled as the result of some fresh information, an obdurately lingering feeling may remain, just as a forgotten dream can seem to leave a feeling residue on waking — although whether we describe the residue as part of that emotion is perhaps arguable.

states such as hoping, wishing, and regretting). In this respect, these states exemplify the familiar intentionalist model. As the objects of mental agency, they can be summoned, examined, affirmed, doubted, endorsed, rejected, applauded, or embraced. The cognitive or belief states making up depression and mania can also be distanced from the subject this way. My beliefs that I am worthless, or an unsung genius, can be criticized as overgeneralization, as contradicted by the facts, as inconsistent with my other beliefs, or with my ideals and values. (It is those states that cognitive therapy is able to work on revising, apparently quite effectively.)

Such reflective appraisal of one's mental states is a form of epistemic agency, as we saw. And such normal exercises of epistemic agency are involved in the ongoing process by which the self is defined and constructed, encompassing what Moran calls the 'processes of review and revision that constitute the rational health of belief and other attitudes' (Moran, 2001, p. 108). Reflective self-awareness presupposes, and the narrative self is the product of, deliberative, authority-conferring agency.[53]

By contrast, moods work against these forms of epistemic agency. Such determinations will tend to succumb to the influence of the mood. We often cannot, cannot directly, or cannot without difficulty 'shake off' moods. Their elusive ubiquity and strangely fungible 'objects' seem to prevent our distancing ourselves from them by naming, doubting, or disbelieving. We are either in a mood — or not. Ratcliffe captures the epistemic inextricability of the person trapped in the moods of these disorders with his description of a mood as unable to be discarded because it is 'a context of intelligibility that continues to be presupposed by all experience and thought', and something that no 'experience, thought, or conceptualization can simply *transcend*' (Ratcliffe, 2010a, p. 362, emphasis added).[54]

Our passivity in relation to all moods, combined with their elusive ubiquity, begin to show why their status as pervasive affections might render the moods of depression and mania so inescapable, compromising the ability to exercise the particular self-constituting form of unifying epistemic agency described by Moran (2001). Yet, other qualitative and quantitative matters also distinguish the dysfunctional moods of depression and mania from more normal states. First,

---

[53] Frankfurt casts this achievement in terms of something more elevated, responsible personhood (Frankfurt, 2006). But again, this emphasis on the normative constituents of character go beyond the remit of the present discussion.

[54] So do some of the metaphors of depression memoir writers: William Styron describes being '…engulfed by a toxic and unnamable tide' (Styron, 2001, p. 14).

perhaps, is their intensity, emphasized in clinical observation and autobiographical writing alike. Ratcliffe stresses the phenomeno-logical inconspicuousness of some moods, we saw, which stand as preconditions of other states. Yet, rather than merely constituting inconspicuous background elements this way, the moods of affective disorder seem to declare themselves insistently, and it is their forceful presence that interferes with the self's integrity.[55]

Second is their particular, narrowly circumscribed subject matter. The very mood congruity noted earlier as a potentially unifying fea-ture of mood disorder is also a constraint. The recurrent themes of these moods are limited in range.[56] Ratcliffe also captures this focal narrowing. Gone, he says, speaking of the way possible content is blocked for the depression sufferer, is 'the conceivability of any alter-native to depression', and although the depression sufferer 'is able to speak of what has been lost, there remains something she cannot fully conceive of, an *appreciation of things that none of her thoughts or words are able to evoke*' (Ratcliffe, 2010a, p. 360). And, running par-allel to Ratcliffe's analysis, the same limited range exhausts the possi-bilities available to the mania sufferer. Apparently fed by reasoning and memory bias, he is locked in his irrepressible optimism.[57]

Summing up these variations: the moods of depression and mania are more intense, narrowly directed, and resistant to change. If my prevailing moods are intense, obdurate, and unremittingly gloomy, pessimistic, and fearful, then adopting a perspective detached enough for me to assess their effects on my judgments and responses will be diminished. And similarly, if my moods are unwarrantedly optimistic, they will colour attempts at a more realistic assessment of myself and the world around me. Inasmuch as my agency is thus reduced then so is the integrity and wholeness of my self.

The epistemic deficits identified here admit of degree as much as do the moods effecting them, of course. The person afflicted with depres-sive and manic moods may be only mildly disadvantaged by these

[55] Ratcliffe accommodates this by distinguishing deeper moods, using depressive moods as examples. Shifts of mood at this deeper level, he allows, may be phenomenologically salient.

[56] When suffering one of her bouts of melancholia, Gilman, quoted earlier, remembers being encouraged by a sympathetic friend to read an agreeable book and occupy her mind with pleasant things. But the friend, she explains, '...did not realize that I was unable to read, and that my mind was *exclusively occupied* with unpleasant things' (Gilman, 1935, p. 90, emphasis added).

[57] Despite the reckless extravagances of her earlier manic episodes, Kay Redfield Jamison writes that when manic she was unable to entertain realistic assessments of what would ensue: 'I couldn't worry about money if I tried. So I don't. The money will come from somewhere; I am entitled; God will provide' (Jamison, 1995, p. 74).

states, her self-integration little affected. And, as the effectiveness of cognitive therapy and much autobiographical evidence indicate, certain epistemic practices go some way towards remedying the limitations imposed by moods. Similar to other efforts we all make to deal with recalcitrant states (such as arranging a wake-up call), this is what has been called 'imperfect rationality'.[58] We cannot dispel our moods directly, or at will, but we can engage in practices affecting and effecting them.[59] Eluding our moods, and anticipating and countering their effects, may require more persistence, effort, and ingenuity for the depression or mania sufferer, but can sometimes be achieved.[60]

Here too, however, aspects of depressed and manic frames of mind involving motivational structures seem likely saboteurs. A person must *wish* to employ indirection in these ways to affect his mood, he must *care* to bring about these changes in himself. So the characteristic lethargy and indifference of depression will detract from effective indirection — the depressed patient often does not care enough to make that effort. And mania represents a different, but nonetheless parallel, problem. Manic moods are agreeable, and compelling, reducing motivation to change. The manic patient *could* use indirection to dispel her ebuliant moods, but she is not inclined to.[61]

6. Conclusion

Certain pathologies, it has been said, are 'self-specific insofar as they are devastating or disruptive for the person's self experiences' (Gallagher, 2011, p. 19). These are the schizophrenia-spectrum disorders, and disruptions that seem to occur at a level beneath reflective awareness. They are indeed disruptive of self. But so, in different ways, are other disorders. One purpose of this discussion was to show that although not so floridly and irremediably so, and for all that they involve the self of reflective awareness, affective or mood disorders will also likely jeopardize self-integration and reveal fissures absent from more normal and normally integrated selves.

---

[58] See Elster (1984).

[59] Importantly, these efforts include enlisting the help of other people.

[60] Cognitive therapy relies on the observation that feelings and thoughts have a mutually reinforcing relationship, as Paul Biegler puts it, so that in depression 'pessimistic and negative cognitions can trigger and perpetuate negative affect, and negative affect can lead to a tendency to focus and ruminate on negative cognitions' (Biegler, 2011, p. 67). And practising 'mindfulness', by distancing oneself from negative thoughts and feelings, can sometimes succeed in breaking the cycle. See Teasdale *et al.* (2002).

[61] This recalcitrance on the part of the manic patient is the bane of the clinician's existence.

A second, broader goal here involved going beyond the way depression and mania transgress social norms (of functionality, appropriateness of affect, and cognitive bias). When combined with differences of quality and quantity in the moods and motivations that beset the depression and mania sufferer, the particular, epistemic deficiencies identified here seem likely to hinder certain forms of self-knowledge and self-integration. And these deficiencies, I suggest, may help explain why the extreme moods found in states of depression and mania contribute to our inclination to regard these conditions as disorder.

Acknowledgments

I am grateful to members of PHAEDRA, Jane Roland Martin, Ann Diller, Barbara Houston, Susan Fransoza, and Beatrice Kipp Nelson for help with earlier drafts of this chapter, as well as Somogy Varga and Amélie Rorty. My thanks also to fellow participants at the 'Complex Self' conference sponsored by the Danish National Research Foundation and the University of Copenhagen's Center for Subjectivity Research in December 2011, and the Philosophy of Psychiatry Workshop sponsored by Macquarie University's Centre of Excellence in Cognition and its Disorders and Centre for Agency, Value and Ethic in February 2012, particularly the formal response to my talk by, and informal conversation with, Professor Catriona Mackenzie.

Louis A. Sass and Elizabeth Pienkos

Varieties of Self-Experience

A Comparative Phenomenology of Melancholia, Mania, and Schizophrenia, Part I

1. Introduction

The difference between affective and schizophrenic forms of disorder is one of the classic issues in psychopathology. Ludwig Binswanger even called it 'the central problem of clinical psychiatry' (Tatossian, 1997). In a famous passage, Karl Jaspers (1946/1963) describes the 'most profound distinction in psychic life [as] that between what is meaningful and *allows empathy*', and what 'in its particular way is *ununderstandable*, "mad" in the literal sense, schizophrenic psychic life' (p. 577). This, in his view, distinguishes affective illnesses, which 'we can comprehend vividly enough as an exaggeration or diminution of known phenomena', such as intense emotion, from the supposedly more *in*comprehensible disorder of schizophrenia. But Jaspers also recognized that this distinction, though fundamental, was extremely difficult to conceptualize: he speaks of 'a basic difference... which even today we cannot formulate clearly and precisely' (*ibid.*, p. 578). The present chapter (together with its sequel) is an attempt to explore this distinction from a phenomenological standpoint, that is, to examine both differences and affinities in the subjective experiences characteristic of these two major groups of psychopathology.

Despite some important work (e.g. Minkowski, 1933/1970; Tellenbach, 1980; Kraus, 1991; Tatossian, 1997; Fuchs, 2001; 2005a; Stanghellini, 2004), affective conditions have been relatively neglected in phenomenological psychopathology, with far less attention directed to subjective life in affective disorders than in the schizophrenia spectrum. More common have been empirical studies enquiring into symptoms and signs that can be objectively observed or

operationalized. While such studies benefit from their ability to compare objectively measureable dimensions, they typically neglect subjective experiences, and so may miss some of the subtle changes
patients undergo. In this chapter we shall give equal emphasis to subjectivity in the affective conditions and in schizophrenia, with each
serving as the foil to the other. One of our purposes is to offer a preliminary mapping or synopsis of key features of subjective experience in
psychotic forms of affective disorder, especially melancholia but also
mania — something that is not available in the recent psychopathological literature.

Our attempt is exploratory. We offer a critical survey of what has
been said in the phenomenological tradition about subjective life in
these conditions, with an eye toward both contrasts and affinities. We
present, whenever possible, patient reports that either illustrate the
relevant theoretical claims or suggest their limitations (mostly taken
from the published literature, but occasionally coming from our own
patients or informants). We are obviously interested in fundamental
differences that distinguish typical affective (melancholic or manic)
phenomenology from what is found in schizophrenia. These differences can be both profound and striking. They are, however, quite
well known. We therefore pay special attention to phenomenological
domains in which the characteristic experiences can appear rather
similar, and where the differential may be difficult to achieve. These
difficult instances, we believe, are especially worthy of study both as
potential aids for differential diagnosis and for furthering our theoretical understanding of both psychopathological conditions; by probing
these affinities, subtle distinctions may become more apparent.

In order to survey the inner landscape of these disorders, it is necessary to divide it into separable domains, even while recognizing that
these domains are likely to be overlapping and interdependent in various ways. In this chapter we will borrow the mapping of domains
offered in a recently developed research tool of phenomenological
psychopathology: the Examination of Anomalous Self-Experience or
EASE (Parnas *et al.*, 2005). The EASE distinguishes five experiential
domains of self-experience: *Cognition and Stream of Consciousness,
Self-Awareness and Presence, Bodily Experiences, Demarcation/
Transitivism*, and *Existential Reorientation*.

The EASE was developed as a technique for carrying out in-depth,
qualitative interviews with live subjects; it targets experiences that are
thought to be highly characteristic of schizophrenia-spectrum illnesses. Research with the EASE and related instruments has shown
that self-disturbances, as there defined, are, in fact, far more common

in schizophrenia-spectrum disorders than in either depression or bipolar disorder (Parnas *et al.*, 2003; Handest and Parnas, 2005; Raballo, Saebye and Parnas, 2011). The EASE can, however, also be viewed as an exceptionally clear and detailed delineation of major domains of psychopathology from a phenomenological standpoint. Its specific items provide an excellent set of definitions and also of key schizophrenic or schizotypal examples with which to compare experiential reports in affective disorders. Whereas the EASE focuses on *sub*-psychotic phenomena, here we are interested both in sub-psychotic and psychotic experiences associated with melancholia, mania, and schizophrenia. Also, although our discussion follows the general EASE mapping, it is not restricted to the particular items included in the EASE, which are primarily directed toward schizophrenia-spectrum self-experience. Here we take a broader approach to the possibility of anomalies in each of these domains of self-experience, so as to include anomalies found in affective illness but possibly not in schizophrenia.

The EASE focuses on anomalies of *self*-disturbance. In the next chapter we supplement these five domains with three others that target anomalies not of self but of world experience: *Objects and Space*, *Events and Time*, and *Aspects of General Atmosphere*.[1]

We wish, then, to offer three perspectives in these chapters: I. a review of some major differences in anomalous self-experience between affective and schizophrenic conditions; II. a consideration of experiences in which the two conditions may nevertheless resemble each other, thus undermining the clarity of the distinction between the two domains; III. suggestions, some quite speculative, about how these apparently similar phenomena might nevertheless be distinct, and perhaps are distinguishable in clinical and research settings.

As noted, the psychiatric understanding of the affective/schizophrenic border has been characterized by various ambiguities and vacillations. We shall suggest that there are various explanations for this. One reason is that affective disorders (contrary to what Jaspers says) may *not*, in fact, always be fully understandable as 'exaggeration or diminishment of known phenomena' of emotional life. This is particularly apparent in severe states of psychotic depression (melancholia), when the patient seems to move beyond any recognizable emotional or affective state into what can seem an utterly remote and

---

[1] A full survey of important world-disturbances in psychopathology would need to address some additional domains, including the experience of other human beings (persons) and of language. For reasons of length, we deal with these latter issues in two further articles, now under preparation.

void-like condition. Mania at the extreme can bring on forms of cognitive or behavioural disorganization and self-disorder that may be sharply at odds with the classic manic experiences of increased vigour, euphoria, and flight of ideas. Distinguishing these experiences from schizophrenic depersonalization, derealization, disorganization, and self-alienation can pose a special challenge for phenomenological investigation. It may, however, help to sharpen our grasp of both conditions.

2. Diagnostic Controversies and Other Complicating Factors

The EASE interview, like much phenomenological psychiatry, is meant to reveal an underlying *trouble générateur*, an organizational matrix or structure of experience; as such, it focuses on the subtle mutations of experience that may or may not be directly reflected in symptoms such as hallucinations or delusions. There is, of course, controversy about the very existence of these matrices of experience. Currently it is common to question the validity of the traditional psychiatric distinction between schizophrenia and the affective disorders (Allerdyce *et al.*, 2007; van Os, 2012). Some contemporary empirical research suggests that many symptoms, or even groups of symptoms, are insufficient for distinguishing between these disorders (e.g. Taylor, 1992; Kendell and Jablensky, 2003; Dutta *et al.*, 2007; van Os, 2009).[2] This is not, of course, a new issue: both the location and existence of boundaries between these disorders have been disputed for over one hundred years. Still, Kraepelin's (1913) basic distinction — whether framed as a dichotomy or as a continuum between schizophrenic and affective types — continues to be the dominant view in contemporary psychiatry and psychology. It is well to bear in mind Karl Jaspers' (1946/1963) assessment of this long-running debate: 'for many years the border between manic-depressive insanity and dementia praecox [the older term for schizophrenia] has vacillated considerably in a kind of pendulum movement without anything new emerging' (p. 567). Jaspers recognized the difficulty of precisely defining the border between these conditions; he also acknowledged the near impossibility of deciding on a diagnosis in certain cases. He did not, however, doubt that there is something valid about this distinction to which we seem always to return, writing that 'there must be

---

[2]   Recent studies employing phenomenological methods have, however, been capable of distinguishing schizophrenia-spectrum disorders from bipolar disorder (Parnas *et al.*, 2003; Haug *et al.*, 2012) and have been able to predict transition to schizophrenia psychosis in ultra high-risk populations (Nelson, Thompson and Yung, 2012).

some kernel of lasting truth not present with previous groupings' (*ibid.*, p. 568).

This chapter contributes to this debate by exploring the possibility that there may indeed be underlying differences that require more sensitive and detailed forms of exploration. In this sense, the very idea that such distinctions exist operates as a working hypothesis, one that is, however, highly congruent with traditional views in psychopathology for the past century (Bleuler, 1911; Kraepelin, 1913; Minkowski, 1927; Jaspers, 1946/1963). Even if it were the case that key pathogenetic processes are shared across these disorders (e.g. salience dysregulation; van Os, 2009; 2012), it may nevertheless be true that the consequences of these processes are moulded differently in accord with distinct underlying experiential orientations or *troubles générateurs*.

In this chapter, we do not seek to determine whether or not such categories should be retained — the latter is obviously an issue that can be debated on a variety of different grounds. Rather, we seek to explore whether certain distinctive kinds of experience can be reliably associated with each of these disorders as traditionally defined. We acknowledge that a certain confirmation bias may prejudice us in the direction of finding differences. This and the following chapter are, however, exploratory, meant to provide hypotheses for future confirmation or disconfirmation. The subtler differences we explore concern levels of experience that are not addressed in the literature critical of these diagnostic entities. Future research may need to take these into account.

We would not argue, of course, that particular experiences in these different conditions can *always* be distinguished in phenomenological terms. One perennial issue, in fact, is whether the distinction between schizophrenia and affective psychosis is sharp or qualitative, or whether there is a continuum, and whether 'schizoaffective' psychosis is a legitimate category (Tsuang and Simpson, 1984; Dutta *et al.*, 2007). Here we take no position on these questions. We have tried, however, to focus on clear-cut examples of the forms of psychosis we consider, and to the extent possible have avoided using examples or analyses of intermediate cases.

One limitation of our study, as with all phenomenological research, is that we must rely largely on patients who are able to describe their experiences; this can involve a selection bias in favour of patients who may not be typical of the entire diagnostic group at issue. Although this issue must be borne in mind, it must also be recognized that this is a necessary feature of phenomenological work, one that can only be avoided at the risk of ignoring the subtle features of a patient's subjectivity.

We must recall, as well, that manifest forms of psychopathology are typically the joint products of numerous factors and processes — not merely of some inherent psychopathological kernel (if such exists), but also of various *sequelae*, including both consequential and compensatory reactions. Consider how very common, and how varied in its manifestations, depression can be in schizophrenia: although the depression of a schizophrenia patient may sometimes have a rather different quality than that of a pure affective patient, in other instances it may be much the same (e.g. the secondary depression elicited by isolation and problems in living). Paranoia is common in schizophrenia, melancholia, and mania, as are certain forms of depersonalization in schizophrenia and melancholia. Indeed such defence reactions are universal or near-universal processes, part of the general human condition. Yet it is true, as well, that the *choice* of these mechanisms, and also the way they are *inflected* in particular cases, can reflect something deeper or more distinctive about the individual or disorder in question.

All this is related to the overlapping issues of co-morbidity and internal complexity. We note, for instance, that some patients with *paranoid* forms of schizophrenia may lack the more extreme forms of self-disorder and world-transformation found in disorganized cases. The melancholia of patients with manic or hypomanic phases may differ from those patients who lack these phases. Schizophrenia patients with predominantly positive versus negative versus disorganized symptoms obviously differ from each other in various ways. There are also significant differences between patients with affective reactions (manic or melancholic) who are prone to psychosis versus those who are not.

It would be impossible to take all these potential subtleties and distinctions fully into account in a brief survey and report such as ours. The play of sameness and difference is virtually kaleidoscopic in nature; it would result in cognitive paralysis. Although we do not ignore all such nuances and qualifications, here we opt for a kind of (Weberian) ideal-type analysis. As Max Weber (1904/1949) noted with regard to such notions as 'charisma' and 'capitalism', such phenomena never exist as 'pure' entities in the real world, yet it is essential to employ such abstractions when analysing empirical reality. This ideal-type analysis emphasizes features that are 'typical' of the phenomenon studied, but without applying equally well, or in just the same way, to all instances of the type. We do not claim that all of the distinctions we suggest will hold invariably, in a truly pathognomonic sense, nor that the feature will be *constantly* present in any particular patient. Here we have the more modest — and more realistic — goal of discerning features of melancholia, mania, or schizophrenia that are highly *distinctive* of the disorder in question.[3]

In this chapter, we have chosen to focus specifically on the experiences of 'melancholia' and 'mania'. 'Melancholia', a term employed since classical times (Radden, 2009), has recently has been used to specify severe, endogenous, or psychotic depression (Sierra, 2009). DSM-IV-TR (2000) uses the specifier 'With Melancholic Features' to describe a Major Depressive Episode that is more severe and qualitatively distinct: with 'a near-complete absence of the capacity for pleasure, not merely a diminution' and with a 'distinct quality of mood... qualitatively different from the sadness experienced during bereavement or a non-melancholic depressive episode' (*ibid.*, p. 419). Our use of 'melancholia' reflects the severity of the disturbance and its likelihood of generating striking experiential anomalies. We use 'mania' to refer to particular experiences that can occur in someone diagnosed with Bipolar Disorder. Here, however, we are specifically interested in these manic experiences themselves, rather than in the diagnostic entity as a whole.

A famous line from the psychiatrist Harry Stack Sullivan states that people with schizophrenia, like all people, are 'more simply human than otherwise' (1953). This reminds us that the structure and pathogenesis of schizophrenia, like all forms of psychopathology, will involve some psychological mechanisms found elsewhere as well — e.g. in affective psychosis, depersonalization disorder, etc. But this does not mean that there is not also an 'otherwise', to use Sullivan's term. The comparative phenomenological method is, we believe, an indispensable tool in isolating this core that, without explaining the *totality* of schizophrenic pathology, may well contribute to giving schizophrenia a unique, Gestalt-like essence. And perhaps it can make a similar contribution in the cases of melancholia and mania. It is worth noting, however, that there does seem to be something more unique or at least 'otherwise' about schizophrenia: whereas most of the phenomena found in melancholia and mania can occur in schizophrenia patients, though less prominently, there do seem to be certain features, often having a certain bizarre or uncanny quality, that seem to be quite distinctive of schizophrenia in particular (Rümke and Neeleman, 1942/1990; Jaspers, 1946/1963; Mellor, 1970).

---

[3] On the ideal-type notion in psychiatry, see Wiggins and Schwartz (1991).

As noted, our study is exploratory, an exercise in generating hypotheses for further investigation. It has several weaknesses that are perhaps inevitable in this sort of project.

Although some of our generalizations are corroborated by controlled empirical research (e.g. by EASE interviews comparing schizophrenia with affective patients), many are supported only by anecdotal reports and theoretical rationales. These would need to be tested in various ways, not only with in-depth qualitative interviews with carefully diagnosed patients, but also through various forms of experimental research.

We are aware of the inherent difficulty of operationalizing some of our more speculative claims, which can refer to subtle features of experience that are not likely to be spontaneously or readily described by individuals untrained in phenomenology, and that may, in some instances, even verge on ineffability. We believe, however, that an empiricist-oriented restriction of theoretical speculation would not be appropriate at this stage of research, when it is difficult to know precisely what can and what cannot be operationalized. Perhaps the major lesson of the modern philosophy of science, since the rejection of the logical-positivist programme, is the complexity of the relationship between theory and observation. Work that is highly theoretical, speculative, clinically oriented, and anecdotal — such as ours — is certainly not *opposed* to empirical study, but should play a role in the formulation of its hypotheses and particular methods. For as we know from Kant, experience without theory is blind, just as theory without experience would be mere intellectual play.[4]

3. Cognition and Stream of Consciousness (EASE Domain 1)

We begin with Domain 1 of the EASE (Examination of Anomalous Self-Experience; Parnas *et al.*, 2005), which contains experiences of anomalous *Cognition and Stream of Consciousness*. Items in this domain — which are thought to be characteristic of schizophrenia-spectrum disorders in particular — generally involve disturbances of the normal process of thinking or related processes such as memory, attention, and language.

I: Thought disorder has, of course, been traditionally associated with schizophrenia, and is often thought to distinguish schizophrenia

---

[4] Kant's famous line from the *Critique of Pure Reason* (1855), 'Thoughts without content are empty, intuitions without concepts are blind' (A51, B75), has been glossed more or less as paraphrased above in *General Systems* (1962).

from the affect- or emotion-related disturbances characteristic of mood disorders. So-called *formal* thought disorder is largely manifest in verbal output, but can clearly be suggestive of cognitive and experiential anomalies as well. Schneider's first-rank symptoms of schizophrenia specify several forms of disturbed experiences of thinking that are explicitly subjective in nature, including audible thoughts, thought withdrawal, and thought diffusion (Schneider, 1959). Such disturbances seem to contrast sharply with the cognitive disturbances typically noted in affective disorders, *viz.* slowed thinking in depression and racing thoughts in mania. Although schizophrenia patients may also experience change in the speed or quantity of their thoughts, what is more distinctive is the *qualitative* change such as described in EASE items *Loss of Thought Ipseity* and *Spatialization of Experience*.

II: However, in more severe forms of affective disturbance, some of these distinctions may not be so clear. Indeed, formal thought disorder has been noted in both psychotic and non-psychotic patients with mania. A study by Holzman, Shenton and Solovay (1986) using the Rorschach Thought Disorder Index examined patients with mania, schizoaffective disorder, and schizophrenia, and noted high levels of thought disorder in all groups, including non-psychotic patients with mania. Common factors among the various diagnoses included vagueness, loss of set, inappropriate distance, and incongruous ideas. Such characteristics echo Binswanger's (1964) earlier description of manic thought, in which he noted that manic 'flight of ideas' involved not merely a simple increase in thought quantity or speed, but was also frequently disordered and confused, jumping from one idea to the next with little goal-directedness or respect for the rules of grammar or logic. DSM-IV-TR (2000) describes manic thinking as like 'watching two or three television programs simultaneously. Frequently there is flight of ideas evidenced by a nearly continuous flow of accelerated speech, which abruptly changes from one thought to another' (p. 358). This mode of thinking bears some similarity to the description of *Thought Pressure* found in the EASE, which describes thoughts that arise 'in quick sequences', and that 'lack... a common theme and hence... coherence or meaning for the client' (Parnas *et al.*, 2005, p. 240).

This form of disordered thought is illustrated in the following statement by a patient with mania: 'I can write up or down. I can call the jolly folks or the sad folks. I have one church on Madison Avenue, another in downtown. You don't go messing around with churches. No I wasn't asleep. I just disappeared...' (Akiskal and Puzantian,

1979). These utterances seem to demonstrate a lack of common meaning or theme similar to what can characterize schizophrenic thinking.

A study by Silber *et al.* (1980) observed several features of their depressed patients that shared commonalities with schizophrenic thought disturbances: 1. 'cognitive rigidity' and 'preoccupation with certain repetitive thoughts', similar to the EASE item *Ruminations/Obsessions*; 2. poverty of speech that seems to resemble schizophrenic *Thought Block* (an EASE item); 3. difficulty focusing that might resemble *Attentional Disorders* (also an EASE item), such as one patient who noted, 'I could not follow conversation, could not pretend any interest. There was no talking with anybody' (Smith, 1999). Sarah Kane, a British playwright known to be severely and psychotically depressed, described her experiences in the play *4.48 Psychosis* (published posthumously after her suicide at age 28). Her statement 'Behold the Eunuch / of castrated thought' (Kane, 2001) suggests a similar feeling of the inadequacy of her thinking.

In addition, Piguet *et al.* (2010) noted that, in contrast to the typical notion of slowed or decreased thinking in melancholia, many depressed patients in fact experience an *increase* in the number of thoughts. These are experienced as coexisting simultaneously in an unpleasant continuous flooding, in which earlier thoughts linger in the mind instead of being replaced by subsequent ones — something that has been called 'thought crowding'. One patient described it as though 'all the problems of the universe came crowding into my mind' (*ibid.*, p. 192). Such 'thought crowding' might not be easily distinguished from schizophrenic 'thought pressure', in which 'many thoughts (or images) with different, unrelated or remotely related meaning content… pop up and disappear or… seem to the patient to occur at the same time (simultaneously)' (Parnas *et al.*, 2005, p. 240). This similarity between crowded thoughts and thought pressure is highlighted in Les Murray's account of depression in his book *Killing the Black Dog*: '…now my mind became congested, jammed with ideas I couldn't formulate clearly or nimbly enough, so that they tumbled over each other and made me incoherent' (Murray, 2009, p. 3).

The following quotation from Sarah Kane's grueling account of psychotic depression suggests another way in which depressive thinking can become strange and even object-like:

> [A] consolidated consciousness resides in a darkened banqueting hall near the ceiling of a mind whose floor shifts as ten thousand cockroaches when a shaft of light enters as all thoughts unite in an instant of accord body no longer expellent as the cockroaches comprise a truth which no one ever utters. (Kane, 2001, p. 205)

Such statements suggest a sense of alienation from one's thoughts, to the point that they may feel creepy, thing-like, and not completely under one's control. This appears similar to the EASE item *Spatialization of Experience*, where 'thoughts, feelings, or other experiences or mental processes are... described in spatialized terms (e.g. location, spatial relation or movement)' (Parnas *et al.*, 2005, p. 242).

Furthermore, it has often been claimed that the first-rank symptoms (FRSs) — which involve severe abnormalities of the sense of possession or control over one's own experience or behaviour, or of one's separation from other minds — are pathognomonic of schizophrenia; but this claim has also been contested on the grounds that similar experiences can be found (though perhaps less frequently) in affective psychosis or PTSD (Taylor and Abrams, 1973; Abrams, Taylor and Gaztanaga, 1974; Carpenter and Strauss, 1974; Abrams and Taylor, 1981).

III: However, a review of the concept of first-rank symptoms by Koehler (1979) provides one way again to differentiate schizophrenic from severe affective symptoms; he suggests that many of the aforementioned overlaps may stem from ambiguities in the definitions of the FRSs. According to some experts, only the more narrowly defined symptoms are specific to schizophrenia as opposed to affective psychosis. Thus for Taylor and Heiser (1971), Mellor (1970), and Wing, Cooper and Sartorius (1974), one must distinguish between '*influenced* experiences' in which the patient experiences his *own* thoughts or feelings as imposed upon him by some outside agency, versus the more distinctive *alienated* experiences, in which thoughts or feelings that were *not* his own somehow come from or belong to an outside force. Of related interest is the observation that, whereas thought diffusion (the sense that one's thoughts are spreading out from one's head) is found in both affective psychosis and schizophrenia, thought broadcasting (the sense that others are *participating* in one's thoughts) is unique to schizophrenia (Fish, in Wing, Cooper and Sartorius, 1974; Hamilton, 1984).

Such a view is consistent with that of Alfred Kraus (1991), who states that although the I-sense may indeed be weakened in melancholia, such patients do not experience the frank loss of mineness (*Meinhaftigkeit*) that does occur in schizophrenia (p. 73). It seems that extreme forms of melancholia and perhaps also mania can indeed involve various forms of alienation from thoughts and feelings, but not the extreme loss of minimal self, of existing as a distinct subjective point of view. By contrast, this disturbance of the core or minimal dimension of selfhood, or *ipseity*, seems to be a key aspect of a disturbed experience of thoughts and cognition for many schizophrenia patients. Clear instances of what the EASE (Parnas *et al.*, 2005, p. 240) terms 'loss of thought ipseity' — where the patient feels that 'certain thoughts [are] deprived of the tag of mineness' — are very rare if not absent outside the schizophrenic spectrum. Even the above quotation from Sarah Kane ('a consolidated consciousness... near the ceiling of a mind') appears to lack the extreme degree of reification and loss of mineness that can be described in schizophrenic spatialization of experience.

This may be related to a difference in the *kind* of confusion that is felt in schizophrenia versus mania. The mania patient's rapidly shifting attention in flight-of-ideas is a form of distraction — an inability to ignore environmental stimuli that are capable of arousing lively but ephemeral interest in the patient, but that, in a normal individual, would remain on the margin of awareness, outside the focus of attention. The distinctive schizophrenic 'perplexity' (*Ratlosigkeit*, as it was called in classical German psychopathology, a term that means helplessness, not knowing what to do, being at a loss) seems less a matter of being distracted by the outside world than of lacking an orienting centre or vital core, the sense of relevancy (of having a thematic field at all) that requires an organizing motivational perspective (Sass, 2004a).

It is all a matter of mattering, we might say, or rather of *how* things matter. Whereas for the individual with mania, with his intensified emotional reactivity, there are too many things that matter, and that come to matter too quickly and fleetingly, for the individual with schizophrenia, it is rather that nothing may matter, or at least matter in a normal fashion. This may be related to a certain emotional flattening that can occur in schizophrenia. Things, after all, normally matter *to* a person and *within* a distinct point of view, and the subjective loss of self-affection (of minimal or core self), which is normally bound up with emotion and grounds one's sense of having an orienting project, tends to undermine one's orientation to the external world. This is not a dimming-down but a qualitative transformation of subjective life. Sophie, a young woman with schizophrenia, reported to us that in schizophrenia a *particular* object may attract attention because of what is experienced as its strangeness or unfamiliarity, or, alternatively, there may be a 'global sense that everything is strange and unfamiliar/ineffably "off"... [resulting in] an inability to attend to anything in particular [and a tendency] to flit from object to object, unsure of why they are all so disturbing'. In either case the object or objects-in-general appear to have lost their normal affordance qualities, which are generally correlated with normal emotional reactions and practical concerns, and instead loom up as objects of a disconcerting fascinating or detached scrutiny.

Distinguishing schizophrenic perplexity from *melancholic* confusion is somewhat more difficult, however. In the latter condition we encounter, if not a *loss* of minimal self, at least an ebbing of its vital dynamism and orienting appetites — all of which obviously diminish the significance things can be felt to have in subjective life, often resulting in a general sense of confusion. For example, one melancholic patient remarked, 'I saw his lips moving, but his words were lost on me... Some other voice held my ear, and my mind was a tangle, a welter of confusion and overwhelm' (Smith, 1999, p. 4). Les Murray, who suffers from depression, describes 'my brain [as] boiling with a confusion of stuff not worth calling thought or imagery: it was more like shredded mental kelp marinated in pure pain' (Murray, 2009, p. 7). 'I can't make decisions... I can't think', writes Sarah Kane (2001, p. 206), and later, 'tongue out / thought stalled / the piecemeal crumple of my mind' (*ibid.*, p. 225). The subjective experience of depressive inadequacy and schizophrenic perplexity may in fact approach each other very closely, at least in some instances. Given the limitations and general vagueness of much verbal report, one should expect to find many indistinguishable descriptions.

We believe, however, that there are some subtle yet profound differences; and that in depression the experience will be more bound up with issues of vitality or fatigue, whereas in schizophrenia there is an even more fundamental disturbance of ipseity or minimal self, manifest both as an exacerbation of hyperreflexivity (exaggerated and dysfunctional forms of self-consciousness) and as an undermining of basic self-affection (of mine-ness, or first-personhood) (Sass and Parnas, 2003; 2007). Consider the following quotation from Antonin Artaud, who suffered from schizophrenia, in which he describes his own experience of mental confusion and related thought blocking:

> [T]he thought, the expression stops because the flow is too violent, because the brain wants to say too many things which it thinks of all at once, ten thoughts instead of one rush toward the exit, the brain sees the whole thought at once with all its circumstances, and it also sees all the points of view it could take and all the forms with which it could invest them, a vast juxtaposition of concepts, each of which seems more necessary and also more dubious than the others, which all the complexities of syntax would never suffice to express and expound. (In Sass, 2003, p. 173)

This sort of hyperreflexivity, in which one's own ongoing mental life comes to be objectified and treated as a thing, can be manifest as the 'spatialization of experience' described above. Schizophrenic patients have described this in various ways: 'Thoughts are encapsulated.' 'Thoughts "spiral around" inside his head.' 'Thoughts always pass down obliquely into the very same spot' (Parnas *et al.*, 2005).

Consider, by contrast, the following account from a depressed patient, which does contain some superficial resemblances:

> I was seized with an unspeakable physical weariness. There was a tired feeling in the muscles unlike anything I had ever experienced. A peculiar sensation appeared to travel up my spine to my brain. I had an indescribable nervous feeling. My nerves seemed like live wires charged with electricity... The most trivial duty became a formidable task. Finally mental and physical exercises became impossible; the tired muscles refused to respond, my 'thinking apparatus' refused to work, ambition was gone. (Landis, 1964, p. 272)

Here the patient's description of her nerves as like 'live wires' and of her brain as a 'thinking apparatus' do suggest some alienation from her body and mind. Similarly, Sarah Kane's (2001) description of 'the ceiling of a mind whose floor shifts as ten thousand cockroaches when a shaft of light enters' evokes a yet more extreme degree of the psychophysical alienation. Still, these patients describe what *they* felt: each is always the subject of consciousness, never questioning that her nerves or brain or thoughts are integral parts of her subjectivity. The depressive experience described here is related to a loss of 'vital impulse', a diminished engagement with the world that decreases motivation and desire, making thoughts, emotions, and body seem nervously charged or dark and creepy, but also sluggish, closed up, and unresponsive. Such experience appears to be subtly but distinctly different from the particular kind of confusion that can be felt in schizophrenia (perplexity/*Ratlosigkeit*), and also from the feeling of thoughts being fully autonomous and alien that can occur with the loss of ipseity or minimal self typical of schizophrenia.

4. Self-awareness and Presence (EASE Domain 2)

The second EASE domain is the one most directly concerned with self-awareness and presence, with what, in the normal case, could be described as 'automatic un-reflected self-presence and immersion in the world' (Parnas *et al.*, 2005, p. 243). This includes a sense of being at one with one's own experience in its full immanence as well as a feeling of immediate engagement with the outside world. Disturbances in this domain clearly reflect what is meant by the concept of schizophrenia as a 'self disorder' in the sense of disordered ipseity or minimal self.

I: A particularly clear description of an experience of ipseity disturbance comes from the autobiography of Elyn Saks, who suffers from schizophrenia:

> And then something odd happens. My awareness (of myself, of him, of the room, of the physical reality around and beyond us) instantly grows fuzzy. Or wobbly. I think I am dissolving. I feel — my mind feels — like a sand castle with all the sand sliding away in the receding surf. *What's happening to me? This is scary, please let it be over!* I think maybe if I stand very still and quiet, it will stop. (Saks, 2007, p. 12)

Affective disorder can also involve disturbance of some aspects of the self, but it is important here to clarify *which* aspects of self are affected. Various authors make a clear distinction between a core or minimal dimension of selfhood — what we call ipseity — and another layer, built upon this foundation, that concerns one's sense of continuity over time (Ricoeur, 1992; Zahavi, 2005). In schizophrenia what seems to be disrupted is the most basic level of self-consciousness, the pre-reflective consciousness that is the source and anchor of all our experience: as Ellen Saks says, 'there's no center to take things in and process them and view the world' (in Sachs, 2007). In melancholia, the disturbance may often occur more at the level of narrative identity — at the level of 'the self as a construction, the product of conceiving oneself in a certain way' (Stanghellini, 2004, p. 23). The understanding of who I am and how I relate to others, and of my continuity over time, will be disturbed, but the person nevertheless preserves the minimal sense of existing as a living, subjective point of view distinct from the external world.

II: It should be noted, however, that there are experiences in severe melancholia that can look very similar to schizophrenia. Silber *et al.* (1980) describe a state of 'affective inaccessibility' in which one moves well beyond sadness or any recognizable form of dysphoria: the melancholic loses 'the ability to experience and recognize affects' (*ibid.*, p. 161), to the point that one may wonder whether it even makes sense of speak of 'depression'. As Sarah Kane wrote, 'I used to be able to cry, but now I am beyond tears' (Kane, 2001, p. 206). Something similar may occur in mania, when the patient seems to lose all capacity to rejoice, because there is no longer an authentic self that can experience the state of joy. Von Gebsattel (in Tatossian, 1997) goes even further, speaking of the possibility of a complete loss of feeling in melancholia, and alongside it, loss of the capacity for meaningful action in the world. This evokes a kind of fundamental emptiness of the self and loss of meaning in the world, which is perhaps what Sarah Kane meant when she wrote, 'corrosive doubt / futile despair... nothing can fill this void in my heart' (Kane, 2001, p. 219).

In the following quotation from by John Custance, a bipolar patient with psychotic features, we see some of the above themes, together with a suggestion that selfhood simply disappears:

> ...the material world seemed less and less real... the whole universe of space and time, of my own senses, was really an illusion... There I was, shut in my own private universe, as it were, with no contact with real people at all, only with phantasmagoria who could at any moment turn into devils. I and all around me were utterly unreal... My soul was finally turned into nothingness — except unending pain. (Custance, 1952, pp. 72f)

III: One might doubt, then, whether it is possible to distinguish the above-mentioned disruptions of self and world from what is found in schizophrenia.

One distinction can perhaps be drawn from the psychoanalytically-oriented account of McGlashan (1982), who discusses '*aphanisis*', a term he uses to describe experiencing a sort of 'pseudo-depression' or 'psychic blankness' common to many chronic schizophrenics. Many of its traits look similar to the melancholic affective inaccessibility described above, such as 'motivational inertia, interpersonal isolation, anhedonia, and reports of feeling empty, stuck or blank' (*ibid.*, p. 120). McGlashan maintains, however, that there is a fundamental difference between these two. He argues that the *aphanisis* of schizophrenia is, at its foundation, an autistic, object-less state, a stance of isolated 'blankness' that occurs as a defence against vague and undifferentiated feelings of discomfort. In severe depression, by contrast, even the shutting down of feeling is always permeated with a sense of interpersonal loss, and this gives these experiences a less autistic quality.

Silber *et al.* (1980) take a similar view, suggesting that in severe depression even the experience of affective inaccessibility occurs as a defence against the pain associated with object loss, certain deprivations, or the experience of failure. The implication is that these painful feelings are still present in severely melancholic patients, though relegated to a level of consciousness or background awareness no longer available to normal focal awareness. This is perhaps the unending pain of which John Custance (1952) complains, despite his sense of unreality and of being a 'soul... turned into nothingness'. But not just *object loss*; also the *loss of feeling itself* is a source of pain in severe depression, as such patients are painfully aware of this loss (Stanghellini, 2004).

It would clearly be wrong, however, to portray the schizophrenic condition as one that is devoid of pain. Here it might be better to resort to a way of describing this distinction that is stated in Jaspers (1946/1963) and brought insightfully into relief by Stanghellini (2004): namely, that between the *feeling that one is unable to feel*, which is itself a source of pain in severe melancholia, and the *inability (at times) even to feel that one feels or exists*, which can be a source of somewhat paradoxical misery for many persons with schizophrenia. Borrowing this formulation, we might say that the melancholic still possesses a fairly robust, basic sense of ipseity or self-possession; this, in fact, provides the position *from which* he can recognize his diminished vitality or affective response. The schizophrenia patient, by contrast, lacks something closer to the core — the sense of inhabiting his own, first-person perspective. But we should not think that the latter condition is devoid of suffering or any kind of subjective response. As Sophie, the young schizophrenic referred to earlier, wrote in response to precisely this point: 'So there is perhaps [in schizophrenia] a sense in which one cannot feel that one feels, but also an almost fully externalized cognition of precisely how (non-affectively) agonizing it is to not be able to feel.'

A further source of anguish for both schizophrenia and affective disorders may be the experience of excessive self-consciousness. However, while melancholic patients may experience a largely *social* self-consciousness (a consciousness of self as *object* of other consciousnesses), patients with schizophrenia may more often experience what the Japanese phenomenological psychiatrist Kimura Bin refers to as 'simultaneous reflection', namely, a self-consciousness of the self *as* consciousness, and in the very *act* of being conscious. This experience of hyperreflexivity (described in Sass, 1992) might be described as involving a split from within, in which consciousness itself becomes divided and self-aware in unusual ways by virtue of taking *itself* as its own object. Most auditory verbal hallucinations in schizophrenia appear to involve this form of hyperreflexivity, possibly due to a kind of self-conscious externalization of 'inner speech', which normally serves as the very medium of thought itself (Lang, 1938; Sass, 1992; Morrison and Haddock, 1997).

More general, and even more profound, than this experience of hyperreflexivity is the experience of the complete collapse of minimal self and related feeling of fragmentation that can occur in schizophrenia — of the kind that is implicit in Elyn Saks' report mentioned earlier, where she feels like she is dissolving, like 'a sand castle with all the sand sliding away in the receding surf'. Antonin Artaud's description of his own 'central collapse of the mind' and 'erosion, both essential and fleeting, of my thinking' (Artaud, 1965, pp. 10–11), more than relating to a disturbance merely of cognitive thought, describes a feeling that the coherent self, the centre from which all organized thought arises, has begun to disintegrate or collapse. Although melancholic patients may at times describe a certain deadness of the self or feeling of void, the latter sort of fragmentation, with all its implications for thought, feeling, and experience of the world, seems to be specific to schizophrenia.

5. Bodily Experiences
(EASE Domain 3)

I: Domain 3 of the EASE describes various disturbed *Bodily Experiences*, typical of schizophrenia, which are said to deviate from a 'normal sense of psychophysical unity and coherence, [from] a normal interplay or oscillation of the body as "lived from within" as a subject or soul…and of the body as an object' (Parnas *et al.*, 2005, p. 252). The items in this domain involve feelings of bizarre estrangement: the body may no longer seem fully to belong to the patient; physiological processes may be felt as strangely concrete or objectified; one's physical movements may become confused with those of external objects or other persons.

Various phenomenological authors have described schizophrenia as involving extreme disembodiment, a sense of radical separation from one's own being as a physical entity (Sass, 1992; Stanghellini, 2004; Fuchs, 2005a). As we have seen, the very experience of the minimal self can seem dubious for such persons; yet it often tends to be identified more with a mental or spiritual than with a corporeal presence (Laing, 1965). For example, one schizophrenic patient was described as having 'difficulty in realizing that she is in her body, and she may be thinking "it's strange that I am here"'. Another spoke of '"a lack of coherence" or split between his physical part, visible to others, and himself, i.e. all that happens in his mind. He feels that his body is a shared property, something anonymous, distanced from him' (Parnas *et al.*, 2005, p. 253).

This does not mean, however, that the body simply disappears, as if it could be simply or persistently ignored. Rather, the body may become the object of a kind of alienating or objectifying, hyperreflexive gaze that turns what might have been implicitly experienced sensations into objectified quasi-entities that are witnessed rather than lived. The body may also be experienced as an alien, controlling entity that subjects the experiential self to its demands or commands. A classic example of the 'influencing machine delusion' illustrates these developments (see Sass, 1992). Here the patient Natalija's earlier experiences of alienation from body sensations led eventually to the delusion that a machine-like version of her own body lay in another room, and that all her own actions, feelings, and perceptions were but copies or epiphenomena of what was happening to the distant Natalija-machine.

Stanghellini (2004) has described these two aspects of schizophrenic disembodiment as those of being either (or both) a 'disembodied spirit' or a 'de-animated body'. Both Sass (2007) and Fuchs (2005a) have described how, in schizophrenia, somatic sensations that would normally ground emotional response can become detached and object-like, leading to a sense of distance and artificiality, and losing their usual emotional significance or resonance. Similarly, other physiological drives like hunger and sexual desire may lose their contextual meaning and come to be experienced as object-like states of tension.

In melancholia and mania, bodily experience is also frequently disturbed, though in ways that tend to look different from the more alienated or objectified experiences in schizophrenia. Stanghellini (2004) aptly described the melancholic experience of feeling 'confined within a body that has lost its own fluidity, mobility, and flexibility' and now acts less as a medium of openness than as 'an obstacle between the self and the world' (p. 139). There is a key difference here, though it is easier to state than always to discern: whereas the person with schizophrenia feels *detached* from his body, the melancholic feels somehow over-identified with it. Rather than being disembodied, the melancholic individual is *overly* embodied or corporealized (Fuchs, 2005a). As in the case of extreme fatigue, one can feel that one is *nothing but* one's body, into which one sinks and which also sinks into itself. One has come to feel incapable of the animated activity whereby the healthy lived body, without leaving itself behind, nevertheless transcends itself toward the external world. The melancholic body has become

> solid and heavy; it resists any attempt at reaching out to touch the external world [and] closes itself up, thus taking on the aspect of a corpse. The fluid body coagulates itself either into a single part of itself, or into

an organ, which is then felt to be heavy, weighty, oppressive, and suffocating. (Stanghellini, 2004, p. 139)

In losing the normal sense of feeling, the melancholic body is no longer imbued with the 'spirit' that animates it and drives it forward. Such
a body turns inflexible, heavy, and burdensome, taking on aspects of a
corpse. Fuchs (2005a) speaks of 'corporealization', stating that such
patients feel detached from their emotions and their environment. The
lived body no longer provides access to the world, as in Merleau-
Ponty's (1945/1962) embodied being, but rather blocks any kind of
meaningful action in the manner of an obstacle.

II: In practice, however, the boundary between schizophrenic and
melancholic experiences of the body can seem to blur. Although melancholic patients may most frequently experience a kind of debilitat-
ing fatigue, stasis, heaviness, and lack of motivation, they sometimes
undergo stranger experiences that suggest something more like a basic
disturbance of ipseity. 'Body and soul can never be married', writes
Sarah Kane (2001, p. 212) in describing body-alienation experiences
reminiscent of schizophrenia. Kane writes: 'I am deadlocked by the
smooth psychiatric voice of reason which tells me there is an objective
reality in which my body and mind are one. But I am not here and
never have been' (*ibid.*, p. 209). Another depressed patient recalls:

> There in the parking lot I was standing at attention. I was being made to
> move; there was nothing for it but to move. My legs snapped out stiffly,
> one by one, in sidelong kicks… My arms traced long stiff arcs through
> the sky; my elbows dropped woodenly into my ribs. Then, apparently, it
> was time for some choreography. My arms and legs began to move
> together, then alternately. I must have resembled some short-circuited
> windshield wiper, or some marionette gone awry. But who — where —
> was the puppeteer? Who was in control of this body? (Smith, 1999, p.
> 18)

Here we see how the body in melancholia can be an obstacle, preventing the person from engaging meaningfully in the world. With its suggestion that someone *else* is controlling the body, this report takes us
beyond typical melancholic corporealization and appears to overlap
with schizophrenic disembodiment.

III: Still, we suggest that these experiences *can* be differentiated. It
is noteworthy that in the report from the depressed patient just above,
the experience described pertains more to *control* of one's body than
to a basic sense of alienation from it: it is always, and still, *my* legs, *my*
arms, and *my* elbows to which the patient refers, as if basic *Meinhaftigkeit* were retained.

Another way of distinguishing between melancholia and schizophrenia would move beyond discrete complaints of disturbed embodiment to consider how these might be related to *other* aspects of the patient's life, such as temporality and intersubjectivity. The intense feeling of guilt and inability to transcend the past that Fuchs relates to melancholic corporealization does not appear so prominent in the types of descriptions provided by schizophrenia patients. Also, the melancholic experiences are perhaps more closely related to an implicit sense of disturbed relationship to others: it is *other people* who will see me as guilty; *other people* to whom I am no longer able to relate as I feel stuck in my own body.

Schizophrenic disembodiment, by contrast, seems to involve — at least in many cases — a disturbance of self-experience that is somewhat less related to others or the actual external world. Such experiences in schizophrenia may certainly *affect* how one engages with one's external situation; but the initial disruption seems more intrinsically internal, involving the body's role in the constitution of minimal selfhood.

6. Demarcation/Transitivism; Existential Reorientation (EASE Domains 4 and 5)

In this final section we briefly discuss some of the outstanding experiences described in two EASE domains: 4. *Demarcation/Transitivism*, and 5. *Existential Reorientation*. We combine discussion of these domains because of an overlap in themes. Domain 4 describes the 'loss or permeability of the self-world boundary' (Parnas *et al.*, 2005, p. 254), and suggests confusion between the self and another, or the feeling of being overwhelmed due to being somehow 'too open or transparent' (*ibid.*, p. 255). Domain 5 refers to 'a fundamental reorientation with respect to [the patient's] general metaphysical worldview and/or hierarchy of values, projects, and interests' (*ibid.*, p. 255), and relates to solipsistic beliefs or experiences, such as feeling that the world is illusory, or that one has extraordinary creative or telepathic powers. Both these domains seem largely to involve a diminution of the usual sense of separation between inner and outer or between subjective and objective reality.

I: Regarding transitivism, experiences of actual confusion between self and other do not seem to be characteristic of patients with mood disorders, whether depressed or manic. Often, in fact, depressed patients describe a painful *increase* in the boundaries between self and other, as in this report:

Gradually that barrier became like a thing of stone or wood in my mind and although it was intangible it was the most real thing in my life. I could see people through that invisible wall, I could speak to them and they to me, but the mental and spiritual I, the essence of me, could not reach them... (In Landis, 1964, p. 151)

II: But some psychotic patients with mania do describe experiencing a kind of 'mystic union' with others or the universe that suggests considerable diminishment of normal ego boundaries. During one manic phase, for instance, John Custance felt a 'breach in the barriers of individuality':

It is actually a sense of communion, in the first place with God, and in the second place with all of mankind, indeed with all of creation... I have on occasion noticed a curious sympathy between my own mind and those of others in an excited mental states... There have been times... when other patients have said things to me without any prompting which corresponded in a very remarkable way with what was in my own mind at the time, as though some sort of telepathy was involved. (Custance, 1952, p. 37)

Other patients with mania stated, 'You just have a feeling you're part of the earth, not a person on your own, sort of melt into it' (Landis, 1964, p. 281) and 'I seem to merge into everything' (Parnas et al., 2005, p. 290). But there also seem to be some subtle difference that may distinguish the merger experiences typical of mania versus schizophrenia.

III: One difference is that patients with mania do not seem to report any sense of *confusion* about their own point of view, in the sense of losing track of who one is. Perhaps associated with this is the presence of a mood-tone that is ecstatic or benign, or at least not frightening or unpleasant. Landis (1964) has related such experiences to a kind of religious or spiritual ecstasy, as is implied by Custance's use of the term 'communion' to describe his relation to 'mankind' and the universe. Typically the manic experience seems to involve an enjoyable feeling of expansion such that one's experience touches and mingles with others. There is little indication of a disorganization of fundamental selfhood, and these patients do not seem at all confused about who they are.

By contrast, the feeling of uncertainty about boundaries often has a dysphoric quality in schizophrenia patients. The patient seems to become anxious about not knowing who he is, or feels threatened and invaded by other people or external stimuli, as in the EASE item *Threatening Bodily Contact*, where 'bodily contact feels threatening to one's autonomy and existence' (Parnas et al., 2005, p. 254). An additional difference seems to be that the schizophrenic experience of union frequently has a more distinctively solipsistic tone, with the world felt to be merely an extension of the self and having no separate reality of its own. This is reflected in many items in Domain 5 of the EASE, *Existential Reorientation*. For example, one former doctor described in the EASE had *Feelings of Centrality*: 'a transient "as if" sentiment that he was the only true doctor in the entire world and the fate of humanity depended on him' (*ibid.*, p. 255). The psychiatrist Hilfiker (in Jaspers, 1946/1963) describes experiences in his schizophrenia patients that are congruent with this item of the EASE: e.g. patients who believe that 'their death would be the death of the world; if they die, everyone else dies'. Other patients made such remarks as, 'When my eyes are bright blue, the sky gets blue'; 'My eyes and the sun are the same'; and 'My body bears fruit... it is a world-body... they have to have someone to support the world; the world must be represented or the world will disappear' (*ibid.*, p. 296). Such quotes strongly suggest the solipsistic quality that can lie behind schizophrenic feelings of union. 'The self is identified with the All', writes Jaspers (*ibid.*) of schizophrenia. 'The patient is not just someone else (Christ, Napoleon, etc.) but simply the All. His own life is experienced as the life of whole world, his strength is world-sustaining and world-vitalizing. He is the seat of this supra-personal power' (*ibid.*, p. 296).

In mania, by contrast, the dominant experience seems more a feeling of resonating or being at one with the All. If in mania there is a sense of *merging* with the Godhead, in schizophrenic solipsism it is more a matter of *being* the only Godhead, the creator of all things in the experiential field. Whereas the manic experience involves *merger* with the world, schizophrenic solipsism seems more a matter of *reducing* the world to one's own consciousness or ken. The following report, from a grandiose patient with mania, does put some pressure on the distinction just drawn. We would argue, however, that it falls short of *identifying* the self with God or the constituting centre of the universe; also there is no denial of the reality of the external universe: 'I feel so close to God, so inspired by His Spirit that in a sense I am God. I see the future, plan the Universe, save mankind; I am utterly and completely immortal; I am even male and female' (Custance, 1952, p. 51).

7. Conclusion

Throughout this chapter, we have considered various ways in which subjective life in affective disorders and in schizophrenia, in particular self-experience, can be similar, in spite of what psychiatry has traditionally recognized as a profound and basic distinction between the two. But we have also attempted to show how, on closer examination, the two can probably be distinguished, albeit in some ways that are more subtle and elusive than those traditionally proposed. Perhaps the best way of summarizing this distinction across all the domains we have reviewed is by returning to Jaspers' (1946/1963, pp. 111, 122) formulations of the melancholic's 'feeling of having no feeling' vs. the schizophrenic experience of being 'no longer able to feel he exists'. It is true that affective patients can experience profound change in the way they experience themselves and the world around them. We suggest, however, that they will typically maintain the sense of basic self that generates or underlies *all* experience, including that *particular* experience which involves recognizing the deadening *of* one's experience. In schizophrenia, by contrast, the most essential disturbance seems to affect minimal or core self in a more fundamental way, undermining of the most intimate and foundational 'I' (Sass and Parnas, 2003). It may be that this fragmentation and collapse of basic ipseity is the *trouble générateur* which the most distinctive disturbances of schizophrenia will reflect.

Acknowledgments

For helpful comments, we thank Matthew Ratcliffe, several participants in the March 2011 Phenomenology of Depression Workshop in Durham, UK, where early forms of these chapters were initially presented, and two anonymous reviewers.

Louis A. Sass and Elizabeth Pienkos

Space, Time, and Atmosphere

A Comparative Phenomenology of Melancholia, Mania, and Schizophrenia, Part II

1. Introduction

In this chapter we continue the project begun in the previous chapter. This is to compare the phenomenology of severe forms of melancholia and mania with the phenomenology of schizophrenia, paying particular attention to areas of overlap in which experiences in these disorders can seem to converge. The previous chapter focused on disturbances of the *self*. Now we turn to anomalous experiences of the *world*, addressing changes in these various psychiatric conditions in the experience of objects and space, of time and events, and of pervasive atmospheric qualities.

Phenomenology has long recognized the inseparability of self and world. Husserl (1931/1962) noted that all consciousness is a consciousness of *something*, suggesting that cognition and subjectivity are intrinsically tied to world-oriented experiences; Heidegger (1962) spoke of human existence as being-in-the-*world* or *Dasein*. While much current phenomenological psychopathology has focused on disturbances of self in schizophrenia, patients often describe concurrent changes in their perception of and engagement with events, things, and the overall 'feel' of the world. Such transformations in schizophrenia and affective disorders have been classically described by Jaspers (1946/1963), Minkowski (1933/1970), and Matussek (1987), among others. More recently, these sorts of changes have been highlighted by the Bonn Scale for the Assessment of Basic Symptoms (an assessment tool that catalogues subjective disturbances in schizophrenia) (Gross *et al.*, 2008), and by such writers as Fuchs (2005a; 2007),

Ratcliffe (2010b), Stanghellini (2004), and Sass (1992). Here we consider three particular domains of world experience: space, time, and atmosphere. These domains have frequently been described as essential components of subjective experience of the world in classic phenomenological research (e.g. Jaspers, 1946/1963; Ellenberger, 1958; Tatossian, 1997). They represent what we consider to be the major dimensions of world experience, with the significant exception of those that have a more explicitly interpersonal focus (the latter to be treated, for reasons of length, in later papers on interpersonal experience and the experience of language).

Like the last chapter, this chapter is exploratory, drawing its conclusions and speculations from a survey of work coming largely from phenomenological psychiatrists and psychologists as well as from first-person accounts of patients diagnosed as suffering from schizophrenia or affective disorder. This chapter has the same ambitions, and suffers from the same limitations, as were described in the two introductory sections of the last chapter; these points will not be discussed again in detail here. As explained there in more detail, our ambition is to contribute to both the diagnostic differential and general psychopathological understanding of the disorders at issue. Just as in the previous chapter, our focus is not on the traditionally described symptoms of schizophrenia and severe affective disorders (such as hallucinations and delusions), but on more subtle, experiential anomalies. By considering these subtle alterations of world experience, we hope to illuminate a more general underlying orientation to experience.

As in the previous chapter, here we survey a considerable array of clinical, theoretical, and empirical work in psychopathology, and we present illustrative patient reports of subjective experience. Our approach is fairly speculative and anecdotal, and obviously needs to be corroborated by empirical research — to which it should serve as a necessary theoretical preliminary. Once again, discussion of each domain of experience is separated into three parts in a dialectical structure: I. obvious and traditionally recognized differences between subjective experience of time, space, and atmosphere in schizophrenia and affective disorders; II. experiences that seem particularly similar between these two domains of disorder; and III. subtler ways in which the disorders seem nevertheless distinct. We remind the reader that we are pursuing a kind of 'ideal-type' analysis. We seek broad generalizations about tendencies and dominant characteristics, without claiming to uncover sharp boundary lines or address all subtypes or internal complexities.

2. Objects and Space

I: Changes in the perception of objects and space are not infrequent in schizophrenia. The Bonn Scale (Gross *et al.*, 2008) lists the experiences of micropsia, macropsia, and dysmegalopsia, disruptions of normal spatial properties (the relative size or shape of objects) that, presumably, are *not* as commonly described in affective illness. In *General Psychopathology*, Jaspers (1946/1963) remarks on these changes in schizophrenia, and also notes the experience of infinite space, citing one schizophrenia patient who said: 'Space seemed to stretch and go on into infinity, completely empty. I felt lost, abandoned to the infinities of space, which in spite of my insignificance somehow threatened me' (*ibid.*, p. 81). Jaspers also describes 'space with an atmosphere' (a phrase taken from Binswanger): the sense that space is charged with a special meaning or mood-like significance. One schizophrenia patient described this in the following terms:

> Suddenly the landscape was removed from me by a strange power. In my mind's eye I thought I saw below the pale blue evening sky a black sky of horrible intensity. Everything became limitless, engulfing... I knew that the autumn landscape was pervaded by a second space, so fine, so invisible, though it was dark, empty, and ghastly. (*Ibid.*, p. 82)

Schizophrenia patients may also describe how they are drawn to notice the empty space surrounding objects or in a scene, rather than the people and things within it:

> [A] schizophrenic reported: 'when he looked at objects, things often seemed so empty. The air was still between things, but the things themselves were not there'. Another patient said: He only saw the space between things; the things were there in a fashion but not so clear; the completely empty space was what struck him. (*Ibid.*, pp. 81f)

Schizophrenia patients may also report an experience in which objects appear fragmented, flat and unrelated, arrayed in space as on a vast, even infinite plane, or reduced to their pure geometrical qualities. 'My perception of the world seemed to sharpen the sense of the strangeness of things', states Renee, author of the *Autobiography of a Schizophrenic Girl* (Sechehaye, 1962, p. 83). 'In the silence and immensity, each object was cut off by a knife, detached in the emptiness, in the boundlessness, spaced off from other things' (*ibid.*, p. 83). Here everything seems somehow equally distant, as if Renee were detached from any normal subjective standpoint.

II: Significant transformations in the experience of space and objects may, however, also occur in the affective disorders, and sometimes in ways that can seem similar to schizophrenia. Ellenberger

(1958) describes how space may feel full or empty, that it may be experienced as expanding or constricting, depending on the state of mind of an individual. Similarly, in mania everything may appear to be more near or readily available than would usually be the case. Consistent with the mania patient's general sense of grandiosity, his belief that he can do or be anything he desires, such a person may feel that all objects are somehow within reach, as if space and distance no longer presented any obstacle and everything lay at one's fingertips.

Melancholic patients, by contrast, may experience everything as being somehow unreachable and far away, with objects seeming duller, smaller, and somehow insignificant. Straus (1958) speaks of how the experience of distance reflects the degree that one feels able to 'reach' or act upon objects, describing how the feeling of passivity (frequently found in depression) 'removes the reachable to a limitless remoteness' (*ibid.*, p. 165). Furthermore, with the dimming down of emotional life, everything loses the intensity of its motivational valence and consequently appears both dull and distant. Some of these melancholic reports can seem difficult to differentiate from experiences of limitless space and meaningless objects that are found in schizophrenia. For example, Cutting (2002) describes an encounter with a melancholic patient as follows: 'When I wanted to weigh him... he got on the scale, shifted the weights, and correctly found his weight. However, he was no sooner finished than he began, "What use is all that? This scale is only a lot of iron and wood"' (p. 155). This description suggests a focus on the material rather than the affordance quality of objects, which may be associated with a more general, alienated perspective on the value of human activities; such a perspective can, at times, erode the ready familiarity of the world (Toulous, 1893, in Cutting, 2002).

III: We suggest, however, that there may be an important albeit subtle difference to be discerned: the difference between a spatial world that is experienced as if from no place in particular versus one that, though distant and deadened, is nevertheless viewed from a *particular* standpoint, and is still imbued with recognizable (though less salient) affordance-meanings.

It may be useful to recall the geometer's distinction between anisotropic space, meaning space that is imbued with a point of view, versus isotropic space — the latter implying an objective view that is not grounded anywhere in particular and allows for uniformity in all directions (Ellenberger, 1958), a sort of alienated 'view from nowhere' (phrase from Nagel, 1986). While patients with mania and melancholia are trapped *within* their point of view, unable to escape from its affective colouring and adopt a more objective perspective, schizophrenia patients seem at times almost to lose the sense of having any subjective centre at all. This can be coordinated with a perception of the world as flat, geometrically oriented, meaningless, and at times bizarre and uncanny. The affective colouring in melancholia or mania reflects an internal feeling state, either duller for the melancholia patient or brighter and more vibrant for the patient with mania. In these affective disorders we do not, however, seem to find the sort of evenly distributed infinitude described by the schizophrenia patient Renee.

3. Time and Events

Now we turn to disturbances of time and the experience of events. The Examination of Anomalous Self-Experiences (EASE; Parnas *et al.*, 2005), which targets experience in the schizophrenia spectrum, devotes but one, rather heterogeneous item to these disturbances: *Disturbance in Experience of Time*, where it is noted that time may seem to be moving more slowly or quickly than usual, to be standing still, or to be fragmented. It also describes disruption in existential time, such that 'life appears to be restricted to the present, without guiding future projects, or the present is overwhelmed by stereotyped/repetitive reliving of congealed past, or the experience towards the future is felt as blocked or not available at all' (*ibid.*, p. 243).[1] Several phenomenological texts, both classic and contemporary, have explored these disturbances and how they might relate to the fundamental disturbance of schizophrenia and affective disorders. We focus first on the theoretical writing of Minkowski, especially *Le Temps Vecu* (1933/1970), then on more recent writings by Thomas Fuchs.

I: Minkowski's analysis of time and its disorders was greatly influenced by the work of Henri Bergson. Bergson considered human subjectivity to be composed of two contrasting but complementary principles, space and lived time, which also reflected the contrast between 'intelligence and intuition, the dead and the living, the immobile and the flowing, being and becoming' (Minkowski, 1933/1970, p. 272). Minkowski describes the fundamental disorder or *trouble générateur* in schizophrenia as a 'loss of vital contact with reality', a profound disturbance of the patient's sense of vitality and of his dynamic relationship between self and world: 'The schizophrenic not only seems completely immobilized in himself but seems as if

---

[1]   Temporality can be conceived of as a feature of either the lived world or self-experience, as both Husserl and Heidegger make clear. Here we treat it (somewhat arbitrarily) as an aspect of the lived world.

deprived of the necessary organ to assimilate anything dynamic' (*ibid.*, p. 276). Instead such a person manifests a kind of 'morbid rationalization' or 'morbid geometrism', with emphasis on the spatial and the static such that 'everything spontaneous, everything unforeseen, is excluded from his life [which] is transformed into a shapeless mosaic composed of logical precepts and scraps of thought' (*ibid.*, p. 278).

In comparing affective disorders to schizophrenia, Minkowski first suggests that the former should be characterized by a *hypertrophy* of vitality, movement, and harmony between self and world (*ibid.*, p. 290). This follows Kretschmer's distinction of schizoid versus cycloid personality traits, such that 'the schizoid is rather unaffected by his surroundings and remains in merely superficial contact with it' while 'the cycloid [associated with affective disorders] always retains his contact with the surrounding world' (Urfer, 2001, p. 283). Bleuler too has suggested that schizophrenia is characterized by a loss of 'syntony', the ability to remain in contact with the environment, while affective disorders involve increase in this trait (Bleuler, 1911).

II: However, Minkowski goes on to question the simplicity of this opposition between schizophrenia and affective disorder. Although the affective patient maintains closer 'contact with ambient life' than does the schizoid or schizophrenic individual, this contact is nevertheless instantaneous and superficial, not 'a fully developed contact' but one that is 'degraded, deformed, in comparison to true syntony' (Minkowski, 1933/1970, p. 291).

According to Minkowksi, the patient with mania loses the capacity for 'unfolding in time' or *durée*, and his vital contact with reality necessarily shrinks as a result, 'absorb[ing the world] so avidly… that he does not penetrate it at all' (*ibid.*, p. 294). This is apparent in manic distractibility, for such patients typically 'perceive only in a fugitive and imprecise manner, seeming scarcely to care very much about what goes on around them' (Kraepelin, in Minkowski, 1933/1970, p. 295) or to grasp ambient events in a deeply meaningful way. The melancholic patient also experiences profound temporal disturbance in which 'ego-time seems slower than world-time' (Minkowski, 1933/1970, p. 297). This causes such a patient to lose future-orientation and to fall out of sync with the environment.

This experience can appear quite similar to some time disturbances in schizophrenia. One schizophrenia patient states, 'There is no more present, only a backward reference to the past; the future goes on shrinking — the past is so intrusive, it envelops me, it pulls me back' (Jaspers, 1946/1963, p. 84), suggesting an experience of the past as dangerously engulfing. Minkowski (1933/1970) notes that in melancholic patients this inhibition and slowing-down result in a feeling of passivity and impotence, and even in a loss of the normal connectedness and meaningful continuity of time and events. 'I live in instantaneousness', states one severely depressed patient. 'I don't have the feeling of continuity any more... At every new instant that I live, I have the feeling that I have just fallen from the sky' (*ibid.*, p. 333). He continued: 'I am incapable of assimilating either movement or the speed of events that occur around me... When someone does something beside me, I am completely disoriented because I am incapable of following the movement... I see a tree, but I cannot see an automobile that is moving at all' (*ibid.*, p. 333). These reports certainly resemble the 'morbid geometrism' and alienated disturbance with spontaneous and dynamic aspects of life that is characteristic of schizophrenia, as reported by a schizophrenia patient also quoted by Minkowski: 'I have a tendency to immobilize life around me... Stone is immobile. The earth, on the contrary, moves; it doesn't inspire any confidence in me... A train passes by an embankment; the train does not exist for me; I wish only to construct the embankment' (*ibid.*, p. 279).

It seems, then, that both melancholic and schizophrenic patients can lose the ability to 'assimilate anything dynamic', perhaps feeling their life to be transformed into something like a 'shapeless mosaic' (*ibid.*, pp. 276, 278).

III: One possible way of distinguishing between these disorders is insightfully developed in recent work by Thomas Fuchs. Fuchs (2007) suggests that the disturbances in schizophrenia can be attributed to a fundamental fragmentation of the 'intentional arc', a phrase from Merleau-Ponty that describes the underlying temporal continuity that permits the seamless connection, via 'passive synthesis', of the present with the immediate past and immediate future. Edmund Husserl referred to this temporal synthesis (we will call it the 'temporal arc') as involving 'retention' and 'protention', which he distinguished from the more thematic and less automatic processes of 'recollection' and 'expectation' (Zahavi, 2005). Retention and protention are intrinsic elements of the 'now', of what William James called the 'specious present' and likened to 'a saddleback and not a knife edge' (James, 1898). As Fuchs (2005a; 2013a) notes, his views are congruent with the ipseity-disturbance hypothesis (Sass and Parnas, 2003). One might say, in fact, that the microstructure of minimal self or first-person givenness just *is* the structure of inner time-consciousness (Zahavi, 2005): the minimal self can only exist as a temporal flux, yet this flux also *depends* on the minimal self as the medium through which it is manifested.[2]

The intimate connection between basic temporality and minimal self is clear in Elyn Saks' account of her schizophrenic experience:

> This experience is much harder, and weirder, to describe than extreme fear or terror. But explaining what I've come to call 'disorganization' is a different challenge altogether. Consciousness gradually loses its coherence. One's center gives way. The center cannot hold. The 'me' becomes a haze, and the solid center from which one experiences reality breaks up like a bad radio signal. There is no longer a sturdy vantage point from which to look out, take things in, assess what's happening. No core holds things together, providing the lens through which to see the world, to make judgments and comprehend risk. Random moments of time follow one another. Sights, sounds, thoughts, and feelings don't go together. No organizing principle takes successive moments in time and puts them together in a coherent way from which sense can be made. And it's all taking place in slow motion. (Saks, 2007, p. 13)

This foundering of the temporal arc has numerous implications or *sequelae*, including the feeling that there are gaps between one moment and the next, and difficulty anticipating and integrating future events. The patient is left experiencing worldly events as though seen under a strobe light, or perhaps like a series of photographs shown one after another in no clear order. Sequences of events, even of the patient's *own* actions, can lose their automatic flow; and the patient may have to make effortful attempts to put them together into a meaningful sense of sequence.[3]

Disruption in the temporal arc will also have implications for higher-order or more reflective/thematic aspects of temporality that are founded on this more basic sense of existing in time. The schizophrenia patient who states, 'You are dying from moment to moment and living from moment to moment, and you're different each time' (Fuchs, 2013a, p. 84) seems to be experiencing a basic disturbance of ipseity/temporality. But this, in turn, will have reverberations at the more reflective and temporally extended level of narrative continuity

---

[2] According to Zahavi: '…inner time consciousness simply *is* the pre-reflective self-awareness of the stream of consciousness, and Husserl's account of the structure of inner time-consciousness (protention–primal representation–retention) should consequently be appreciated as an analysis of the microstructure of first-personal givenness' or 'pre-reflective self-awareness' (Zahavi, 2005, p. 65, also p. 54).

[3] An interesting demonstration of this mutation of basic temporal anticipation is the schizophrenia patient's ability to tickle herself, apparently because she can lose the ability to own or predict the consequences of her own hand and finger movements (Blakemore, Wolpert and Frith, 2000).

over larger stretches of time, and involving recollection and expectation rather than the more basic retention and protention.

By contrast, in his analysis of temporality in *melancholia*, Fuchs (2007; 2013a) emphasizes not the very *structure* of the temporal arc, with its protention and retention, but the loss of drive, motivation, or vitality and an associated slowing down of physiological processes. These are manifestations of a 'loss of conation': diminution of 'the basic energetic momentum of everyday life', of the drive, appetites, or desires that makes one pursue various goals, and which are inextricably linked to the basic sense of 'aliveness' or fundamental self-affection. Such persons also tend to feel rigid in comparison to the world around them and to lose their affective resonance with others and even themselves, resulting in the experience of 'affective depersonalization'.

As the melancholic mood takes over, there is the feeling of being oppressed by an inescapable past, and a loss of orientation to the future. The future may in fact come to seem like yet another manifestation of the past, so predetermined and inevitable is its feel. The overarching mood tone of this melancholic lived world is one of guilt, of being tied to one's past transgressions against others whose consequences will be forever repeated in the future. As Binswanger notes, melancholic thoughts are overwhelmingly characterized by empty possibility: 'If only I had done/not done this' (in Fuchs, 2013a), where the patient is completely stuck in his futile regret of the past. Sarah Kane, the playwright who so vividly evokes her psychotic depression in her play *4.48 Psychosis*, described this boundless shame, guilt, and regret, in which 'a wound from two years ago opens like a cadaver and a long buried shame roars its foul decaying grief' (Kane, 2001, p. 209). The transgressions at issue may be more imaginary than real, but they are typically felt to reside in an unchangeable past. 'I gassed the Jews', writes Sarah Kane. 'I killed the Kurds, I bombed the Arabs, I fucked small children while they begged for mercy, the killing fields are mine' (*ibid.*, p. 227). And elsewhere in Kane's play, she writes: 'Victim. Perpetrator. Bystander' (*ibid.*, p. 231).

We may summarize this distinction as follows: schizophrenia patients can certainly experience many of the temporal distortions associated with melancholia; some, for example, may be consumed by the past. But what is more distinctive of persons with schizophrenia is their propensity to experience a disturbance of time at the very level of ipseity and basic temporality, that is, in the disruption of the temporal arc, of the 'coupling or mutual relation of conscious moments creating a span of lived time which is necessary for the continuity of self-awareness' (Fuchs, 2013a, p. 98). This disruption has a multitude of consequences, including loss of fundamental dynamism and diminished contact between oneself and the world. In melancholia, by contrast, the core disturbance has more to do with motivational drive, and it affects primarily the social and narrative dimensions of experience rather than ipseity itself. The melancholic is not driven to the pursuit of any need, desire, or goal, and in this sense lacks propulsion toward the future. However, he or she still experiences what William James called 'the specious present' and what Husserl termed 'width of presence', or the 'duration-block' (Husserl, in Zahavi, 2005). In melancholia, the past becomes more determining, and the future less open; in mania it is the reverse. The relative *weighting* of past, present, and future can also change in schizophrenia, but this is not the most fundamental change. In schizophrenia the very vector-like nature of the present moment, understood as James's specious present or the Husserlian now, can actually collapse or disappear. And as a result, rather than merely slowing or speeding the flow, life itself can turn into a series of stills as time turns wholly strange and unpredictable. '[T]he play of time was so uncanny... an *alien time* seemed to dawn', said one patient with schizophrenia (Jaspers, 1946/1963, p. 86).

These are subtle but profound differences. Consider the difference between the following two reports. On the one hand, a melancholic patient says, 'I cannot see the future, just as if there were none. I think everything is going to stop now and tomorrow there will be nothing at all' (*ibid.*, p. 86). On the other hand, a schizophrenia patient states, 'While watching TV it becomes even stranger. Though I can see every scene, I don't understand the plot. Every scene jumps to the next, there is no connection. The course of time is strange, too. Time splits up and doesn't run forward anymore. There arise uncountable disparate now, now, now, all crazy and without rule or order' (Kimura, in Fuchs, 2007, p. 233).

These temporal alterations have implications for the patients' overall experience of the general causal structure of events. In melancholia and mania the dominant causal structures of interpretation are fairly straightforward: in depression, inexorable causal determinism (e.g. preoccupation with bodily aging; impossibility of escaping consequences of past events); in mania, an exaggerated sense of the power of one's own will, implying that events are largely under one's control. Both modes of experience can and do occur in schizophrenia, sometimes in extreme form, as when the patient experiences the self as a machine or a god-like entity. But in schizophrenia one may also find a profound and confusing sense of the sheer randomness of events, as if all causal linkages are destroyed or were effaced. The difference can be summarized as follows: in schizophrenia, a mode of temporality (perhaps better, of *a*-temporality) that, together with collapse of protention and retention, loses all organization and meaning; in melancholia, a foundering of drive and associated projection of the self into the future, that leaves one dominated by the past, futility, and fatigue.

4. Atmosphere

We turn now to the topic of atmosphere, of aspects of experience or subjective life that seem to concern the feel of everything and cannot readily be ascribed to any particular domain, such as space, time, persons, or language. Some psychiatrists have suggested that such holistic changes can be sensed from without, as when Tellenbach spoke of 'atmospheric diagnosis' and Rümke of the 'praecox feeling' (Cermolacce, Sass and Parnas, 2010). Here we consider the subjective side of these changes in mood or atmosphere as they may occur in both schizophrenia and affective psychoses.

I: The atmosphere of the depressive and the manic worlds are typically described either as grim and deadened or as abnormally bright and vibrant, respectively. By contrast, schizophrenic persons are often described as manifesting 'flat affect' — a term that refers primarily to diminished affective *expression*, but is frequently assumed to be associated with an underlying diminishment of emotional or affective *experience*. As mentioned in the introduction, according to Jaspers (1946/1963) the alterations typical of affective illnesses can be 'comprehend[ed] vividly enough as an exaggeration or diminution of known phenomena', such as intense emotion (p. 578). By contrast, the key features of the typically schizophrenic ambiance do not seem comprehensible in such obviously emotion-related terms. This would include several aspects of the oft-discussed 'delusional mood' or 'delusional atmosphere', the atmospheric feeling state that precedes or accompanies the development of delusions in schizophrenia (though perhaps not exclusively in schizophrenia), as well as of forms of 'perplexity' and 'derealization' considered to be fairly specific to this illness.

A crucial feature of the 'delusional mood' is a quality of disconcerting and suggestive specificity. In this state of what might be termed 'uncanny particularity' (Sass, 1994), objects or events can appear as though they were special in some way, commanding one's attention and jumping out with a strange significance: 'Every detail and event takes on an excruciating distinctness, specialness, and peculiarity — some definite meaning that always lies just out of reach, however, where it eludes all attempts to grasp or specify it' (Sass, 1992, p. 52). This change can be quite subtle: 'The environment is somehow different — not to a gross degree — perception is unaltered in itself but there is some change which envelops everything with a subtle, pervasive and strangely uncertain light' (Jaspers, 1946/1963, p. 98).

Often there is a 'just so' quality ('I noticed particularly', the patient will say; *ibid.*, p. 100), with everything seeming to exist or somehow to be placed in a specific rather than random way. Given this felt specificity, the subject will sense that such an experience *must* refer to or mean something, but is typically unable to determine what that meaning might be. Experiences may also be imbued with a *déjà-vu* quality or can take on Capgras-like qualities in which everything seems like a copy or clone of something now absent. For example, schizophrenia patients will describe 'so-called' things or 'so-called' people, as when Daniel Paul Schreber spoke of the 'supposed patients' and a man 'who was supposed to be the Medical Director of the Institute' (in Sass, 1994, pp. 104f). The subject may also feel that such experiences have a certain 'for-me-ness' to them, namely, that they are somehow targeting the subject and intentionally eliciting his attention for some unknown reason having either cosmic or more mundane, paranoid significance.

Other atmospheric features characteristic of schizophrenia pertain more directly to the reality-feeling itself, which is perhaps the most foundational of all issues and one that can be felt in very pervasive yet concrete terms. The entire fabric of space and time may seem subtly yet utterly transformed, with 'the feeling of reality... either heightened, pulsing with a mysterious, unnameable force, or else oddly diminished or undermined — or, paradoxically, things may seem... both "unreal and extra-real at the same time"' (Sass, 1992, p. 44). The world may, for instance, seem intensified yet somehow artificial, as is suggested by one schizophrenia patient's description of the world as a 'puppet theatre' (Fuchs, 2005a).

In a previous article we have discussed how, in schizophrenia, the world may seem merely a solipsistic extension, without separate reality of its own. Another crucial feature of the schizophrenic world is captured by the notion of 'double or multiple bookkeeping', the quality whereby persons with schizophrenia seem able to live in two or more realities, at the same time or in quick succession and sometimes without confusion between the two. This is most obvious in the case of certain chronic deluded patients, who though preoccupied with their fantasies nevertheless comport themselves in perfect accord with intersubjective reality. It can also appear in more subtle, quasi-perceptual forms, as when patients are aware of two distinct ways of seeing another person, in a kind of 'seeing-as' whereby, for example, they may see the therapist as both dead and yet not-dead (Sass, 2013; Sass and Pienkos, 2013). The sort of wavering or equivocation regarding the nature of external reality seems much less common in affective psychosis, whether melancholia or mania.

As a result of these overall perceptual and more general, experiential changes, normal objects and events shed their common-sense meanings. The classic psychopathological literature speaks of a specifically schizophrenic 'perplexity' and 'loss of natural self-evidence' (Blankenburg, 1986; Stoerring, 1987), a feeling of confronting a world that is, by turns, fragmented, meaningless, or unreal, yet often insinuating. Maldiney (in Raballo and Nelson, 2010) speaks of a loss of 'transpassibility' in schizophrenia, by which he means loss of the spontaneous attunement or fluid understanding of the world whereby new things become spontaneously incorporated into one's world-view as comprehensible and meaningful. Instead of a 'familiar space of naturally given saliences, [the world becomes] enigmatic and impenetrable; the very feeling of self-coherence [may] blur and eventually fall apart' (Raballo and Nelson, 2010, p. 251).

II: But there are a number of features of affective psychosis that bear striking resemblance to these 'atmospheric' changes that are often assumed to be specific to schizophrenia. Paranoia, with its sense of being at the centre of a threatening or insinuating world, is especially common in mania but also in depression. Indeed, as noted earlier, some psychiatrists have even argued that many or most cases of supposed *paranoid* schizophrenia are really forms of affective psychosis (Lake, 2008).

One of the most distinctive features of *melancholic* forms of depression is the *unfamiliar* nature of the sadness or dysphoria that occurs (DSM-IV-TR, 2000, p. 491). Since this unfamiliarity or strangeness is not merely quantitative, it appears to conflict with Jaspers' talk (see above) of mere 'exaggeration or diminution of [such] known phenomena' as sadness or grief. On the other side, the supposed diminishment of affective intensity that is sometimes ascribed to schizophrenia in particular (i.e. the internal or subjective dimension of 'flat affect') has been contradicted by recent research, involving both self-report and physiological measures, which suggests that schizophrenia patients actually react just as intensely as do normal individuals (Kring *et al.*, 1993; Kring, Kerr and Earnst, 1999).

Forms of derealization certainly occur in severe melancholia. As one depressed patient states, 'I feel miserable and ill; instead of a heightened sense of reality I seem "to move among a world of ghosts and feel myself the shadow of a dream"' (Custance, 1952, p. 61). Another described living 'in a Plutonian psychical twilight. Even the sun was off-color to me' (Kaplan, 1964, p. 83). Many studies have also noted the frequency of depersonalization and derealization experiences at the onset of depression, and as contributors to the formation of depressive delusions (see Sierra, 2009). Like schizophrenia patients, melancholic persons also describe fears and delusions related to death, annihilation, and even a kind of world catastrophe. One melancholic patient reports: '...the room opened on to... space, blank, void. I could never get back, never find myself or anything. The room moved a little as if it were gradually slipping into that all-enveloping nothingness...' (Kaplan, 1964, p. 162). Others say: 'I conceived the delusion that I was about to be buried alive, not in the earth but walled in a small chamber; and I believed that "they" were coming for me' (*ibid.*, p. 86). '...I had a sudden vision of the end of the world, a catastrophe caused solely by my fate' (*ibid.*, p. 86).

Patients with mania often describe the other side of this kind of atmospheric change, namely, an *increase* in liveliness or a *heightened* sense of reality, sometimes involving *jamais-vu* experiences. As one patient states,

> I seem to merge into everything. [There was] an intense consciousness of power and absolute ecstasy... Things appear more real, as if you were just becoming alive and had never lived before. The whole being expands... Everything is more intense... Everything is absolutely new, every minute is as if everything has just started. (Landis, 1964, p. 290)

The bipolar patient John Custance describes a 'heightened sense of reality' in his manic phases, when 'the outer world makes a much more vivid and intense impression on me than usual' (Custance, 1952, p. 31). 'At present,' he writes, 'faces seem to glow with a sort of inner light which shows up the characteristic lines extremely vividly' (*ibid.*, p. 31). This report is at least reminiscent of 'mere being' experiences in schizophrenia, where things can seem 'illuminated and tense', 'alive... in their existence itself' (Sechehaye, 1962, pp. 40, 41), oddly unfamiliar, or otherwise hyper-real.

It is not surprising that these experiences of paranoia and derealization will often be accompanied by forms of cognitive confusion, in affective disorder as in schizophrenia. The altered feel and significance of the world makes it difficult either to assess reality or to cope with it in standard ways. One depressed patient described this experience as follows: 'I seemed to catch out of the tail of my eye a cold black draughty void, with a feeling that I stood on the brink of it in peril of my reason…' (Kaplan, 1964, p. 88). Such subtle changes in the surrounding environment can cause a feeling that one no longer knows how to *be* in the world, and the sense that one is going crazy.

III: Closer analysis suggests some subtle yet significant differences that can sometimes distinguish these experiences in schizophrenic versus affective conditions. In schizophrenia, paranoid interpretations will often be closely associated with certain cognitive/perceptual changes by which they seem to be inspired and that they often serve to rationalize or justify. These changes — including uncanny particularity, doubling, and *déjà vu* — do not seem common (or perhaps even present) in either melancholia or mania. In the latter conditions, paranoid trends appear to be more directly related to the projection of negative self-evaluations or some combination of grandiosity with irritability (and, perhaps, submerged feelings of inferiority). Although the latter motivations can certainly be present in schizophrenia, they seem less dominant or decisive than in the affective conditions.

Furthermore, although the derealization that is common in melancholia can certainly be profound, it seems to lack the extremely uncanny quality characteristic of schizophrenia. Instead of entering into a new and bizarre universe where objects are stripped of all meaning, there is a more straightforward sense that everything is imbued with sadness, guilt, heaviness, or lack of vitality. 'Everything I saw seemed to be a burden to me,' said one melancholic patient, ' the earth seemed accursed for my sake: all trees, plants, rocks, hills, and vales seemed to be dressed in mourning and groaning, under the weight of the curse, and everything around me seemed to be conspiring my ruin' (Landis, 1964, p. 272). Objects may lose meaning and interest, becoming symbols of depression or losing all imaginable appeal. Although things may no longer matter in melancholia, they maintain their basic meaning as things: a tree is still a tree, a face is still a face. This contrasts with the loss of affordances and fragmentation that sometimes prevails in the schizophrenic world — where, as one patient put it, one can feel 'surrounded by a multitude of meaningless details' (Sass, 1992, p. 50) or in which even a human face may lose its coherence: 'I saw the individual features of her face', writes the schizophrenia patient Renee, 'separated from each other: the teeth, then the nose, then the cheeks, then one eye and the other' (quoted in Sass, 1992, p. 50).

The loss of meaning and vital significance found in both schizophrenia and melancholia may be associated with a preoccupation with death, annihilation, and ultimate catastrophe. In melancholia, however, death and destruction appear to be more closely related to guilt, pain, and deprivation, including the feeling of having lost enlivening appetites or the sense that one no longer deserves to live or has been passed up by life, creating a sense of deadness. The Cotard delusion of being dead is common in severe depression as well as in certain organic conditions. Similar experiences of catastrophe and annihilation can certainly occur in schizophrenia patients — indeed 'world catastrophe' is one of their classic delusional themes; but here one often finds a solipsistic element that imbues things with a different accent. 'If you do not keep in touch with me, you will perish', said one schizophrenia patient. And two others: 'Once I am dead, you will all lose your minds'; 'They have to have someone to support the world; the world must be represented or the world will disappear' (in Sass, 1992, p. 303). This solipsistic feeling — that if one desisted from creating everything, the world would cease to exist — seems absent or very rare in melancholia.

As noted, schizophrenia patients can also experience a *heightening* of reality that can seem reminiscent of mania. But in mania there seems a greater emphasis on the sensory qualities of an object, such as aesthetic aspects of colours or shape, and a more distinctly ecstatic vision of the world. In schizophrenia the focus may be more on ontological qualities; the mere existence of a thing may jump forward as practical meanings in the world recede from awareness. A similar experience is described in the famous scene from Sartre's *Nausea* in which the narrator Roquentin stares at the roots of a chestnut tree until they lose all functional qualities and seem to manifest the sheer fact of being there before him in space (discussed in Sass, 1992, p. 187). Another such instance occurs in a classic account from the schizophrenia patient Renee, who describes objects as becoming detached from their normal usages and looming forth in the sheer fact of their existence:

> When, for example, I looked at a chair or a jug, I thought not of their use or function — a jug not as something to hold water and milk, a chair not as something to sit in — but as having lost their names, their functions and their meanings; they became 'things' and began to take on life, to exist... Their life consisted uniquely in the fact that they were there, in their existence itself. (Sechehaye, 1962, pp. 40f)

The 'mere being' of such objects or people can make them seem, in a disconcerting way, both unreal and hyper-real, both dead and alive. Melancholia can involve similar forms of uncertainty. But schizophrenic individuals often seem to inhabit, we might say, an even deeper region of the 'uncanny valley' — which is a term that virtual reality and video game designers use to refer to that unsettling, liminal realm (much to be avoided in computer graphic design) in which one is uncertain of whether something or someone is alive or dead, real or unreal (Mori, 1970).

Residing deep in the uncanny valley seems to be a disconcerting experience, a source of anxiety and ontological uncertainty. Such reactions can certainly be intense. They are, however, distinct from the more standard, emotional reactions that, at the extreme, are termed the 'passions'. Here we encounter one of the most misunderstood features of schizophrenia: the fact that, although such persons may well have diminished *emotional* experience, this does not mean that their *affective* life is any less intense. As Sass (2004b; 2007) has pointed out, emotions can be understood as a subset of the more general category of affective reactions: namely, as those affective reactions that are targeted at specific persons or events that are experienced by the subject as existing independently of him or her (in the 'external' or 'objective' world) and that are felt to have real but unpredictable consequences for the subject's survival or flourishing. Various aspects of schizophrenic experience seem liable to detach the patient from this mode of experience. These include the tendency for bodily experiences, kinaesthetic or proprioceptive, to replace external objects as the focus of attention; for external objects to lose the coherence or affordance-qualities that make them emotionally relevant; and finally, for some patients to withdraw into what they experience as a subjectivistic or even solipsistic world. Although all these experiences undermine one or another requirement for truly *emotional* experience, they are often associated with highly charged yet nonemotional (in the above sense of 'emotional') *affective* responses, such as awe, amazement, or general ontological insecurity about the very existence of the world or the self. These latter responses, affective yet non-emotional, seem to be far more characteristic of schizophrenia than of melancholia or mania. Such an interpretation is consistent with both subjective reports and neurophysiological findings (e.g. re electrodermal response) concerning so-called 'flat affect' in schizophrenia (Sass, 2007).

Still another crucial aspect of schizophrenic experience pertains to the general sense of presence, reality, or substantiality that the objects of experience are felt to have. The overall feel of the schizophrenic world has been aptly described as 'peculiarly insubstantial, evanescent, and hovering' (in Schmidt, 1987, p. 115). Persons with schizophrenia may seem to be open to a variety of ways of experiencing even the same events or set of objects, and may slide all too readily between perspectives on the world, or even experience two or more perspectives simultaneously (as indicated by 'fluidity' and 'contamination' codes on the Rorschach test; Solovay *et al.*, 1986). This contrasts sharply with the fatal certitude so characteristic of psychotic depression, in which the feeling of absolute and incontrovertible finality (usually involving guilt and a sense of doom) can be so dominant.

5. Conclusion

In the previous chapter we discussed a range of features of self-disturbance in schizophrenia and affective psychosis. These included disturbances of a person's relationship to thoughts and thinking, feelings of alienation from the body, changes in emotional experience, and distortions of the basic sense of existing as a subjective presence. We concluded by describing the difference between schizophrenia and melancholia as akin to the distinction between the 'the feeling that I cannot feel' (melancholia) and the sense of being 'unable to feel that I feel' (or even to *feel* that I *don't* feel: schizophrenia) — the latter involving a more profound disturbance that is closer to the innermost kernel or zero point of self-experience.

In this chapter we focused on the perception of and engagement with the outside world, including space and objects, events and time, and general atmosphere. Most of these experiences can be described as involving forms of alienation and experiences of strangeness and the uncanny. Both schizophrenic and melancholic patients may experience a sense of being cut off from the world around them. Melancholic patients may feel out of sync with the world, or they may feel a significant decrease in motivation that renders them incapable of engaging with people and objects, thus creating an unbridgeable gap between themselves and the world. Schizophrenic patients, on the other hand, may have always felt separate or distant from people and things; and their experience of alienation may be bound up with a hyperreflexive scrutiny of the strangeness of the world. Such experiences may also be accompanied by loss of common-sense meanings of objects and fragmentation of time and space.

Experiences of the background sense of reality, or atmosphere, may also be transformed in these disorders. The world may seem unreal or hyper-real. It may seem void of all meaning, or else as though it contains special, even paranoid, meaning for the patient alone. However, whereas these changes will typically occur as a result of emotional disturbances in melancholia and mania, and will thus typically be tinged with either a depressive or an excited mood state, such experiences in schizophrenia are often notable for their sheer uncanniness, which seems both to result from and to augment the difficulty of existing in the world. In schizophrenia the general atmospheric qualities seem subtly and ineffably strange, as in the experiences of uncanny particularity and *déjà-vu*, even to the point of fragmentation or meaninglessness.

In both chapters, we have focused on similarities that can complicate differential diagnosis of schizophrenia versus affective disorder, and that may also suggest some shared psychopathological processes or mechanisms. But we have also suggested that a nuanced understanding of underlying structural changes can help to differentiate the two disorders, and perhaps ultimately contribute to a more precise grasp of the different pathogenetic pathways they may involve. For example, hallucinations in a patient with mania may not imply the same type or degree of foundational alteration in cognitive and experiential orientation as occurs in schizophrenia. Such differences may be crucial in understanding the greater chronicity of schizophrenia, and its propensity to place the patient more profoundly at odds with common-sense, practical reality and the social world. The ability to make such distinctions is essential for both treatment and research into these disorders. We hope that our exploratory forays will spur further, empirical research on both the affinities and differences of subjective experience in schizophrenia and severe affective disorders.

Giovanni Stanghellini
and René Rosfort

Borderline Depression

A Desperate Vitality

A desperate vitality.
— P.P. Pasolini (1964)

1. Introduction

This chapter suggests viewing borderline personality and borderline depression in terms of emotions. From this perspective, borderline personality is characterized by dysphoric mood, and borderline depression by fluctuations between dysphoria and anger. Since dysphoria is a broad and vague concept, we individuate the dysphoria proper to borderline persons as a disquieting feeling characterized by a kind of intentionality devoid of the moderating power of language and representation. Borderline persons, we argue, experience their mood as a disordered flux, an overwhelming power that is at the same time a disturbing, disorganizing, and compelling source of vitality.

On one side, this power is a violent spasm that takes control of the body and destroys the embodied structure that organizes our intentional engagement with the world. It is experienced as an energy that takes the representation of oneself to pieces, reducing it to an assemblage of disordered emotions and drives. On the other side, however, it is also a power that expresses an encouraging vitality seducingly in touch with invigorating sensations.

In order to illustrate our argument, throughout the paper we shall use quotes from the case story of a 40-year-old man collected in a psychotherapeutic setting by GS for several years. This testimony has been selected because it is representative of our experience more generally. We suggest that this case story is paradigmatic of the emotional complex in borderline patients, including extreme emotional fluctu-

ations between dysphoria and anger. In particular, in this patient
dysphoria appears as intentionality somehow incapable of being articulated. He experiences himself and others as blurred and fragmented,
which provokes excruciating feelings of incoherence, emptiness,
uncertainty, and inauthenticity. At the same time, though, the patient
shows spontaneous surges of vitality, although disorganized and
aimless:

> *You ask me what I feel when I feel like this… I want to be polite with
> you… I don't know, I can't say. I hope you're not like the other doc… She
> saw something 'metaphysical' in my mood. Why the fuck she thought so,
> I don't know! She said it was 'ineffable' and 'undefinable'. She may be
> right. But it doesn't help. I told her 'I just feel bad and I can't tell you
> why', but she wanted me to tell her 'the story' of this feeling. What an
> asshole! To insist like this! It made me feel even worse, it made me feel
> stupid. I got angry at her and at myself too, because I couldn't figure out
> 'why' …*
>
> *I had this energy in all my body, not a pleasant energy, rather an
> uncomfortable feeling of excess. A sort of sexual excitement, but not
> exactly so. Something electric moving in my flesh. A current or a heat!
> Something biting, scorching, burning, I don't know. Life itself must be
> like this, if you're able to understand it or somehow control it! But, for
> me, the only way to cope with this energy is to masturbate till it fades
> away.*

The borderline type of existence is under the spell of the paradoxical
nature of this power, destructive and creative at the same time — a
power that brings with it a *desperate vitality*.

In what follows, we will first eliminate some possible misunderstandings about the psychopathological and nosological status of
depression in borderline persons. We will contrast the type of depression in borderline persons with another prototypical form of major
depression, namely melancholia. We go on to explicate our understanding of what human emotions are and our three-levelled approach
to making sense of those emotions — phenomenological, ontological,
and normative. Having explained our understanding of emotions, we
then describe the particular phenomenology characterizing the emotional complex of borderline existence in the course of depressive
acute states as well as in non-depressive phases, focusing especially
on the oscillations between dysphoric mood and angry affect that
bring about quite differently experienced phenomena and life-worlds.
Finally, the chapter is concluded with a sketch of the frustrated emotional normativity characteristic of the borderline type of existence.
Here we look more carefully at the (neglected) vital character of
dysphoria, which we believe to be an indispensable feature in order to

understand and treat borderline persons. This vitality engenders an intense need to satisfy the affective, biological values brought about by vigorous feelings of being alive. These values run counter to and often clash with the ethical norms and social rules that structure the world in which the borderline person lives, provoking a frustrated sense of inauthenticity, worthlessness, and inanity of life.

2. Borderline and Melancholic Depressions

'Depression' is a polysemic term signifying a wide range of forms of distress. Also, depression as a syndrome is a very heterogeneous clinical phenomenon that requires the setting of external boundaries (when does depression become a mental disorder?) as well as internal ones (how many types of depressive syndromes are there?). Therefore, we need an 'in-depth exploration of the subjective experience of depressed persons and of its differences with respect to the perception of ordinary sadness' (Maj, 2012, p. 225), as well as a phenomenological discrimination between different forms of 'depressed' mood. It is unlikely that a standard interview conducted using a checklist of depressive symptoms may clarify the matter, so '[t]here is no other way than to talk to the patient' if we want to grasp the qualitative nuances between different forms of depressive feelings (Parnas, 2012, p. 231).

Depression in borderline persons typically takes one distinctive form. Although it may seem a paradox, a subgroup of persons diagnosed with major depression may not be 'depressed' in the most common sense of the term, i.e. aboulic and apathic. Besides typically depressed patients, who complain about low energy and sadness, when depression develops out of a borderline personality disorder patients may display a chaotic vitality together with an irritable and angry mood (e.g. Kernberg, 1975; Gunderson, 1984; Blatt and Zuroff, 1992). If we strictly confine ourselves to *major depression* as it is defined in current diagnostic manuals, there are at least two types that must be kept separate. In a seminal paper, Gunderson and Philips (1991) contrasted 'empty' depression, which affects persons with borderline personality disorder, with 'guilt' depressions that mirror more classical forms of mood disorders. Comparing a sample of patients with borderline personality disorder vs. non-borderlines, both developing a major depressive episode, Westen and collaborators (1992) confirmed that depression in borderline patients is characterized by emptiness, loneliness, and desperation in relation to attachment figures, together with labile, diffuse negative affectivity. The phenomen-

ality of depression is 'distinct in borderline patients, centering on concerns about abandonment and rejection, a sense of emptiness and
meaninglessness, and a view of the self as fundamentally evil or
despicable' (Westen *et al.*, 1992, p. 382). 'Guilt' depression, on the
other hand, has its own long-established specific clinical profile
whose main features, next to guilty feelings or delusions of guilt, are
lack of vital drive and exacerbated experience of loss of emotional
grasp and resonance — also called feeling of the loss of feeling. This
depressive syndrome, reflecting the traditional prototype of depression or *melancholia*, was described and discussed in detail by classics
of phenomenological psychopathology, including Tellenbach (1961/
1976), who associated it with a specific type of personality which was
on his suggestion named the *Typus Melancholicus* (TM). This association has been confirmed in several studies[1] supporting the hypothesis
that TM is typical of a majority of depressed patients, plausibly constituting a specific vulnerability factor. According to Tellenbach (1961/
1976) and Kraus (1977), the TM is characterized by the person's need
for meticulous organization of his own life-world and the fixation on
harmony in interpersonal relationships (orderliness); the commitment
to prevent guilt-attributions and guilt-feelings (conscientiousness); an
exaggerated norm adaptation and external norm receptiveness (hyper/
heteronomia); and by the emotional and cognitive incapacity to perceive opposite characteristics concerning the same object or person
(intolerance of ambiguity). Such core-properties, which have been
operationalized (Stanghellini and Bertelli, 2006), are radically different from those characterizing borderline persons.[2]

Differences in emotional profile in borderline vs. melancholic
depressions have also been empirically established. If compared to
borderline patients who develop depressive episodes, melancholic
patients show very low rates of anger and dysphoria. They complain

---

[1]   Tölle (1987), Sauer, Richter and Sass (1989), von Zerssen and Possl (1990), Sato *et al.*
(1992; 1993), Fukunishi *et al.* (1993), Nakanishi, Isobe and Ogawa (1993), Mundt *et al.*
(1997), von Zerssen *et al.* (1994; 1997), Stanghellini, Bertelli and Raballo (2006), for
example.

[2]   Obviously, these two types of depression do not cover the whole depressive spectrum.
There are, for instance, forms of melancholic depression that do not have guilt (i.e. the loss
of moral integrity) as their main theme, but are characterized more by hypochondriac and
bankruptcy delusions (i.e. the loss of bodily and financial integrity). What is relevant,
though, in the context of our argument is that we are witnessing a profound transformation
of the clinical forms of depression: whereas in handbooks of psychiatry published until 30
years ago melancholia was the typical, if not the paradigmatic, form of depression (e.g. Ey,
Bernard and Brisset, 1960; Mayer-Gross, Slater and Roth, 1954), in more recent times we
have seen an epidemic of non-melancholic forms of 'atypical' depression in which guilt,
loss, and vital sadness are not the central phenomena, but rather a confusing mixture of
emptiness, abandonment, persecution, restlessness, impulsivity, dysphoria, and anger.

about their lack of emotional resonance with other persons and the environment, and, most importantly, they feel guilty for this lack of emotional involvement. The depressive experience of borderline patients is imbued with a tense, irritated mood, feelings of emptiness, higher proneness to externalize anger, resentment towards the environment, relatively high reactivity to environmental solicitations, and usually low levels of guilt feelings (Stanghellini, Bertelli and Raballo, 2006).

These empirical findings should allow us to seek out more nuanced differences between the two sets of abnormal phenomena. Depressed mood is a complex emotional state that includes at least the following principal features: feeling of prostration (as in lack of vital drive), loss of pleasure and interest (anhedonia), moral pain, and the pathogenic situation in which depressed mood occurs. When the phenomenality of these features is considered more carefully, though, we can see significant differences between the two major prototypes of depression in question.

Lack of vital drive. It is a feeling of diminished vitality, freshness, physical and psychical integrity. This lack, in turn, entails feelings of despondency, feebleness, physical malaise. The general character of abnormal vitality is present in both forms of depression, but with a major difference as far as its embodied features are concerned. Embodiment in melancholic persons is dominated by the structure of over-identification. They feel that they are *nothing but* their body which is experienced as abnormally materialized and reified, heavy and rigid, devoid of emotions, energies, and drives. This loss of bodily elasticity and resonance implies painful sensations of derealization (feelings of detachment from other persons and external reality). In borderline depressions, rather than a feeling of diminished vitality, we find a threatening sense of uncontrollable energy that dissipates the person's sense of agency and may therefore end up in a sensation of complete exhaustion and prostration. We do not find an over-identification of oneself with one's own body. Rather, one's own body, as the source of vitality and drive, is felt as if out of voluntary control, lying somewhere between self and something which is not the self (*'not a pleasant energy, rather an uncomfortable feeling of excess'*). In borderline depression the body is experienced as charged with an energy that does not seem to belong to oneself, that is, it disrupts a person's sense of being a self by transforming that person's body into an anonymous source of vitality (*'Something biting, scorching, burning, I don't know'*).

Anhedonia. The incapacity to feel pleasure is another key feature that distinguishes borderline from melancholic pathology. It is considered a feature of emotional anaesthesia, i.e. a painful feeling of the loss of the capacity of feeling. Anhedonia is typically absent in the melancholic type of personality when not undergoing depressive episodes. The melancholic type of personality usually exhibits hyperthymic temperamental traits (Stanghellini, Bertelli and Raballo, 2006) including sociability, hyperactivity, and over-involvement, but not anhedonia. Complaints of loss of emotional resonance (e.g. the incapacity to have empathic feelings with others) are typical in acute episodes of melancholic depression. The type of anhedonia exhibited by borderline persons is different from this. Anhedonia may be an accompanying feature of dysphoria in borderline persons, but in that case it typically has a *hyperbolic character* (Zanarini and Frankenburg, 1997), since it triggers an escalation of behaviours that are meant to contrast it — the most prevalent being (although not exclusive to borderline depression) alcohol and drug abuse, a turbulent erotic life, and self-mutilations. When anhedonia appears in borderline persons as a feature of a depressive episode, it typically consists in a kind of irritating emptiness that oscillates between painful feelings of abandonment and self- and other-destructive acting-outs, including a mixture of anger and humiliation. If this emptiness is to be understood as some form of anhedonia, it is certainly very different from the kind of anhedonia that we find in melancholic depression, since the borderline's feelings of emptiness are more akin to an overcharged, hypersensitive, and frustrated emotional resonance — as if it consisted of raw feelings that blunt the emotional life because of their unmediated intensity.

Moral pain. Guilt is the moral feeling that typically arises when we think that we have in some way wronged another person. As such, it is the fundamental theme in those forms of major depression affecting the melancholic type of personality. Depressive episodes in borderline persons are not characterized by this kind of guilt feeling. Typical borderline persons think that they suffer because they *have been wronged* by the other person. Guilt is on the side of the other — usually a significant other. Sometimes, though, borderline persons are also affected by a moral pain that has been called 'persecutory guilt' (Grinberg, 1964). Persecutory guilt is the delusional theme whereby the patient feels persecuted for a fault she senses to have really committed, though without being explicitly aware of being responsible for her fault. To explain this point, we need to distinguish two different emotional complexes involving moral pain: one is characterized by a constellation of guilt, humiliation, and anger; the other by guilt, shame, and remorse. This first complex is typical in borderline depression, whereas the second can be found in melancholic depression.

While the feelings of guilt involved in melancholic patients tend to evoke shame when thinking about the wronged other, persecutory guilt is characterized by a feeling of being humiliated by the other with regard to oneself. Also, guilt and shame in melancholic patients are self-referential: they feel guilty and ashamed in front of themselves. Persecutory guilt and humiliation in borderline patients involve the other: they feel wronged and humiliated by the other, whose *look* is responsible for revealing to everybody their faults and for laying bare 'petty' moral flaws in their character.

> *You see, sometimes people watch me in a strange way... not all people, someone who knows me... as if they want to penetrate me, to see inside me... this makes me feel insecure, naked, as if they really want to humiliate me... What do they know about me? Do they really think they know me? Not even I know myself! Am I supposed to conform to their petty rules? Who authorized them to judge me?*

Typically, as is the case with this patient, feelings of humiliation are accompanied by anger. We will come back to the central role of anger in the sections ahead.

Pathogenic situation. Another important feature that can help to disentangle borderline from melancholic depression is the kind of situation that generates each of them.[3] Normally, the depressive decomposition of the TM is triggered by experiences of *loss*, which she construes as *her own* wrong behaviour, whereas the borderline person is sensible to experiences of *abandonment*, which she construes as wrong behaviour on the part of *the other person*. For borderline persons, other people oscillate between opposite polarities: a hoped-for source of selfhood through recognition, but also of humiliation and thus of disunion and despair. These themes are reflected in the borderline person's feelings and delusional themes when she experiences acute depressive decomposition.

3. Emotions, Bodily Feelings, and Normativity

Our understanding of what emotions are has a significant bearing on our interpretation of borderline depression, so without going into detail about the century-long debate in philosophy of emotion

---

[3] For a general discussion of the 'context criterion' in depression, see Maj (2012).

between feeling theories (e.g. James, 1884; Damasio, 1994; and Prinz, 2004) and cognitive theories (e.g. Solomon, 2007; Gordon, 1987; Nussbaum, 2001), in this section we shall very briefly try to position ourselves with respect to, perhaps, the most central issue in this debate. The issue is whether emotions are constituted principally by *bodily feelings*, i.e. non-intentional, physiological changes in the body (feeling theories), or principally by *cognitive states*, i.e. intentionally or cognitively structured conscious experiences (cognitive theories). Now, the embodied character of human emotions can hardly be put in doubt, since — as de Sousa has noticed — 'of all the aspects of what we call the "mind", emotions are the most deeply embodied' (de Sousa, 1987, p. 47). It is equally difficult, however, to contest that many human emotions are indeed constituted by some form of intentional structure or cognitive structure.

In fact, it has been argued that the distinction between cognitive emotions and bodily feelings seems rather awkward (e.g. *ibid.*; Stocker, 1996; Goldie, 2000; Ratcliffe, 2008a). We agree with this stance, and believe that it is perhaps best simply to accept that what we call an emotion is a heterogeneous phenomenon that involves constellations of bodily feelings that can be *more or less intentionally structured*. To sort out and make sense of those constellations of feelings, we combine a phenomenological approach to emotional experience with an insistence on the normative complexity of emotional experience entailed by the ontological ambivalence constitutive of human emotions (de Sousa, 1987; 2007; 2011).

We work with a three-level approach to emotions (Stanghellini and Rosfort, 2013): what emotions feel like (phenomenological), what emotions are (ontological), and how to live with emotions (normative). We need to combine the phenomenological perspective with both an ontological and a normative perspective if we want to make sense of the complexity of human emotions. Articulating what different emotions feel like is, in our opinion, our best means to making sense of those emotions. However, as de Sousa points out, due to their embodied nature, 'what emotions feel like cannot give us full access to their nature' (de Sousa, 2010, p. 100). Next to the phenomenological level, we must take into account the ontological level, i.e. the impersonal biological features of an emotional experience:

> [E]motions are not altogether knowable on the basis of what is available only in the moment's consciousness. Indeed, emotions are shaped by history on at least two levels: that of the individual development from zygote through infant to adult, but also on the phylogenetic scale of our evolution into the animals that we are. Consequently it is not surprising

that emotions are not entirely transparent to consciousness. (*Ibid.*, p. 100; see also de Sousa 2011, pp. 130–6, and de Sousa, 2006)

This ontological complexity manifests itself phenomenologically in the sense that many emotions, or aspects of an emotional experience, are cognitively impenetrable (Goldie, 2000, pp. 110–1) and do not accommodate our cognitive and intentional structures. Emotions are expressions of the biological vitality that informs and to a certain degree orients human life — as well as the life of other animals. The problem with explaining human emotions within a theoretical framework that neglects either the cognitive or bodily aspect of emotions emerges at the normative level. Precisely, it surfaces in regard to how we should live and cope with our emotional experience, that is, how we should try to make sense of what we feel and to take responsibility for our emotional reactions — even though, and exactly because, they have a tendency to spiral out of control. Emotions are what makes life interesting and enriches our experience of the world and other people exactly because they make my experiences matter to me. Emotions make experience matter to me because they reveal that I am inescapably involved in the world that I experience. Experience is never neutral, but always personal in the sense that my experience is shaped by the person that I am. Sartre was keenly aware of this personal aspect of emotional experience, which was part of his sceptical stance towards emotions:

> [T]he consciousness leaps into the magical world of emotion [*le monde magique de l'émotion*], plunges wholly into it by debasing itself. It is a new consciousness in front of a new world — a world which it constitutes with its own most intimate quality, with that presence to itself [*cette présence à elle-même*], without distance, of its point of view upon the world. (Sartre, 1939/1971, p. 78; translation modified)

Emotions can distort our experience, complicate our understanding of what is going on, and make us say or do things we know to be inappropriate or wrong. Emotions can destroy our life — as well as make it a life worth living. What makes emotional experience 'magical' is also what makes it terrible. To live with our emotions, we have to try to make sense of what we feel, why we feel it, and how to handle the involuntary aspects of who and what we are that our emotions reveal. In this sense, we are in full agreement with the *ethical emphasis* of the cognitive theories. Emotions require that we appropriate and take responsibility for what we feel. However, while most cognitive theories reject the possibility that bodily feelings are constitutive of our norms and values, we suggest that it is exactly because the a-rational character of our bodily feelings is an inherent part of our values that emotional experience is so fraught with normative challenges.

Emotions and feelings are fundamental to the values and norms by means of which we orient ourselves in the world, and in relation to other people and ourselves. In addition to the epistemic function of revealing our concerns and what we care about, emotions are also constitutive of some of the values — and at times even the norms (the emotional aspect of a norm can itself become a norm, e.g. 'to *be* right it has to *feel* right') — that inform and shape our existential orientation. As David Pugmire puts it, besides being 'our way of awakening to the values we find', emotion 'also imbues certain things with value, inasmuch as they matter to us specifically for the kind of emotion they arouse in us' (Pugmire, 2005, pp. 16, 22).

In other words, emotions are what make us care about the conventions, rules, values, and norms that structure and orient our experience of the world, other people, and ourselves (de Sousa, 2011, p. 8). This is not to say that values and norms are merely emotional. On the contrary, values, and norms in particular, are the more stable, i.e. less emotion-dependent, points of orientation that enable us to distance ourselves from what we may feel in a given situation (Blackburn, 1998, pp. 67–98). Values are typically more intrinsically personal than norms in that they express and constitute my personal view on the world, while norms represent the interpersonal structures that orient and govern my existence in a world shared with other persons. Norms — whether external (social or cultural) or internal (personal) — are primarily appropriated and cultivated cognitively as part of our development and enculturation. To live in a world shared with other people we must understand and appropriate the norms that structure this world. Values, on the contrary, can be pre-reflective or non-propositional (although they can be cognitively articulated) in the sense that many of my values are an ineradicable part of my embodied existence. Besides the more or less rational values that I experience and learn to appreciate through my coexistence with other people in a shared world, my body automatically generates a-rational, *vital* values solely by the sheer fact of functioning. As Ricoeur argues:

> Need [*besoin*] is the primordial spontaneity of the body; as such it originally and initially reveals values which sets it apart from all other sources of motives. Through need, values *emerge* [*apparaissent*] without my having posited them in my act-generating role: bread is good, wine is good. Before I will it, a value already appeals to me solely because I exist in flesh [*j'existe en chair*]; it is already a reality in the world, a reality which reveals itself to me through the lack [*le manque*]

...The mystery of incarnate Cogito ties willing to this first stratum of values with which motivation begins. (Ricoeur, 1950/1966, p. 94)

It is the complexity of a-rational bodily values and rational (social or ethical) norms that frustrates the emotional experience of borderline persons. The intensity of their bodily feeling makes it extremely difficult, at times impossible, for the borderline persons to live with the spontaneous, emotional values that these feelings bring about. The emotional intensity does not allow them to distance themselves from what they feel here and now, and therefore they are not able to appropriate their feelings in the light of the values, conventions, and norms that constitute the world in which they live. They live under the spell of what, in the closing section, we shall call a *frustrated normativity*.

Linking emotions and biology in this way is obviously not a new approach but, as mentioned, the central argument of the feeling theories. The feeling theories argue for the close relation, already noted by Darwin (1872/1998),[4] between, on the one hand, basic evolutionarily developed biological values and, on the other, human emotional experience and behaviour. Here is not the place to go into the complex, and highly contentious, debate about emotions and biological values. For the purpose of our argument it should suffice to say that we agree with the emphasis on the significance of basic biological values for human emotional life. As Panksepp has recently put it:

> By necessity, our search has to be initially guided by our own emotional experiences. But a full scientific understanding must include, to a substantial extent, neuroscientific hypotheses based on emerging understandings of the primal sources of the diverse affective experiences of the brain that make emotional arousals so incredibly powerful and interesting. Perhaps many psychologists would still like it to be some other way — that feelings just like our ideas are simply conceptual acts. But few are willing to probe this well hidden underbelly of mind in animals. (Panksepp, 2012, p. 5)

On Panksepp's account, this 'hidden underbelly' of mind is constituted by endogenous emotional systems generating cross-species affective values that still have a significant bearing on human emotional life (Panksepp, 1998; Panksepp and Biven, 2012, pp. 425–74). Our astonishing capacity to think about our feelings, to experience particularly human emotions, and to educate our emotional behaviour, enables us to diminish the sway that affective values hold over our behaviour, but unlike the stoic aspirations of some cognitive theorists

---

[4]   Panksepp (1998, pp. 121–222); Prinz (2004, pp. 160–78); Robinson (2005, pp. 28–56); Damasio (2010, pp. 108–29); LeDoux (2012), for example.

(Nussbaum, 2001) we do not think it possible entirely to eradicate the motivational force of our cognitively impenetrable feelings. These feelings are, as Goldie puts it, 'at the heart of emotion' (2000, p. 12).

However, contrary to some advocates of the feeling theories, we do not believe, and neither does Panksepp, that this presence of biological values at the heart of emotional experience makes the peculiar intentional structure and cognitive functioning of human emotions superfluous or in any way irrelevant. Rather, we believe that an essential character of emotions emerges when we consider *how one should cope* with one's emotional experiences. We, as human persons situated in a world shared with other persons, are *responsible* for our emotions — not for what we feel, but for what we decide to do with what we feel. This is the *normative level*, namely a person's responsibility to articulate, make sense of, and eventually cope with her emotions which sometimes trouble her fragile and vulnerable sense of being a person. The existence of a human person is structured and oriented by ethical norms and social rules which, in turn, presuppose an autonomy on the part of the person, that is, presuppose that we are capable of deciding whether to consent or to react against the emotion we are feeling. The problem is, however, that emotions often complicate this sense of autonomy. As we all know, emotions can make us feel like strangers to ourselves, surprise and frighten us by their intensity (and sometimes by their lack of intensity), and make us behave in ways we did not think possible. To make sense of — and eventually deal with — this alienating aspect of our emotional experience, we need to take seriously the fact that, due to the evolutionary history out of which particularly human emotions developed, our emotions are permeated by vestigial traces of the biological functions that organize and inform all mammalian life. In other words, emotions are constituted by complex intentional and rational features as well as biological and a-rational ones (de Sousa, 2007, pp. 6–9) — and by a fragile dialectic between the two. The normative level brings out the peculiar fact that human emotions are constituted by the fragile complexity of biological as well as personal and societal factors. This fragility emerges into the foreground of the borderline emotional experience.

4. The Borderline Emotional Complex

In this section we return to the phenomenological level of enquiry. In the first part, we will describe in detail anger and dysphoria, the main emotions characterizing borderline persons. Then we identify a core emotional complex manifested by borderline persons, composed of dysphoric mood as an enduring and permanent trait, and angry affect as an intermittent state. Acute depressive episodes in borderline persons are finally described as characterized by angry outbursts accompanied by feelings of humiliation or by exacerbations of dysphoria culminating in feelings of emptiness and boredom.

Anger is an emotion normally conceived as involving a personal offence, or having been somehow wronged by another person, and as such it often motivates a desire for retaliation. In its Latin and Greek roots (*angor, anchō*), both referring to strangling, we can find a strong association with aggression. Episodes of anger tend to be short-lived, all-consuming, and focused on a particular target. Anger and aggressive behaviours characterize the acute phases of the borderline person's existence. Despite its complex cognitive, personal, and normative aspects (Solomon, 2007, pp. 13–28), anger is, in most cases, a readily identified emotion because of its unambiguous intentional object (when angry, I am normally angry with someone because of something he has said or done) and rather clear behavioural manifestations (increase of muscle tension, scowling, grinding of teeth, glaring, clenching of fists, changes of body posture, flashing, paling, etc.) (Tavris, 1989).

Dysphoria[5] manifests itself as a prolonged, unmotivated, indistinct, and quasi-ineffable constellation of feelings that convey a nebula of vague impulses, sensations, and perceptions that permeate a person's whole field of awareness. The psychological and psychopathological characterization of dysphoria is quite difficult because of its subdued manifestation and loose connection to our behavioural patterns. The word 'dysphoria' derives from the ancient Greek δύσφορος (*dysphoros*), formed as δυσ- (*dis-*), difficult, and φέρω (*phero*), to bear. It is an oppressive, and sometimes unbearable, mood. So, even in its etymological roots the word 'dysphoria' is quite polysemous, vaguely defining an emotional condition in which a person is heavily oppressed, and in which that person may either react and show his feelings, or passively suffer and submit to them (Stanghellini, 2000). Phenomenal characterizations of dysphoria mainly focus on its being felt as a burden one cannot get rid of because it is not external to one's own self. It is an obstacle to movement and, at the same time, it may generate impatience, restlessness, and an incoercible impulse to move

---

[5] The term dysphoria is sometimes used in English, particularly in psychiatry, simply as the most generic term for any kind of negative emotion. It is, however, an impoverishment of psychopathological phenomenology to conflate, for example, sadness, anger, and grief into one single term. We therefore suggest a more restrictive use of dysphoria as specified in this chapter.

away without a definite goal. It is also experienced as an uncomfortable feeling characterized both by being painful and sorrowful, as
well as discontented and indignant. This complexity elicits opposite
kinds of movement such as inaction/action, resignation/resistance,
suffering/retaliation. Because of these ambiguities, the definition of
dysphoria is quite controversial. Some use this term to simply qualify
bad mood, or even as an equivalent for depressed mood. However, by
conflating dysphoria and depressed mood one risks neglecting the
phenomenal and behavioural differences between various kinds of
depressive states, for example, the significant differences between
melancholic and borderline depression that we explained above. A
more precise definition of dysphoria as a symptom is: 'a feeling state
of unpleasant, nervous tenseness, a limitation of emotional resonance
to hostile responses, and increased readiness to aggressive acting out'
(Berner, Musalek and Walter, 1987, p. 97). A dysphoric person feels
sulky and unsatisfied. Additionally, dysphoria is often accompanied
by irritability — oversensitivity or irascibility leading to explosive
and aggressive reactions. Irritability and dysphoria are often associated with internal agitation. Accordingly, dysphoric persons often
complain of feelings of tension and uneasiness. Dysphoria, irritability, and internal agitation form together a symptom-complex that in
borderline persons is also accompanied by emotional lability, i.e. a
marked emotional instability characterized by short-lived emotional
states and large emotional fluctuations, and by hyper-emotionality,
i.e. the abrupt emergence of uncontrollable emotional reactions disproportionate to the intensity of the stimulus.

The phenomenal characteristics of dysphoria and anger, the differences between the two, and the oscillations from one to the other may
become more perspicuous if we introduce here a phenomenological
distinction between mood and affect. We would argue that dysphoria
is a mood, whereas anger is an affect.

While affects are responses to a phenomenon that is perceived as
their motivation, moods do not possess such directedness to a motivat-
ing object.[6] Even though the terminology of influential phenomenologists differs,[7] their analyses of these experiences concur in their

---

[6]   The term 'affect' is rather ambiguous in English. It can be used as a very general term cov-
      ering the subjective, first-person experiential aspect of an emotional episode as opposed to
      the physiological, objective aspect. As we did with the term dysphoria, here too we sug-
      gest a more restrictive use of this term, which will become clear in what follows.

[7]   Scheler (1916/1966) *Affekte/Gefühle*; Heidegger (1927/1986) *Affekte/Stimmungen*;
      Sartre (1939/1971) *affects/emotions*; Strasser (1956/1977) *Gefühle/Stimmungen*; Ricoeur
      (1960) *sentiments schematisés/sentiments informes*, for example.

general characteristics. The principal phenomenological difference between moods and affects revolves around the *intentional character* of these two kinds of emotional experiences: whereas affects typically involve an explicit intentional object that directs and informs a specific affect, moods are normally not directed at or informed by any particular object; or to put it differently, the intentional structure of moods is significantly attenuated or diffuse compared to the one found in affects (Rosfort and Stanghellini, 2009).

With this very brief outline in place, we shall try to pinpoint the main characteristics of anger (affect) and dysphoria (mood) in terms of their different intentional structure. Dysphoria, especially in borderline persons, fragments their representations of themselves and others, thus contributing to their painful experience of incoherence and inner emptiness. In the befuddled atmosphere of their dysphoric mood, borderline persons often experience their own self as dim and fuzzy, and feel deprived of a defined identity and unable to be steadily involved in a given life project or social role. Also, they may see others as cloudy, and their faces as expressionless. No particular action is dictated by dysphoric mood. On the contrary, it complicates the relation between feeling and action because it introduces an ambiguous, and highly frustrating, emotional vacuum in the form of doubt, hesitation, and questions.

> *When I am in this state I feel lost. Lonely. Desperate. Nobody is there for me, or better: they are all around but useless. I can't understand them and they can't understand me. I see them, but their expression does not really come through to me... Quite the same with myself: I feel as if everything matters and nothing matters... Again: nothing metaphysical! I simply cannot understand and I simply have no reason to do anything.*

Anger may restore the cohesion of the self, determine a clear-cut, unambiguous image of the other person, and dissipate all doubts and sentiments of absurdity — at the cost, however, of representing the other as unambiguously menacing. Anger tends to preserve and maintain a precarious cohesion of the self (Pazzagli and Rossi Monti, 2000, p. 223), in the sense that venting one's anger is a way of feeling alive and of affirming one's right to exist as the unique person that one is. In anger episodes, the vague and confused sense of values and norms that characterizes borderline existence is suddenly replaced by a crystal clear, although elementary, normative universe in which it is painfully obvious to the borderline person who is 'good' (oneself) and who is 'bad' (the other). This sudden feeling of infallible rightfulness helps the borderline person to find his or her lost identity in a world that momentarily regains its structure and meaning.

Anger does not necessary imply an acute depressive episode, since short and intermittent angry outbursts are the rule during the existence of persons with borderline personality disorder. Nevertheless, severe anger may sometimes trigger acute, though transitory, decompositions, entailing paranoid ideas or delusions or persecutory guilt. In the light of anger, which dissipates the hazy atmosphere of dysphoria, the other suddenly comes into focus as a persecutor. The gaze of the other mercilessly lays bare the patient's inner insufficiency and thus makes her feel humiliated. So, the sense of identity established by anger is highly unstable due to the fact that the cohesion brought about by anger is constantly threatened by the instability brought about by humiliation.

We can sum up the dialectics between dysphoria and anger in borderline existence in the following way:

(1) Dysphoria as a *permanent trait*: the dysphoric emotional complex (dysphoria, irritability, internal agitation, and emotional lability) is the *background mood trait* characterizing persons with borderline personality disorder. It is the long-lasting and profound emotional tonality or basic temperament in which the borderline person is enmeshed, and as such it influences both the voluntary and involuntary aspect of that person. The existence of borderline persons exhibits prolonged states dominated by dysphoric mood. This is an emotional state saturated with a brimming constellation of feelings without any explicit object or target, a state of tension that may lead to spontaneously vigorous outbursts as well as to pale stagnation or emotional depletion.

(2a) Anger as an *acute intermittent state*: intermittently, borderline persons enter acute episodes of excitement in which anger may prevail. Anger is the affective state that punctuates the existence of the borderline person. Angry outbursts, emanating from the dysphoric background, are typically accompanied by feelings of humiliation and may generate acute micro-psychotic episodes during which the borderline person may develop paranoid symptoms, including transitory delusion-like and hallucination-like phenomena. Persecutory delusions may develop out of these episodes, in which the persecutor is typically a significant other (the patient's partner, relative, or therapist, for example).

(2b) Dysphoria as an *acute intermittent state*: alternatively, the person may collapse into acute episodes during which their dysphoric mood exacerbates, culminating in a painful paralysis of action characterized by feelings of emptiness, boredom, dissatisfaction; or in other words, a mixture of, or a rapid oscillation between, dysphoric mood and more focused affects like disgust, fear, and occasionally anger (concerning oneself or others). This may entail tormenting ideas of meaninglessness, persecutory guilt, and, in the most severe cases, suicidal ideation.

To make sense of this tense dialectic between dysphoria and anger, we need to explain the peculiar vitality that, as we argued, was the principal feature distinguishing borderline depression from other kinds of depression.

5. Frustrated Normativity:
The (Neglected) Vital Character of Dysphoria

Moods — to use Bin Kimura's terminology — are pure *noesis*, or *noematically* empty intentionality. By this we mean that, if noematic representations 'control the noetic act so that it does not deviate from its relationship with life' (Kimura, 2000, p. 88, our translation), then moods are noetic acts without, or at least with severely diminished, representational, linguistic, or reflective control.

This characterization of pure noesis or noematically empty intentionality tallies well with the experience that borderline persons have of their own dysphoric mood: an untamed source of vitality, a disturbing and yet exuberant force:

> You see, when you have tried this, I mean when you have the feeling you have succeeded in submitting to this force, you cannot easily change direction. I lived for years confined in my house, behaving exactly as you could expect from a 'depressed' person. I stood alone, dirty, miserable, no care for myself. It took years before I realized that it was because I was scared of what my body could do if I went out. I was not 'inhibited', as the other doctor said. I felt tremendously frenzied. I was alive again. And it scared me to death. I had no words to say what happened. I felt an unbearable energy coming out from I do not know where. It was like an animal inside me... When I could leave my home for the first time it was because I accepted a date. I started a life whose only reason was sex. Or better: it was not the reason, it was simply the only way I could regain the outer world. I realized I could channel my energies in my sexual encounters. They were not pleasant: they were just necessary! I could get no pleasure, do you understand? It was like a compulsion — the only way to cope with my body. Now, you let me understand I should stop this. Did I get it right? But I am not sure I can. I am afraid that if I stop I will lie in my bed for the next twenty years.

As argued above, dysphoria is a peculiar form of mood, characterized by a fierce sense of vitality not found in other depressive syndromes. We believe that it is possible to make sense of this sense of painful vitality if we examine more closely the relation between intentionality and embodiment in the borderline emotional complex, that is, if we look at what we have called the ontological aspect of human emotions.

The emotional fragility or stable instability experienced by borderline persons is caused by a raw, unmediated bodily vitality that does not accommodate to pre-reflective intentional structures or cognitive efforts. Their dysphoric mood is characterized by extreme presence of a primary, bodily force that fragments the intentional structure of human embodiment, the lived body, exposing an animal vitality, a mere body entirely at the mercy of the basic biological values that nourish and to some extent orient human emotional life. There is little possibility for action in this kaleidoscopic universe of raw feelings. Objects become unfocused and intentional structures crumple under the intensity of this emotional pressure. Bodily reactions take dominance over bodily action, and the intimate sense of being an embodied self is eclipsed by the sense of having an intimidating body. This chaotic vitality, being devoid of intentional structure and content, desperately seeks an object, mostly a person, at which to direct its surplus of energy. This means that the borderline person feels the presence of a spontaneous energy without any clear direction or definite target. It is emotional energy that throws itself at the other with an overwhelming intensity. Often, this impulse takes on a sexual form which the borderline person defines as 'love'. The loved object is the form that the desperate vitality takes for the borderline person.

The brimming intensity of the dysphoric mood demands the same intensity of the intentional correlate to its affects. Something of the desperate and frustrated energy of the dysphoric mood is transferred to the intentional structures of the interpersonal relation. The intensity of the borderline person cannot be disappointed. It is all-or-nothing. This immensely intense character of the interpersonal relationships makes them highly precarious. The slightest change in the emotional atmosphere, a wrong word, a delay, and the borderline person feels attacked or humiliated, and reacts with anger. Because of its intensity, this vitality exceeds the bounds of what can be represented, and is experienced as quasi-ineffable ('*I just feel bad and I can't tell you why*').[8] It blurs and obliterates, not only the body from where it comes,

---

[8] This view may complement the psychoanalytic concept of death drive (*Todestrieb*), i.e. the drive towards self-destruction or towards the return to the inorganic. When thus

but also the self, and others, to whom it is directed (*'I can't understand them... I see them, but their expression does not really come through to me... Quite the same with myself'*). Due to the violent, all-consuming character of this vitality, borderline persons live in a world of pure presence. What some clinicians and researchers sometimes fail to appreciate in the dysphoric mood of borderline persons is the juvenile, vital tenderness, and thus the disquieting fragility, of their sensibility; the puzzling manifestation of an amorphous *now* — liberated from the encumbering conditions of past and future that normally structure and orient human feeling, thought, and behaviour. It is both a threat to the self and the source of vitality, the vital force that they cannot renounce (*'Now, you let me understand I should stop this... I am afraid that if I stop I will lie in my bed for the next twenty years'*). Thus, it is impossible both to appropriate it and to distance oneself from it.

First and foremost, this emotional state is characterized by brimming waves of feelings — and not merely by feelings of void and inner emptiness. Before feeling empty, borderline persons feel too full of emotions. Kimura captures this brimming emotional state in his description of the *intra festum*:

> [T]he feast constitutes the most privileged occasion for the realization of ecstasy as excess or chaotic immediateness. Here one witnesses, among other things, the manifestation of vital exaltation, inebriation, rapture, sexual debauchery, play, violence, crime and death; we could say the destruction of everyday routine in general by means of a passion for the sacred or, conversely, for the sacrilege. In short, it is a triumph of *Chaos* over *Nomos* and *Cosmos* which characterizes the region of the feast. Here, the principles of life and death are in no way antagonists and they do not exclude one another. On the contrary, the correlation between them is such that an increase in one elicits that of the other. (Kimura, 1992, p. 148, our translation)

The norms by which the borderline person is driven are not the ethical norms or social conventions that structure and organize our interpersonal world. Rather, borderline persons refuse such conditions, thus entering into collision with what they consider the hypocrisy and the inauthenticity of the pallid emotions by which other persons live:

> *Since my wife left me, I sometimes pick up my two girls from school. There, it's full of parents talking nonsense to each other: petty, insignificant things such as food, holidays, maids. It irritates me. Why can't they talk about things that make a difference in life? The only valuable topic*

---

considered, the death drive is not opposed to the life instinct, rather it is an ungovernable excess of vitality (*'It was like an animal inside me'*) which — as Lacan would say — is not marked by the symbolic (*'I had no words to say what happened'*).

to talk about is our own feelings. I cannot stand small talk. I am dis-
gusted. It's fake. I know this implies that my younger daughter and I
always go home alone — and this makes her sorry. But I simply cannot
cope with it.

The borderline person's normativity is an *emotional normativity* constituted by the intensity of affective values which are nevertheless
constantly frustrated by the ethical norms and the social rules and conventions that structure the world in which they live. The borderline
person cannot — or will not — let his bouts of energy be restricted by
or conformed to the needs of other people, ethical norms, or social
conventions, all of which he considers inauthentic and therefore as an
unwarranted challenge to his truly natural being, his spontaneity.

This kind of emotionally frustrated normativity can be the initial
cause of borderline depression. It is the presence of a vitality that
merely strives to affirm its own emotional intensity, to satisfy its own
rudimentary feelings of being alive and the anonymous values
revealed and engendered by these feelings, without any regard for the
ethical or social norms that govern the world in which the borderline
person desperately tries to live. Feelings and values are the same for
the borderline person. They can only feel the meaning of values.
Norms are inauthentic because they disregard the intimate feelings of
the person whose behaviour they are meant to inform and orient. The
incapacity to distance herself from her own feelings means that the
borderline person is not capable of appropriating those very feelings
in the light of the norms that are part of being a person in a world
shared with other persons. She is condemned to simply live the intense
but disrupted life of her feelings. The norms, ethical as well as social,
that allow us to distance ourselves from our feelings and needs in the
light of our care for living 'a good life' with other people, are somehow undermined by the intensity of the borderline feelings. Norms
and conventions are merely viewed as annoying attempts to drain the
vitality that sustains the borderline world. The normative frustration
experienced by borderline persons continuously generates desperate
attempts to maintain their vitality in the face of what they consider to
be the encumbering strictures and platitudes of everyday life. It is a
desperate vitality engendering a complex type of depression characterized by emptiness, concerns of abandonment and rejection, despair
and meaninglessness, a labile sense of identity, and diffuse negative
emotionality, constantly punctuated by feelings of humiliation, and
marked by aggressive outbursts.

6. Conclusion

In this chapter we tried to characterize the borderline emotional complex, and argued that borderline persons can be described in terms of their emotional experiences as affected by dysphoric mood as a permanent trait, that is, by a brimming constellation of feelings without explicit object or target. As we have seen, dysphoria generates impatience, discontent, restlessness, and an incoercible impulse to move away without a definite goal. We described dysphoria in borderline persons as a form of noematically empty intentionality that is felt as a *source of vitality*, disturbing and yet exuberant. We suggested that focusing on the vital character of dysphoria implies being able to consider the precarious sense of selfhood and identity of borderline persons as a positive aspect, a less deadly feature than mere identity confusion and the manifestation of a death instinct. It is an expression of unmediated life, of an overwhelming sense of being alive. Dysphoric mood as a desperate source of vitality is the emotional root of the well-known borderline stable instability.

We also interpreted the decomposition of borderline personality into acute episodes of depression as the oscillation between the confusing background of dysphoria and a more normative emotion such as anger. We contrasted depression in borderline persons with depression in the melancholic type of personality. Depression in borderline persons is often characterized by *angry outbursts* typically accompanied by feelings of humiliation and occasionally delusion-like or hallucination-like phenomena. Alternatively, *exacerbation of dysphoric mood* may be accompanied by feelings of void, boredom, and disgust.

Finally, we argued — against the background of our understanding of human emotions as both biological and personal — that feelings of desperate vitality in borderline persons may generate a kind of *frustrated normativity* marked by intense affective values disruptive of ethical norms and social rules, all of which the person considers as an unwarranted challenge to their spontaneity. This kind of emotionally frustrated normativity may expose borderline persons to traumatic experiences of relational failures and solitude generating emptiness, despair, and meaninglessness, feelings of humiliation and aggressive outbursts — which are the main features of borderline depression.

Havi Carel

Bodily Doubt

The deepest human problems lurk behind the obvious.
(Blankenburg, 2002, p. 303)

1. Introduction

Anyone who has written a philosophy paper is probably familiar with the feeling of doubt that comes over you as you start to write. Even if you have written dozens of articles before, there is a moment a crippling doubt appears. Will I be able to write this? I am not sure I measure up to the task. This feeling of doubt dissipates and the paper is somehow written. But can this doubt simply be dismissed as an illusion, academics' *nikephobia*, or does it indicate that something deeper is going on? Why does this doubt invade us when we embark on a perfectly familiar task?

This feeling of doubt takes on a particular inflection in cases of mental and somatic disorder. For example, some people with depression seem to describe this sense of inability, but in an intensified and more pervasive form. For example:

> When I'm depressed, every job seems bigger and harder. Every setback strikes me not as something easy to work around or get over but as a huge obstacle. Events appear more chaotic and beyond my control: if I fail to achieve some goal, it will seem that achieving it is forever beyond my abilities, which I perceive to be far more meagre than I did when I was not depressed. (Law, 2009, p. 355)

Here is another example, this time of a somatic illness. If you have ever been very ill with the flu you may have been lying in bed and thinking about something you need to do, maybe grocery shopping. You may contemplate executing the task, but at the same time feel serious doubt about whether you could actually perform the task, given how ill you are. Again, a sense of doubt about a routine activity pervades you.

In this chapter I explore this type of feeling, focusing on a particular feeling which I characterize as bodily doubt. I suggest that we have an ongoing tacit certainty about our bodies (e.g. that we will be able to digest our lunch, that our hearts will carry on beating, that our legs will carry us, etc.) that is not rationally justified. Similar to Hume's critique of our instinctive faith in induction, I suggest that a sense of unjustified and nonetheless powerful faith underlies our relationship with our bodies. This feeling of certainty we have about our bodies can be construed as a belief we cannot help but hold, but are unable to epistemically justify.

I use the case of illness, in which this certainty breaks down, to examine the normal feeling of certainty, which is tacit and thus diffi-cult to scrutinize. What the case of illness reveals is that the kind of belief that underlies our relationship with our bodies is a bodily feel-ing that is anchored in our animal nature. I characterize this feeling of bodily doubt as one that radically modifies our experience. I then present this modification as made up of three changes to experience: loss of continuity, loss of transparency, and loss of faith in one's embodied existence.

The structure of the paper is as follows. In Section 2 I present bodily certainty and discuss its main features: it is unjustified and tacit. In Section 3 I propose that cases of breakdown of bodily certainty are characterized by a special kind of doubt, namely, bodily doubt. I con-clude by presenting the philosophical importance of studying cases of pathology (mental and somatic disorder, as well as other kinds of experience) and suggesting that illness is a philosophical tool for the study of otherwise hidden aspects of human experience.

2. Bodily Certainty

In *Feelings of Being* Matthew Ratcliffe (2008a) describes existential feelings, which are the background feelings underlying our existence. Existential feelings are a pre-given context in which particular inten-tional attitudes are possible. On Ratcliffe's account, existential feel-ings ground the sense of belonging to a world, sense of reality, which characterizes normal human existence (*ibid.*, p. 41). In his account Ratcliffe relies on Heidegger's mood analysis, to provide an account of a feeling that grounds human existence and gives it a sense of sta-bility and normality (*ibid.*, pp. 47–52). The common state of affairs is one in which the world appears familiar, its workings are mostly pre-dictable, and one feels grounded in it. This does not mean that an indi-vidual necessarily feels happy or satisfied. Rather, the focus is on the tacit sense of reality (as opposed to unreality) and understanding of one's being in the world. Importantly, because this feeling is usually tacit (we do not normally go about thinking how lucky we are that our perceptions are orderly and familiar, that our bodies obey us, that the world continues to appear to us, and so on) it mostly goes unnoticed and is not the object of explicit scrutiny. Husserl similarly presents the world as the 'universal ground of belief pregiven for every experience of individual objects' (Husserl, 1948/1997, p. 28). He writes: 'an actual *world* always precedes cognitive activity as the universal ground, and this means first of all a ground of universal passive belief in being which is presupposed by every particular cognitive operation' (*ibid.*, p. 30).

The framework of Ratcliffe's analysis is phenomenological. On this view embodiment is the fundamental characteristic of human existence, so any feeling of being one has must of its very essence be a bodily feeling (*cf.* Merleau-Ponty, 1945/1962). Ratcliffe claims that these feelings are *bodily*, but also give a sense of how the world is and of one's relationship to the world. He writes: 'bodily feelings are not just feelings of internal bodily states; they can also contribute to experiences of things outside the body... certain feelings... are ways of finding ourselves in the world, existential backgrounds that shape all our experiences' (Ratcliffe, 2008a, p. 47). This dual role of existential feelings is of importance to Ratcliffe, as it synthesizes the internal and the external, feeling and cognition.

Because they are often tacit, existential feelings are difficult to study and not often the focus of a philosophical analysis. Indeed, Ratcliffe's monograph is the first of its kind. He claims that existential feelings can best be studied by looking at pathological cases in which the feeling of being has been disturbed. Ratcliffe examines such cases, for example the Capgras delusion (a rare psychiatric disorder in which a person thinks that members of family and friends are impostures) and Cotard's syndrome (another rare disorder in which a person thinks they are dead or that their bodies are rotting, or that their internal organs have been removed). Ratcliffe also discusses more common disorders such as depression and schizophrenia, in which the sense of reality is disturbed.

A particular aspect of existential feelings I would like to focus on here is the feeling of bodily certainty, or of bodily doubt, that accompanies existential feelings. I suggest that a feeling of bodily certainty or uncertainty is a necessary constituent of existential feelings that makes its bearer present in a world by offering her a meaningful horizon in which things and projects can appear. In other words, different degrees and kinds of bodily certainty and uncertainty are integral to all existential feelings.

Let us look at bodily certainty first. We tacitly feel confident (or rather, we do not normally question) that our bodies will continue to function in a similar fashion to the way they have functioned in the past: we expect our stomachs to digest the lunch we have just eaten, our brains to continue to process information, our eyes to continue to see, and so on. This feeling is normally so tacit that it is difficult to describe. Revealing it is the task of this section.

By bodily certainty I denote the subtle feeling of 'I can' that pervades our actions (*cf.* Husserl, 1950/1999). This is the feeling of possibility, openness, and ability that characterizes routine and familiar actions. This feeling is anchored in what Merleau-Ponty called one's 'habitual body', the body's accumulated habits and routines (*cf.* Merleau-Ponty, 1945/1962). The 'I can' feeling implicitly underlies all our movements and plans. If I plan to walk the dog, implicit in that plan is my ability to walk. This 'I can' feeling is not unlimited. We do not have such a feeling when we contemplate flying or breathing under water. But this feeling of possibility and freedom does characterize our attitude towards most of our actions. Even if I plan to run a half-marathon, and doubt whether I would be able to complete the course, this doubt is more of a challenge or motivator than the negation of the 'I can' feeling. In other words, such a doubt does not disrupt the feeling of bodily certainty, but rather extends the sense of certainty by challenging us to develop further abilities. Indeed, challenging bodily activities such as competitive sports define themselves as explicitly pushing the limits of bodily performance.

Normally bodily certainty is tacit, but it can be made explicit and become the object of philosophical reflection. When I type these words I am oblivious to the speed and expertise with which my fingers find the needed keys. But I am easily able to turn my attention to this achievement and pay explicit attention to it (although this disturbs the fluidity of the typing). But most of the time when I type, I pay no attention to my typing and take for granted the speed, ease, and painlessness of this activity. I also know very little about the neurology and physiology involved in typing and have little interest in typing over and above its practical usefulness to me. This kind of taken-for-grantedness — unreflective, disinterested — characterizes bodily certainty. When my husband lifts our son onto his shoulders and runs down the path, he does not consider this an achievement. It is just something he does in the full, but tacit, confidence that he can bear the child's weight, that he is able to run, keep his balance, and so on. He has been able to do this previously, so takes for granted that he will be able to do this now. This type of bodily certainty is pervasive and provides the background confidence with which we perform familiar actions.

This way of talking about bodily certainty may be misleading. It makes it seem as if this feeling is constantly monitored and reflected upon; as if it is an explicit part of experience. But actually most routine actions we perform — walking, talking, eating, and so on — are rarely consciously reflected upon. Rather, they form a transparent background that is just there, in stable form, often for many decades. The sense of certainty, therefore, is not conscious but pre-reflective. It is simply the immediacy and automatic manner in which we turn to familiar tasks. It is not optional, but a basic mode of action that takes agency for granted. We could say that this certainty is most effective when it is unnoticed. In the same way that we do not pause to wonder whether our food was poisoned by the chef in a restaurant (*cf.* Bernstein, 2011), we do not need to check that we know how to chew. Indeed, this would be a cumbersome and unnecessary procedure most of the time. We simply have a sense of certainty and normally also of bodily ease and familiarity that go unnoticed and yet enable action.

This feeling has a phenomenology that can be described when we turn our attention to it, as well as propositional content, although bodily certainty is not primarily a propositional attitude. It is only when we explicitly reflect upon this certainty, or express it to others, that a propositional attitude is involved. This propositional attitude is secondary to a more fundamental, non-propositional form of experience. The phenomenology is straightforward: we feel able, confident, comfortable, and familiar with what we are doing. We have no worries about bodily failure, and we simply perform the task at hand. Moreover, this is primarily a *bodily* feeling. The tacit aspect of the feeling lies here: our body proceeds with pre-reflective confidence and ease; there is no need for reflection. The sense of certainty is primarily to be found in the tacit confidence with which we make a cup of tea, slice an apple, walk the dog, or dial a number. There is no hesitation and no doubt involved. There is no reflection, and there is a clear sense (again, tacit) that the action is meaningful, familiar, and possible. This taken for granted confidence also makes the propositional content seem artificial and uninteresting. We do not congratulate ourselves by thinking: 'I inserted that key in the lock rather well!' or 'I walk like an expert'. Normally we are not called upon to formulate the feeling of certainty or pay it any attention. It is simply there, as a silent enabler of action.

Bodily certainty serves as the ground on which we base many of our assumptions and expectations. What an analysis of it reveals is that our most abstract goals and assumptions are based on a simple bodily feeling of ability. The certainty, a lack of a need to attend to our bodies, is core to our being. This fundamental role of bodily certainty can be seen as analogous to the role of hinge propositions (Wittgenstein, 1969, §341). These propositions are characterized by the fact that they are exempt from doubt and are like hinges on which questions and doubts turn (*ibid.*). The 'hinge' in the case of bodily certainty is not a proposition, but a *bodily feeling* (that can be expressed as a proposition, but is not primarily cognitive), of being comfortable, in control of one's body, having a sense of familiarity and continuity with respect to one's body. A tacit existential feeling of trust (*cf.* Bernstein, 2011), familiarity (*cf.* Ratcliffe, 2008a), and normalcy underlies our everyday activities and actions.

3. Bodily Doubt

One way to make visible the bodily certainty that underpins everyday human experience is by looking at cases of its breakdown, namely, illness. In many somatic and mental disorders the sense of certainty and confidence we have in our own bodies is deeply disturbed. What was previously taken for granted, normally for many years — that my legs can carry me, that my brain will continue working as before, that my lungs can support my body's oxygen requirements — is suddenly and sometimes acutely thrown into question. Such cases of illness make apparent not only the bodily feeling of confidence, familiarity, and continuity that is disturbed, but also a host of assumptions that hang on it. For example, one's future plans depend on bodily capacities and thus are limited by ill health. One's temporal sense is radically changed by a poor prognosis. One's values and sense of what is important in life are frequently modified in light of illness; bodily limitations impact on one's existence generally (Carel, 2008). One's concepts undergo a radical change; the meaning of terms such as 'near' or 'easy' fundamentally change (Carel, 2012).

Bodily doubt is not just a disruption of belief, but a disturbance on a bodily level. It is a disruption of one's most fundamental sense of being in the world. Bodily doubt gives rise to an experience of unreality, estrangement, and detachment. From a feeling of comfortably inhabiting a world, the ill person undergoing such an experience is thrown into uncertainty and anxiety. Her attention is withdrawn from the world and focused on her body. She may feel acutely isolated from others, who maintain their connection to the world, and may become detached from both physical and social environments. The natural confidence in her bodily abilities is displaced by a feeling of helplessness, alarm, and distrust in her body. There are different degrees of bodily doubt. It may vary in duration, intensity, and specificity. Part of our experience of the flu, for example, is the understanding that it is temporary. Thus an experience of bodily doubt associated with the flu differs substantively from bodily doubt experienced in the context of Parkinson's disease, for example, or another serious chronic condition. Bodily certainty can be regained in many cases, but the expectation that the doubt may return substantively changes the kind of experience involved in each case. Similarly for intensity: a bad case of tonsillitis may involve bodily doubt at the time without a longer term shift in the structure of one's experience.[1] A more radical doubt, where the intensity of the experience is greater and the feeling is expected to return, may change the structure of one's experience in a profound way. Finally, bodily doubt can be all-pervasive, or it may relate to specific aspects of bodily functioning. It is possible to experience doubt about a certain action (walking up the stairs) without calling into question other, even interrelated, aspects of bodily existence (such as balancing). What I suggest is that this wide range of experiences share common features that make the experience of bodily doubt philosophically revealing by exposing the structure of how things normally are.

Bodily doubt has additional features that make it philosophically revealing. First, the feeling can descend at any moment. In some cases its appearance may be gradual, but it may come upon a person with complete surprise (injuries caused by an accident are such cases). Its precariousness and unpredictability make it more threatening and us less capable of incorporating it into our familiar world. Second, the feeling of bodily doubt invades the normal sense of things, the everyday. It results in feeling exposed, under threat. It is uncanny and may give rise to a kind of anxiety. In this respect bodily doubt is different to normal kinds of bodily failure (slipping on the street, failing to learn a dance move, feeling too exhausted to go to a party) that may seem similar to bodily doubt. In normal failure one is still immersed in the world. The failure is incorporated into one's current existential feeling, which is often an undifferentiated background feeling. In contrast, bodily doubt disrupts the normal sense of being in the world and replaces immersion with suspension. So in normal conditions one

---

[1] Less serious conditions can also be philosophically revealing, as they disclose more minor interruptions to the flow of experience. Sartre (1943/2003) gives the example of a headache as disrupting reading.

may experience bodily failure that may be frustrating and humiliating (if you have ever tried to fix a bike puncture you will know the feeling), but one remains immersed in the task and in the world. Bodily doubt throws one out of immersion and into suspension and the familiar world is replaced by an uncanny one.

So is bodily doubt a type of anxiety? What picks out experiences of bodily doubt from other types of anxiety is that they are expressed as genuine *embodied* doubt about bodily capacities that are normally taken for granted. Heidegger described anxiety as a state of loss of meaning (1927/1962). But bodily doubt, in contrast, has meaning: the meaning is the doubt itself. The doubt is neither irrational nor meaningless. It can be clearly explained and expressed. Bodily doubt can be helpfully contrasted with panic attacks, which have a similar phenomenology. Whilst the experience of bodily doubt and of a panic attack may be similar (acute sense of disruption, anxiety about one's ability to breathe or stay conscious, etc.), the two can be distinguished on non-phenomenological grounds. Bodily doubt is situationally appropriate and associated with true beliefs, whereas panic attacks are situationally inappropriate and frequently associated with false beliefs (e.g. 'I am about to die', thought by a young, healthy individual).

Third, bodily doubt reveals the extent of our vulnerability, which routines, psychological defence mechanisms, and safety measures we put in place aim to mask. Once experienced, bodily doubt often leaves a permanent mark on the person experiencing it; it is the loss of a certainty that has hitherto never been disturbed. Moreover, the *possibility* of it being disturbed has not been countenanced. In this sense it is like other kinds of trauma (being the victim of violence, bereavement, being involved in an accident, and so on). What these cases have in common with bodily doubt is that they overthrow our most basic assumptions about the regularity, predictability, and benevolence of the world. J.M. Bernstein describes trauma victims as undergoing an experience 'revealing underlying and intractable dimensions of vulnerability, dependence, and potential helplessness that are normally hidden from consciousness' (Bernstein, 2011, p. 399). Bodily doubt similarly reveals vulnerability, but of a specifically bodily kind. Illness has also been likened to a loss of innocence; the return to the naïve, and in retrospect gullible, state of confidence one was in before is impossible (McKinnon, private communication). There is no turning back once genuine bodily doubt has been experienced; one's basic orientation in the world has changed and the possibility of catastrophic bodily failure is now part of one's horizons.

Fourth, bodily doubt makes the person experiencing it feel incapable. Confronting the loss of abilities and the frustration involved in 'being unable' ('I cannot') contrasts with the normal (healthy) feeling of competence and ability, even when this ability is punctuated by occasional failure. For example, I decide to go for a walk after dinner to stretch my legs. Of course I cannot walk indefinitely, but my bodily certainty is such that the project (going for a walk) dominates the action. I walk until I am satisfied, so in effect I have walked without limit. In a state of doubt I want to go for a walk, but I am restricted by my bodily limitation. I plan before I act (how far I can go; will it be too steep? What if I get too tired? What if I need the toilet? etc.) such that the action becomes entirely determined by my bodily limits. The limitless sense of myself, of my open horizons, as extending beyond myself and into the world collapses back onto my actual physical being; it becomes an act of conscious planning to see how far I can, or dare, project myself onto the world.

An important question is what is the relationship between bodily doubt and bodily incapacity? Bodily doubt can be experienced in the absence of a known bodily incapacity, as might be the case in depression. Bodily doubt can also diminish as one adjusts to certain incapacities (e.g. in certain forms of disability) and may be completely absent in the case of congenital disability. So there are grounds for differentiating between states of 'being unable' and states of not knowing, or suddenly feeling doubtful about, whether one might be able to. I suggest that bodily doubt is part of serious illness and constitutes the transition from health (bodily capacity) to illness (bodily incapacity), via the experience of bodily doubt. In anxiety disorders, where there is no underlying somatic illness, the disorder can be described as a series of experiences of bodily doubt that continue occurring because there is no transition to bodily incapacity.

More generally, the sense of inability may stem from a bodily dysfunction (e.g. loss of mobility), but also from an incapacitating mental disorder, such as depression. Depression often gives rise to severe feelings of helplessness and ineptitude which can be crippling. Moreover, the physical symptoms of depression can be severe and comparable with somatic inflammatory disease (Ratcliffe *et al.*, this volume). Whether caused by 'somatic' or 'mental' factors, the feeling of inability is prominent and affects both the actions a person can take and the actions she thinks she can take. Bodily doubt affects the spectrum of possibilities available to a person in the concrete sense of being unable to perform an action as well as in the existential sense of a perceived narrowing down of possibilities. Bodily doubt challenges the everyday veneer of normality and control that we cultivate as individuals and as a society. As such it can reveal the true state of affairs, which is one of vulnerability, existential uncertainty, and dependency on others (Bernstein, 2011).

Phenomenologically speaking, bodily doubt is experienced as anxiety on a physical level, hesitation with respect to movement and action, and a deep disturbance of existential feeling. This doubt distorts the sense of distance and time, in a way akin to other kinds of psychological stress. However, the important feature of bodily doubt is that it is not a *mere* psychological state, although it certainly has psychological features. It cannot be reduced to a mental state or propositional attitude. Even in the case of bodily doubt arising from a mental disorder such as depression, it is still a *bodily* feeling. The sense of fatigue, feeling 'off', and so on, which characterize many kinds of depression, are distinct bodily sensations. In short, any mental disorder has a bodily phenomenology. Trying to explain bodily doubt as a psychological state is phenomenologically inaccurate and nosologically wrong, because it ignores a host of somatic symptoms and sensations.

Bodily doubt is a *physical* sensation of doubt and hesitation arising in one's body. It is not solely cognitive, although it can be expressed in propositions. Here is an example. Patients with severe respiratory disease commonly report fearing that they will be unable to breathe. This feeling cannot be described simply as a 'panic attack' because in these cases there is rational ground for the fear. The fear stems from a physical experience of acute breathlessness that at its extreme leads to respiratory failure. In such cases bodily doubt is an expression of disease limitations that shatter the normal belief that one will continue to breathe. It is immensely unpleasant and terrifying, but the psychological features of this experience are a result of the bodily doubt, not the doubt itself.

Bodily doubt not only changes the content of experience, it also pierces the normal sense of bodily control, continuity, and transparency in a way that reveals their contingency. It shows our tacit faith in our own bodies to be a complex structure that becomes visible when it is disturbed. It changes the normal experience of continuity, transparency, and trust that characterize this structure. Here are three such changes:

1. Loss of continuity: human cognition and action are characterized by continuity of experience and purposeful action (Sartre, 1943/2003; Merleau-Ponty, 1945/1962; Noë, 2004). In bodily doubt this continuity is lost and replaced by a suspension of normal action and a modified awareness of self and environment. In this suspension, experience is sliced by discontinuity. The characteristic smoothness of everyday routine is disrupted. Everyday habits become the object of explicit attention and conscious effort; the ongoing tacit sense of normalcy is lost. In this situation one is unable to pursue their goals; the normal flow of actions leading to the goals is disturbed. Minor tasks require planning and attention to detail, as well as contingency plans. The normal flow of everyday activities is halted by bodily uncertainty and when it is resumed it is altered by the experience of doubt. The *possibility* of doubt colours further experience, even if continuity is restored. The possibility of feeling this doubt is a constant reminder of the contingency and fallibility of the original continuity.

In mental disorder, in particular in anxiety and depression, the pattern is different. These conditions may lead to a state characterized by Heidegger (1927/1962) as anxiety. In anxiety one's sense of purposeful activity is lost, leaving the person unable to act. Action is grounded in meaning: I tap keys on my computer keyboard in order to write this paper. I write this paper in order to convey certain ideas. I convey certain ideas in order to contribute to a debate in philosophy, and so on. But, as Heidegger points out, ultimately, this nested set of goal-directed activities comes to an end. Ultimately human existence is ungrounded. This realization leads to what Heidegger calls anxiety (*Angst*). In anxiety purposefulness is removed and with it the meaning of entities. They turn from being ready-to-hand (*Zuhanden*) entities we use (keyboard, desk, reading lamp) to being present-at-hand (*Vorhanden*) entities which confront us with their lack of usefulness, and hence their lack of meaning. In anxiety the intelligibility of the world surrounding us is lost, because the practical coherence of entities has been lost when the sense of purposefulness is gone.

This experience has been documented by people with mental illness. Ratcliffe (2013b) discusses the sense of unreality that characterizes schizophrenia, citing a patient who says:

> When, for example, I looked at a chair or a jug, I thought not of their use or function — a jug not as something to hold water and milk, a chair not as something to sit in — but as having lost their names, their functions and meanings. (Cited in Ratcliffe, 2013b)

This is an example of an extreme break with previous continuity of purposeful action and meaning. It reveals the taken for granted sense of order and meaningfulness that characterize our commerce with the world of things and other people.

The loss of continuity also leads to a break with past abilities, which are not guaranteed to return in the future. Indeed, reliance on past abilities (e.g. the ease with which one could walk to the cinema) is broken by bodily doubt. This brings about a loss of habits and expectations which make up one's everyday dealings with the world and requires broad adjustment to the new conditions (Carel, 2008). The outcome of such adjustment may be reducing the number of outings and level of challenge, social withdrawal, and overall reluctance to go beyond the narrow band of 'safe' activities. Finally, whereas bodily certainty synthesizes present and future through goal-directed action, in doubt the present moment (incapacity) is split off from the future (goals). In doing so, living bodies (future-directed, world-facing, projected) become fragile physical entities (inert, self-facing) that are non- projecting and dislocated from embodied action. In other words, the body turns from being a ready-to-hand entity, poised to act and immersed in a world, to a present-at-hand uncanny entity that has lost its capacity for intentional action and is suspended from the world. The focus shifts from experiencing oneself primarily as an intentional subject to experiencing oneself as a material object.

2. Loss of transparency: the healthy body has been characterized as transparent (Sartre, 1943/2003) or even absent (Leder, 1990). Leder writes: 'while in one sense the body is the most abiding and inescapable presence in our lives, it is also essentially characterised by absence. That is, one's own body is rarely the thematic object of experience' (*ibid.*, p. 1). This transparency is somewhat idealized in philosophical descriptions of health, since even this transparency is often pierced by experiences in which the body comes to the fore, sometimes in negative ways. Even in normal everyday experience there are many ways in which the world resists us. Often the interaction between us and the world is smooth and automatic and regulated by well-developed behavioural repertoires. In these cases there is little need for conscious attention. But even in health the world may resist this smooth articulation and require conscious awareness. Perhaps the small knocks and resistances that befall us in minor accidents, bodily failures, bodily needs, and the inability to easily learn new bodily skills disrupt this transparency in minor ways. Illness, in contrast, creates areas of dramatic resistance in the exchange between body and environment, so is wholly different to these small knocks. Even if the transparency of the healthy body is somewhat exaggerated, it is still the case that we intend towards the world through our body and it serves as a medium through which we encounter the world, whilst remaining in the background. The body 'plays a constitutive role in experience precisely by grounding, making possible, and yet remaining peripheral in the horizons of our conceptual awareness' (Carman, 1999, p. 208). Or as Merleau-Ponty said, the body is 'our general medium for having a world' (Merleau-Ponty, 1945/1962, p. 146).

  In cases of bodily doubt, the body's taken for granted capacities become explicit achievements. What was previously performed with little or no thought now requires conscious planning. For example, in the case of bodily doubt, shopping for groceries may become a full-blown project, demanding planning, explicit attention to detail, and contingency plans. Moreover, the action is understood in terms of its limits which also leads to a loss of spontaneity and changes the meaning of routine tasks.

  Additionally, the body becomes *explicitly thematized* as a problem. The tacit taken for granted attitude we have towards it (we expect our bodies to perform complex actions, to be pain-free, to allow us to concentrate, and so on) is replaced by an explicit attitude of concern, anxiety, and fear. In bodily doubt we may even worry about aspects of our body that are normally invisible (e.g. liver function) and alter our behaviour accordingly. Merely knowing about a particular risk associated with an illness, whether real or imagined, is often enough to modify bodily habits so they are slower, more hesitant, or otherwise censored. This, too, is a kind of bodily doubt. The psychological result of this is harmful: the attitude of the ill person towards her body is negative and this appraisal is often reinforced in the medical encounter (Carel, 2012). For example, most test results measure how much certain organ functions deviate from the normal range (e.g. kidney and liver function are measured as percentage of predicted value). Medical encounters usually focus on the dysfunction at hand, thus becoming an unpleasant reminder of the extent of bodily incapacity or disease progression. These encounters contribute to the explicit thematization of the body as a problem and reduce the ill person's ability to experience the body as transparent.[2]

  Finally, there is a melancholic element to this loss of transparency. The body as it was before is often viewed nostalgically, as a lost era (ageing is a similar case in point), and the experience of adjusting to this loss has been likened to mourning (Little *et al.*, 1998). The transparency and spontaneity of bodily certainty is replaced in illness with opacity and passivity (Sartre, 1943/2003, p. 359). To paraphrase

---

[2] I am not critical of the medical need to measure dysfunction, but I think it is important to appreciate the effect this has on the ill person.

Sartre, bodily doubt 'fastens on to consciousness with all its teeth', and the body becomes a source of uncertainty, pain, and suffering (*ibid.*, p. 360).

3. Loss of faith in one's body: the loss of faith pertains to the tacit set of beliefs we hold about our bodies. These beliefs support everyday actions as well as more specialized goals and projects. Whatever the action, it is hard to carry it out in the context of doubt. Not being sure one is able to achieve the simplest of tasks leaves one in turmoil and the implicit certainties underpinning the everyday damaged.[3] This loss of faith is not an experience of mental breakdown, although it could be triggered by some kinds of mental disorder. The phenomenology of these experiences is so firmly rooted in the body that it would be misleading to say that they are some kind of mental error. The loss of faith is a way of experiencing one's body which replaces the previous certainty. This is an experience of vulnerability, hesitation, and doubt, experienced on a bodily level. This experience amounts to a disruption of one's sense of belonging to the world and the disappearance of the sense of ordinariness.

The loss of faith in one's body reveals the contingency and fallibility of our normal trust in our bodies. In this sense, the loss of faith as the failure of bodily certainty makes explicit the weak epistemic status of our everyday beliefs. I suggest that bodily doubt is a practical enactment of Hume's critique of induction. As Hume writes: 'As to past *Experience*, it can be allowed to give *direct* and *certain* information of those precise objects only, and that precise period of time, which fell under its cognizance: but why this experience should be extended to future times, and to other objects, which for aught we know, may be only in appearance similar; this is the main question on which I would insist' (Hume, 1777/1975, pp. 33–4, italics in the original). Bodily doubt reveals the bodily certainty previously taken for granted and inductively learned to be epistemically unjustified.

Hume concludes that 'wherever the repetition of any particular act or operation produces a propensity to renew the same act or operation, without being impelled by any reasoning or process of the understanding, we always say, that this propensity is the effect of *Custom*' (*ibid.*, p. 43). I suggest that such custom underlies our tacit beliefs about our body's continued functioning and our sense of bodily certainty. Hume comes close to stating this when he asks: 'The bread, which I formerly eat, nourished me... but does it follow, that other bread must also

---

[3]   'Turmoil' is the term ancient sceptics used to characterize discrepancies in their impressions that lead to doubt. For the sceptic, investigation leads to suspension of judgment, which resolves the turmoil and brings about *ataraxia* (Vogt, 2010).

nourish me at another time…?' (*ibid.*, p. 34). Finally, in the *Dialogues Concerning Natural Religion* Hume also argues (through the words of Philo) that 'vulgar' prejudices, which are continually reinforced by experience, must be respected 'since [such prejudice] is founded on vulgar experience, the only guide which you profess to follow' (Hume, 1779/2008, Part Six). Bodily certainty could be seen as such a 'vulgar prejudice'.

I suggest that bodily certainty is an instance of the epistemically ungrounded beliefs Hume argues we hold. And the loss of faith experienced in bodily doubt reveals the tenuousness of this belief. The tacit belief in the continued functioning of our body enables us to function normally and pursue everyday goals and plans. We hold other kinds of tacit beliefs, e.g. that our house is still standing although we are now in the office. The question whether these beliefs are irrational, or how powerful Hume's critique is has been discussed at length. The analogy to Hume I wish to draw here is to the *fallibility* of such beliefs. As Bernstein (2011) points out, there is a fundamental sense of trust which underlies our commerce with the world, and this tacit network of trust relationships enables us to go about our business without being paralysed by doubt. On Bernstein's view, trust is a non-propositional attitude, a basic feeling that permeates our interactions with other people. What this trust enables us to do is to find ourselves in a world that is peaceful and stable enough to enable us — amongst other things — to philosophize. Husserl comments in a similar vein: 'it is this *universal ground of belief in a world* which all praxis presupposes, not only the praxis of life but also the theoretical praxis of cognition' (Husserl, 1948/1997, p. 30). Lived doubt, of which bodily doubt is one instance, is pervasive and disrupts everyday action. Thorsrud claims that 'all intentional, purposeful action presupposes some sort of belief' (Thorsrud, 2009, p. 173). If action depends, in part, on belief, then the suspension or loss of belief must disrupt action. As such bodily doubt goes to the heart of everyday action.

4. Pathology as Method

So far, this chapter has explored the systematic invisibility of bodily certainty. To paraphrase Bernstein's (2011) words about trust, bodily certainty best realizes itself through its disappearance. In order to study this certainty we should turn to cases in which it is absent, namely, cases of mental or somatic disorder. What can pathologies tell us about the normal way of things? If normally I do not doubt that my body will continue to support and obey me, what does a disruption of this cause? Bodily certainty is part of a tacit sense of belonging to the world that is normally unnoticed (Ratcliffe, 2008a). What cases of mental and somatic pathology enable us to see is that what ordinarily binds you to the world can become visible and hence the object of study. I would like to end by suggesting that certain types of pathology are crucial for the philosophical study of human existence. In such cases the body becomes unnatural and is thematized in new ways. This enables us to explore dimensions of it that would normally go unnoticed. The term 'pathology' does not only refer to certain cases of illness. It may include other kinds of alienated or explicitly thematized embodiment. For example, in her essay 'Throwing Like a Girl', Iris Marion Young (2005) describes embodiment that is experienced as unnatural and gazed upon. Her study of the cultural pathologization of female embodied experience includes phenomenological analyses of aspects of embodiment that are both fundamental and mundane.

Pathological cases of embodiment provide a philosophical tool with which to illuminate normal embodiment (Carel, 2013). But is this tool available to everyone, or only to those who experience pathology? Is the first-person experience of bodily doubt a prerequisite for certain kinds of philosophical insight? Or should we maintain that second- or third-person access is sufficient? If one lacks the first-person experience, how does one come to appreciate the relevant phenomenology? I would like to suggest that in order to glean philosophical insight from bodily doubt one does not need to have the first-person experience herself. There is good evidence that empathy can train and redirect modes of thinking, moral insight, and sensibilities in philosophically important ways (e.g. Nussbaum, 1990; Ratcliffe, 2012b). So the philosophical method proposed here is universally available. The philosophically relevant features of bodily doubt can be conveyed by using literature, film, testimonies, and so on. However, I also think it would be true to say that there is something ineffable about radical bodily experiences that can only be fully appreciated if one undergoes the experience oneself (childbirth is one such case). It may be that some of the experience cannot be propositionally expressed. This is a limitation that is inherent to this method, but does not seriously hinder it. The method is still widely accessible and useful across a range of philosophical issues.

Merleau-Ponty's (1945/1962) study of Schneider (based on Gelb and Goldstein's case study) shows this method at work. Schneider, a World War I soldier, suffered a brain injury which restricted his actions in unusual ways. He lived a seemingly normal life, working and living independently. However, Schneider was limited in an interesting and pervasive way. For example, he was unable to change his daily routine (e.g. stray from his normal route home). He could not initiate sexual relations although his sexual function was intact. Merleau-Ponty characterizes Schneider's malaise as existential, arguing that Schneider's ability to initiate, imagine, and fantasize has been lost. '[Schneider] is "tied" to actuality, he "lacks liberty", that concrete liberty which comprises the general power of putting oneself into a situation' (*ibid.*, p. 135).

For Merleau-Ponty, Schneider's peculiar pathology[4] reveals our bodies as 'the potentiality of a certain world' (Merleau-Ponty, 1945/ 1962, p. 106). What we are normally able to do is to 'reckon with the possible', which thus acquires a certain actuality. In Schneider's case the field of actuality is limited and has to be made explicit through a conscious effort. It is this conscious, explicit effort and the correlating achievement of action that make pathological cases useful (Gallagher, 2005). By making explicit and artificial what normally goes unnoticed, such cases draw our attention to how things normally are. Pathological cases show that an experience of smooth interwoven experience and action is not a taken for granted ground, but an *achievement* (Ratcliffe, 2013). Because the end product seems so natural, we need pathological cases with which to expose the underlying process that gives us a normal world.

5. Conclusion

This essay presented bodily certainty and its absence, bodily doubt, as a core feature of existential feelings. I described bodily doubt as a loss of continuity, loss of transparency of the body, and loss of faith in one's body. I suggested that bodily certainty is an instance of Hume's general claim about our animal nature: we feel certain that our bodies will continue to function. This certainty is not epistemically justifiable but is impossible to relinquish. The experience of bodily doubt makes this tacit certainty explicit and enables us to study it. I argued that the exploration of pathology is useful for highlighting tacit aspects of experience that otherwise go unnoticed. Finally, I put the specific claim about the usefulness of examining bodily doubt in broader context, suggesting that it provides a philosophical tool for studying human experience. The study of pathological cases is crucial for illuminating normal function, because it brings to the fore implicit processes and assumptions that are not normally available to us. Since

---

[4] It was thought that Schneider's pathology was vision agnosia, but recently Marotta and Behrmann (2004) have argued that he suffered from integrative agnosia.

bodily doubt is primarily an experience arising from mental and somatic disorder, philosophy has much to learn from the study of illness.

What I hope this essay has shown is the extent to which we are dependent on our bodies, not only for everyday functioning but also for the broader sweep of life, including our goals, plans, and expectations. Bodily certainty grounds and enables human activity. Ultimately, this ground is beyond our control and its potential fallibility is ever present. Human existence is characterized by a brute dependence on utter unreliability, on our feeble, transient organismic structures. We put much effort into denying how feeble our bodies and minds are. Perhaps it is time to turn to this fact and study it in order to reveal the philosophical significance of human vulnerability.

Acknowledgments

This chapter was written during a period of research leave funded by the Leverhulme Trust. I am grateful to the Trust for awarding me a fellowship. I thank Jeremy Dunham, Samir Okasha, Richard Pettigrew, Andrew Pyle, Matthew Ratcliffe, S. Kay Toombs, Greg Tuck, and Sean Watson for discussing the chapter with me and making helpful suggestions. I also thank two anonymous reviewers and audiences at Warwick and UWE, Bristol, for their comments on the chapter.

Matthew Ratcliffe, Matthew Broome, Benedict Smith and Hannah Bowden

A Bad Case of the Flu?

The Comparative Phenomenology of Depression and Somatic Illness

1. Introduction

Clear phenomenological boundaries between broad categories of *psychiatric* illness — such as 'depression' and 'schizophrenia' — may be difficult to draw, but surely it is safe to assume that depression is distinct from experiences of *somatic* illness? In this chapter, we suggest not. First of all, we draw upon a body of first-person testimony in order to emphasize that depression, as experienced by sufferers, is very much a *bodily* condition. Although it is not exclusively bodily, we argue that the same applies to experiences of somatic illness. Then we turn to recent scientific work on the relationship between depression and inflammation, which suggests that depression and bodily infection can be associated with similar neurobiological changes in brain areas connected with the regulation of mood, caused in both cases by increased levels of pro-inflammatory cytokines. Of course, it could be argued that, even if bodily experience in depression has much in common with certain forms of somatic illness (both phenomenologically and neurobiologically), depression has additional features. However, established diagnostic criteria are so broad that they encompass a heterogeneous range of experiences. Symptoms that are largely or wholly attributable to inflammation could, we suggest, meet the DSM-IV criteria for a major depressive episode. Hence some cases of 'depression' may well be phenomenologically indistinguishable from what we would expect to find in a case of undiagnosed infection by some pathogen. In certain other cases, differences may be symptomatic of greater duration of symptoms in depression and/or changes in self-interpretation and social relations associated with the diagnosis. However, different symptoms, which might well occur in the absence of inflammation, could equally meet the same diagnostic criteria. It is doubtful that this diverse phenomenology is united by a common aetiology. Hence, if the category 'major depression' is supposed to identify a unitary form of illness that can be reliably treated in a particular way, it is too broad to do the required work.[1]

2. The Bodily Phenomenology of Depression

It is often remarked that the expression or even experience of depression is cross-culturally variable. For instance, a 'predominance of somatic symptoms' is evident in some non-western narratives of depression (Kleinman, 1988a, p. 41). However, it is important not to understate the pervasiveness and salience of bodily symptoms in contemporary western depression narratives too. They are frequently emphasized in published autobiographies. For example:

> Why do they call it a 'mental' illness? The pain isn't just in my head; it's everywhere, but mainly at my throat and in my heart. Perhaps my heart is broken. Is this what this is? My whole chest feels like it's being crushed. It's hard to breathe. (Brampton, 2008, p. 34)

Bodily symptoms are equally conspicuous in unpublished first-person accounts of depression. In 2011, we conducted an internet questionnaire study, which included the question 'how does your body feel when you're depressed?'[2] Out of 136 people who responded to that question, only two reported no bodily ailments, and two others were unsure. One or more of the words 'tired', 'heavy', 'lethargic', and 'exhausted' appeared in 96 of the other responses. Most of the remainder included comparable terms; there were complaints of lacking energy, feeling drained or fatigued, and having a sluggish or leaden body. In addition to the core themes of heaviness, exhaustion, and lack of vitality, people complained of many other bodily symptoms, including general aches and pains, headache, feelings of illness, sickness or nausea, joint pain, pain or pressure in the chest, numbness, and loss of

---

[1]　See also Ghaemi (2008) for the point that the concept of 'major depression' is 'excessively broad'. Ghaemi argues from the limited efficacy of pharmaceutical intervention to the conclusion that treatment is guided by inadequate diagnostic categories: 'since nosology precedes pharmacology, if we get the diagnosis wrong, treatment will be ineffective' (*ibid.*, p. 965).

[2]　The questionnaire was posted on the website of the mental health charity SANE. Respondents identified themselves as depressed and, in most cases, offered details of their diagnoses. They provided free text responses with no word limit.

appetite. Some also reported a sore throat and blocked nose. Responses varied in detail. Some consisted of only one or two sentences:

> #8. 'Very tired and uncomfortable.'
> #26. 'As heavy as lead. I can't drag it out of bed most of the time.'
> #41. 'Tired, aching.'
> #66. 'Tired and painful. I feel like gravity is pushing me down.'
> #129. 'My body seems very heavy and it's an effort to move.'
> #133. 'Exhausted, drained, no energy.'
> #180. 'Tired but not sleepy. Tight neck and shoulders giving head-aches.'
> #266. 'Exhausted, heavy limbs, aching, headaches, tired, spaced out.'
> #312. 'Heavy, arched and with hot and cold sweats. Vulnerable and hol-low.'
> #357. 'No energy. Just totally run down.'

Others were more detailed:

> #14. 'Slow, heavy, lethargic and painful. Every morning I wake with a sore throat, headache and blocked nose. Everything feels 1000 times harder to do. To get out of bed, hold a cup of tea, it's all such an effort. My entire body aches and feels like it is going to break.'
> #22. 'Lethargic, like it's full of lead. My legs felt heavy all the time and I felt ridiculously tired. It was a horrible cycle — the more I felt tired, the more I stayed in bed, so that when I did get up I'd feel even more lethar-gic. Sometimes I would feel so numb I felt like I couldn't eat anything, or I'd feel "too sad" to eat. I think a lot of people have this impression that depression is a purely mental illness, and I can't explain it but it totally affects you physically as well and your body just goes into melt-down mode.'[3]

Several respondents also reported negative evaluations of their bodies or some property of their bodies. These were mostly self-evaluations, although some also referred to how others saw them. The most fre-quent complaint was that of being 'fat' or 'ugly', the more general theme being disgust at one's body and often also oneself. Some also wrote that their bodies were 'pointless' or 'useless', where bodily use-lessness was closely tied to uselessness of the self. However, in what follows, we will restrict our analysis to the core bodily symptoms that

---

[3] Respondents had various different diagnoses, but most of them stated their diagnosis as 'depression', 'clinical depression', or 'major depression'. Setting aside some cases involving mania and/or psychotic features, there was no discernable correlation between particular diagnoses and the kinds of description offered.

characterize almost every account, and will thus exclude — for current purposes — this dimension of body- and self-evaluation.[4]

On the basis of the testimony we have quoted, it might seem that bodily experience in depression is very similar to the kinds of experience associated with acute somatic illnesses such as influenza. However, perhaps they only *seem* similar because an exclusive emphasis upon bodily experience gives us a very partial picture of the phenomenology of depression. Depression also involves changes in emotion, thought, and volition, and in experiences of the world and other people. All of this is embedded in a more pervasive transformation of the person's experience of and relationship with the world (Ratcliffe, 2010b; 2013a). Sufferers often complain of finding themselves in an impoverished and alien realm, the nature of which they find very difficult to convey to others. The world is stripped of all the practical significance that it was once imbued with, and so they feel curiously detached from everything and everyone, not quite 'there'. In addition, the kinds of significant possibility that things used to offer are sometimes replaced by a sense of inchoate threat. For example:

> I awoke into a different world. It was as though all had changed while I slept: that I awoke not into normal consciousness but into a nightmare... At that time ordinary objects — chairs, tables and the like — possessed a frightening, menacing quality which is very hard to describe vividly in the way that I was then affected. It was as though I lived in some kind of hell, containing nothing from which I could obtain relief or comfort. (Testimony quoted by Rowe, 1978, pp. 269–70)

Many of our questionnaire respondents also reported profound changes in their sense of belonging to a world:

> #17. 'Often, the world feels as though it is a very long way away and that it takes an enormous amount of effort to engage with the world and your own life. It feels as though you're watching life from a long distance. At times it felt as though I was looking through a fish eye lens, and couldn't see clearly around the periphery, or even very well at all. I felt slightly pulled back from reality, as though there was cotton wool between my brain and my senses.'

---

[4] It is debatable whether and to what extent an attitude of disgust or shame directed at the body can be extricated from a more immediate bodily phenomenology. It is arguable that a sense of how others perceive one's body can be integral to everyday bodily experience, rather than being something that one has to infer from it (Sartre, 1989, Part 3; Ratcliffe and Broome, 2012). Perhaps one *feels* fat, ugly, or disgusting in a way that incorporates a sense of how one is perceived by others. On the other hand, it could be that one's body is judged to be disgusting or ugly on the basis of prior experiences and beliefs. It is difficult to discern which applies in any given case.

#138. 'I feel like I am watching the world around me and have no way of participating.'

Along with this, there were complaints of being imprisoned in a realm that offers no possibility of meaningful activity and no hope of escape:

#16. 'It is as if I am being suffocated and I feel trapped with no escape apart from death…'
#28. 'It [the world] feels pointless, there's no future and no hope.'
#75. 'When I'm depressed life never seems worth living. I can never think about how my life is different from when I'm not depressed. I think that my life will never change and that I will always be depressed.'

Hence one could maintain that it is 'psychological' changes like these, rather than associated 'bodily' experiences, that distinguish the phenomenology of depression from that of somatic illness. Furthermore, the bodily symptoms might be interpreted differently once their psychological context is acknowledged, further lessening the alleged similarity.

3. The World of Illness

On the basis of first-person testimonies, many somatic illnesses do appear to have an exclusively 'bodily' phenomenology. It is easy enough to find reports of experiences of influenza and other acute illnesses. For example, a website on 'cold and flu' includes 153 first-person accounts.[5] They mention a range of symptoms, such as headache, sore throat, stomach ache, congested nose, throat, lungs, and/or sinuses, soreness, stiffness, aches, joint pain, feeling hot or cold, sweating, diarrhoea, watery and/or itchy eyes, weakness, and exhaustion. A few posts also complain of crying all the time and wondering when it will end. One person remarks, 'I just want to die', and goes on to say 'this one makes me feel like absolute crap and I am just whinging and complaining and I just want to cry all the time'. But aside from that, the focus is almost entirely upon unpleasant bodily experience.

However, the few authors who explore the phenomenology of somatic illness in any detail tend to relate a more profound and encompassing change in how one finds oneself in the world. To quote Merleau-Ponty (1962, p. 107), illness can amount to a 'complete form of existence'. Consider some remarks by Virginia Woolf, in her essay *On Being Ill*. First of all, Woolf emphasizes both the difficulty of describing our bodily experience and its neglect in literature: 'English, which can express the thoughts of Hamlet and the tragedy of

---

[5] http://coldflu.about.com/u/ua/flu/flusymptomsstories.htm (accessed 11 Dec 2011).

Lear, has no words for the shiver and the headache' (Woolf, 1930/ 2002, p. 6).[6] She adds that the phenomenology of illness is not restricted to the body; it also transforms experience of the world and other people. Reflecting on being in bed with influenza, Woolf notes how 'the world has changed its shape'; 'the whole landscape of life lies remote and fair, like the shore seen from a ship far out at sea' (Woolf, 1930/2002, p. 8). We find similar themes in J.H. van den Berg's (1966) essay on the phenomenology of illness, *The Psychology of the Sickbed*. His emphasis is upon the experience of serious, chronic illness.[7] However, much of his discussion is equally intended to apply to more mundane cases of acute illness. Here too, a shift in how one finds oneself in the world is described. Along with altered bodily experience, the world looks different — familiar things seem somehow strange, distant. There is a sense of being dislodged from the realm of everyday activity: 'I have ceased to belong; I have no part in it.' The world has, van den Berg says, 'shrunk to the size of my bedroom, or rather my bed' (1966, p. 26). This shrinkage is attributable to one's no longer being practically, purposively immersed in various projects that more usually determine whether and how worldly entities appear significant and solicit activity. A purposive striving towards the future that previously characterized experience and activity has been lost, and one therefore feels oddly rooted in the present. Things also become salient in new ways. How they appear is no longer constrained by their practical salience in the context of one's habitual concerns, and so all sorts of ordinarily overlooked details begin to show up:

> The blankets of my bed, articles so much devoted to utility that they used to disappear behind the goal they served, so that in my normal condition I could not possibly have said what color they are, become jungles of colored threads in which my eye laboriously finds its way. (*Ibid.*, p. 29)

One's body is experienced in a new way too. What was taken for granted becomes conspicuous: 'The healthy person is allowed to be his body and he makes use of this right eagerly; he *is* his body. Illness disturbs this assimilation. Man's body becomes foreign to him' (*ibid.*, p. 66). In addition, van den Berg conveys the extent to which experience of body and world in illness are both regulated by relations with

---

[6]   Scarry (1985) makes a similar point about the experience of pain, claiming that it cannot be adequately expressed by language.

[7]   See also Carel (2008) for a detailed account of the first-person experience of serious, chronic illness, which emphasizes the extent to which illness changes one's world.

other people. Especially in cases of more serious, chronic illness, how the patient 'experiences his sickbed depends to a great extent on the behavior of the visitor: the way he enters, the way he finds a seat and the way he talks' (*ibid.*, p. 18).[8]

Why should a change in the overall way one's body is experienced be associated with an all-pervasive transformation of one's experienced relationship with the world? The answer, we suggest, is that bodily experience and world experience are inextricable. The phenomenology of the body is not restricted to its being an object of experience; it is also experienced as a medium of perception, that through which other things are perceived. This is a consistent theme in the phenomenological tradition. As Husserl (1989, p. 61) puts it, 'the Body [*Leib*] is, in the first place, *the medium of all perception*; it is the *organ of perception* and is *necessarily* involved in all perception'. Inspired by Husserl, Merleau-Ponty (1962, p. 146) adopts a similar but more elaborate account, according to which the body and its habitual dispositions and activities amount to 'our general medium for having a world'. Drawing on such work, Ratcliffe (2008a) argues that terms such as 'bodily feeling' and 'bodily experience' are equivocal; a distinction needs to be made between the *feeling* body and the *felt* body, where the former is a medium through which something else is experienced, while the latter is an object of experience. It is thus a mistake to think of bodily experience as something that occurs in isolation from world experience; the two are often inseparable.[9] One might object that the 'feeling body' does not feature in experience at all, that the body is either a central/peripheral object of experience or disappears altogether from experience. Sartre (1989, p. 322), amongst others, leans towards such a view, in maintaining that when we are unthinkingly immersed in our projects, our bodily phenomenology amounts to no more than an organized system of practical possibilities sewn into the experienced world. However, it is more plausible, in our view, to retain a distinction between the feeling body and the phenomenologically absent body. A bodily feeling can be both an object of experience and — at the same time — a way in which something else

---

[8]   Elsewhere, van den Berg (1972) offers a phenomenological account of *psychiatric* illness, which emphasizes forms of experience that are remarkably similar (Ratcliffe, 2010a).

[9]   Although Ratcliffe's account of bodily feeling as world-involving draws explicitly upon work in the phenomenological tradition, others have made complementary points in different ways. For example, Goldie (2000; 2009) maintains that not all feelings are 'bodily feelings' with an exclusively bodily phenomenology. There are also, he says, 'feelings towards', where the phenomenology of the feeling is inseparable from its world-directed intentionality.

is experienced. Indeed, it can be experienced *as* that through which something else is experienced (Ratcliffe, 2012c).

We suggest that this general kind of approach is plausible when interpreting experiences of illness, including psychiatric illness. People with depression often try to express something that is neither an experience of the body in isolation from the world nor vice versa, but a way of experiencing both. For example:

> Now, sitting in my pine-paneled room, I felt myself hurtling once more into the abyss. The mental pain was physical, as if the marrow of my bones were being ground into dust. (Thompson, 1995, p. 246)

Hence it is arguable that psychiatric illness can involve changes in bodily feeling that at the same time amount to alterations in 'how one finds oneself in the world' (Ratcliffe, 2008a). For instance, Sass (2004b) suggests that a loss of bodily affect in schizophrenia is bound up with what he calls 'unworlding', where the world appears stripped of practical potentialities. And Fuchs (2005a) maintains that depression likewise has an essentially bodily phenomenology — it involves a process where aspects of bodily experience that usually operate as a medium for world experience instead become uncomfortably obtrusive, altering world experience in the process. Depression, he says, involves 'reification or corporealization of the lived body' (*ibid.*, p. 95). Thus the fatigue and discomfort described by most of our questionnaire respondents also amounts to disruption of the body's role as a medium of experience and activity, and thus to a change in how they experience and relate to the world. For example, one person responded to our question about bodily experience with 'Tired — really, really tired — the stairs in my house seem like a mountain' (#147). The stairs are perceived in this way *through* the tired, cumbersome, incapable body. The kind of tiredness that people complain of is more extreme than mundane tiredness; it is the loss of an ordinarily taken for granted vitality that at the same time amounts to a draining away of practical possibilities from the experienced world (Ratcliffe, forthcoming). As Fuchs (2005a, p. 99) puts it, there is a diminishment of 'the *connative dimension* of the body', of a sense of the world as an arena of variably enticing practical possibilities.

If somatic illness can similarly involve not just bodily experience but a change in how one 'finds oneself in the world', how are we to distinguish its phenomenology from that of psychiatric illness and, more specifically, depression? Of course, experience of serious, chronic illness is routinely distinguished from depression, as exemplified by the observation that depression is sometimes but not always co-morbid with it (National Collaborative Centre for Mental Health, 2010). Indeed, it is possible to have a general sense of well-being in the context of illness, something that is incompatible with a diagnosis of depression.[10] However, we want to focus on something more specific here. We are concerned with what distinguishes the phenomenology of depression from a certain kind of all-over bodily experience commonly associated with a wide range of illnesses, a general 'feeling of being unwell' that characterizes acute infections such as influenza as well as chronic illness, but need not be a *constant* accompaniment to the latter.

Now, nothing we have said so far is incompatible with the view that illnesses such as influenza involve an experience of the body, pure and simple. That some bodily experiences are inseparable from world experience does not rule out the possibility that others are principally or even exclusively of the body.[11] Perhaps what Woolf, van den Berg, and other phenomenologically inclined writers describe are exceptions to the rule. Should the view that certain somatic illness experiences are interestingly similar to depression therefore be dismissed? We suggest not. As Woolf points out, the phenomenology of somatic illness has been neglected, to the extent that we lack the language required to adequately convey it. But aren't influenza symptoms routinely and unproblematically described, as illustrated by the 153 accounts mentioned earlier? In fact, people seldom offer anything approximating a *description*. Instead, they *name* various phenomena and emphasize how unpleasant they are. Furthermore, a diagnosis of influenza gives one a disease entity and aetiology to refer to, along with an established canon of *bodily* complaints to list. In the case of depression, no disease process has been identified, and there is instead an emphasis on 'psychological' changes that many sufferers complain are difficult or even impossible to convey to others. Hence it is likely that a diagnosis of depression disposes one to emphasize symptoms

---

[10] Thanks to Havi Carel (personal communication) for drawing our attention to this. The possibility of well-being in illness shows that there is no simple correlation between the presence of disease, conceived of biologically, and a certain kind of experience. We are using the term 'illness experience' in a fairly permissive way here, to refer to kinds of experience that are attributable, at least in part, to the presence of some disease, kinds of experience that may turn out to be quite heterogeneous. Some of these experiences may arise in other contexts too, and so an 'illness experience' should be thought of as a kind of experience that is frequently rather than invariably associated with disease. When it comes to 'psychiatric illness', matters are more complicated still as it is often unclear what — if anything — the relevant disease process consists of.

[11] For example, Goldie (2009) emphasizes that many feelings have world-directed intentionality but resists the view that they all do, maintaining that there are exclusively 'bodily' feelings too.

that can be more easily circumvented when reporting an experience of influenza. It is also interesting to note that people with depression often report confusing its onset with that of influenza or some other infection. As one of our questionnaire respondent comments, 'It [the body] aches. I can feel fluish. My stomach and throat can ache and I feel anxious' (#228). Indeed, someone Ratcliffe spoke to at the time of writing this chapter (who had suffered from depression once before) reported how he had recently thought he was becoming depressed and was very relieved when he then developed a cough and a runny nose. Hence the conclusion to be drawn at this stage is that we cannot rule out the possibility of differences between accounts of somatic illness and depression being largely attributable to established styles of report, rather than to marked phenomenological differences.

We will now consider some recent neurobiological evidence, which suggests that some cases of 'depression' are indeed phenomenologically indistinguishable from forms of experience that are, in other contexts, construed as symptoms of somatic illness.

4. Depression, Inflammation, and the Feeling of Illness

It is easy to distinguish most cases of influenza from depression, as influenza involves more than just a vague feeling of being unwell. There are a range of more specific symptoms too, and the same applies to other illnesses. Indeed, one might argue that the 'feeling of being unwell' to which we refer is an abstraction from experience, rather than something that can be experienced in isolation and legitimately compared to depression. However, we reject that view, on the basis of both experience and immunobiology. What we have in mind is something that is often experienced before the onset of various more specific symptoms, which can also linger for a time after those symptoms have disappeared. It is not pathogen-specific; many acute and chronic illnesses are characterized by much the same kind of experience, which involves lack of vitality, inability to concentrate, diminished inclination to act, and a sense of being disconnected from things. The relevant experience is largely attributable to an immune response common to many illnesses, which involves the increased release of protein molecules called pro-inflammatory cytokines by white blood cells (particularly monocytes). These cytokines play a regulatory role, serving to increase the body's inflammatory response to infection. It has long been recognized that inflammation in illness is correlated with behavioural changes (which have also been observed in animal studies) and with lowering of mood (Harrison *et al.*, 2009). Correla-

tion does not add up to cause, but the view that pro-inflammatory cytokines are causally involved in feelings of lethargy and low mood is supported by experimental studies where inflammation is induced in healthy subjects (by injecting them with a vaccine, for example), and mood changes are monitored. Participants report or display symptoms such as 'fatigue, psychomotor slowing, mild cognitive confusion, memory impairment, anxiety, and deterioration in mood', which are strikingly similar to depression (*ibid.*, p. 407). Indeed, longer term inflammatory responses in patients treated with interferon (an artificial inflammatory cytokine) are associated with diagnoses of major depressive episodes in approximately 50% of cases. There is also a characteristic time course; lethargy and various other symptoms are more salient in the first few weeks, while anxiety and depressed mood become more pronounced after one to three months of treatment. The mechanism whereby pro-inflammatory cytokines induce sickness behaviour is not fully understood. However, it is accepted that they are able to act across the blood-brain barrier, and it seems that sickness-associated experiential changes owe much to their influence upon activity in specific areas of the brain, including some of those implicated in mood regulation.

Interestingly, depression is also — sometimes, at least — associated with heightened levels of inflammatory cytokines. Several markers of inflammation are found in depressed patients, regardless of age of onset, severity, and type (Raison, Capuron and Miller, 2006; Miller, Maletic and Raison, 2009). This is perhaps unsurprising, as acute/chronic psychological stress also triggers increased release of inflammatory cytokines and episodes of depression are frequently preceded by stressors (Raison, Capuron and Miller, 2006; Miller, Maletic and Raison, 2009). It has therefore been suggested that depression is wholly or partly attributable to over-activation of the immune system: 'depressive disorders might be best characterised as conditions of immune activation, especially hyperactivity of innate immune inflammatory responses' (Raison, Capuron and Miller, 2006, p. 24). In support of this hypothesis, there are studies reporting that antidepressants in conjunction with anti-inflammatory drugs are more effective in treating depression than antidepressants alone (e.g. Müller *et al.*, 2006). And, as Raison, Capuron and Miller (2006) observe, the inflammation hypothesis of depression also helps to account for the increased prevalence of depression in medical illness (which they claim to be five- to tenfold), given the near ubiquity of inflammation in illness.

When it comes to determining whether and to what extent the phenomenology of depression is akin to that of a general 'feeling of being unwell', the neurobiology can help to arbitrate. Changes in brain activation associated with inflammation-induced mood changes were investigated by Harrison *et al.* (2009), who conducted an fMRI study monitoring brain activation in subjects who had been injected with typhoid vaccine (which causes an inflammatory response). They found that areas showing increased activation corresponded to those identified by Helen Mayberg and colleagues as centrally involved in depression, principally the subgenual cingulate (e.g. Mayberg, 2003a; Mayberg *et al.*, 1999; 2005). These changes in brain activation were correlated with first-person reports of fatigue, low mood, anxiety, and other symptoms. Harrison *et al.* (2009, p. 407) thus propose that there is a 'common pathophysiological basis for major depressive disorder and sickness-associated mood change and depression'.[12] We do not want to put too much weight upon neurobiological data. Nevertheless, we take the following methodological principle to be generally sound: where there *seems to be* no phenomenological difference between experiences of type A and type B, an absence of associated neurobiological difference supports the view that there is indeed no difference.

Where does this leave matters? In the remainder of this section we will critically reflect upon some of the conclusions that might be drawn. The most radical view would be that depression and a feeling of being ill are one and the same. Depression, it might be argued, is the kind of experience someone has when chronically inflamed. In support of this view, many of our questionnaire respondents emphasized a general feeling of being unwell that appears to be indistinguishable from the kind of experience typical of a range of illnesses (at least in the absence of further qualification):

#155. 'Tired, achy, unwell.'
#352. 'I notice small aches and pains more and also feel nauseous and have an indefinable feeling of being unwell.'

---

[12] It is also interesting to note that the same inflammatory cytokines (e.g. IL-6) have also been implicated in alcohol hangovers. Verster (2008) suggests that a hangover involves two largely independent factors: dehydration symptoms and the effects of increased concentrations of pro-inflammatory cytokines, although he adds that the picture is complicated by additional factors such as tiredness, food, smoking, and congeners (colourings and flavourings in drinks). Depression is sometimes compared to a bad hangover. For example, one of our questionnaire respondents describes it as a 'permanent hangover' in order to 'illustrate the sense of everything closing in and the feeling of hopelessness' (#60). Another says that it is 'like when you have just had a load to drink the night before and just woken up with a desire to stay put and sleep' (#242).

#334. 'When I first started to suffer from depression I always used to say that it felt as though something "wasn't quite right" in that I generally felt under the weather. It felt as though I was always coming down with a cold in that I felt "below par". My swings in mood are generally accompanied by headaches, sometimes quite bad, and I will always wake up with them. If that is the case I know that my mood is changing and that my headache will not go until I go to sleep that night.'

This view would cast doubt upon the legitimacy of 'depression' as an illness category. Given that forms of experience associated with influenza, tonsillitis, and a range of other infections are not categorized as 'depression' but as symptoms of infection by some pathogen, it would surely be dubious to insist that all those other inflammation experiences where the aetiology is unknown constitute a single medical condition. Of course, one could maintain that depression is not to be identified with its symptoms; it is instead what causes them. Radden (2009, pp. 79–80) makes the helpful distinction between an aetiological/causal conception of depression and an 'ontological descriptivism' that identifies depression with a cluster of symptoms. But to appeal to aetiology here would be to mortgage the integrity of the construct 'depression' upon future discovery of a common cause of all those phenomena currently falling under the category 'symptoms of inflammation not currently attributed to known pathogens'. And that would surely be wishful thinking. Depression is frequently associated with some stressor, but there is a need to distinguish between proportionate and disproportionate reactions to events, and there are thus different kinds of causal story to be told about stressors, perhaps many different kinds.[13] In other cases, 'depression' might arise due to undiagnosed or as yet unidentified pathogens, or some other trigger of inflammation. So, even if all cases were principally attributable to inflammation, we would expect depression to be causally diverse. It is already well established that inflammation has a variety of causes and there are no grounds for thinking that cases of 'inflammation: cause unknown' are exceptions to the rule. Hence, if the radical view was the correct one, 'depression' would be best construed as a temporary placeholder, to be jettisoned once we have a more refined understanding of the different phenomena that it encompasses.

However, an obvious objection to the radical view is that symptoms such as low mood are not constant accompaniments to all instances of

---

[13] Horwitz and Wakefield (2007) observe that a proportionality criterion has been removed from the DSM classification system, so that it does not give us the means to distinguish an appropriate reaction to circumstances from an excessive reaction. Consequently, both get diagnosed as depression.

inflammation. Hence the phenomenology associated with inflammation does not add up to that of depression. One could respond to this by maintaining that the relevant phenomenology is a *common* symptom of inflammation, rather than a *universal* symptom. In those cases where that phenomenology is associated with infection by some pathogen, it is generally regarded as a symptom of somatic illness rather than depression. So the position would be that depression is indistinguishable from the kinds of experience associated with *some* inflammatory responses to infection, rather than every such response.

A further objection is that not all cases of illness that involve the general feeling of being unwell, which the radical view takes to be indistinguishable from depression, are co-morbid with depression. Therefore, depression must be different from the experience of inflammation. However, in cases where a somatic illness has already been diagnosed, the fact that symptoms p, q, and r can be attributed to that illness rather than depression need not imply a phenomenological difference between the two. In the absence of a diagnosed somatic illness, exactly the same symptoms might be attributed to depression instead, as exemplified by the DSM instruction to disregard what would otherwise be depression symptoms when they can be attributed to another medical condition (DSM-IV-TR, 2000, p. 351). Nevertheless, the possibility of co-morbidity still implies that at least some cases of 'depression' involve something more. Otherwise, depression could not be diagnosed in conjunction with *any* of those inflammatory conditions that are themselves associated with an alteration in how one 'finds oneself in the world', and it frequently is. Indeed, one might argue that, contrary to the radical view, depression *always* involves something more, that a general feeling of sickness is common to depression and somatic illness but never sufficient for depression.

Where there are phenomenological differences between an instance of depression and a general feeling of being ill, it is arguable that at least some of them are attributable to duration of symptoms. As noted earlier, it has been proposed that the symptoms of inflammation follow a temporal pattern, with mood changes that lead to a diagnosis of major depression becoming more pronounced in the longer term. So perhaps the initial sickness feeling is not sufficient for depression but predisposes one towards other phenomenological changes that are. Maybe the kinds of inertia and despair associated with depression are only phenomenologically intelligible in the context of already having a body that is drained of its vitality and a world that is no longer alive with possibilities for bodily activity.[14] Alternatively, there could be a simple causal relation here. It is surely plausible to maintain that living with chronic illness *makes* some people depressed. And perhaps, in certain other cases, the illness causes physiological changes that lead to depression. A causal account of either kind would commit us to the view there is more to depression than an overall feeling of being unwell (regardless of how long one might be inflamed for). And it is quite clear that there can be. For example, depression symptoms such as despair do not relate in a systematic way to a prior experience of inflammation. Such feelings can take several different forms. One might lose hope in relation to a project that is central to one's life and thus lose a whole system of long-term hopes and aspirations, or one might lose 'hope', in the deeper sense that one is unable to entertain the possibility of hoping for anything. In the latter case, 'hope', rather than a system of hopes, is gone from one's world. And there are several variants of the latter — one might lose all sense of there being non-trivial hopes; one might lose all hope in the context of one's own life but retain hope in relation to the lives of others; or one might live in a world where all hopes seem fragile, where all projects rest upon something that is uncertain, untrustworthy, and perhaps even malevolent (Ratcliffe, 2013a). Any one of these might be associated with a diagnosis of depression. It is arguable that certain forms of despair are indeed closely associated with inflammation. Put crudely, bodily fatigue might eventually add up to a sense that one cannot do various things. So everything seems impossible and hope in one's ability to achieve anything is progressively eroded. However, it is far from clear that all instances of despair take that form. Indeed, there are surely 'existential' forms of despair that do not depend essentially upon feeling drained of bodily vitality.[15] To all this, we can add that there is a need for caution regarding the inflammation data. As Raison *et al.* concede, some studies have failed to find a correlation between inflammation and major depression. They thus acknowledge that 'strong pronouncements about the role of the immune system in depression might be premature'; inconsistent findings suggest that 'inflammation contributes to some, but not all, cases of depression'

---

[14] A comparison could be drawn here with Sass's (e.g. 2003) account of negative symptoms in schizophrenia, according to which later psychotic symptoms are only intelligible in the context of early symptoms such as affective changes and a draining of practical significance from the world.

[15] This difference may relate to the distinction between 'demoralization' and 'depression' drawn by Kissane and Clarke (2001) and Clarke and Kissane (2002).

(Raison, Capuron and Miller, 2006, p. 25).[16] Furthermore, it is likely that the phenomenology associated with inflammation is itself variable, perhaps markedly so.

To further complicate matters, diagnosis can itself shape how a person experiences, interprets, and responds to her condition. Although people with influenza sometimes ask 'when will this end?', the timescale is fairly predictable. Appreciation of one's predicament as longer term and of unknown duration might itself shape how it is experienced. Diagnosis of depression involves greater uncertainty, and the sense that 'this might never end' or 'this will never end' could surely precipitate or fuel feelings of despair.[17] In addition, depression can be interpreted by the sufferer in a way that differs from how somatic illnesses are generally conceived of. Influenza is a foreign invader that inflicts symptoms upon one from the outside, whereas many depression narratives construe depression as integral to the self. As Radden (2009, p. 16) puts it, accounts of depression often have a 'symptom-integrating structure', rather than one that sets the illness apart from the self. This interpretive tendency may partly account for the frequency of complaints of worthlessness, guilt, and inability in depression. Whereas influenza temporarily stops one from doing things that one is capable of doing or prevents one from acting in ways that are consistent with who one takes oneself to be, depression is often taken by sufferers to be inextricable from who they are and what they are capable of. Much the same point applies to social relations. A person might feel socially uncomfortable or estranged from others due to an external constraint that gets in the way of her normal social dispositions, or she might construe herself as cut off from others due to an enduring attribute of herself. Thus it is arguable that certain symptoms of depression can be accounted for in terms of how one conceives of one's predicament, and that these are partly responsible for setting it apart from experiences of somatic illness. In addition, there are various social and interpersonal norms associated with diagnoses of depression and psychiatric illness more generally, which regulate the behaviour of friends, family, and clinicians, and might equally shape one's experience and behaviour.

---

[16] Krishnadas and Cavanagh (2012, p. 495) suggest that only around a third of people with diagnoses of major depressive disorder have raised levels of inflammatory biomarkers.

[17] With this in mind, and also the earlier observation that more severe depression symptoms may be associated with longer term inflammation, it would be interesting to explore the comparative phenomenology of longer term infections such as glandular fever (infectious mononucleosis), as well as that of chronic fatigue syndrome (myalgic encephalopathy).

5. The Heterogeneity of Depression

How do we arbitrate between the various options outlined above? In asking that question, we get to the heart of the problem. Current conceptions of depression, and also more specific subcategories such as 'major depression', are too permissive to facilitate the required distinctions. They accommodate and fail to distinguish a variety of predicaments, which are likely to differ from the phenomenology of somatic illness in different ways and to different degrees. Consider the DSM-IV-TR criteria for a major depressive episode:

> [For at least two weeks] there is either depressed mood or the loss of interest or pleasure in nearly all activities. In children and adolescents, the mood may be irritable rather than sad. The individual must also experience at least four additional symptoms drawn from a list that includes changes in appetite or weight, sleep, and psychomotor activity; decreased energy; feelings of worthlessness or guilt; difficulty thinking, concentrating or making decisions; or recurrent thoughts of death or suicidal ideation, plans, or attempts. (2000, p. 349)

The majority of these symptoms are implicitly or explicitly phenomenological, and they are all under-described. For example, 'depressed mood' can surely refer to a range of experiences. And consider feelings of guilt and worthlessness. It is possible to distinguish between several importantly different kinds of guilt feeling. One might feel guilty about something specific, or perhaps guilty about something that one finds hard to pin down. Alternatively, one might have a generalized feeling of guilt that encompasses many deeds. Another variant is where one feels that one *is guilty*, pure and simple; one's essence is guilt, a guilt that does not attach to a specific set of deeds (Ratcliffe, 2010b). Any of these could feature in a depression narrative. So 'guilt' in depression, like 'despair', refers to a range of experiences. Given the phenomenologically permissive way in which depression is described by diagnostic systems such as DSM-IV and ICD-10, the general feeling of being unwell, associated with illnesses such as influenza, does indeed meet the criteria for a major depressive episode, at least in those cases where another illness has not been diagnosed. It can certainly involve depressed mood and loss of interest in activity for at least two weeks, along with other symptoms including decreased energy, difficulty thinking, and changes in sleep patterns. And the neurobiological similarities further point to the view that there is no principled way of distinguishing between the two phenomenologically. That they share neural correlates suggests they are indeed what they seem to be: much the same. To add to the problem, a predicament that did not involve this general sickness feeling could equally meet those same criteria. One could surely lose interest in activity without having a general feeling of illness, and — depending on the circumstances — this might be associated with weight change, guilt, lack of concentration, and even thoughts of suicide. So it may well be that certain experiences of 'major depression' are only superficially similar. In the absence of a common phenomenology or aetiology that unites them and sets them apart from other forms of illness, it is not clear what does unite them, other than entrenched diagnostic practices.

What we have here is a dynamic and diverse phenomenology, which is associated with a range of causes, and embedded in systems of meaning that involve various norms of self-interpretation and performance. The radical conclusion that there is no difference between the phenomenology of depression and a chronic, pronounced feeling of sickness should therefore be rejected, not simply because 'depression is something else', but because depression is too untidy. The category 'depression' does accommodate 'no difference' cases, but it accommodates various other cases too. The literature on depression and inflammation tends to assume the legitimacy of the diagnostic category 'major depression'. Indeed, Raison, Capuron and Miller (2006) even engage in some speculative evolutionary theorizing about how depression might involve an adapted immune response that has become maladaptive in modern social environments. Harrison *et al.* similarly accept the category 'major depression' and consider what the mechanisms underlying it might be: 'neurobiological circuits supporting adaptive motivational reorientation during sickness might be "hijacked" maladaptively during clinical depression' (Harrison *et al.*, 2009, p. 413). However, the findings of such studies, when united with the kind of phenomenological reflection pursued here (which fails to discern a clear phenomenological difference), render that category highly problematic. It is based largely upon phenomenological considerations but encompasses a heterogeneous range of phenomena, whilst failing to distinguish them from other phenomena that it is not supposed to encompass. In addition, it gives us no basis for thinking that these phenomena are aetiologically united.

Further phenomenological and neurobiological research is needed in order to discern what, if anything, might distinguish the range of somatic illness experiences from the range of depression experiences. In the absence of the clarification and refinement that such research might bring, 'depression' risks being a 'catch-all' term. This raises serious concerns in relation to the treatment of depression. As the diagnosis accommodates many different experiences and causes, there is every reason to suspect that an effective treatment for one of them will not be an effective treatment for some or all of the others. That conclusion is consistent with recent literature reporting the limited, variable, and/or unpredictable efficacy of current antidepressant treatments.[18]

Acknowledgments

This chapter was written as part of the project 'Emotional Experience in Depression: A Philosophical Study'. We would like to thank the AHRC and DFG for funding the project. We are very grateful to our project colleagues in the UK and Germany, an audience at the University of Osnabrück, and to Havi Carel, Charles Fernyhough, Neil Harrison, and two anonymous referees for helpful discussion and advice. Thanks also to Outi Benson for helping us to design the questionnaire study, to the mental health charity SANE for hosting it, and to all those who responded to it.

---

[18] See, for example, Ghaemi (2008), Kirsch (2009), and Undurraga and Baldessarini (2012). Kirsch goes so far as to claim that antidepressants are no more than 'active placebos'. However, if subtypes of what we currently call 'major depression' are better distinguished, we might find that they are effective for some types but not others. Hence reports of their limited effectiveness or even ineffectiveness could be partly attributable to an inadequate nosology, as Ghaemi (2008) suggests.

Thomas Fuchs

Depression, Intercorporeality, and Interaffectivity

1. Introduction

Depression is generally classified as an affective disorder (ICD-10, DSM-IV-TR). According to current psychiatric opinion, its core is constituted by a disturbance of mood and affect, typically connected to negative cognitions, self-evaluations, and emotions such as anxiety, shame, and guilt. Optional symptoms may include bodily or vegetative disturbances such as loss of appetite, weight, or libido, insomnia, and psychomotor inhibition; then the diagnosis receives the supplement 'with somatic syndrome' (ICD-10). On the other hand, the predominant psychological and psychotherapeutic approaches to depression are based on cognitive models: here, the core of the disorder is regarded as a combination of faulty information processing and distorted thinking (Clark and Beck, 1989; Beck and Alford, 2009, pp. 224ff). Consequently, Cognitive Behaviour Therapy is the generally recommended treatment (Beck *et al.*, 1979).

Both approaches have in common that they regard depression as an 'inner', mental, and individual disorder. Despite these predominant views, however, affective or cognitive symptoms are by no means found in all patients suffering from depression. Instead they may complain of constant fatigue, sickness, numbness, various kinds of pain or dysaesthesias. In these cases, the diagnostic vocabulary resorts to notions such as 'masked' or 'somatized' depression in order to rescue the concept of a primary emotional disturbance. However, transcultural studies, in particular the large WHO comparison study from 1997 (Gureje, Simon and Üstün, 1997), have pointed out that the core syndrome of depression is rather not of a 'psychological' nature. Loss of vitality, appetite, and drive, fatigue, sleep disturbances, and various somatic complaints such as feelings of pain, burning, tension, numbness, or heaviness are overall much more frequent than depressive mood or guilt feelings. In Turkey, Greece, Nigeria, China, and India, for instance, over 85% of depressed patients consult the doctor with somatic complaints. Only in France and Italy is the rate below 60% (Kirmayer and Groleau, 2001). Already in earlier studies, somatic symptoms and psychomotor inhibition were found to be prevailing in Africa and South America (Binitie, 1975; Mezzich and Raab, 1980; Escobar, Gomez and Tuason, 1983). One may conclude that depression is primarily experienced as a *bodily disturbance* in a majority of cultures, rather than only shifted or projected to the body secondarily (Pfeiffer, 1984).

At the same time, however, the vast majority of patients are well able to consider current stressors as causes of their condition. They will also complain about not being able to fulfil their tasks and to take part in social life any more (Kleinman and Good, 1985; Kirmayer, 2001). Thus, in various cultures the somatic and the psychosocial experience of the illness apparently constitute an integral unity, and the lived body functions as a particular medium for the expression of interpersonal states and conflicts. The split between somatic or external and mental or internal symptoms turns out to be the result of a specifically western cultural development. It presumes an inner realm of the psyche as separated from the body as well as from the social environment, or in other words, an inner mind for which the body only serves as a field of projection. 'Somatization' then denotes a shift of psychological content or meaning onto the body, leading to the rather Eurocentric view that members of non-western cultures have only insufficient introspective or verbal capacities to perceive and express their feelings in a mature way.

In general, western psychopathology views mental illness primarily as a process within the individual (or his brain) which only secondarily affects the bodily and the social space. Quite different concepts can be found in cultures whose members do not experience themselves as much as separate individuals but rather as parts of social communities. Disorders of mood or well-being are then conceived less as intra-psychic, but rather as bodily, expressive, interpersonal, or even atmospheric processes. Thus, in traditional Japanese or Chinese psychopathology the surrounding climate and social atmospheres such as the *ki* (or *qi*) are regarded as carriers of mental illness: *ki* means 'air', 'breath', but also 'mood' and 'atmosphere', and thus constitutes the 'in-between' from which mental disorders may take their origin (Kimura, 1995; Kitanaka, 2012, pp. 23ff).[1]

Phenomenological psychopathology has a traditional affinity for such concepts, since it regards the lived body not only as the primary domain of self-experience, of well-being or ill-being, but also as the medium of our elementary contact to the world (Merleau-Ponty, 1945; Stanghellini, 2004; Fuchs, 2002c; 2005). Background feelings of the body such as ease or unease, relaxation or tension, expansion or constriction, freshness or tiredness provide a tacit evaluation of how 'things stand' in our life; they colour and permeate all world-directed experience (Damasio, 1999; Ratcliffe, 2008a; Fuchs, 2012). Moreover, the body is always already oriented towards other bodily beings, connected to them from early childhood on through desire, imitation, and empathy. The mutual bodily resonance in social encounters, mediated by posture, facial, gestural, and vocal expression, engenders our attunement to others and functions as a carrier of basic interpersonal atmospheres such as warmth, ease, familiarity, and belonging, or in the negative case, coldness, tension, unease, or unfamiliarity. *The body is embedded in intercorporeality, and thus becomes the medium of interaffectivity.* From this point of view, so-called mental disorders should rather be regarded as alterations of the patient's lived body, lived space, and being-with-others. 'The patient is ill; this means, *his world* is ill', as van den Berg has put it (1972, p. 46). In this sense, the illness is not in the patient, but the patient is in the illness, as it were; for mental illness is not a state in the head, but an altered way of being in the world.

On this background, I will describe depression as a disturbance of intercorporeality and interaffectivity. I will argue that depression is not an 'inner', psychological, or neurobiological disorder, as it is considered in western psychiatry, but a 'detunement' (*Verstimmung*) of the resonant body that normally mediates our attunement and participation in the shared social space. Instead of expressing and connecting the self with others, the depressive body turns into a barrier to all impulses directed to the environment, resulting in a general sense of detachment, separation, or even expulsion. Before analysing depression on this basis, I will give a short overview of the phenomenology of intercorporeality and interaffectivity.

---

[1] Lee, Kleinman and Kleinman (2007) have explored how the traditional medical ideas about *qi* are expressed through a language of embodied emotion by people who suffer from 'depression' in contemporary China. Preverbal pain, sleeplessness, and social distress or disharmony play a major role in the patients' descriptions.

2. Intercorporeality and Interaffectivity

To begin with, we should abandon the idea that emotions are only 'mental' phenomena, and the world is bare of any affective qualities. The introjection of feelings into an inner 'psyche' is a heritage of Platonic and, later on, Cartesian dualism and its invention of the soul. In fact, we do not live in a merely physical world; the experienced space around us is always charged with affective qualities. We feel something 'in the air', or we sense an interpersonal 'climate', for example, a serene, a solemn, or a threatening atmosphere. Feelings befall us; they emerge from situations, persons, and objects which have their expressive qualities and which attract or repel us. This *emotional space* is essentially felt through the medium of the *body* which widens, tightens, weakens, trembles, shakes, etc. in correspondence to the feelings and atmospheres that we experience. There is no emotion without bodily sensations, bodily resonance, and affectability. Of course, when I am moved by an emotion, I may not even be aware of my body; yet being afraid, for instance, is not possible without feeling a bodily tension or trembling, a beating of the heart or a shortness of breath, and a tendency to withdraw. It is *through* these sensations that I am anxiously directed towards a frightening situation. The body is a 'resonance body', a most sensitive sounding board in which interpersonal and other 'vibrations' constantly reverberate (James, 1884; Fuchs, 2013b).[2]

Kinaesthesia is an important component of this resonance. Emotions are dynamic forces that motivate and move us in our ongoing interactions with the environment, inducing us to move forwards or backwards, upwards or downwards, or to behave in more specific ways. In this view, emotions are first and foremost embodied motivations to action (Sheets-Johnstone, 1999). As such, they are not only felt from the inside, but also displayed and visible in expression and behaviour, often as bodily tokens or rudiments of action. The facial, gestural, and postural expression of a feeling is part of the bodily resonance that feeds back into the feeling itself, but also induces processes of *inter-bodily resonance* (Froese and Fuchs, 2012). Our body is affected by the other's expression, and we experience the kinetics, intensity, and timing of his emotions through our own bodily kinaesthesia and sensation. Thus, intercorporeality is the essential basis of empathy.

---

[2] In his well-known paper 'What is an Emotion?', William James referred to the inner organs of the body as '…a sort of soundingboard, which every change of our consciousness, however slight, may make reverberate' (James, 1884).

This can perhaps best be studied in early childhood. Emotions primarily emerge from and are embedded in dyadic interactions of infant and caregiver. Stern (1985) has shown in detail how emotions are cross-modally expressed, shared, and regulated. Infants experience joint affective states in terms of dynamic flow patterns, intensities, shapes, and vitality affects (for example, crescendo or decrescendo, fading, bursting, pulsing, effortful or easy) in just the way that music is experienced as affective dynamics. This includes the tendency to mimic and synchronize each other's facial expressions, vocalizations, postures, movements, and thus to converge emotionally (Condon, 1979; Hatfield, Caccioppo and Rapson, 1994). All this may be summarized by the terms *affect attunement* or *interaffectivity* (Stern, 1985, p. 132). Thus, emotions or affects are not inner states that we experience only individually or that we have to decode in others, but primarily *shared states* that we experience through mutual intercorporeal affection. Even if emotions become increasingly independent from another's presence, intercorporeality remains the basis of empathy: there is a bodily link which allows emotions to immediately affect the other and thus enables empathic understanding without requiring a theory of mind or verbal articulation (Fuchs and De Jaegher, 2009).

The linkage between body, self, and other also characterizes the phenomenology of moods. It is a common understanding in phenomenology that moods are not inner states, but permeate and tinge the whole field of experience. Thus, moods are atmospheric in nature, radiating through the environment like warmth or cold, and conferring corresponding expressive qualities on the whole situation. It is no coincidence that we often use words taken from weather such as 'bright', 'sunny', 'gloomy', 'clouded', or 'dark' to denote mood states as well as the atmosphere of situations. On the other hand, moods also include background feelings of the body, such as feelings of lightness and freshness in elation, or of heaviness and weariness in depression. The phenomenology of moods is well expressed in the German notion of *Stimmung* which implies metaphors of attunement, concordance, and orchestration. Moods may be said to 'tune' body, self, and environment to a common chord, similar to a tonality linking a series of notes and chords to the major or minor key. Thus they tend to establish a consonance of bodily feeling, emotion, and environmental atmosphere.[3]

---

[3] Of course it may occur that one's mood is in contrast to the atmosphere one encounters in the environment, as when a sad person enters a cheerful party, but usually there is at least a tendency of mood and surrounding atmosphere to converge.

Moreover, moods link the background feeling of the body to the potentialities of a given life situation. 'The mood has already disclosed, in every case, Being-in-the-world as a whole, and makes it possible first of all to direct oneself towards something' (Heidegger, 1962, p. 176). Moods are thus both feelings of the body and ways of finding oneself in the world. They indicate 'how things stand' in our life and how we are disposed to react to the present situation. Such feelings do not only include typical moods such as elation, serenity, sadness, or melancholy, but also what Ratcliffe (2008a) has termed *existential feelings*: feelings of wideness or restriction, freedom or imprisonment, vulnerability or protection, familiarity or estrangement, reality or unreality, feeling alive or feeling dead. However, it seems important to note that all these background feelings are not just related to an anonymous world, but to the world that we share with others, or to the interpersonal world. They are *existential feelings of being-with*. It is primarily in our coexistence with others that we feel close or distant, familiar or alienated, open or restricted, and even real or unreal. Thus, interaffectivity is not merely a particular section or application of our emotional endowment. Rather, it is the encompassing sphere in which our emotional life is embedded from birth on. This sphere has its centre in the lived body: through its affectability and resonance it mediates our participation in a shared space of affective attunement.

To summarize: in contrast to the common cognitivist picture in which our mental states and emotions are located within our head, phenomenology regards feelings as residing in between individuals. Human beings do not have moods or emotions independent of their embodied relations and interactions with their fellow human beings. Emotions are ways of being in the world, emerging on the basis of a pre-reflective attunement with others, indicating the current state of our relations, interests, and conflicts, and manifesting themselves as attitudes and expressions of the body. This view appears to be quite common among cultural anthropologists as well: numerous ethnographic studies, particularly in the Pacific and Africa, have noted that emotions are a primary idiom for defining and negotiating relations of self-with-others in a moral order (see Lutz and White, 1986, and Lindholm, 2007, for an overview). In these studies, emotions emerge as socially shaped and regulated; they are less construed as inner states, as conceived by western psychology, but result from people's engagements with others. Similarly, in these cultures, the source of emotional disturbance, imbalance, or illness is assumed to lie primarily in the social world.

One might argue here that it is not possible to define emotions as well as affective disturbances *as such*, apart from their respective cultural background, thus maintaining that both psychology and psychopathology are culturally relative. If emotions, mood, or depression are then conceived as inner and rather cognitive states in western cultures, couldn't this be due to a different kind of experience in western individuals which has developed in this way over the past centuries? And shouldn't we regard depression as being a different illness in different regions of the world? Granted, the rise of dualism and individualism in western societies has also changed our subjective experience to a significant degree. The way we conceive of our emotions and of our body certainly influences our affective and bodily self-awareness, at least on the conscious level. On the other hand, conceptualization and language do not construct subjective experience *de novo* — rather, they emphasize and highlight certain of its aspects to the disadvantage of others. Thus, the embodied and extended nature of our pre-reflective emotional experience has not vanished completely in the course of western cultural history. It still lies hidden beneath our predominant self-concept which regards emotions as inner or mental states that we should be able to control as autonomous persons. Once we change our concepts, we could well retrieve these hidden layers of our own experience. Consequently, I argue that depression is not basically different in western and non-western cultures but that it should rather be conceived as a disorder of embodiment and interaffectivity in western societies as well — what we lack in our culture is just the non-dualistic vocabulary to adequately describe it. Phenomenology precisely offers a way to regain access to this pre-reflective dimension of experience, namely through methodically 'bracketing' our culture-bound and science-based assumptions about the nature and causes of affective experience (Fuchs, 2002c).

3. Depression as a Disorder of Intercorporeality and Interaffectivity

On the basis of the above considerations, I will now describe depression as a disorder of intercorporeality and interaffectivity. In short, the depressive state may be characterized by a general constriction or 'congealment' of the lived body, leading to a numbing of emotional resonance and loss of attunement. This alters the patient's existential feelings of being-with, resulting in a general sense of detachment, segregation, or even expulsion. In this way, the lived body also expresses the experiences of loss and separation which trigger depressive episodes on a psychosocial level.

a) Corporealization

In severe depression, the lived body loses the lightness, fluidity, and mobility of a medium and turns into a heavy, solid body which puts up resistance to all intentions and impulses directed towards the world. The depressive patient experiences a local or general oppression, anxiety, and constriction (e.g. a feeling of an armour or tyre around the chest, of a pressure in the head, etc.). The materiality, density, and weight of the body, otherwise suspended and unnoticed in everyday performance, now come to the fore and are felt painfully. In this respect, depression closely resembles somatic illnesses such as infections which affect one's overall bodily state. Corresponding reports from patients may well be elicited provided that the interviewer takes their bodily experience seriously; they will complain about feelings of fatigue, exhaustion, paralysis, aches, sickness, nausea, numbness, etc. (see Ratcliffe *et al.*, this volume). Moreover, in depression the exchange of body and environment is blocked, drive and impulse are exhausted. Sense perception and movement are weakened and finally walled in by the general rigidity which is also visible in the patient's gaze, face, or gestures. In order to act, the patients have to overcome their psychomotor inhibition and to push themselves to even minor tasks. With growing inhibition, sensorimotor space is restricted to the nearest environment, culminating in depressive stupor. In sum, depression may be described as a reification or *corporealization* of the lived body (Fuchs, 2005a).[4]

The constriction and encapsulation of the body corresponds to the psychosocial experiences that typically lead to depression. These are experiences of a disruption of relations and bonds, including the loss of relevant others or of important social roles, furthermore situations of a backlog in one's duties, falling short of one's aspirations, or social defeat (Tellenbach, 1980; Bjorkqvist, 2001). In terms of temporality, one may speak of a social desynchronization (Fuchs, 2001): the movement of life is blocked and the person is unable to keep pace with others. These situations of social separation or defeat are perceived as particularly threatening since the patients feel they do not have the

---

[4] This description refers to the most frequent type of severe depression which is characterized by psychomotor inhibition. There is another type with prevailing agitation and anxiety ('agitated depression') in which the patients experience the same constriction but the loss of drive is less marked, so that they try in vain to escape from their tormenting bodily state by aimless activity.

necessary resources for coping ('learned helplessness', Seligman, 1975). Depression is the consequent psychophysiological reaction: at the biological level, it involves a pattern of neurobiological, meta-bolic, immunological, biorhythmic, and other organismic dysfunc-tions which are equivalent to a partial decoupling or separation between organism and environment.[5] These dysfunctions are experi-enced as a loss of drive and interest (anhedonia), psychomotor inhibi-tion, bodily constriction, and depressive mood.

b) Intercorporeality and Interaffectivity

The bodily constriction results not only in felt oppression, anxiety, or heaviness, but more subtly in a loss of the inter-bodily resonance which mediates the empathic understanding in social encounters. The depressive body lacks expression and offers no clue for the other's empathic perception. The continuous synchronization of bodily ges-tures and gazes which normally accompanies interaction breaks down. The patients themselves realize this congealment of their expression; moreover, their own mimetic perception and resonance with the other's body is lacking (Persad and Polivy, 1993; Csukly *et al.*, 2009; Bourke, Douglas and Porter, 2010). Thus, they feel unable to emotionally communicate their experience and try in vain to com-pensate for the loss of resonance by stereotyped repetition of their complaints.

The loss of bodily resonance or affectability concerns, more gener-ally, the experience of affective valences and atmospheres. The deeper the depression, the more the attractive qualities of the environment faint. The patients are no longer capable of being moved and affected by things, situations, or other persons. This leads to an inability to feel emotions or atmospheres at all, which is all the more painful as it is not caused by mere apathy or indifference (as for example in frontal brain injury) but by the tormenting bodily constriction and rigidity. Kurt Schneider wrote that the 'vital disturbances' of bodily feelings in severe depression are so intense that psychic or 'higher' feelings can no longer arise (Schneider, 1920). The patients then complain of a 'feeling of not feeling' and of not being able to sympathize with their relatives any more. In his autobiographical account, Solomon describes his depression as '...a loss of feeling, a numbness, [which]

---

[5]   This comes about through a prolonged organismic stress reaction, affecting, above all, the CRH-ACTH-cortisol system, the sympathetic nervous system as well as the serotonin-transmitter regulation in the limbic system, and resulting in a desynchronization of diurnal hormone and sleep-wake cycles (Wehr and Goodwin, 1983; Glannon, 2002; Berger, Calker and Riemann, 2003).

had infected all my human relations. I didn't care about love; about my work; about family; about friends...' (Solomon, 2001, p. 45). Hence, the patients lose the participation in the shared space of affective attunement.

Of course, there are emotions that remain despite the loss of affectability, in particular feelings of guilt, anxiety, or despair. However, these emotions show some characteristic features: (1) they do not connect, but rather separate the subject from the world and from others; (2) their felt bodily quality is characterized by constriction and rigidity, thus corresponding to the depressive state of corporealization; (3) they are embedded in the prevailing depressed mood rather than arising as independent feelings; therefore their intentional objects are just as ubiquitous as arbitrary. A depressive patient describes what may be called an elementary, bodily experience of guilt:

> It comes from below, from the gut, like a terrible oppression rising to the chest; then a pressure arises, like a crime that I have committed. I feel it like a wound on my chest, that is my tortured conscience... then this attracts my memories, and I have to think again of all that I have missed or done wrong in my life... (Fuchs, 2000, pp. 116f)

This shows that an elementary feeling of being guilty can be rooted in bodily experience itself and only secondarily materializes in corresponding yet arbitrary memories of omissions or failures.[6] Similarly, the bodily state of diffuse, vital anxiety finds its concrete objects in all kinds of imagined disaster (financial ruin, lethal disease, etc.) which the patient anticipates as inevitable. The simultaneity of a loss of affectability and the presence of anxiety or guilt feelings, contradictory at first sight, can thus be explained by their mood-congruent, bodily character. In severe or psychotic stages of depression, such constricting emotions turn into continuous states of agony, and it may be doubted whether they could still be called emotions at all.

c) Derealization and Depersonalization

Since the affective contact to the environment is also essential for our basic sense of reality and belonging to the world, a loss of body resonance always results in a certain degree of derealization and depersonalization. Therefore affective depersonalization is a core feature of

---

[6] In general, memories are facilitated by the bodily and emotional state that corresponds to the condition in which they were acquired; *cf.* the research on state-dependent learning and mood-congruent memories (e.g. Bower, 1981; Blaney, 1986). This is particularly valid for depression (e.g. Barry, Naus and Rehm, 2004).

severe depressive episodes (Kraus, 2002; Stanghellini, 2004). However, there is a special kind of melancholic depression in which depersonalization is the prominent symptom; in German psychopathology it is called '*Entfremdungsdepression*' (depersonalized depression; Petrilowitsch, 1956). Here the emotional quality of perception is lost completely, objects look blunt or dead, and space seems hollowed out, as it were; in the words of a patient:

> There is only emptiness around me; it fills the space between me and my husband; instead of conducting it keeps me away. I am kept away from the whole world; there is an abyss in between. (von Gebsattel, 1954, p. 25)

The patient feels like an isolated object in a world without relationships; there is only an abstract space around her, not a lived, embodied space any more. Perception only shows the naked framework of objects, not their connectedness or their 'flesh'. The depersonalization in severe depression culminates in so-called nihilistic delusions or Cotard's syndrome, formerly called '*melancholia anaesthetica*' (Enoch and Trethowan, 1991). The patients no longer sense their own body; taste, smell, even the sense of warmth or pain are missing, everything seems dead. Having lost the background feeling of the body that conveys a sense of connectedness and realness to our experience, the patients may contend that the whole world is empty or does not exist any more. This lets them conclude that they have already died and ought to be buried.

> A 61-year old patient felt that her inner body, her stomach and bowels had been contracted so that there was no hollow space left. The whole body, she said, was dried out and decayed, nothing inside did move any more. The body felt numb, she sensed neither heat nor cold, meals had lost their taste. Finally she was convinced that all her relatives had died, that she was alone in the world and had to live in a dead body for ever. (Fuchs, 2000, p. 112)

The experience of derealization may in some cases lead to a combination of Cotard's with Capgras' syndrome (Enoch and Trethowan, 1991; Joseph, 1986; Wright, Young and Hellawell, 1993; Young, Leafhead and Szulecka, 1994): the patients are convinced that their relatives have been replaced by impostors or phantoms. This phenomenon points to the pre-reflective nature of interpersonal trust: the perception of another's appearance as familiar and natural depends on the basic inter-bodily resonance that mediates our affective attunement to others. It is part of our pre-predicative relation to the world and to others that we take the other's identity for granted provided there is sufficient similarity in his appearance. The complete loss of affective resonance, however, may let others appear as fakes or actors who are part of an illusionary theatre. The Dutch psychiatrist Piet Kuiper, who suffered from psychotic depression, reports this experience:

> Someone who resembled my wife was walking beside me, and my friends visited me… Everything was as it normally would be. The figure representing my wife constantly reminded me of what I had failed to do for her… But what looks like normal life is it not. I found myself on the other side. And now I realized what the cause of my death had been… I had died, but God had removed this event from my awareness… A harsher punishment can hardly be imagined. Without being aware of having died, you are in a hell that resembles in all details the world you had lived in, and thus God lets you see and feel that you have made nothing of your life. (Kuiper, 1991, p. 136)

What we can notice here is the inherent connection of interaffectivity, basic trust, and the sense of realness (Varga, 2012): the world is experienced as familiar and real as long as it is permeated by the affective resonance and the practical significances shared with others — in other words, as long as it remains the common life-world. Our bodily background feelings connect us to others and lend familiarity to the world. At the same time, this normally taken-for-granted connection constitutes the horizon of our world, which in Husserl's words is always an 'open horizon of co-subjects' (Husserl, 1973, p. 497). In this sense, our experience of the world means always already a *co-experience*. However, once the interaffective basis of co-experiencing the world is lost, as in Kuiper's case, the sense of reality dissolves and gives way to a virtualization of one's being-in-the-world. Cotard's and Capgras' syndrome — though the former usually occurs in affective disorders, the latter in paranoid disorders — share the loss of basic familiarity and therefore may sometimes shade into or accompany each other (Young, Leafhead and Szulecka, 1994).

d) Delusions of Guilt

With Cotard's syndrome, we have already entered the domain of psychotic depression. In the last section, I want to look at a more typical example of depressive delusions from an interaffective point of view, namely at delusions of guilt.

As I mentioned at the beginning, feelings and ideations of guilt are, from a transcultural perspective, rather special symptoms of depression occurring in western societies. Nevertheless, as we have seen, they also have their basis in bodily and interaffective experience. Under suitable cultural conditions, primary or existential feelings of guilt may emerge from the pervasive state of bodily constriction and separation from others. For the basic experience of guilt may also be described as the fear or state of being rejected, ostracized, or expelled from the community. The various forms of sanctions which foster the development of conscience in early childhood imply, as a rule, a withdrawal of affection, a rejection or punishment. These experiences of being separated from others and thrown back upon oneself are felt as a painful bodily constriction and anxiety. They may even be related to a primeval, instinctive *fear of segregation* that was experienced when a member of a tribe got lost or was expelled from the group (Bilz, 1971, p. 356).

As we have already seen above, the depressed patient's bodily constriction, vital anxiety, and loss of interaffective attunement are particularly suited to reactivate these primary feelings of guilt.[7] This holds true even more for the 'Typus Melancholicus', the personality that is particularly prone to fall ill from depression in western society (Tellenbach, 1980; Mundt *et al.*, 1997; Kronmüller *et al.*, 2002). This personality type is characterized by excessive conscientiousness, orderliness, hypernomic adherence to social norms, and dependency on stable interpersonal relationships. For these patients, the affective ties to others are essential, even vital, and becoming guilty means to be excluded from the indispensable community with others. In depression, the patients experience bodily constriction as an elementary separation and rejection which activates an archaic, punishing, and annihilating conscience (Fuchs, 2002b).

The crucial presupposition for depressive delusions, however, concerns the intersubjective constitution of reality. Precisely, the social reality of guilt does not mean a fixed state or quantity but is negotiated through a shared process of attribution and justification which defines the omissions or faults as well as their degree of severity. Similarly, dealing with guilt (through responsibility, regret, compensation, forgiveness, rehabilitation, etc.) involves an intersubjective agreement and mutual alignment of perspectives. This in turn requires a deeper fundament which is generated by our pre-reflective affective connectedness with others, in particular by a basic sense of *mutual trust*. The depressive patient, however, loses this pre-reflective connection and becomes locked in his bodily constriction and corporealization. Thus, he is literally deprived of the free scope that is necessary for taking

---

[7]   This is in line with recent research on the embodiment of emotions, showing that bodily postures, expressions, sensations, and interoceptive states influence one's emotional state in various ways, 'bottom-up', so to speak (Damasio, 1999; Niedenthal, 2007; Craig, 2008).

another's perspective and relativizing his own point of view. Others are separated by an abyss and can no longer be reached. Guilt, instead of being an intersubjective *relation* that can be dealt with, becomes *a thing* or *an object* the patient is identified with, as shown by the following case example:

> Soon after his retirement, a 64 year-old patient fell ill with a severe depression. Coming from a poor background, he had achieved to become staff executive of a big company by hard work. He reported that he had only been on sick leave for 10 days in 45 years of work. In contrast, his depression was characterised by a feeling of decay. All his power had vanished, the patient complained, he had no longer command of his arms and legs. He had burnt the candle at both ends, had not taken care of his family, and now he deserved to get his comeuppance. He accused himself of being responsible for the failure of an important deal of his company two years ago which would inevitably lead to its bankruptcy. He would never be able to cancel this debt again. Moreover, he complained that he had no more feelings for others. 'I am only a burden for them, a millstone around my family's neck… for me, life is over.' He finally thought that the death sweat already appeared on his forehead, one could even see the cadaveric lividity on his face. He should be driven in the mortuary in the basement and be abandoned there. (Case example from my own clinical work, T.F.)

The capacity of taking the perspective of others is not only a cognitive feat but depends on a common interaffective sphere that is part of the 'bedrock of unquestioned certainties' (Wittgenstein, 1969; Rhodes and Gipps, 2008). It provides a foundational, non-representational structure of mutual understanding that underpins our shared view of reality. In delusional depression, however, the loss of the pre-predicative relation to others makes it impossible to take their perspective and to gain distance from oneself, thus forcing the patient *to completely equate his self with his current depressed state*. This present state means being thrown back upon oneself, feeling rejected and expelled. The delusional patient, as shown in the case example, is identified with his existential feeling of guilt to the extent that he is *guilty as such*. There is no remorse, recompense, or forgiveness, for the guilt is not embedded in a common sphere which would allow for that. Delusions of guilt result from a disruption of intersubjective relations at the basic level of interaffectivity.

This is characteristic of depressive delusion in general: corporealization and loss of attunement to others prevent the patient from taking their perspective. As a result, a state of self beyond the present one becomes unimaginable. It has always been like this, and it will stay like this forever — to remember or hope for anything different is deception. The patient is inevitably identified with his present state of bodily constriction and decay, with his state of feeling guilty as such, or, in nihilistic delusion, with his state of feeling dead. Hypochondriacal or nihilistic delusions, delusions of guilt or impoverishment are all just different manifestations of a complete objectivation or reification of the self that can no longer be transcended. Depressive delusion is therefore rooted in the loss of the shared interaffective space and in the utter isolation of the self that results from it.

4. Conclusion

Depression is not an 'inner', psychological, or mental disorder, but a 'detunement' of the lived body that normally mediates our participation in a shared space of attunement. The corporealized, constricted body loses its affectability and emotional resonance; this undermines the patient's existential feelings of being-with, resulting in a general sense of detachment, separation, or even expulsion. The typical cognitive symptoms of depression are only a result of this basic bodily alteration.

The constriction and encapsulation of the lived body also corresponds to the typical triggering situations of depression. These are mostly experiences of a disruption of relations and bonds: a loss of relevant others or of important social roles, experiences of backlog or defeat, resulting in a desynchronization from others and in a blocked movement of life. To these situations of threatening or actual separation, the depressive patient reacts as a psychophysiological unity. For without doubt, depression is a bodily illness also in the biological sense, implying functional disturbances on different levels and a partial decoupling of organism and environment. But at the same time, the biological dysfunctions which result in the felt bodily constriction are just the meaningful expression of a disorder of intercorporeality and interaffectivity on the psychosocial level. Our participation in interaffective space is mediated by a fundamental bodily resonance. In depression, this attunement fails, and the lived body, as it were, shrinks to the boundaries of the material body.

In concluding, we may ask why psychopathology has traditionally disregarded this bodily and intersubjective basis of depression and focused on individual psychological symptoms instead. After all, a careful interview will find those complaints in most cases, and in primary care systems reporting somatic symptoms is even the predominant mode of presenting a depression (Kapfhammer, 2006). The main reason for this neglect might be seen in the fact that psychiatry still has no concept of the lived body, nor of the organic unity of the embodied person. The traditional dualism of mind and body has only been replaced by a reductionist monism which now regards the brain as the true heir of the soul — again disregarding the living unity of the organism (Fuchs, 2011). No matter whether depression is attributed to the soul or to the brain — in both cases it is disconnected from the body and put into an inner container. As a result, the embodied experience of patients is at best regarded as a secondary 'somatization'.

In contrast to this, intercorporeality and interaffectivity are the crucial dimensions of an ecological, non-reductionist view of depression. Hence, if we still want to call it an affective disorder, we should not understand this term as an intra-individual state, localizable within the psyche or the brain, but as a detunement (*Verstimmung*) in the literal sense — a failure of bodily attunement to the shared space of interaffectivity.

Acknowledgments

This work was supported by the Marie-Curie Initial Training Network 'TESIS: Towards an Embodied Science of InterSubjectivity' (FP7-PEOPLE-2010-ITN, 264828). I also would like to thank two anonymous reviewers for their valuable comments on an earlier version of the chapter.

Thomas J. Csordas

Inferring Immediacy in Adolescent Accounts of Depression

In this chapter I address the experience of depression among adolescent psychiatric inpatients who participated in an ethnographic study in the American Southwest. My discussion is directed at the question of how our account can become a phenomenology of depression, that is, an account at a certain level of analysis that is not better described as clinical, symptomatic, diagnostic, therapeutic, epidemiological, pharmacological, psychodynamic, socioeconomic, etc. I want to assert that the principle descriptor of this level of analysis is experiential immediacy based on intersubjectivity (Csordas, 2008; in press; Duranti, 2010; Kirmayer, 2008), where immediacy is understood as direct contact with a phenomenon, and a phenomenon (such as depression) is an appearance in reality. For our purposes, immediacy includes not only the sense in which experience is unmediated or direct, but also the sense of temporality either in the narrative present (reported immediacy) or the actual present.

In so far as it undergirds any possibility of inferring experiential immediacy, intersubjectivity (in general but especially with respect to the case of a condition like depression) does not allow us to answer the question 'What is it like to be someone else?', but instead allows us to ask the question 'What is it like for someone else to be?' (*cf.* Linger, 2010). The first question implies that what we want to know is what it would be like *for me* to be another person; the second is about what it is like for that person to be him or herself. This has to be an inferential process because it is based on empathy and intuitive listening rather than our identity with that person; intersubjectivity is not shared subjectivity but, as Merleau-Ponty observed, the recognition that an interlocutor is 'another myself'. It is also inferential both because a person is unlikely to be able to respond to a direct question about what it is like to be him or her, and because such an answer in any case would already be in the register of reflexivity and not immediacy.

This approach to immediacy presupposes a theory of language. At least in anthropology, it is often taken for granted that language is a public medium that shapes, constructs, or distorts experience, which remains private and even inchoate; we only ever have access to language and never really to experience or the subjectivity that underlies it. In the Saussurian idiom, this standpoint privileges the abstract and systematic character of language (*langue*) over the interactive and intersubjective character of speech (*parole*), such that language is primarily a code to be deciphered. In the Whorfian idiom of linguistic relativity, it adopts an over-literal understanding of the insight that each language creates a distinctive reality for its community of speakers, rendering language not only a framework for experience but also a kind of cage for it. I prefer a warmer theory of language, one closer to the assertion by Heidegger in his 'Letter on Humanism' (e.g. 1977) that 'language is the house of being'. If this is taken explicitly to refer to the relation between language and thought, we can revise it to 'language is the city of being' to refer to the relation between language and intersubjectivity. Language can, again in Heidegger's terms, 'disclose' rather than mask or determine elements of experience if it is understood not in abstract, mentalistic terms but as a kind of bodily secretion imbued with intersubjectivity. It is in this sense that language is the form of, now borrowing a phrase from Merleau-Ponty, our 'sonorous being'. The intersubjective immediacy of language in this sense is one condition of possibility for inferring subjective immediacy in an interlocutor.

To be more precise, this approach to language and intersubjectivity allows for a kind of empathy understood as intuitive listening conducive to the task of inferring immediacy. Recognizing the value of this task is in accord with a tendency within anthropology and philosophy to conceive empathy not only as a cognitive or imaginative capacity but also as a form of practice in the life-world. Recent anthropological work by Hollan and Throop understands empathy as 'approximating the subjective experience of another form a quasi-first-person perspective' and 'a first-person-like perspective on another that involves an emotional, embodied, or experiential aspect' (Hollan and Throop, 2008, pp. 387, 391) that takes into account not only the capabilities of the empathizer but 'the imaginative and emotional capabilities of the person to be understood as well' (Hollan, 2008, p. 475). From a philosophical standpoint, Ratcliffe (2012b) moves beyond mundane empathy that presupposes a shared or mostly shared world to a radical empathy that recognizes a variable sense of belonging to a shared world, and is predicated on adopting a phenomenological stance that conceives reality as constituted by a structured and transformable horizon of possibilities. In both the anthropological and philosophical approaches, experience can be encountered in behaviour or through language, potentially allowing for elaboration of differences among perceptual, narrative, or dialogical empathy. I will propose a method to engage the latter, dialogical empathy, in inferring immediacy from interviews with depressed adolescents.

1. The SWYEPT Study

We are concerned here with the experience of adolescents aged 12–18 who have been admitted as inpatients at a university psychiatric hospital for children in New Mexico and who participated in the project Southwest Youth and the Experience of Psychiatric Treatment (SWYEPT). The Children's Psychiatric Hospital of the University of New Mexico was founded in 1978 with an orthopsychiatry orientation and the availability of multiple forms of treatment intervention, with a psychoanalyst as medical director. In the intervening three decades the treatment programme has evolved in a direction typical of many psychiatric institutions. There has been a movement away from psychoanalytic and insight-oriented therapies toward cognitive behavioural approaches and more recently dialectical behavioural therapy. The average stay for patients has declined from one year to thirty days for residential patients.

Young people were usually brought to the hospital by their families, though not infrequently the police were involved. Patients and their families entered the SWYEPT project upon consultation with hospital staff to determine whether their clinical conditions were stable enough to participate. Although our first encounters were in the hospital and although we were interested in their experience of treatment, ours was not strictly speaking a clinical ethnography of this hospital. In other words, we did not focus on the hospital's clinical culture, the development and implementation of the treatment programme, or the interaction among staff, between staff and patients, or among patients themselves. Our work transcended the clinical setting, following the patients into their families and sometimes into other institutional settings, and following them over time with interviews at approximately six months and again at one year after their discharge. Furthermore, although we were interested in culture in the form of ethnic differences among patients — Native American, Hispanic or Latino, and Euro-American or white — ethnic differences were relatively inconsequential beside issues of family disorganization, poverty, and social marginality. This is hardly to say that culture is not a factor, for the patterns of interaction, narrative, expectation, complaint, and interpretation we are discovering in the lives of these families are profoundly cultural and indeed speak volumes about culture.

Of the 47 adolescents in the study, there are 25 boys and 22 girls, roughly equally distributed among Hispanic, Euro-American, and Native Americans, along with a considerable number claiming mixed ethnicity to include African Americans and Southeast Asians. A majority of the children had been hospitalized prior to this admission. We are finding a pervasiveness of chaotic family environments across ethnicities and communities involving drug use, violence, gang activity, neglect, sexual abuse, and family and residential instability, though such factors are by no means always present and exhibit a variety of relations to depression (Jenkins, in press). The category of 'psychiatric disorder' is inadequate to the task of describing 'life experience' in our population of patients in treatment. This is not because of a predetermined anthropological mistrust of psychiatric diagnostic categories as cultural artefacts and repositories of ethnocentrism and ethnopsychology. On the one hand, psychiatric categories are relevant in so far as for professionals and families alike they are deployed as rhetorical weapons, metaphorical containers, emotional relief, opportunities for blame, epithets to throw, therapeutic tools, points of reference. On the other hand, as descriptors of the existential realities of people's lives, the nature of their affliction, and the problems they are struggling with, they are invariably imprecise and two-dimensional.

2. Depression among Adolescents

Using the version of the Structured Clinical Interview for DSM adapted for children (KID-SCID), we determined that 28 of our 47 participating adolescents were afflicted with either major depression or dysthymia. Of those 28, only 4 had no other co-morbid diagnosis. In preparing this article I found myself faced with the choice of focusing on those four, as it were, 'pure cases', or making a more general analytic pass through the material for our depressed youth. When I began looking at interviews, however, I found that the first of these patients and his family, based on their experience with the mental health care system, were endorsing depression, anxiety not otherwise specified, alcohol-related neurobiological spectrum disorder, Asperger's syndrome, and attention deficit hyperactivity disorder. The next patient endorsed seven diagnoses including depression, anxiety, premenstrual dysphoric disorder, oppositional defiant disorder, bipolar II, and 'I don't know the rest' — so much for diagnostic tidiness.

I then went entirely in the opposite direction and decided, across all the depressed participants, to examine all the instances in which they discussed depression *per se*. In this light I began by culling our interview material for passages that included the words depression, depressed, and depressing as used by interviewers and participants, including both patients and parents, and examining both diagnostic interviews (the aforementioned KID-SCID designed to determine the presence of psychiatric disorder) and ethnographic interviews (using open-ended, conversational style questions to elicit discourse on life and illness experience).

Our first observation addresses the question of the relative salience of the term depression to patients in relation to whether its occurrence can be considered an artefact of the interview process. That is, when we literally counted occurrences of these words across interviews for ten of our participants, we found the following. Comparing the formal psychiatric diagnostic interview (KID-SCID) with the open-ended ethnographic interview, we found that in half of the cases patients used depression words more often in the ethnographic than the psychiatric interviews, and in one case the word depression appeared with the same frequency in each. Across all the interviews, in six of ten cases the interviewer used depression words more often than the patient, but in four the patient used the terms more often. Finally, in nine of ten cases over all the interviews patients used depression words more frequently than did their guardian. This is admittedly a rather weak fact, but it allows us to suggest that adolescent patients did not have depression words 'put in their mouths', simply responding to an interview format or to the suggestion of interviewer or parent.

Given this observation, it is clear that depression is sometimes discussed as a diagnosis and sometimes as a feeling or experience, and sometimes as what we might call a discursive token. As a diagnostic term, depression names an illness or disorder understood as either psychological, biological, or a combination of both, and designated as an object or target of treatment. As an experiential term, depression is most likely to appear in association with anger and with behaviours such as sexual acting out, violence, and drug use. Parents tend more to describe behaviours that verify the diagnosis or from which they infer a psychic state, while youth tend to describe feelings of depression and the consequences of those feelings for behaviour, relationships, or hospitalization and treatment. As a discursive token, depression is part of a discursive regime in which patient, family members, and mental health professionals participate and that includes medications and treatments as well as other diagnoses that add to or compete with one another in the characterization of the patient and his or her illness and also in the negotiation of everyday life for the patient and family members.

A host of issues relevant to inferring immediacy present themselves in just a first pass through this material. Without assigning order or priority, we can note first the use of images and metaphors, as in the youth who refers to the experience of 'slipping' into a depressive state, the sense that certain events may 'trigger' an onset, the description of an episode of behavioural deterioration and loss of control as a 'blow-up' or a 'meltdown', invoking the sense of depression as 'being stuck in this dark place', or seeing the issues of self-esteem, depression, and sexually acting out as 'connected in a circle'. Narrativity may be either fragmented or coherent and is expressed in a number of ways, with respect to specific events involving problematic behaviours, conflicts, or traumas, with respect to a trajectory through different diagnoses, illness, and treatment episodes, and getting better or worse overall. Intersubjectivity can be inferred along an axis of emotional attachment to isolation, and takes on a specific and immediate character in interviews where parent and child want to be interviewed together rather than separately. Levels of arousal are discernible both in events recounted and the tone of voice in the interview itself.

The intersection of temporality and causality is worth explicit mention. The first level of distinction is between children who indicate that in their recollection they have always been depressed and those who can identify a precipitating incident such as a trauma, family conflict, death of a family member, or post-partum depression. Once the depressive condition is recognized, there is the additional distinction between experiencing it as an ongoing state or dividing it into episodes, and furthermore each episode may be understood as occurring spontaneously or having a specific trigger. Finally, there is reversibility of the causal vector such that one can say that because of being depressed he or she did not engage in social activities or that because one did not engage in social activities he or she became depressed.

Likewise, one can say that he or she was hospitalized because of depression or depressed because of being hospitalized. Again, one can say that because one was depressed he or she engaged in negative behaviour or that one's negative behaviour caused depression. Either of these formulations can be reciprocal and engaged in a way leading to a vicious cycle that exacerbates depression, or can be recognized as reversible in a way that stimulates motivation to overcome depression. In the case of negative behaviour, an additional factor is whether the young person construes it as either morally bad or undermining of self-esteem. Most notably these behaviours include self-cutting or other self-harm, violence against others, drug or alcohol abuse, excessive sexual activity, sexually molesting a younger child, arson, or vandalism. Such behaviours in themselves may or may not have a negative moral valence: self-cutting can be judged as an emotional relief rather than as morally bad; arson can be described legalistically as a felony rather than morally as bad.

As in the case of adults, it is not uncommon for these adolescents to mention anxiety in conjunction with repression. However, it is striking that even more salient is the close association of depression with anger. Anger is both a common aspect of emotional experience in adolescent depression and closely related both to the experience of violence and the enactment of violence. That is, one can report the experience of becoming depressed by being exposed to violence or of becoming violent as a consequence of being depressed. That being said, however, among participants in our study anger appeared just as commonly among those without a research diagnosis of depression, so though we can say that this emotion is cited by 57% of our participants, we can at this point only say that it is a significant theme among psychiatric inpatients in general; if it has a quality inflected by depression in a way that is distinguishable for that group of patients, our analysis has not yet reached the point of being able to identify it.

3. Rules of Inference

Given our opening discussion of language and empathy as conditions of possibility for an intuitive listening that allows for the intersubjective inference of immediacy, our analysis cannot be devoid of method. Based on a preliminary examination of our interview data guided by contemporary work in phenomenological anthropology (Jackson, 1996; Katz and Csordas, 2003; Csordas, in press), I deduced four methodological rules of inference to guide the following reading of experiential immediacy in how SWYEPT participants talked about depression:

1) Observe word choice, which can reveal both contextual features of the social situation and nuances of interpersonal relationships.
2) Anticipate surprises, which can reveal presuppositions and taken-for-granted ideas different from those of the interlocutor/interviewer.
3) Attend to affect, expressed both in narrative and by tone of voice, which informs about intensity of distress and style of engagement.
4) Respect reflexivity, the expression of which indicates complexity of experience and the content of which is a motivationally consequential interpretation.

Several abbreviated examples of how these rules can be applied will clarify.

One young person said, 'I just get in these moods where I don't want to move. I hate that'. Here the reference is not to a capacity but to a mood, not to an inability but to a lack of motivation, and not to accomplishment of any task but to any physical movement at all. The affective tone is unambiguous, and in vivid contrast to what one might conclude is lethargy, hate connotes an active and energetic resistance to incapacitation.

Another young person commented that, 'Eh, the medication controls me (laughs) like depression-wise'. What we can infer from the choice to say that it controls me rather than it controls my depression, and from the reflexive laughter in response to this phrase, is a self-aware ambivalence about the notion of control. There is an overtone of embarrassment about needing to be controlled, an acknowledgment of the medication's beneficial efficacy, and an element of resignation at having surrendered some autonomy to the medication.

Again, we heard 'I felt like I had to be perfect and if I wasn't, I was the devil or something'. Here depression is related to the pressure of behavioural standards imposed by parents, but sufficiently internalized to be experienced as oppressive. In this instance we can infer such a sense of condemnatory oppressiveness from the use of the word 'devil', which at the least bears negative implications for self-esteem and at the most insinuates the literal presence of demonic evil.

A statement during a follow-up interview in response to a question about how a young person's situation had changed since our last encounter was that the problem was 'Just anger, basically. I'm not depressed anymore. I'm pretty happy, actually'. Here there is a clear sense expressed that there has been improvement, with depressed or sad feeling having given way to happiness, but with the addition of 'actually' suggesting that this might be an awareness occurring as an insight in the moment of the interview itself. At the same time there is from the observer's standpoint an apparent incongruity in the persistence of anger as an underlying emotional state independent of depression, particularly since in the clinical view anger and depression can be intertwined.

Finally, consider the comment from another participant that 'I kinda realized that I don't really have a good distinction between depression and anger'. Here is an example of reflexivity in which depression is clearly again understood as an emotion rather than a disorder, and in relation to anger as a distinct emotion. The implication is both that the two are distinct and that they should be distinguished, with a subtext that failure to distinguish them also complicates being able to distinguish between normal occurrences and pathological exaggerations of either.

4. Describing Depression

In what follows I shall present more extended excerpts from interviews in which somewhat more elaborated and contextualized inference can be made about experiential immediacy. The first is from a boy of mixed Hispanic and Anglo parentage who was fifteen years old when he entered the SWYEPT project. He lived with two younger brothers, two younger sisters, and two fathers: his mother had undergone gender reassignment surgery and his parents were living as a gay male couple. The domestic environment is turbulent, and this boy has violent tendencies himself — he had been hospitalized because of a violent episode at school in which he beat up another student and threw bricks through the school bus window, as well as threatening to kill himself. His demeanour as we observed it was particularly intense and on-edge, and he looks older than his age, very tall with a fair amount of facial hair. All three of our research team members who met him reported that he became either agitated or depressed during their interview. Here is an excerpt from one of those occasions, our second ethnographic interview:

> Interviewer: Um, and so you mentioned that you were mostly dealing right now with anger and depression?
> Participant: Yes.

I: And how are you dealing with those?

P: Like, how well?

I: Well, like, what types of things are you doing, and how well.

P: I'm using coping skills such as, like, deep breathing, (Mmhmm.) um, arts and crafts cause, um, I love art (Mmhmm.) and, um, reading. (Mmhmm.) And writing. Those are the things that I use.

I: OK.

P: And when it gets really bad I punch walls or punch out windows.

The young man's tone of voice was quite matter-of-fact in this exchange, evident both in his crisp question to clarify whether the interviewer's 'how well' was meant in an evaluative or enumerative sense, and in his specification of four 'coping skills'. Education in a repertoire of coping skills, and not only for 'anger management', is a large part of the kind of therapy adolescents with whom we worked receive in both inpatient and outpatient settings. There is a discourse of coping skills just as there is a discourse of diagnostic categories and types of medication. Each of the three constitutes an idiom applied by patients and their families to understanding and negotiating their experience. In this instance his expressive mastery of the idiom implies mastery of the behavioural repertoire of skills, in contrast with others who acknowledge exposure to coping skills but not necessarily to using them. Thus he produces a striking incongruity when he adds to the list precisely the kind of action coping skills are intended to forestall, including punching walls and windows as just one among the ways he copes with anger. His personal construction of the category of coping skills cannot but influence his experience in the immediacy of an angry moment. This is likely the case even if he were to acknowledge that punching walls is not the best among these skills, and even if his remark was intended partially tongue-in-cheek for performative effect or to recognize that in fact the coping skills are not always successful.

Here is another excerpt featuring the same participant, this time from his psychiatric diagnostic interview:

P: I can snap out of bad moods pretty quick. (OK.) Depression, I can snap out of pretty fast. I just need to think about something else (Mmhmm.) or, um, just get out and do something. (OK.) When I was depressed for that long I wasn't doing anything. (OK.) And that was before I knew what I had to do to stop it. (OK.) I was doing what I, what my depression was urging me to do not what I thought would be best.

I: Mmhmm. During the times when you're feeling kind of irritable and you're yelling, feeling like you're yelling at people, do you, how do you feel about yourself?

P: (yawns) Ashamed and disappointed.

Our participant invokes a classic presumption of North American ethnopsychology, namely that one can and should be able to 'snap out of' a depressed mood. He clearly distinguishes his current ability to do so from an earlier period of severe depression. During that period he 'wasn't doing anything', prevented by depression from doing what he was still able in thought to recognize as the best course of action, and hence reduced to inertia. Note that despite the apparent personification of depression in so far as it was 'urging' him not to act, there is no sense that he was being urged by inner voices as in psychotic hallucination; in this context the concept of depression participates in a discourse of diagnoses and of moods/emotions, but not in a discourse of voices or spirits. It is also of note that, although he specifies two techniques he uses to snap out of bad moods, these are different from the coping skills for dealing with anger he enumerated in the previous excerpt. Indeed, he not only avoids evoking the language of coping, but chooses to say what it was like 'before I knew' rather than 'before I learned' how to stop it and snap out of it. This indicates a subtle phenomenological difference between the linked emotions of anger and depression beyond the aggressively active nature of anger and the incapacitatingly passive nature of depression. Finally, the yawn that accompanies his acknowledgment of shame and disappointment as evaluative emotions renders their mention so matter-of-fact as to suggest that they are secondary, derivative, and unremarkable in comparison to anger and depression, though it is also possible that the yawn's occurrence could on the one hand be entirely coincidental, or on the other hand that it could itself be a sign of embarrassment.

The second participant I will discuss is a Hispanic female who was seventeen years old when she joined the study. At the beginning of her participation she lived with her mother and infant son, and suffered from post-partum depression; by the time of her follow-up interview she lived with a boyfriend who was not her child's father. The youngest of three daughters of a single mother with multiple boyfriends and alcoholism, her childhood had been quite unstable. She had 'grown up fast', observing sexual activity from the age of four and caring for her alcoholic mother, with whom she has a close but volatile relationship. She was sexually molested herself at age eleven by one of her mother's boyfriends, and again as a young teenager by someone that she had 'trusted, he took advantage of me'. She had experienced traumatic abandonment at age fifteen, having believed that her adoptive father was her biological father and being informed by him that he wasn't and would not be available to her financially or emotionally; he remarried. She began cutting herself 'to take the pain away'.

Her depression was precipitated by the end of her relationship with the baby's father just before her delivery hospitalization, though he remained involved with his son afterwards.

The following account is from her final ethnographic interview, reflecting back on the post-partum depression that led to hospitalization:

> Well, it all started, like, probably about early July, I would say, I started feeling that like, it's, I guess um, how can I explain it, like I feel like I can't breathe, like it's the anxiety, like I started to feel like that I wasn't really optimistic about anything. I was just really down, and I knew that I was going bad, and then all of a sudden I started having, like, these crazy thoughts, like, different ways of how I would kill myself, or um, thoughts of me hurting my son. It just, it just, like, all happened at once. And when it happened, I just, like, I, I, I think I looked like I was half dead when they, when they, um, took me to the emergency room 'cause I just looked like crap really. I didn't — I couldn't function, like I didn't, I didn't want to be around my son. Um, all I would do is cry. And I even tried to jump out the car. I, I just, a lot happened, and that's when I knew that I just had to go, I had to get help, even though, you know, it risked a lot with [my son].

This passage describes the onset of a depressive episode in particularly vivid detail. It opens with a tight constellation of physical sensation (breathing), emotion (anxiety), and attitude (lack of optimism), mood (being down), and clear anticipation (she *knew* she was 'going bad'). One can thus infer that although crazy thoughts about suicide or harming her son then began, 'all of a sudden' and 'all at once', they did not appear 'out of nowhere' but marked the transition into a full-scale crisis. A different constellation characterizes this crisis, including deterioration in physical appearance (looking 'like crap'), incapacitation (couldn't function), withdrawal (from her son), emotional expression (incessant crying), suicidal behaviour (attempt to jump out of the car). Her recognition of crossing this threshold is clear once again in that she *knew* she needed help despite the risk of having her son taken away. Intense ambivalence surrounding her two-month-old infant coloured the incident, and she interpreted feeling stimulated sexually when she was breast-feeding as abnormal and inappropriate so had to 'quit that cold turkey'. Her depression worsened along with preoccupation and rumination over whether she might hurt her son, until in a panic she asked her mother for help and was taken to the emergency room and hospitalized.

This participant was among those who expressed a positive attitude to antidepressant medication, though she has not consistently adhered to taking them:

> They said that, if I did, stop my medications again like I did last time, then I'm, it, it, the, the, that all that stuff would probably most likely come back. And I believe that it will too especially since things are so stressful right now, and, I mean, I know when I'm starting to feel depressed, and I can feel it. So now, like, so now that I know I can just, you know, call my therapist and be like, 'I'm starting to feel those feelings again'. I can just, like, nip it in the bud right there before it gets worse. Where it got that worse because I just, I just let it kept, keep getting worse and worse.

Evident here is an attunement to the effect of medication in suppressing symptoms and stress in provoking them. That her illness remains unresolved and that it can re-emerge can be inferred from her sensitivity to 'feeling those feelings', the double use of feel indicating a reflexive awareness of their onset. In the same vein, the sense that her condition is a persistent one rather than one that is resolved is evident in her comment not that the depression could occur again 'because' she was under stress but could 'come back... especially since' she was under stress. Note in comparison with the previous participant that she does not invoke 'coping skills', but instead refers to an ongoing therapeutic relationship; this may reflect gendered difference in behavioural style, personality difference, availability of resources, or type of depressive experience. It is not accidental that the colloquialism deployed by the young man was to 'snap out of it' while this young woman's goal was to 'nip it in the bud'. While his experience took the form primarily of depressed moods and angry episodes, her experience was with prolonged episodes of incapacitating ruminative depression.

5. Conclusion

Based on these brief considerations, it is evident that a considerable amount of information about experiential immediacy in depression can be inferred from a close reading of how people — even adolescents whose expressivity as a group is often regarded as undeveloped at best and sullenly reserved at worst — talk about their illness. From a methodological standpoint this approach departs from the intersection of a phenomenology of language and a phenomenology of illness. Even given the constraints of the interview format, attention to spontaneous word choice, unexpected articulations, emotional quality/intensity, and reflexivity disclose something of the concrete immediacy of affliction; and even presupposing that some participants have developed a standardized way of telling their story, one can discern rhetorical motifs implicating immediate illness experience as expressed in narrative form. In so far as this level of meaning defines the life-world of patients, it cannot but have clinical significance, at least with respect to rapport between patient and clinician and at best with respect to strategies for management and treatment of the illness.

Much more can be done with such material than I have managed to do in this brief essay. Fully developed case studies could take fuller account of the interaction between developmental, biographical, and pathological features of the experience of the young people who participated in the SWYEPT project. Such case studies would not only allow greater elaboration of nuance in description of the immediate experience of depressive symptoms, but could also include how that experience is bound up with other domains of the life-world such as relationships, religion, morality, reflexivity, identity, and treatment. Comparison across case studies would likely result in a typology of personal and idiosyncratic expressive modes refracted by gender, class, and ethnicity, as well as styles of engagement with clinically derived discourses of coping, medication, and diagnosis. It would also allow us to specify experiential modulations across different variants and degrees of severity of depressive experience, and across instances of co-occurring diagnosis such as anxiety, post-traumatic stress, and substance abuse disorders. Finally, comparable material from parents and caregivers is needed to flesh out the context of familial life-worlds and the co-production of domestic milieus that are hostile and undermining or supportive and nurturing. Such analyses will be forthcoming as our analysis of SWYEPT data progresses.

Aknowledgments

Research for this chapter was supported by National Institute for Mental Health Research Grant 1 RO1 MH071781, Thomas J. Csordas and Janis H. Jenkins Co-PIs. We are grateful to Dr. David Mullen and the staff of the Children's Psychiatric Hospital of the University of New Mexico Medical School, and all the participants in the SWYEPT project who took the time to speak with us on several occasions about their experience. Special thanks are due to members of our research team including Bridget Haas, Whitney Duncan, Heather Spector Hallman, Allen Tran, Jessica Novak, Nofit Itzhak, Celeste Padilla, Ricki Bettencourt, Michael Storck, Elisa Dimas, and Mary Bancroft.

Philip Gerrans and Klaus Scherer

Wired for Despair

The Neurochemistry of Emotion and the Phenomenology of Depression

1. Introduction

Persistent and pervasive feelings of estrangement, depersonalization, emptiness, grandiosity, or desolation are not in themselves emotional experiences. Rather they condition the space of emotional possibilities. Someone who feels the world to be a desolate or dangerous place, for example, becomes liable to experience episodes of sadness or fear.

Such pervasive feelings are often described as moods and contrasted with emotional feelings that arise as part of an emotional episode with a specific object and discrete duration. This contrast, however, does not quite capture the way pervasive feeling states influence the experience of emotion. Such states darken or lighten the emotional landscape, affecting the ability of emotional feelings to colour features of that landscape. Only when the nature of these pervasive feelings changes radically, as in depression, anxiety, or other psychiatric disorders, does their fundamental importance become apparent. Even then, however, because moods, unlike emotions, do not have specific objects and are produced by tacit cognitive processes and experienced bodily, their meaning is not readily available to introspection or reflection. Matthew Ratcliffe has introduced the concept of 'existential feelings' to capture some of the elusive properties of these persistent and pervasive phenomenal states (Ratcliffe, 2005; 2008a; 2009a,b).

Ratcliffe describes existential feelings as 'pre-intentional' rather than intentional to capture the way they preconfigure the range of emotional experiences for a subject. Ratcliffe also suggests that a simple distinction between bodily experiences and experiences of the world cannot do justice to the phenomenology of existential feelings.

This extends a point familiar to theorists of emotion to the case of existential feelings: emotional feelings are bodily feelings, but they also represent the significance of the objects of emotion for us. Similarly, pre-intentional feelings are bodily feelings that also carry information, not about specific objects, but about our mode of emotional orientation to the world. As Ratcliffe (2010d) puts it, 'something can be both a bodily feeling and, at the same time, an experience of worldly possibilities'. We might say that existential feelings signal the way the emotional world is preconfigured.

Emotions are not moods, and emotional feelings are not existential feelings, but there is a connection between emotions and moods phenomenologically and conceptually which has proved hard to articulate (Frijda, 1993a). By redirecting attention to the configuring role of persistent and pervasive feeling states, the concept of existential feeling is helpful in linking the phenomenology to the neurobiology and explaining some puzzles about the way treatment for mood disorders works.

In this chapter we give an account of the cognitive properties of some neural mechanisms that enable existential feelings to configure the emotional world in this way. The account takes as a case study change in depressive mood consequent on the administration of selective serotonin re-uptake inhibitors (SSRIs) in antidepressant treatment. Where such treatment works the world is experienced in a different way before and after treatment. We argue that such changes reflect the influence of SSRIs on neural circuits involved in emotional processing.[1] The important point is that the cognitive properties of these circuits explain how existential feelings preconfigure the emotional world.

The account depends on a particular theory of emotional processing: the Multicomponential Appraisal Theory (MAT). Appraisal theory is familiar to theorists of emotion as the theory that emotions are representations of the significance of events for the organism. The intentional content of an emotion represents a core relational theme (CRT) (Frijda, 1986; 2001; 2009; Scherer, Schorr and Johnstone, 2001). The CRT of fear is danger or threat, of sadness, loss, and so on.

---

[1]   It should be noted that there are empirical grounds for scepticism about the role of antidepressants in mood disorder. For sceptics like Kirsch (2009b; Kirsch *et al.*, 2008) antidepressant effects are essentially placebo effects. Both sceptical and standard accounts in fact need an account of the mechanisms and cognitive processes involved in mood. Once that account is provided it becomes an open possibility that plasticity in those mechanisms and resultant cognitive changes could be produced by pharmacology or placebo. In what follows, however, we assume the standard account in which depressive mood remits following antidepressant treatment.

This core relational theme is sometimes called the *formal object* of an emotion. *Concrete objects* of emotion are the specific objects or events appraised as instantiating the formal object. For example, in an episode of sadness a specific event such as a death is *appraised* as an irreversible loss for the subject of the emotion (Kenny, 1963; Prinz, 2004). Appraisal theory is well placed to explain how emotions derive their intentional content.

Early appraisal theorists assimilated appraisals to judgments: beliefs about the properties of the objects of emotion (Kenny, 1963; Solomon, 1988; 1989). Consequently appraisal theory has been criticized as overly intellectualistic and as ignoring the felt aspect of emotion. Grief, for example, is a visceral state whose essence is a feeling, not a judgment, runs the objection. Equally an emotional feeling may arise or persist in the absence of, or in opposition to, a judgment. Thus accounting for the intentionality of emotional feelings in terms of judgments is an oversimplification.

MAT avoids this objection since it locates many dimensions of appraisal at different, subpersonal, levels of cognitive processing (Grandjean and Scherer, 2008, p. 488; Sander, Grandjean and Scherer, 2005). It retains the idea that appraisals are mental representations of subjective relevance, but suggests that many such representations depend on processes which use coding formats and timescales which make them unavailable for explicit reflective thought. Most emotional appraisals are in fact conducted by neural circuits which automatically link perception to the automatic regulation of visceral and bodily responses so that they issue almost instantaneously in feelings which reflect the nature of that appraisal.

An example of a subpersonal appraisal process is provided by responses to perceived changes in emotional expression or posture of conspecifics. The mind has mechanisms that constantly compute the relevance of such changes for the subject and initiate appropriate responses. When we recognize a familiar person and see her smile, for example, the significance of that information for us has been represented and that representation used to initiate a response within a few hundred milliseconds (Adolphs, 2010; Sander *et al.*, 2003; 2007; N'Diaye, Sander and Vuilleumier, 2009).

When information processing in this type of circuitry becomes rigidly biased, the repertoire of possible appraisals is limited, effectively limiting the range of possible emotional responses for the subject. Feeling states reflect those biases, lingering and becoming entrenched even in the absence of specific emotional elicitors. In depression, for example, the subject becomes 'wired for despair' as very fundamental appraisal systems become biased to the detection and processing of negative information and consequent disengagement from the world, especially the social world. The consequence is to install automatic bodily and behavioural emotional responses whose sustained presence is experienced as the depressive mood (Colombetti and Thompson, 2008). Or, as Ratcliffe might put it, as existential feelings of despair and desolation.

2. Feelings as Emotion Components

One difference between MAT theories of emotion (and mood) and various feeling theories is that appraisal theories treat feelings as one of many *components* of emotion (Frijda, 1986; 1993b; Frijda *et al.*, 1989). These components are cognition (at different levels of complexity and explicitness ranging from low-level reflexive processes to high-level reflective deliberation), motivational action tendencies, physiological response patterns, motor expression, and feelings (Sander, Grandjean and Scherer, 2005; Brosch *et al.*, 2010). The emotional phenotype for any emotion refers to the way these components are *coordinated* (see below) in the face of their objects, formal and concrete, in an emotional episode.

The essential feature of appraisal theories is that the coordination of emotion components is explained in terms of appraisals. That is, representations of the significance of an object for the subject of the emotion. A prototypical episode of fear organizes components adaptively to respond to the danger. These components include high-level cognition (beliefs about the nature and significance of the object and consequences of action); lower-level cognition (detection of hostile facial expression, vocalization, or posture, and continued monitoring for threat by specialized neural circuits); characteristic autonomic and somatovisceral changes, sensed as feelings; and motor responses, including facial expression. The adaptive coordination of these components in an episode of fear depends on the appraisal of a stimulus as dangerous. The point to note is that these components, while they can occur independently under other conditions, co-occur in a typical pattern in an emotional episode in virtue of the appraisal.

Thus the feeling characteristic of an emotion is a component of the overall emotional state, consequent an appraisal. It is a way of being aware of the bodily state produced by the representation of an emotionally salient property (Colombetti and Thompson, 2008). A bodily feeling in an emotional episode does double duty. It tells the subject about her body *and* about the object or state of the world whose appraisal led to that body state. This dual role for bodily feeling is explained in different ways by different theorists. Prinz (2004), for example, following basic emotion theorists, gives a teleological theory of the emotional intentionality of bodily feelings. Peter Goldie (2000) developed a subtle phenomenological account of what he called 'feeling towards' in episodes of emotion. The MAT explains the intentionality of emotional experience in virtue of the representational content of processes of appraisal that generate it.

Cognitive neuroscience has identified circuits, essential for this coordination of feeling with other components of emotion, which function as 'hubs' of distributed circuits that determine the *subjective relevance* of information. Lower level hubs implement rapid online appraisals while upper level hubs link this information acquired by low-level appraisal systems to higher level, cognitively explicit, forms of appraisal, including belief fixation.

A crucial lower level appraisal hub is the amygdala. Initially the activity of the amygdala was interpreted narrowly as a substrate for 'fear' of standard elicitors. Subsequently this interpretation was replaced by a wider one which treats it as the basis of context-sensitive 'aversion' or 'negative affect'. Further evidence of its role in many conditions involving the rapid and automatic processing of self relevant information, including positive and rewarding information, led to further theoretical revision. It is now described as a *hub* of an appraisal system (Hsu *et al.*, 2005; Adolphs, 2010; Brosch *et al.*, 2010; Vuilleumier *et al.*, 2003). An example is the processing of information in facial expression. Typically faces are scanned for emotionally significant information (such a smiles, frowns, direction and return of gaze) in parallel with other face processing operations such as the detection of identity. As faces are scanned and information gathered, appropriate autonomic and physiological responses are initiated. The scanning process and the initiation of downstream response are coordinated by activation in the amygdala. Thus, although the amygdala does not itself represent all information necessary to establish the emotional relevance of a stimulus, it coordinates the relevant distributed processing. It is thus the hub of a distributed appraisal processing system whose operations are fast, automatic, and not available to conscious control. We can call these types of appraisals *peripheral* in the jargon of cognitive neuroscience since they are rapid, quasi-perceptual, and not under voluntary control.

A higher level hub of appraisal is the ventromedial prefrontal cortex, a structure which traffics the information acquired by low-level hubs to so-called central or higher level processes. In effect the

ventromedial prefrontal cortex recapitulates at a higher level the properties of the amygdala. In so doing it associates emotional information
with explicitly represented information used in reflective decision
making and planning (Ochsner *et al.*, 2002; Bechara *et al.*, 2000). It
thus allows the subject to make more explicit appraisals using so-
called 'central' processes. In general peripheral appraisals involve
posterior circuitry that evolved to manage the sensorimotor interface
with the world, while central appraisals depend on prefrontal structures which evolved to allow stimulus-independent metacognition.
What appraisals at these different levels of explicitness have in common is the representation of the significance of an object or situation
for the subject.[2]

As Grandjean and colleagues put it summarizing studies on the
communication between the amygdala, hippocampus, and prefrontal
systems:

> empirical findings of neuronal synchronisation in the human brain in
> response to emotional stimuli highlight the importance of functional
> coupling between different distant and local neuronal assemblies and
> suggest continuous cross talk between different brain regions during the
> processing of emotional stimuli. (Grandjean and Scherer, 2008, p. 488;
> see also Sander, Grandjean and Scherer, 2005)

Thus the concept of interacting neural circuitry specialized for peripheral and central appraisal is empirically supported. Not only that, but
this circuitry drives the coordination of emotion components.

3. Feelings and Moods:
State and Trait Appraisal Bias

People develop *appraisal biases*, tendencies to evaluate objects in
characteristic ways and to coordinate emotion components accordingly (Scherer and Brosch, 2009). When we say that someone is
depressed or anxious we do not mean that they are unhappy or worried
about a specific object. Rather we mean that any object they encounter
tends to be appraised in ways that initiate the coordination of components of unhappiness or anxiety. Similarly we explain optimism as a
trait not in terms of attitude to a specific object but as an appraisal bias
(perhaps installed history of rewarding interactions with the world).

---

[2] The idea that the ventromedial prefrontal cortex computes subjective relevance of cen-
     trally represented information predicts that deficits would manifest as an inability to take
     and incorporate a *personal perspective* on centrally processed information (Goel *et al.*,
     1998; Koenigs *et al.*, 2007; Buckner, Andrews-Hanna and Schacter, 2008; Adolphs *et al.*,
     2002).

The concept refers to characteristic patterns of emotional responses based on biased processing of information.

Anxiety provides an example. Someone with an anxiety disorder has a persistent feeling characteristic of appraising situations as threatening and/or beyond her control. The feeling may wax and wane according to the way attention is captured or directed, but it unfortunately persists in the phenomenological background. Its persistence can be explained by the way in which both peripheral and central appraisal systems are 'rewired' from below, primed to detect and respond to threats. Someone with an anxiety disorder, for example, will typically show unusual patterns of face scanning, avoiding the eyes. This avoidance pattern is produced entirely below the threshold of conscious control by peripheral visuomotor systems driven by the amygdala. Typically in such cases hyperactivity of the amygdala itself is driven by lower level brainstem systems. A consequence of very low-level peripheral appraisals driven by the amygdala is mutually-reinforcing physiological changes. As a result an anxious person experiences a characteristic bodily feeling which is a consequence of the fact that her body is primed for avoidance even though there may not currently be a threatening stimulus.

We are not claiming here that dispositions *per se* have a phenomenology, but that the typical pattern of appraisals installed by an emotional disposition, or appraisal bias, has a persistent residual phenomenology. Feelings produced by physiological responses initiated by peripheral appraisals tend to linger and exert an influence on central appraisals whose net effect is to reinforce the feeling. The anxious person will tend to 'dwell in imagination on possible disasters' as Ryle (2009) put it, a tendency which has feedback effects throughout the hierarchy of appraisal systems.

Goldie (2000) gives the excellent example of someone who continues to feel angry long after the initial episode (in his case an upsetting marital argument). This person remains tense and irritable for the rest of the day. They grip the steering wheel tightly driving to work, swear at other drivers, don't show their normal good humour in social encounters. Were they to attend to their feelings they might detect their over-arousal. Often such a residual feeling is at odds with the current situation because it is the lingering result of temporally distant appraisals whose content is not available to consciousness. And precisely because of this residual over-arousal, which tends to short circuit reflective deliberation and crowds out the capacity for positive appraisal, such a person might then start to react angrily to neutral situations, or be inattentive to positive information, reinforcing the problem.

This is an example of an episode of emotion producing a relatively short-lived existential feeling of irritability. Other more dramatic cases may arise where sustained grief at the death of a loved one ultimately installs a pervasive appraisal bias leading to depression and the characteristic existential feeling of emptiness and desolation. In such cases an emotional feeling with a specific object leads to an existential feeling which influences the overall pattern of emotional appraisals.

4. Neurochemistry, Appraisal, and Feeling in Depression

These facts suggest that the existential feelings characteristic of depression could result from biases in appraisal which may operate well below the threshold of explicit cognition. And in fact recent work on the pharmacology of depression has adopted this hypothesis to explain why it is that the phenomenology of depression is so persistent and pervasive in the face of antidepressant treatment.

One clinical approach to depression is the administration of drugs which increase levels of 5hydroxytrypamine (5HT), also know as serotonin, in the synaptic cleft. The role and efficacy of these drugs is controversial but the consensus is that, typically after some delay, they help resolve or alleviate symptoms.

One governing hypothesis here has been that these drugs elevate mood, perhaps not immediately or directly but eventually, with favourable flow-on effects for the rest of the subject's psychological economy. Perhaps if the subject *feels happier* and more optimistic, her patterns of thought and behaviour will realign appropriately, removing negative appraisal biases.

This presupposes two things: first that antidepressants change mood, and second that mood has a *primary* causal force in coordinating other symptoms of depression. Let us call the conjunction of these two claims the 'mood is chemistry hypothesis' (MIC). If MIC is right we should be able to remove depression by changing the characteristic mood by intervening at the neurochemical level.

It is certainly true that moods can be changed by neurochemical intervention. Feeling states are often instantaneously sensitive to neurochemical changes. However, we do not think the evidence supports the idea that SSRIs are effective in depression as a result of direct alteration of feeling states. Nor does it support the idea that a change in feeling state leads directly to a change in appraisal bias.

In fact in the case of SSRIs the direction of explanation goes the other way. SSRIs do not change appraisal biases by changing mood. Rather they change mood by changing appraisal biases. In particular, antidepressants change peripheral appraisals by changing the information processing properties of peripheral appraisal circuits. The best example comes from recent work on the effects of antidepressants on the interaction between the amygdala, the hub of the peripheral appraisal system, and the systems it regulates.

There is now a body of work which explains the fact that mood does not resolve immediately following antidepressant treatment in terms of the timescale of effects on peripheral appraisal systems of antidepressants. For example, after one week's administration of serotonin, which changes the balance of norepinephrine and serotonin action in the amygdala, patients' amygdala response to masked fearful faces was reduced and the responses of the facial fusiform areas to happy faces was increased. This is an example of the role of the amygdala as a hub of peripheral appraisal. These effects occur well below the threshold of explicit awareness. Patients' explicit judgments about emotional expressions also change accordingly. Patients are more likely to correctly identify positive emotional expressions, for example. Memory for positive words also increased (see Harmer *et al.*, 2009, for a discussion). These effects have now been demonstrated repeatedly (Di Simplicio *et al.*, 2011; McCabe *et al.*, 2011; Pringle *et al.*, 2011; Harmer, 2008).

However, although peripheral appraisals of facial emotional expression change quite quickly, the depressive mood persists for a much longer period, suggesting that 'antidepressants are able to modify behavioural and neural responses to emotional information *without any change in subjective mood*. Moreover the changes in emotional processing can be seen across different stimuli types and extend outside conscious awareness' (Harmer *et al.*, 2009, my italics).

Summarizing recent work in the area, Harmer and collaborators pointed out that delay in the remission of mood is not a puzzle if mood is understood as a downstream effect of changes to peripheral appraisal systems with consequent reorganization of emotion components, including feelings. They concluded that 'antidepressant drug treatments may target these *underlying processes supporting mood rather than targeting mood directly*' and 'the therapeutic effect of noradrenaline and serotonin enhancement may depend on how far positive shifts in *automatic emotional processing* [peripheral appraisal in our terminology] can lead to altered conscious emotional appraisal and improved mood' (*ibid.*).

This view of the evidence about the relationship between peripheral appraisal and mood is consistent with MAT. For MAT, feelings of sadness, grief, or despair are a 'global broadcast' of the organismic state that results when cognitive, psychomotor, and affective systems (mal)function in withdrawal mode. At the level of conscious awareness the subject experiences the consequences of biased peripheral appraisals as low mood.

Central appraisals, which depend on communication between central and peripheral appraisal systems, are also affected in depression. For example, the ability to remember and make use of positive autobiographical information is compromised by changes in circuits linking the amygdala, hippocampus, and prefrontal cortex (Ressler and Nemeroff, 2001; Davidson *et al.*, 2000; D'Sa and Duman, 2002; Fuchs *et al.*, 2004; Roozendaal *et al.*, 2009). These circuits implement the communication between the hubs of peripheral and central appraisal and are crucial to the learning and recall of affective contingencies. In fact, the volume of these circuits is often reduced in severe depression (Bremner *et al.*, 2000; Sheline *et al.*, 1996; Videbech and Ravnkilde, 2004). This is consistent with findings that depressive subjects cannot down-regulate their ventromedial prefrontal cortex when appraising potentially negative or depressing stimuli (Sheline *et al.*, 1996; Videbech and Ravnkilde, 2004; Northoff, 2007). Negative autobiographical information is excessively salient to these people. It is not an accident that patients with ventromedial lesions, as well as having characteristic cognitive and behavioural deficits, *are not depressed*. This is explained in terms of a 'lack of the cognitive/affective symptoms associated with self-awareness' (I paraphrase the conclusion of Koenigs and Grafman, 2009, p. 46).

Depressive mood, or existential feelings of despair, reflect an appraisal bias. Since appraisal biases operate in a hierarchical, recurrent fashion and are mutually reinforcing with other components of the emotional systems such as feelings, psychomotor tendencies, and cognition, there is no *a priori* reason to think that intervention at any point in the system is a privileged way to change an appraisal bias. Indeed practitioners of CBT intervene at the level of explicit judgment, changing the pattern of explicit appraisal. Sometimes this approach succeeds in alleviating depressive mood, which suggests that mood is not independent of high-level cognition.

Similarly it *may* be possible to remove the appraisal bias by changing mood directly, as MIC suggests. However, as a matter of fact this does not seem to be how SSRIs work. SSRIs work not by changing mood but by changing the receptive properties of neurons in appraisal circuits, both making them more responsive to positive information and enabling plasticity effects in distributed circuits to which they project. It can take weeks or months to undo entrenched biases in the coordination of emotion components which have been established by patterns of negative peripheral appraisal (Harmer *et al.*, 2009). Downstream bodily feeling and mood aspects persist because they are causally dependent, not only on the prior action of SSRIs on appraisal processes, but on the introduction of a new pattern of appraisal.

This is why Castren (2005) argued that the key to understanding the role of SSRIs in depression is rejecting the MIC hypothesis. Levels of serotonin do not represent positive appraisals. But where appraisal circuits have become biased to process negative information, changing the balance of serotonin/norepinephrine changes the properties of circuits which regulate coordination of emotion components: '[A]ctivity dependant neuronal communication might underlie depression... and antidepressants might work by improving information processing in the affected neural networks' (*ibid.*, p. 2002). Harmer's interpretation of this evidence is novel in psychiatry, which has tended to ignore information processing approaches that emphasize cognitive architecture, in favour of either neurochemical (versions of the MIC hypothesis) or cognitive behavioural approaches which target what we have called central appraisals.

The crude idea that 'mood is chemistry' is perhaps a straw man, but seeing what is wrong with it helps us identify something crucial about the nature of emotions. Emotions have multiple interacting components implemented by interacting neural circuits, and feeling is only one of these components.

Consequently it is not surprising that changing neurochemistry does not always change mood immediately in cases where mood is a consequence of appraisal bias. An organism which is withdrawn, anhedonic, avolitional, has psychomotor poverty and rigid patterns of aversive behaviour, and pessimistic and self-accusing thoughts rapidly receives environmental and bodily feedback that it is failing. Thus all of its appraisal systems represent failure and consolidate the depressive pattern of organization of emotion components.

Ultimately, the beneficial effect of SSRIs in depression treatment is to alter the information processing properties of neural circuits responsible for peripheral appraisals. The effects of pharmacological treatment are very indirect because they depend on neural plasticity in these networks: synaptic connections need to be rebuilt and potentiated. Not only that, but in so far as depression arises in a personal and social context, *activity-dependent* plasticity effects require either changes in the *milieu* or significant cognitive and behavioural work to uninstall dysfunctional appraisals. Restoring the *ability* to detect positive emotional expression will not help unless the patient is consistently exposed to a positive social milieu sufficient to rehabilitate the relevant circuitry.

5. Conclusion

The relationship between feeling states such as mood, physiology, and neural processes is controversial for many phenomenologists. While no one would deny that feeling states are neural representations of body state, the nature of the intentional relationship between feelings and their objects is obscure. While most theorists of emotion and certainly those influenced by phenomenological traditions would accept that feelings in these cases are 'directed', the nature of the representational relationship between bodily feeling and the world is not always clear. The aim of this chapter has been to clarify that relationship for the case of depressive mood.

In this respect the category of existential feelings, understood in the way Ratcliffe describes, as forms of emotional orientation to the world, or the taking of the world as a set of possibilities for engagement, provides a potential link if understood as a manifestation of appraisal bias. MAT offers an information processing approach with potential to bridge the gap between neurophysiology and phenomenology precisely because it involves forms of tacit representation and processing known to be intimately involved in the regulation of bodily feeling, The fact that resolution of mood relates indirectly to administration of SSRIs turns out, slightly paradoxically, to be another point in favour of MAT. The relationship between neurochemistry and alteration in mood depends on plasticity effects that change the bias in neural circuitry which forms a hub of peripheral appraisal. The nature of peripheral appraisal biases helps account for the fundamental pre-intentional role of existential feeling.

Michael Gaebler, Jan-Peter Lamke, Judith K. Daniels and Henrik Walter

Phenomenal Depth

A Common Phenomenological Dimension in Depression and Depersonalization

Patients suffering from depersonalization disorder report alterations in their sensory, self-referential, and emotional processing that can be described as a lack of *relatedness* in combination with reduced experiential richness. Similarly, patients suffering from certain types of depression can be characterized as experiencing alienation from both their surroundings and their emotional experience. Building on these phenomenological observations and clinical characteristics, we propose the conceptualization of a common dimension underlying these and similar clinical phenomena. This dimension, which we call 'phenomenal depth', cuts across diagnostic boundaries, potentially allows for quantification, and may thus facilitate neurocognitive investigation. The experience of phenomenal depth can be altered severely in psychological disorders. Based on our clinical observations, we assume that all objects of experience (including one's own or others' feelings, one's body, and objects of the outside world) have adherent to them a sense of depth of that experience. The degree of this subjective richness or experiential vividness, which we consider a structural feature of consciousness (*cf.* Fuchs, 2002c; 2010; Seth, 2009), can be captured along the dimension of phenomenal depth. Its impairment is a common feature in depression and depersonalization disorder.

In the following, we review pathological constraints of phenomenal depth in certain types of depression and in depersonalization disorder in order to extract commonalities.[1] We thereby wish to put forward the idea that different experiential qualities can be related to the dimen-

---

[1] While qualitatively similar experiences are also regularly reported by anxiety patients as occurring during panic attacks or post-traumatic dissociation, they typically last only a

sion of phenomenal depth, spanning sensory and self-related or emotional processes.

Alterations of phenomenal depth find their expression in altered sensory perception (visual 'flatness' or lack of three-dimensionality, increased perceived distance from acoustic sources, etc.) but also in altered self-related and self-referential processes (such as emotional experience, meta-cognition, and alienation from thought processes). Thus, phenomenal depth does not only tie together alterations in sensory and self-related or emotional processing but may also enable us to locate different clinical conditions on a common phenomenological dimension. We thereby build on earlier work by Church (2003) and Kunzendorf *et al.* (2010) who characterized the phenomenal world of a depressed person as 'meaner and grayer', 'thin and dry' (Church, 2003, p. 175; cited from Ingmar Bergman's *Scenes from a Marriage*), 'undifferentiated', 'flat' (Church, 2003, p. 179), and 'lacking depth' (*ibid.*, p. 177) compared with a healthy person's world of experience. What Church calls 'perceptual failures' (*ibid.*, p. 175) does not refer to deficits in attention or to distortions of sensory systems at a low level (like impaired stereopsis). Describing a lack of differentiation that affects all senses, she points out that there is a 'difference between being preoccupied or absent-minded, where very little is noticed, and being depressed, where what is noticed seems deficient' (*ibid.*, p. 175). Using a combination of self-report questionnaires and measures of the perception of visuo-spatially ambiguous shapes, Kunzendorf *et al.* (2010) also show empirically that depression is associated with a 'flatter' self-perception and a 'flatter' phenomenal world (pp. 447, 455).

Importantly, phenomenal depth is a meta-cognitive or meta-affective experience, that is, it is not about the intensity of (deep) feelings but about the feeling of depth. This conception aims at capturing the degree of experiential immersion or embeddedness of an individual in his or her environment.[2]

As we will detail below, the experience of limited phenomenal depth in certain types of depression and in depersonalization disorder entails more than a shift in sensory perception. Although phenomenal depth is certainly related to visuo-spatial depth perception, the two are not identical and should not be confused. A classical phenomeno-

---

few minutes in these patients. Here, we will focus on depression and depersonalization disorder, that is, disorders in which such symptoms are typically chronic.

[2] A related notion of experiential vividness, called *gradual presence*, and its potential bodily constitution in a sensorimotor or enactivist framework has recently been discussed by Fingerhut (2012).

logical treatise of the dimension of (visuo-spatial) depth states that 'it is, so to speak, the most "existential" of all dimensions, because... it is not impressed upon the object itself, it quite clearly belongs to the perspective and not to things' (Merleau-Ponty, 1945/1962, p. 298). The wider scope of the term *depth* already implied in Merleau-Ponty's observation supports that we extend it beyond the visuo-spatial domain. Therefore, the notion of phenomenal depth explicitly includes more extensive experiential alterations with respect to oneself and the world in broader sensory, affective, and cognitive domains and we consider it suitable to capture the pervasive disconnectedness as it occurs in depersonalization and other psychopathological states. Phenomenal depth is also not identical with the intensity of a particular experience: experiences that have a particularly high or low phenomenal depth are not just more or less intense but qualitatively different. As a phenomenological concept, phenomenal depth is meant to focus not on the content but on the form and structure of experience (*cf.* Fuchs, 2002c; 2010). While the focus of this chapter lies on the decrease in phenomenal depth as it occurs in certain psychiatric diseases, the concept can potentially be extended towards increases in phenomenal depth as they may occur in other psychopathological states (e.g. in mania), after drug use, or in otherwise altered states of consciousness, for example through meditative practices. We assume that phenomenal depth also varies within a normal range in our daily life, even though these variations need not always be fully conscious.

Understanding the fundamental changes similarly appearing in certain types of depression and in depersonalization disorder as alterations along the common dimension of phenomenal depth may thus provide a handle for the experimental manipulation and measurement of subjective emotional experience and alterations thereof.

In what follows, we will first describe depersonalization in more detail, both as a symptom and as a syndrome, often overseen by psychiatrists. Then, we will give a short historical and conceptual overview of the (phenomenological) overlap of depersonalization and depression. Thereafter, we will discuss how conceptualizing both depersonalization and depression (and potentially other psychopathologies) as alterations along the shared phenomenological dimension of phenomenal depth may be useful for their neurocognitive investigation and will relate it to the idea of the brain as a prediction machine.

1. Phenomenal Depth in Depersonalization (Disorder)

Patient reports of depersonalization in the literature and in our own studies, as well as the most commonly used specific self-report questionnaire, the Cambridge Depersonalization Scale (CDS; Sierra and Berrios, 2000), lead us to understand depersonalization and derealization as involving a loss or reduction of phenomenal depth. Particularly the aspects of detachment from self and world together with a persistent emotional numbing and 'flat or lifeless' perception (CDS item 2) provide hints for this connection.

Although phenomena reminiscent of depersonalization have been described at least since the early nineteenth century, the term only appeared in 1898 when it was introduced into the medical realm by French psychiatrist Ludovic Dugas using an expression he encountered in the personal diaries of French-Swiss philosopher H.F. Amiel (cf. Sierra and Berrios, 1997).

While depersonalization is often reduced to *feelings of unreality* (e.g. Radovic and Radovic, 2002), the term has been used to describe a much broader but phenomenologically stable (Sierra and Berrios, 2001) cluster of mental disturbances, centring around a felt disconnectedness from one's own mental processes, emotions, and body.

In addition, these subjective experiences of estrangement or detachment from oneself are frequently accompanied by derealization, the sense that one's surroundings are unfamiliar or that the world appears unreal.

Around three quarters of the general population experience mild or transient depersonalization-derealization symptoms at least once in their lives (Hunter, Sierra and David, 2004). Such symptoms can, for example, be induced by hypnosis (Röder *et al.*, 2007), fatigue (Mayer-Gross, 1935), jet lag and sleep deprivation (Bliss, Clark and West, 1959), sensory deprivation (Reed and Sedman, 1964). They may appear after persistent stress or drug use (such as cannabis or hallucinogenic substances; e.g. Mathew *et al.*, 1999), but also spontaneously during fMRI experiments (Michal *et al.*, 2005) and in reaction to traumatic incidents (Daniels *et al.*, 2012). Up to 56% of psychiatric inpatients report current experiences of depersonalization (Davidson, 1966), and it has been suggested that in the context of mood and anxiety disorders the presence of depersonalization symptoms correlates with higher disease severity and poorer response to treatment (Mula, Pini and Cassano, 2007).

Under certain conditions, depersonalization can also be considered a pleasant experience and there certainly are culturally approved religious or ritual activities which explicitly evoke or seek these phenomena. In this line, a transcultural approach found that reported depersonalization experiences are susceptible to cultural variation in that the prevalence of depersonalization in psychiatric inpatients (Sierra *et al.*, 2006) and the frequency of depersonalization during panic (Sierra-Siegert and David, 2007) was found to be significantly lower in non-western and more collectivistic countries as compared to more individualistic societies.

In some people, however, these phenomena become persistent and interfere with their individual and social functioning, thus reaching the threshold for diagnosis of a mental illness.

2. Depersonalization as Syndrome: Depersonalization Disorder

While depersonalization and derealization frequently occur as co-morbid symptoms in other psychiatric disorders, they can amount to a chronic mental illness in their own right: the ICD-10 (WHO, 2007) classifies the 'depersonalization-derealization syndrome' as an independent neurotic illness (F48.1), while the DSM-IV (APA, 1994) distinguishes between 'depersonalization disorder' (DPD), considered a dissociative disorder (300.6), and 'derealization' (without depersonalization), which is separately listed in examples of a 'dissociative disorder — not otherwise specified' (DDNOS, 300.15).[3] The diagnostic criteria in both ICD-10 and DSM-IV comprise loss of emotion with feelings of estrangement/detachment from one's thinking, body, or surroundings. They also mention a perceived spontaneous change of experiential quality (ICD-10: 'unreal, remote, or automatized'; DSM-IV: 'as if... in a dream', 'external world as strange or unreal', 'other people seem unfamiliar or mechanical') with normal sensorium and the retained capacity of emotional expression. Importantly, both diagnostic manuals require patients to show intact reality testing, that is, to be free of delusions.

Studies from different countries in North America and Europe have repeatedly found a lifetime prevalence in the range of 1–2% (Hunter, Sierra and David, 2004; Michal *et al.*, 2009). Although this prevalence rate is comparable to that of other psychiatric disorders such as

---

[3] In line with patient reports, the vast majority of cases in the literature, the view of the ICD-10 as well as current recommendations for the revision of the diagnostic criteria in DSM-5 (Spiegel *et al.*, 2011), we will not explicitly distinguish between depersonalization and derealization in this text. We rather take *depersonalization* as shorthand for *depersonalization-derealization*.

schizophrenia or obsessive-compulsive disorder (OCD), DPD is much less frequently diagnosed.

Several more general assessment tools exist for dissociative experiences which include phenomena of depersonalization (e.g. the Dissociative Experiences Scale, DES; Bernstein and Putnam, 1986). However, as mentioned above, with the CDS there is also an established self-report questionnaire to specifically measure depersonalization-derealization symptoms. It captures the frequency and duration of depersonalization experiences, exists both in a state (CDS-22) and a trait (CDS-30) version, and has been translated into several other languages (e.g. Michal *et al.*, 2004; Molina Castillo *et al.*, 2006).

Several items of the CDS pertain to experiential *depth*: while some items of the CDS-30 describe an alteration in the experience of sensory input (item 2: 'What I see looks "flat" and "lifeless", as if I were looking at a picture'; item 19: 'Objects around me seem to look smaller or further away'; item 11: 'Familiar voices (including my own) sound remote and unreal'), others pertain to the feeling of disconnectedness from the outside world (item 1: 'Out of the blue, I feel strange, as if I were not real or as if I were cut off from the world'; item 13: 'My surroundings feel detached or unreal, as if there were a veil between me and the outside world'; item 26: 'I feel so detached from my thoughts that they seem to have a "life" of their own') or one's own bodily actions (item 3: 'Parts of my body feel as if they didn't belong to me'; item 6: 'Whilst doing something I have the feeling of being a "detached observer" of myself'; item 8: 'My body feels very light, as if it were floating on air'; item 24: 'When I move it doesn't feel as if I were in charge of the movements, so that I feel "automatic" and mechanical as if I were a "robot"').

Factor analyses on CDS scores from two large and independent cohorts extracted four (Sierra *et al.*, 2005) and five (Simeon *et al.*, 2008) factors constituting the syndrome. Both studies converge on the core factors of *emotional numbing*, *unreality of self/anomalous body experience + perceptual alterations*, and *alienation from/unreality of surroundings*, and only differ on one remaining factor each: while Sierra *et al.* (2005) focus on anomalous memory disturbances, Simeon *et al.* (2008) emphasize alterations in the temporal domain for their characterization of depersonalization.

DPD typically has its onset in adolescence or early adulthood (Sierra, 2009, p. 50) and it is thought to affect both sexes equally. The initial development can be sudden or gradual and has been reported to occur spontaneously after medical or illicit drug use or during a stressful life period (Simeon *et al.*, 2003; Baker *et al.*, 2003). Specifically, there is recent evidence for an onset of DPD in adolescence after consuming cannabis (Hürlimann, Kupferschmid and Simon, 2012). Depersonalization also occurs in neurological conditions such as migraine (Cahill and Murphy, 2004; Reutens, Nielsen and Sachdev, 2010, for review) or temporal lobe epilepsy (e.g. Lambert and Sierra, 2002). Emotional neglect by parents (Michal *et al.*, 2007; Simeon *et al.*, 2001) as well as increased anxiety during childhood (Lee *et al.*, 2010) emerged as the most significant psychosocial predictors for the development of depersonalization symptoms and a diagnosis of DPD.

Both in its common transient form and in its pathological chronic manifestation, depersonalization refers to a cluster of experiential alterations. Although its symptom descriptions vary in their details, depersonalization exhibits a comprehensive disconnectedness from oneself and the world, which pervades all sensory, affective, and cognitive aspects of experience.

In order to extract the fundamental character of this cluster of disturbances we introduce the underlying dimension of phenomenal depth, understanding depersonalization as involving a reduction in phenomenal depth.

3. History and Concepts of Depersonalization in Depression

Similar alterations, which can be interpreted along the continuum of phenomenal depth, have previously been described in patients with depression. Kraus (2002; 2008) differentiates two conceptually and clinically interesting forms of depersonalization that occur in severe major depression and that have historically been described: consciously experienced depersonalization and pre-reflectively lived depersonalization. In the former, alienation-depression, the patients have insight into the disorder and consciously experience the alienation from their own selves and from the surrounding world, while in the latter, melancholic depression, the patients *live* the alienation without reflecting upon it (as described by von Gebsattel, 1937). While consciously experienced depersonalization may also be secondarily present in otherwise typical cases of major depression, in the following, only those subtypes of depression shall be considered where one form of depersonalization is *formative* for the clinical picture.

Alienation-Depression

The type of severe depression in which consciously experienced depersonalization plays a dominant role has been described by Petrilowitsch
(1956) as alienation-depression (*Entfremdungsdepression*). The characteristic, consciously experienced alienation from oneself and from
the outside world is accompanied by a loss of feeling towards oneself,
other persons, and objects of the world (*cf.* Johnson, 1935), which
may be considered a loss of basic 'existential feelings' (Kraus, 2002;
cf. also Ratcliffe, 2008a; 2009c, for a related notion). In the description by Petrilowitsch (1956), patients typically complain about low
mood or a general inability to experience emotions, reduced physical
and intellectual capacities, and a distorted sense of time. At the same
time, objective measures or observable symptoms provide little evidence for their condition: they seem only slightly depressed and
sometimes taciturn, with, if at all, mildly to moderately impaired
psychomotoric and intellectual performance. In addition, patients
report a marked lack of drive, a loss of spontaneity, a feeling of acting
like an automaton, and an inability to vividly imagine things. However, during conversation they are able to respond adequately and
sometimes even appear to be energetic. Frequent coexisting symptoms are disturbed bodily sensations and hypochondriac anxieties
related to these experiences of somatopsychic alienation as well as
obsessions and compulsions. According to Petrilowitsch (1956) delusions do usually not occur in this type of depression and, in contrast to
typical major depression and also to melancholic depression (*cf.*
Kraus, 2002; Fuchs, 2010), patients suffering from alienation-depression do not experience excessive feelings of guilt. Instead, recognizing their own impairments in certain domains leads to feelings of
insufficiency without regarding this insufficiency as their own fault.
Comparing expectations or norms to deficient actualities is a central
feature of alienation-depression and Petrilowitsch (1956) attempts a
psychodynamic explanation along these lines: on the one hand, the
discrepancy between the experienced existential significance of the
psycho- pathological deficits and the low severity of the observable
symptoms is a determining characteristic of alienation-depression. On
the other hand, Petrilowitsch (1956) postulates that while the *motivational component* of the patient's personality or temperament
('*Antriebsseite der Persönlichkeit*', p. 294) is impaired, the *core personality* (encompassing inherent or acquired dispositions, attitudes,
and morals) remains intact. This means that the patients still have certain expectations how they should behave and feel. However, their

manifest emotions are always weaker than they should be according to the expectations stemming from their intact *core* personality and the expectations are never met — which culminates in the agonizing experience of having lost all feelings ('*das qualvolle Erlebnis des Gefühls der Gefühllosigkeit*'; *ibid.*, p. 297).

The apparent paradox of reduced emotional experience in combination with high subjective distress has also been addressed more recently with respect to depersonalization disorder: quoting Ackner (1954), Medford proposes an attentional imbalance in which 'sufferers tend to focus attention on inner sensations and concerns, at the expense of attending to the external world' (Medford, 2012, p. 141).

While Petrilowitsch's '*Entfremdungsdepression*' was originally conceptualized as a type of depression, the consciously experienced depersonalization phenomena prevail and there is a high overlap with depersonalization disorder. We therefore propose that the symptomatology of alienation-depression, such as the loss of feeling, the impression of acting like an automaton, or the inability to vividly imagine things, can similarly be understood as expressions of reduced phenomenal depth.

Particularly, an imbalance or tension between expectation and actual (affective) experience or behaviour is supposed to play a crucial role in the aetiology or maintenance of the symptoms. We follow Petrilowitsch in assuming that it is this subjectively experienced tension which is felt as reduced phenomenal depth in the case of alienation-depression. Understanding alienation-depression as originating from a reduction in phenomenal depth thus suggests the involvement of a matching or calibration component which may provide hints for a neurobiological conceptualization in the predictive coding framework (*cf.* below).

Melancholic Depersonalization

The type of severe depression in which pre-reflectively lived depersonalization plays a dominant role has been described as *melancholia* or *melancholic depersonalization* by Kraus (2002; 2008). He explicitly uses the older term 'melancholia' (Kraus, 2002, p. 169; 2008, p. 243) in order to distinguish it from mood disorders as they are described in ICD-10 and DSM-IV. Drawing on a continuous tradition (ranging from Heinroth to Schilder, von Gebsattel, von Ditfurth, Hutter, and Schulte) Kraus sees lived depersonalization as the basic disturbance underlying melancholia and thus introduces the more precise term 'melancholic depersonalization' (Kraus, 2008, p. 243), which is characterized by melancholic mood, an inhibition of drive, an altered relation to oneself, a lack of both self-transcendence and of being directed to the world (Griesinger, 1867; von Gebsattel, 1937), delusions, local and somatic dysaesthesia, and complaints about being unable to speak, move, or eat (in the absence of any bodily impairments).

According to Kraus (2002; 2008), the melancholic mood alteration is not just experienced as a particularly high degree of sadness but as something qualitatively different from normal moods such as non-pathological sadness or happiness. Kraus thus considers it insufficient to specify additional somatic or psychotic symptoms — as is done in the ICD-10 — for capturing the difference between melancholia and typical major depression. Although melancholic patients are usually able to differentiate between a melancholic mood alteration and non-pathological low mood, this difference is often difficult for them to describe. The patients experience the melancholic mood alteration as something strange that is forced upon them and takes complete hold of the person while at the same time remaining inaccessible. It is thus impossible for the patients to identify with their own mood and they experience themselves as alienated, empty, and lifeless.

Kraus (2002; 2008) compares this to what Freud (1967) describes as *the emptiness of the I*. The melancholic mood cannot be modulated, which makes it virtually impossible for the patient to experience other emotions, resulting in a loss of feelings. As the condition appears to be unmotivated and inexplicable, it is difficult for others to empathize with the patient about it. Melancholic depersonalization may sometimes be preceded or followed by normal low mood, but this is not at the core of the melancholic mood alteration.

This loss of feelings, the altered experience of oneself, and the lack of both self-transcendence and of being directed to the world, along with the inhibition of drive, can again be understood as signs of reduced phenomenal depth. However, it remains unknown what this descriptive similarity between alienation-depression and melancholic depersonalization means with regard to underlying mechanisms.

In Kraus's framework, a deficient structure of the self is identified as the cause of lived depersonalization underlying melancholia. The capability of self-reference is assumed to be greatly reduced in lived depersonalization. While the *me*, defined by Mead (1934) as the socialized aspect of the person, remains intact, the *I*, the active and creative aspect of the person that brings about a sense of freedom and initiative (*ibid.*), transcending the *me* and being directed towards the future, is severely impaired in melancholic depersonalization. The relation to oneself is disturbed and the capability to 'take a position towards oneself' (Kraus, 2002, p. 169) or towards one's own feelings is diminished, resulting in the above-described symptomatology.

In melancholic depersonalization the reduction or loss of phenomenal depth thus may have different causes than in alienation-depression. Whereas in the latter reduced phenomenal depth results from the experienced tension between expected and actual (affective) experiences, in the former it may result from a deficient structure of the self.

4. The Dimension of Phenomenal Depth in Depression

What should have become apparent in the clinical descriptions presented above is also visible in the statistics of the high co-morbidity between depersonalization and depression (also mentioned above). While historically '[a]n association between depression and depersonalization has been known for a long time' (Sierra, 2009, p. 75), also more recent studies recognize their diagnostic overlap: Mula and colleagues (2010) extracted two distinct but closely related psychopathological dimensions in patients with major depression and bipolar disorder: *anhedonia*, the diminished or abolished capacity to experience pleasant emotions, and *affective depersonalization*, an experienced emotional numbing which generally applies to all emotions.

A more theoretical treatise by Church (2003) describes the phenomenal world of a depressed person as 'lacking depth, both in space and in time' (p. 177) and as 'an undifferentiated and flat sort of place' (p. 179) because '[a]s one's capacity to imagine alternative perspectives on the world diminishes, so too does the experienced depth of that world' (pp. 179f). In contrast, a normal person's experience includes 'a world "behind" the flat surface of appearances' (*ibid.*, p. 180), 'a world of many possibilities' (p. 184). Church thus relates experiential depth to the 'space of possibilities' as it has been repeatedly conceptualized in phenomenological philosophy, for example in Husserl's and Merleau-Ponty's *horizons* or, more recently, in Ratcliffe's (2008a; 2012d) formulation of existential feelings as 'configuration[s] of the possibility space [i.e. the sense of possibilities for perceptual and practical accessibility] that shapes all experience, thought and activity' (Ratcliffe, 2012d, p. 44). Ratcliffe explicitly denies that these configurations of the possibility space differ in depth (*ibid.*), but acknowledges that changes in the configurations of this possibility space do.[4]

Based on Church's conception of phenomenal flatness and on previous studies indicating that 'depressed persons generate imagery more slowly (Cocude, Charlot and Michel, 1997), generate less vivid imagery (Sacco and Ruggieri, 1997), generate less positive fantasies (Starker and Singer, 1975), and imagine positive future events less vividly than negative future events (Holmes *et al.*, 2008)', Kunzendorf *et al.* (2010, p. 455) set out to empirically investigate the relationship between depressive symptomatology and perceptual flatness. Their study combined established self-report questionnaires assessing depressive and anxious traits with new measures of 'flat versus deep' self, person, and object perception. While self and others had to be explicitly rated with pairs of adjectives, semantically spanning the space between flat and deep, object perception was assessed implicitly: the bigger of two ambiguous shapes, an equilateral four-sided and a circular shape, needed to be identified on a graded scale. When perceiving the object as a flat, two-dimensional plane, the area of the circle would be bigger than the one of the square, while a bias towards deeper perception would rather tend towards identifying the three-dimensional volume of the cube as bigger than the one of the sphere. The results demonstrate that a tendency for depressive symptoms (but not for normal sadness) is associated with a *flatter self, person, and object perception* and hence a generally *flatter phenomenal world*.

The study by Kunzendorf *et al.* (2010) can be seen as an initial attempt to relate the concept of experiential or phenomenal depth to psychological traits or tendencies and its results indicate the applicability of phenomenal depth to neurocognitive investigation. Owing to our own research background, we wish to propose the phenomenological dimension of phenomenal depth for clinical investigation, where it aims to capture the level of felt depth of subjective experience across diagnostic boundaries. Accordingly, we suggest that although they are regarded as different syndromes, DPD and certain types of depression share a common core element in that both conditions are characterized by a reduction in phenomenal depth. Our prediction

---

[4]   In the same chapter, Ratcliffe (2012d) develops the concept of 'affective depth' which is only marginally related to the dimension of phenomenal depth as we propose it. For Ratcliffe, the more severe the effect of limiting the possibility space of the patient, the 'deeper' the change in existential feeling. We suggest that experiential depth is flattened or reduced in psychopathologies that involve a detachment from self and world like depersonalization disorder and certain types of depression.

would be that the visuo-spatial bias observed by Kunzendorf *et al.* (2010) can also be found in DPD or in experimentally induced transient depersonalization.

5. The Neurobiology of Phenomenal Depth

Proposing phenomenal depth or a sense of experiential depth and subjective richness as a structural feature of consciousness and its reduction as a common dimension in depression and depersonalization disorder potentially allows for a quantification of phenomenal depth and may thus facilitate neurocognitive investigation.[5]

As phenomenal depth is assumed to constitute a felt aspect of *all* experience, its biological implementation may similarly relate to or feed into structures that generally process the inside and the outside world.

Phenomenal Depth and the Inner Milieu

Hints for a physiological implementation of a basal dimension such as phenomenal depth originate in research on animals and specifically non-human primates (Denton, 2006; Panksepp, 1998), the results of which have recently been extended to humans. These works describe basal bodily feelings in the shape of *homeostatic emotions* (e.g. Craig, 2008), *primal emotions* (Denton, 2006), or *primordial feelings* (Damasio, 2010), which provide information about the internal state of the organism (*interoception*) and influence mechanisms of life regulation (*homeostasis*). In homeostasis, changes in the mechanical, thermal, or chemical state of the internal milieu are registered and dynamically regulated on the basis of the perceived physiological condition of the body as it is conveyed through interoception, a process related to the autonomic nervous system.

Nuclei in the brainstem thereby modulate regulation processes, thus ensuring a basic level of feeling, but simultaneously also forward interoceptive information to cortical areas, of which specifically the insular cortex and the anterior cingulate contribute to a more

---

[5] Furthermore, the concept of phenomenal depth also avoids the recourse to the binary and negative definition as it is commonly used in descriptions of depersonalization disorder (e.g. '*un*-reality' or a lack of felt presence), which only has poor explanatory value (*cf.* Sierra and David, 2010). More specifically, the positive formulation of phenomenal depth avoids the paradoxical situation in which a sense of reality or felt depth is only implied through double negation: for example, according to the ICD-10, DPD patients report that 'objects, people and/or surrounding seem unreal' while necessarily being 'aware of the unreality of the change [namely, the unreality feelings]' (Sierra and David, 2010). In this understanding of the psychopathology, awareness of the 'unreality of the unreality' thus indirectly implies reality, hence 'normal/healthy' subjective experience.

differentiated affective consciousness and the subjective element of instinctive behaviour (*cf.* Craig, 2009; Medford and Critchley, 2010; Damasio, 2010).

Relevant relays in ascending homeostatic projections are, for example, the solitary and parabrachial nuclei, the periaqueductal grey, as well as the inferior and superior colliculi, in which coarse maps of the body are created and integrated before they are forwarded to cortical areas via thalamic relays (*cf.* Craig, 2002; Denton, 2006; Merker, 2007; Panksepp, 1998; for further physiological details).

One of the most important properties of the brain is its extensive structural and functional feedback which is strongly present intra-cortically but becomes particularly relevant in mutual connections between cortex and specific thalamic nuclei (reticularis and intralaminares) or the brainstem. Particularly thalamo-cortico-thalamic loops have been ascribed a role in the formation of subjective experience (e.g. Edelman and Tononi, 2000; Laureys and Tononi, 2008; Llinás, 2002), but recent approaches extend the focus further in the caudal direction and assume that an integration of brainstem-based body representations with cognitive structures at the level of the cortex is of central importance for phenomenal experience (Damasio, 2010; Merker, 2007; Northoff and Panksepp, 2008; Panksepp and Northoff, 2009).

In particular, a recent model by Seth and colleagues (2012) captures this cascading flow of interoceptive information and emphasizes its generative aspects by linking subjective experience to theories of predictive coding. They suggest a neural comparator mechanism predicting informative interoceptive signals in a top-down fashion. A match between top-down prediction and bottom-up internal informative signals leads to the sense of presence, while interoceptive inference in the form of a prediction error is considered 'the constitutive basis of emotion' (Seth, Suzuki and Critchley, 2012, p. 11).

Phenomenal Depth and the Outside World

The approach by Seth and colleagues (2012) is inspired by the *comparator model* of sensorimotor interaction (e.g. Wolpert and Ghahramani, 2000) in which it is assumed that the brain predicts consequences of current actions and compares these predictions to actual outcomes. In the comparator model, a sense of *agency*, similar to the sense of presence for the inner milieu, indicates the successful prediction of consequences in the outer world. Larger theoretical frameworks of brain function (most notably Friston's ideas about *predictive coding* and the *free-energy principle*; e.g. Friston, 2005; 2010) propose that this mechanism is not restricted to the motor domain but rather constitutes a general or global processing principle of the brain. Therefore, it is reasonable to assume that similar mechanisms act on the inner milieu. If predictive coding were a global principle of brain function, and phenomenological depth could be understood as describing experiences connected to the matching of such predictions, the latter would be related to a very basic neurocognitive mechanism.

In their model, Seth, Suzuki and Critchley (2012) propose that external predictive coding (related to agency) and internal predictive coding (related to presence) interact in order to generate full-blown subjective experience. Accordingly, it may be proposed that the phenomenological dimension of phenomenal depth relates to both agency as well as presence, integrating the outer world and the inner self through the principle of predictive coding. Predictive coding might therefore be a formal feature of the neurobiological implementation of phenomenal depth, which we have described as a central quality of all experience — being diminished in both depersonalization and the above-characterized types of depression.

6. Towards a Neurophenomenology of Phenomenal Depth

Neurophenomenology generally investigates how subjective experience is embodied in the physical world. Phenomenological approaches in neuropsychiatry create an '*intermediate level* that relates the level of molecular dysfunctions... to the molar level of descriptive psychopathology and its nosological syndromes' (Fuchs, 2010, p. 548, italics in the original). The dimension of phenomenal depth may provide a useful concept for this research programme as its reduction is a central feature of psychopathologies such as depersonalization disorder and certain types of depression. In addition, as we suggested above, phenomenal depth can be linked to the neurobiology of embodiment via neurocognitive and neurocomputational models.

As with every neurophenomenological enterprise there are two important challenges: first, how can we measure subjective experience, and second, what are the measures to which we want to link those subjective components? Capturing subjective experience usually involves self-reports, for example through questionnaires or structured interviews. Explicit neurophenomenological questionnaires could be developed that assess phenomenal depth in different domains of experience (see Kunzendorf *et al.*, 2010, for a first cut in this direction). Another approach would be to explicitly consider subjective experience as a dependent variable and to experimentally adjust the independent variable in order to measure different degrees of phenomenal depth. While the implicit measures of visuo-spatial bias by Kunzendorf and colleagues (2010) are a start, in more complex set-ups such as multisensory virtual realities, indirect subjective judgments may be assessed, which do not require putting them into explicit propositions as in the case of self-reports (e.g. Ehrsson, 2007).

On the neuro-side there is a whole range of possible approaches including behavioural measures related to the brain and the inner milieu as well as direct and indirect measures of brain activity like EEG/fMRI or brain stimulation methods. These methods can be used to understand how higher-order properties emerge from their neural basis (Walter, 1998; Walter *et al.*, 2009a).

An open question worth investigating is whether the experience of phenomenal depth can be deliberately varied similarly to the experience of emotions. For example, certain types of emotion regulation that aim for a disconnection between the self and the affective dimension of the external world, called *detachment* or *distancing*, can be investigated in healthy subjects (Walter *et al.*, 2009b) but also in patients with depression (Erk *et al.*, 2010) using neuroimaging methods like fMRI. In these studies it has been found that a network comprising the right prefrontal cortex and a region near the right temporo-parietal junction is implied in detaching from affective experience. Accordingly, these regions might be involved in a neurocognitive mechanism that is either directly related to phenomenal depth or that influences connections between the cortex and the brainstem — possibly via the VMPFC — which are likely to regulate experiential depth. Alternatively, the observed activations might also be related to the self-reflective conscious properties of phenomenal depth which is, as described, a meta-cognitive or meta-affective experience.

As has already become apparent, one can also employ psychopathological models of chronically altered phenomenal depth by investigating, for example, subjects with DPD or depression (*cf.* Walter and Michal, in press). This approach has the advantage that phenomena that are typically quite labile and easily influenceable by framing or expectation effects in healthy subjects are more stable and unyielding in patients and therefore easier to correlate with neurobiological measures. On the other side, there are also many confounds in patient studies, and investigations of both healthy subjects and patients will provide complementary clues towards a neurophenom-enology of phenomenal depth.

Based on the considerations above, there are several predictions that can be made with respect to an empirical investigation of phenomenal depth: one is that at the level of the central nervous system the experience of phenomenal depth relates to the interaction of brainstem, thalamus, and cortical areas. Another one is that prediction errors should play an important role in modulating phenomenal depth. At this point these are approximations, but as demonstrated by Seth *et al.*'s (2012) approach, they can be transformed into more precise hypotheses concerning, for example, the role of particular brain regions like the anterior cingulate (ACC) and the insular cortex. Our point in this chapter is thus to suggest a dimension of experience along which an investigation of complex phenomena may become feasible or easier.

Certainly, a challenge for a neurophenomenological account of phenomenal depth is how this dimension can be included into more theoretical or neurophilosophical models of phenomenal experience. We suggest that phenomenal depth might be a formal feature of such models relating to the integration of world-informative body representations into a self-model as it has been formulated and extensively described by Metzinger (e.g. 1999; 2003). Phenomenal depth may be directly related to the property of *transparency* (Metzinger, 2003, p. 163), that is, to the degree to which the representations of bodily states and thus emotions are becoming attentionally transparent to self-reflection or to the degree that they are experienced. From a representational point of view, this would mean that the representational format of the self-model and of external objects are so similar or so interconnected that it virtually becomes impossible to disentangle them by higher-order cognitive processes — something Metzinger calls 'convolved holism' (*ibid.*, pp. 143–50). In contrast, in conditions of low phenomenal depth the formats of representation may be quite dissimilar so that they become opaque and are experienced as different: 'full blown global opacity leads to a "derealization" on the level of phenomenal experience' (*ibid.*, p. 538). If this is the case then it follows that the neuroscientific basis of altered phenomenal depth in psychiatric disorders like DPD or depression has a connection to altered self-representation, as is also suggested in the symptom descriptions by Petrilowitsch (1956) and Kraus (2002; 2008). Therefore, we propose to include some measures of self and selfhood into neurophenomenological investigations of those conditions whenever possible.

We hope that our reflection will motivate investigators to consider phenomenal depth a relevant and useful dimension in neurophenomenological research in psychiatry — but also in general cognitive-affective neuroscience — as it may prove to be a simple way to elucidate complex phenomena. In particular, it can serve as a link in understanding symptoms observed in different psychopathologies, as we have shown for the cases of depersonalization disorder and certain types of depression.

Acknowledgment

This work was supported by a grant from the VolkswagenStiftung (II/84 051).

Anna Buchheim, Roberto Viviani
and Henrik Walter

Attachment Narratives
in Depression

A Neurocognitive Approach

Introduction

John Bowlby's (1980) primary goal in formulating attachment theory was to develop a 'new' model of developmental psychiatry that emphasized the role of real-life events, especially childhood experiences with a parent, as potential contributors to 'mental ill-health'. In the first volume of *Attachment and Loss*, Bowlby (1969) explicated developmental risk in terms of attachment insecurity, defined as feelings of apprehension, anxiety, and fear that result from experiences of compromised maternal care. Attachment theory provides a powerful framework for understanding the nature of close relationships, emotion regulation, trauma, and psychopathology in the context of attachment (Westen *et al.*, 2006). The attachment system is thought to influence the individual's interpersonal perception, expectations, and behaviour (Bretherton and Munholland, 2008). Several studies have demonstrated the central role of attachment patterns in the development of diverse disorders (see review from Dozier, Chase Stovall and Albus, 2008). In particular, they show that disruption in early attachment relationships, via experiences of loss or trauma, influences the development of psychopathological symptoms.

In this contribution we will report on the relationship between attachment patterns in individuals, attachment dysregulation, and emotional disturbances such as depression and review two studies of our own on the neural correlates of attachment.

Four Types of Attachment Patterns

Based on behavioural research in developmental psychology, attachment researchers have developed instruments in order to distinguish four different types of attachment. The classical way to do this is to interview patients in a structured way, the so-called AAI or Adult Attachment Interview (George, Kaplan and Main, 1984/1985/1996; Main and Goldwyn, 1985–1996). Another instrument that we have used in most of our own studies is a semi-structured interview working with pictures to which the participants produce narratives, the so-called AAP or Adult Attachment Projective Picture System (George and West, 2001; 2012). Both models try to capture how the inner working models of attachment are organized based on the content and form of the narratives produced. As a result, participants are classified as belonging to one of four categorized attachment patterns. The first three are patterns that are organized: secure, insecure-dismissing, insecure-preoccupied; whereas the last, the unresolved pattern, is disorganized. A secure attachment pattern is a 'healthy', integrated form of attachment organization, whereas dismissing and preoccupied patterns are dysfunctional, although still organized. The last pattern, the unresolved or disorganized, shows lower emotional integration in the representation of attachment. A more detailed explanation of the types of attachment is given below in the paragraph on the AAP.

It should be noted here that there are also paper and pencil questionnaires that measure adult attachment (Ravitz *et al.*, 2010). However, they differ from the AAI as they measure the explicit, subjective evaluation of what people think about their attachment (called attachment *style*). In contrast, AAI and AAP measure attachment implicitly by coding according to a validated manual how people talk about attachment related issues, thereby measuring attachment *representations*. As so often with implicit and explicit measures there is no evident convergent validity between interview measures and self-report measures of attachment with respect to the organized secure and insecure patterns (Ravitz *et al.*, 2010).

Attachment Patterns in Depression

In recent studies there is growing evidence suggesting that early negative life events may be a marker for chronic depression (Klein *et al.*, 2009). An established risk factor for chronic depression is early life trauma (see Klein, 2010), for example: early loss of a significant caregiver, emotional maltreatment, physical and/or sexual abuse and neglect (e.g. Saleptsi *et al.*, 2004). Such experiences clearly have an impact on the development of inner working models of attachment. On a psycho-behavioural level, significant characteristics of chronically depressed patients in contrast to episodically depressed patients have been identified. These differences comprise interpersonal deficits, a lack of authentic empathy and perspective switching deficits (Zobel *et al.*, 2010), distrust in interpersonal relationships with an expectation to be rejected from others, and a pervasive self-rejection. A recent study investigated the significant impact of childhood trauma (e.g. parental loss) for the chronicity of depression in adults (Wiersma *et al.*, 2009).

The relationship between unresolved (i.e. 'disorganized') attachment and psychopathology is consistent with Bowlby's (1980) original predictions regarding psychiatric instability as a potential response to the death of attachment figures. A recent meta-analysis found that clinical participants showed more insecure and unresolved/disorganized attachment representations than healthy controls (Bakermans-Kranenburg and van IJzendoorn, 2009).

Concerning depression more specifically, studies are inconsistent. Some of them found more preoccupied attachment patterns (Rosenstein and Horowitz, 1996; Fonagy *et al.*, 1996), while others report that depression (episodically depressed and dysthymic) is rather associated with dismissing states of mind (deactivating attachment related themes; see Dozier *et al.*, 2008). In contrast, Fonagy *et al.* (1996) reported a high percentage of unresolved loss (72%) in depressed inpatients using the AAI. A recent study also demonstrated that adolescents with depressive disorders showed a significantly higher percentage of unresolved loss compared to adolescents with obsessive compulsive disorders (Ivarsson *et al.*, 2010). In one of our own studies using the AAP (Buchheim *et al.*, 2012a,b), we also found a high percentage of unresolved loss (54%) in chronically depressed patients (n = 16).

Change of Attachment Status in Psychotherapy

Several recent empirical therapy outcome studies have assessed representation attachment measures before and after therapy. These studies used measures like the AAI or AAP which have been shown to be a useful indicator of outcome in psychotherapy for adults with diverse disorders — including depression, borderline personality disorder, and post-traumatic stress disorder — by measuring changes of the way to talk about attachment experiences.

For example, Levy *et al.* (2006) reported that attachment security can be improved in patients with BPD, particularly in response to transference-focused psychotherapy (TFP). This study was a clinical trial in 90 outpatients with BPD randomly assigned to either TFP, a modified psychodynamic supportive psychotherapy, or dialectical behaviour therapy. Over one year of treatment, the frequency of secure attachment representations (assessed with the AAI) increased significantly but only for patients being treated by TFP. This result was interpreted in the following way: patients in the TFP group were treated by focusing on the change of self- and object representations; how they regulated emotions for themselves and when confronted with significant others. The AAI captured this structural change by showing a shift from insecurity to security.

In a recently published study, we assessed attachment patterns in chronically depressed patients during psychoanalytic treatment using the AAP (Buchheim *et al.*, 2012a,b). The fMRI sample consisted of 16 patients and 17 controls which all were assessed pre–post with fMRI. As expected, chronically depressed patients showed at the beginning of psychodynamic treatment a higher proportion of 'unresolved trauma' compared to controls. This attachment status changed significantly in the expected direction after 15 months of treatment. In the total sample of the study 14 of 18 patients changed from disorganized to an organized attachment status (resolved); only 4 of the patients remained unresolved. Half of the patients showed an 'unresolved trauma' when talking about loss experiences. This result can be considered as preliminary and it remains to be seen if this can be replicated in a larger sample.

Assessing Attachment Patterns in Narratives with the AAP

The Adult Attachment Projective Picture System (AAP) (George and West, 2001; 2012) is a validated measure to assess attachment representations, based on the analysis of narratives produced by patients confronted with a set of eight pictures, one neutral and seven attachment scenes. Individuals are instructed to tell a story: 'Tell me what led up to that scene, what are the characters thinking or feeling, and what might happen next?' (George and West, 2001; 2012). Individuals are classified on the basis of verbatim narratives into one of four attachment group categorizations, as mentioned above (secure, dismissing, preoccupied, and unresolved). Using a manual, individuals are coded by how they represent attachment within the narratives they tell. Secure attachment is characterized by an integrated agency of the self, connectedness, and synchrony with the capacity to integrate dysregulated attachment fear. Dismissing attachment is characterized by functional attachment with little capacity for integration, combined with a prevalence of deactivating defences. Preoccupied attachment is characterized by entangled attachment relationships associated with heightened emotional conflicts. Unresolved attachment is characterized by attachment dysregulation associated with heightened attachment fear, and is a predominant pattern in clinical samples. Unresolved attachment in the AAP coding system is defined as an individual's failure to integrate and resolve any frightening or threatening narrative material, including words and phrases, e.g. death, attack, or devastation.

The following example is an unresolved attachment narrative to the AAP picture 'Cemetery' (see Figure 1) from a depressed patient.

Figure 1. AAP-Picture 'Cemetery' from the Adult Attachment Projective Picture System © George and West (2012), all rights reserved.

*'This man is standing in front of the grave of his wife and he visits her to tell her how much he feels deserted. The grave looks strange and it must be very cold. **What is he thinking or feeling?** He is completely close to the one who he has lost. He speaks with her. He has no idea what to do next and feels desperately lost and helpless. **What is happening next?** He will stand there for a long time. **Anything else?** No.'*

This narrative demonstrates helplessness and unresolved mourning. The man in the story feels desperately lost and shows no way to resolve the hopeless situation. He speaks with the dead person, which is a marker to designate the dissolution of boundaries between the living and deceased. This story shows no indicators of an internalized secure base or capacity to act.

After 15 months of treatment the patient produced the following narrative to the same picture:

*'Oh this person is sad. He is standing in front of the grave of his wife. She is dead since many years. **What is he thinking or feeling?** Yeah, he misses her still a lot. Maybe he is crying, feels alone. He remembers what they shared together, thinks about her. Pause — **What is happening next?** He will stand there for a little while, he is still sad, but then he goes home and tries to distract himself, maybe he meets someone.'*

This story shows a different pattern of attachment representation. The man is sad because of the death of his wife and misses her a lot, but he is not helpless anymore. He remembers what they shared together and what he thinks about her. This is an indicator for having an internalized secure base in the AAP representing the character's attempt at integration at the level of mind. The topic of thought is personal and demonstrates that the character has a relationship, which has influenced the character development in some way. The man's way to cope with his sadness is reflection and to show capacity to act by leaving the cemetery. He is going home, a place of security, and will attempt to connect with other people. (A comprehensive description of the coding procedure along with transcript examples is found in George and West, 2012.)

In the following section we give an illustrative summary of the results from several of our own studies following a specific attachment-theoretical psychodynamic line of thought.

Neural Correlates of Attachment
Dysregulation in Processing Narratives

A few studies have investigated the neural correlates of the appraisal and processing of narratives generated by the AAP in groups of patients and during the therapy of depression to better understand the psychological functions activated by attachment related themes. These studies capitalize on the capacity of functional magnetic resonance imaging (fMRI) to demonstrate the activation of specific brain circuits when participants are exposed to stimuli of a selected type, or are asked to perform chosen tasks (e.g. Posner and Raichle, 1994). Using this approach with a variety of stimuli and tasks it is possible to characterize modes of brain function that span across traditional divisions and provide an objective characterization of the mind embodied in the neural circuits subserving its functioning. The question that these studies potentially address is the relationship between narrative processing, especially in relation to attachment and its elaboration in mental disorders such as depression, and neuropsychological function more generally.

Our first study compared patients affected by borderline personality disorder (BPD) and healthy controls (Buchheim *et al.*, 2008). BPD patients frequently present a history of trauma, and the sample recruited for this study were selected for the existence of past attachment traumas specifically (*ibid.*; Buchheim and George, 2011; 2012). As predicted, BPD patients were classified as 'unresolved' with respect to attachment trauma and showed significant differences to healthy controls, namely, more dysregulated attachment trauma language indicators in monadic picture stories. In this study, participants were scanned while producing narratives elicited by the AAP scenes. The analysis of the narratives showed monadic pictures to be associated with more traumatic material in BPD patients than in controls, which showed distinct activation in several brain areas. The most striking finding was the demonstration of a differential activation in the anterior cingulate cortex (ACC), a part of the limbic system located deep in the midline of the brain, when producing narratives from monadic pictures (Buchheim *et al.*, 2008). The observed ACC activation in our study was located in the anterior midcingulate cortex (aMCC). The aMCC is innervated by the midline and intralaminar thalamic nuclei belonging to the medial pain system, and also receives direct input from the amygdala. This area has been described to be involved in the perception of pain (Vogt, 2005), most notably when the source of pain was psychological rather than physical (Eisenberger, Liebermann and Williams, 2003; Osaka *et al.*, 2004; Ploghaus *et al.*, 1999). These results are consistent with the observation that BPD patients experience psychological pain in association with aloneness and the fear of abandonment. Abandonment fears are the most persistent long-term symptoms in BPD patients and are considered to be clinically relevant (Zanarini *et al.*, 2003). With this study we could contribute to an understanding of the neural basis for this clinical observation using attachment relevant material and fMRI.

Functional neuroimaging based on the AAP was also applied in the study of the effects of psychoanalytic therapy of depression (Buchheim *et al.*, 2012b,c). In this study, the AAP was used to assess attachment narratives in depressed patients for two purposes: to document the change of representational attachment status before and after fifteen months of treatment in psychodynamic therapy as mentioned before, and to assess neural changes of chronically depressed patients during psychodynamic treatment.

During the fMRI session, participants processed short personalized narrative fragments presented together with the AAP scenes that had been extracted from the previous AAP interview. The personalized narrative was composed from three core sentences that represented the attachment pattern of the participants. These were extracted from the audiotaped responses to each AAP picture stimulus by two independent certified judges (e.g. 'He is completely close to the one who he has lost'). These sentences were paired to the respective picture to constitute the 'personally relevant' trials tailored to each participant. The same pictures, paired to sentences describing only the environment of the depicted situation (e.g. 'There is grass growing next to the stone'), constituted the control trials, assumed to not activate the attachment system or to a lesser degree, hence 'neutral' trials, and were identical for all participants. Therefore, the comparison between personally relevant and neutral trials activated circuits associated with narratives of personal history, whose emotional relevance was made more likely by the capacity of the AAP scenes to activate the attachment system. The study focused on patients that had experienced recurrent bouts of depression. These were patients with rather intense feelings of helplessness and fear of losing the love of a significant other (Taylor, 2008).

When exposed to attachment relevant narratives, patients undergoing long-term psychoanalytic psychotherapy were characterized by changes in brain activation that were not present in the control sample of healthy participants. As in the study with BPD patients, the limbic system was involved in the changes in the appraisal of the attachment related material and narrative processing. A portion of the ACC associated by previous fMRI studies with depression (Mayberg, 2003b) and avoidant attachment styles (Gillath et al., 2005) was activated more in patients than in controls before therapy, while at the end of the therapy they showed less activation than the controls (crossed interaction). Importantly, these activation changes were associated with symptom improvement as measured by the Beck Depression Inventory (BDI), thereby linking brain and behavioural measures.

Another area that was revealed to be modulated in its activity by therapy was the anterior hippocampus-amygdala area, a region of the limbic system that is involved in perceiving and processing stimuli of negative emotional valence (Davis and Whalen, 2001), as well as in recall of events that were experienced in a negatively valenced context (Erk, Martin and Walter, 2005). This structure was less active in patients at the end of therapy when exposed to the attachment relevant narratives, while in the healthy control there was no change in function. These changes were accompanied by analogous effects in the prefrontal cortex, which is associated with the cognitive control of emotions (Walter *et al.*, 2009; Erk *et al.*, 2010).

Taken together, the noted difference in brain functioning is consistent with the psychological changes promoted by long-term psychodynamic psychotherapy, especially those therapies favouring acceptance of core issues related to attachment and loss.

General Discussion and Conclusion

We demonstrated different ways to use individual attachment narratives in an experimental fMRI environment. The narratives used were derived from the AAP, a standardized and reliable projective test that allows clinicians to categorize attachment pattern in adults. As experience of loss and trauma disrupts early attachment relationships, influencing the development of several psychiatric disorders (Dozier *et al.*, 2008), it is not surprising that participants with clinically relevant psychopathological symptoms show, in general, more insecure and unresolved attachment representations (Bakermans-Kranenburg and van IJzendoorn, 2009), a finding that was also confirmed in our studies. As attachment representations will influence psychopathology and the effectiveness of psychological therapies, it is of interest to find ways to understand the neurobiological underpinnings of attachment representations.

In our studies with borderline patients (study 1) and chronically depressed patients (study 2) we used two approaches. In the first study we analysed the neural activity during in-scanner talking by taking into account the number of language indicators of traumatic dysregulation in regard to AAP pictures. This method is interesting because it allows a look at brain activity while producing attachment relevant narratives. However, it has some associated methodological issues that restrict the possibility of interpretation, including: the influence of movements, the length of the speaking periods, the uniqueness of each narrative which does not allow for repetitions of stimuli to increase signal to noise ratio. Therefore, a compromise between the need to get individually tailored attachment relevant stimulus material from narratives and signal-theoretic considerations was chosen in the second study, where standardized sentences were extracted from AAP narratives and presented in the scanner in comparison to control sentences.

We interpret our studies' results as indicators for either psychological pain (study 1) or emotional memories, emotion regulation, and cognitive control (study 2). Moreover, it was demonstrated that attachment related brain activations did change over the course of psychodynamic therapy, and that these activation changes were correlated with the improvement of symptoms.

What have we learned from these results? Is it really so astonishing that attachment representation can be traced in the brain? Well, of course every psychological process or disposition has somehow to be reflected in the organization of the brain, but it is not always easy to be able to demonstrate it. Our findings demonstrate correlations in nature, as most neuroimaging studies and also many behavioural experiments. However, by demonstrating changes in attachment related brain activation during the course of therapy, we have introduced a kind of long-term 'effect' showing that brain activations related to attachment can be normalized, altered, or influenced by psychodynamic therapy. In regard to the material, one could ask, have we really measured the neural correlates of attachment or rather the neural correlate of some confounding variable, e.g. an association with disorganized attachment representations? Well, to be sure that it is not the case it would be necessary that the groups investigated differ only with respect to one variable (attachment category), while keeping all other variables constant. To find patients who differ only in the variable investigated and not in any other is the regulative ideal of all clinical neuropsychiatric research, although it is never possible to achieve. Indeed, one is trying to control the most important variables, as we have done, but many of the inferences drawn rest on many explicit or implicit assumptions that research from different angles have yet to prove or disprove. For example, it would be interesting to investigate if the post-therapy brain modulatory effects are also in patients with chronic depression that fall into the category of secure attachment, although these will be rare exceptions. As our studies are the first that try to prove how producing attachment narratives or being confronted with elements of attachment narratives change brain activation and how these changes 'normalize' within the course of therapy in chronic depression, we regard them as a first attempt towards a cognitive neuroscience of attachment representation in a clinical context. It is now up to further studies to try to improve on our design as well as to compare and replicate results across diagnostic categories and symptoms in order to find out if our interpretations hold up to further enquiry.

In conclusion, using the AAP in two individually tailored stimuli approaches demonstrate that attachment measures combining pictures and narrative material, which are relevant for personal attachment categorization, might be an innovative way to address the search for neural correlates while the attachment system of these participants is activated (Buchheim and George, 2011; 2012).

Acknowledgment

We thank Andrew Wold for proofreading the manuscript.

References

(1962) *General Systems*, **7–8**, Society for the Advancement of General Systems Theory.

Abrams, R. & Taylor, M.A. (1981) Importance of schizophrenic symptoms in the diagnosis of mania, *American Journal of Psychiatry*, **138**, pp. 658–661.

Abrams, R., Taylor, M.A. & Gaztanaga, P. (1974) Manic-depressive illness and paranoid schizophrenia, *Archives of General Psychiatry*, **31**, pp. 640–642.

Ackner, B. (1954) Depersonalization: I. Aetiology and phenomenology, *Journal of Mental Science*, **100** (421), pp. 838–853.

Adolphs, R. (2010) What does the amygdala contribute to social cognition?, *Annals of the New York Academy of Sciences*, **1191**, pp. 42–61.

Adolphs, R., Baron Cohen, S., *et al.* (2002) Impaired recognition of social emotions following amygdala damage, *Journal of Cognitive Neuroscience*, **14** (8), pp. 1264–1274.

Akiskal, H. & Puzantian, V. (1979) Psychotic forms of depression and mania, *Psychiatric Clinics of North America*, **2**, pp. 419–440.

Allerdyce, J., Gaebel, W., Zielasek, J. & van Os, J. (2007) Deconstructing psychosis conference February 2006: The validity of schizophrenia and alternative approaches to the classification of psychosis, *Schizophrenia Bulletin*, **33** (4), pp. 863–867.

American Psychiatric Association (1994) *Diagnostic and Statistical Manual of Mental Disorders*, 4th ed., Washington, DC: American Psychiatric Association.

American Psychiatric Association (2000) *Diagnostic and Statistical Manual of Mental Disorders*, 4th ed., text revision, Washington, DC: American Psychiatric Association.

American Psychiatric Association (2013) *Diagnostic and Statistical Manual of Mental Disorders*, 5th ed., Washington, DC: American Psychiatric Association.

Artaud, A. (1965) *Artaud Anthology*, San Francisco, CA: City Lights Books.

Baker, D., Hunter, E.C.M., Lawrence, E., Medford, N., Patel, M. & Senior, C. (2003) Depersonalisation disorder: Clinical features of 204 cases, *British Journal of Psychiatry*, **182**, pp. 428–433.

Bakermans-Kranenburg, M.J. & van IJzendoorn, M. (2009) The first 10,000 Adult Attachment Interviews: Distributions of adult attachment representations in clinical and non-clinical groups, *Attachment & Human Development*, **11** (3), pp. 223–263.

Barry, E.S., Naus, M.J. & Rehm, L.P. (2004) Depression and implicit memory: Understanding mood congruent memory bias, *Cognitive Therapy and Research*, **28**, pp. 387–414.

Bayne, T. (2008) The phenomenology of agency, *Philosophy Compass*, **3** (1), pp. 182–202.

Bayne, T. & Levy, N. (2006) The feeling of doing: Deconstructing the phenomenology of agency, in Sebanz, N. & Prinz, W. (eds.) *Disorders of Volition*, London: MIT Press.

Bayne, T. & Pacherie, E. (2007) Narrators and comparators: The architecture of agentive self-awareness, *Synthese*, **159** (3), pp. 475–491.

Bechara, A., Damasio, H., *et al.* (2000) Emotion, decision making and the orbitofrontal cortex, *Cerebral Cortex*, **10** (3), pp. 295–307.

Beck, A.T. (1986) Hopelessness as a predictor of eventual suicide, in Mann, J.J. & Stanley, M. (eds.) *Psychobiology of Suicidal Behavior*, New York: Academy of Sciences.

Beck, A.T., Rush, A.J., Shaw, B.F., *et al.* (1979) *Cognitive Therapy of Depression*, New York: Guilford Press.

Beck, A.T., Steer, R.A., Kovacs, M. & Garrison, B. (1985) Hopelessness and eventual suicide: A 10-year prospective study of patients hospitalized with suicidal ideation, *American Journal of Psychiatry*, **142**, pp. 559–563.

Beck, A.T., Brown, G. & Steer, R.A. (1989) Prediction of eventual suicide in psychiatric inpatients by clinical ratings of hopelessness, *Journal of Consulting and Clinical Psychology*, **57** (2), pp. 309–310.

Beck, A.T. & Alford, B.A. (2009) *Depression: Causes and Treatment*, Philadelphia, PA: University of Pennsylvania Press.

Berg, J.H. van den (1966) *The Psychology of the Sickbed*, Pittsburgh, PA: Duquesne University Press.

Berg, J.H. van den (1972) *A Different Existence: Principles of Phenomenological Psychopathology*, Pittsburgh, PA:Duquesne University Press.

Berger, M. van, Calker, D. & Riemann, D. (2003) Sleep and manipulations of the sleep-wake rhythm in depression, *Acta Psychiatrica Scandinavica*, Suppl. **418**, pp. 83–91.

Berner, P., Musalek, M. & Walter, H. (1987) Psychopathological concepts of dysphoria, *Psychopathology*, **20** (2), pp. 93–100.

Bernstein, E.M. & Putnam, F.W. (1986) Development, reliability, and validity of a dissociation scale, *Journal of Nervous and Mental Disease*, **174** (12).

Bernstein, J. (2011) Trust: On the real but almost always unnoticed, ever-changing foundation of ethical life, *Metaphilosophy*, **42** (4), pp. 395–416.

Berrios, H. (1985) The psychopathology of affectivity: Conceptual and historical aspects, *Psychological Medicine*, **15**, pp. 745–758.

Biegler, P. (2011) *The Ethical Treatment of Depression: Autonomy through Psychotherapy*, Cambridge, MA: MIT Press.

Bilz, R. (1971) *Palaeoanthropologie*, vol. 1, Frankfurt: Suhrkamp.

Binitie, A. (1975) A factor analytic study of depression across cultures, *British Journal of Psychiatry*, **127**, pp. 559–563.

Binswanger, L. (1964) On the manic mode of being-in-the-world, in Straus, E.W. (ed.) *Phenomenology: Pure and Applied*, pp. 127–141, Pittsburgh, PA: Duquesne University Press.

Bjorkqvist, K. (2001) Social defeat as a stressor in humans, *Physiology & Behavior*, **73**, pp. 435–442.

Blackburn, S. (1998) *Ruling Passions: A Theory of Practical Reasoning*, Oxford: Oxford University Press.

Blakemore, S., Wolpert, D. & Frith, C. (2000) Why can't you tickle yourself?, *NeuroReport*, **11** (11), pp. R11–R16.

Blankenburg, W. (1986) Autismus, in Müller, C. (ed.) *Lexicon et Psychiatrie*, pp. 83–89, Berlin: Springer.

Blankenburg, W. (2002) First steps toward a psychopathology of 'common sense', *Philosophy, Psychiatry and Psychology*, **8** (4), pp. 303–315.

Blaney, P.H. (1986) Affect and memory: A review, *Psychological Bulletin*, **99**, pp. 229–246.

Blatt, S. & Zuroff, D. (1992) Interpersonal relatedness and self-definition: Two prototypes for depression, *Clinical Psychology Review*, **12** (5), pp. 527–562.

Bleuler, E. (1911) *Dementia Praecox or the Group of Schizophrenias*, New York: International Universities Press.

Bliss, E.L., Clark, L.D. & West, C.D. (1959) Studies of sleep deprivation — relationship to schizophrenia, *Archives of Neurology and Psychiatry*, **81** (3), pp. 348–348.

Bolton, D. & Hill, C. (1996) *Mind, Meaning and Mental Disorder: The Nature of Causal Explanation in Psychology and Psychiatry*, Oxford: Oxford University Press.

Bourke, C., Douglas, K. & Porter, R. (2010) Processing of facial emotion expression in major depression: A review, *Australian and New Zealand Journal of Psychiatry*, **44**, pp. 681–696.

Bower, G.H. (1981) Mood and memory, *American Psychologist*, **36**, pp. 129–148.

Bowlby, J. (1969) *Attachment and Loss, Vol. 1: Attachment*, New York: Basic Books.

Bowlby, J. (1980) *Attachment and Loss, Vol. 3: Loss: Sadness and Depression*, New York: Basic Books.

Brampton, S. (2008) *Shoot the Damn Dog: A Memoir of Depression*, London: Bloomsbury.

Braude, S. (1991) *First Person Plural*, New York: Routledge.

Bremner, J., Narayan, M., *et al.* (2000) Hippocampal volume reduction in major depression, *American Journal of Psychiatry*, **157** (1), p. 115.

Bretherton, I. & Munholland, K.A. (2008) Internal working models in attachment relationships: Elaborating a central construct in attachment theory, in Cassidy, J. & Shaver, P.R. (eds) *Handbook of Attachment*, pp. 102–130, London: Guilford Press.

Brosch, T., Pourtois, G., *et al.* (2010) The perception and categorisation of emotional stimuli: A review, *Cognition & Emotion*, **24** (3), pp. 377–400.

Buchheim, A., Erk, S., George, C., Kächele, H., Kircher, T., Martius, P., Pokorny, D., Ruchsow, M., Spitzer, M. & Walter, H. (2008) Neural correlates of attachment trauma in borderline personality disorder: A functional magnetic resonance imaging study, *Psychiatry Research: Neuroimaging*, **163**, pp. 223–235.

Buchheim, A. & George, C. (2011) Attachment disorganization in borderline personality disorder and anxiety disorder, in Solomon, J. & George, V. (eds.) *Disorganization of Attachment and Caregiving*, pp. 343–383, New York: Guilford Press.

Buchheim, A. & George, C. (2012) Using the AAP in neurobiology research, in George, C. & West, M. (eds.) *The Adult Attachment Projective Picture System*, pp. 253–274, New York: Guilford Press.

Buchheim, A., Taubner, S. & George, C. (2012a) Neuronale Korrelate von Bindungsmustern bei depressiv Erkrankten, in Böker, H. & Seifritz, E. (eds.) *Psychotherapie und Neurowissenschaften*, pp. 388–413, Bern: Huber.

Buchheim, A., Viviani, R., Kessler, H., Kächele, H., Cierpka, M., Roth, G., George, C., Kernberg, O.F., Bruns, G. & Taubner, S. (2012b) Neuronale Veränderungen bei chronisch-depressiven Patienten während psychoanalytischer Psychotherapie. Funktionelle Magnetresonanz-tomographie-Studie mit einem Bindungsparadigma, *Psychotherapeut*, **57**, pp. 219–226.

Buchheim, A., Viviani, R., Kessler, H., Kächele, H., Cierpka, M., Roth, G., George, C., Kernberg, P.F., Bruns, G. & Taubner, S. (2012c) Changes in prefrontal-limbic function in major depression after 15 months of long-term psychotherapy, *PLoS One*, e33745.

Buckner, R.L., Andrews-Hanna, J.R. & Schacter, D.L. (2008) The brain's default network, *Annals of the New York Academy of Sciences*, **1124** (1), pp. 1–38.

Butler, R.W. & Braff, D.L. (1991) Delusions: A review and integration, *Schizophrenia Bulletin*, **17** (4), pp. 633–647.

Cahill, C.M. & Murphy, K.C. (2004) Migraine and depersonalization disorder, *Cephalalgia: An international Journal of Headache*, **24** (8), pp. 686–687.

Carel, H. (2008) *Illness: The Cry of the Flesh*, Stocksfield: Acumen.

Carel, H. (2012) Phenomenology as a resource for patients, *Journal of Medicine and Philosophy*, **37** (2), pp. 96–113.

Carel, H. (2013) Illness, phenomenology, and the philosophical method, *Theoretical Medicine and Bioethics*, **34** (4).

Carman, T. (1999) The body in Husserl and Merleau-Ponty, *Philosophical Topics*, **27** (2), pp. 205–226.

Carpenter, W.T. & Strauss, J.S. (1974) Cross cultural evaluation of Schneider's first-rank symptoms of schizophrenia: A report from the International Pilot Study of Schizophrenia, *American Journal of Psychiatry*, **131**, pp. 682–687.

Castren, E. (2005) Is mood chemistry?, *Nature Reviews Neuroscience*, **6** (3), pp. 241–246.

Cermolacce, M., Sass, L.A. & Parnas, J. (2010) What is bizarre in bizarre delusions? A critical review, *Schizophrenia Bulletin*, **36** (4), pp. 667–679.

Charland, L. (2010) Reinstating the passions: Arguments from the history of psychopathology, in Goldie, P. (ed.) *The Oxford Handbook of Philosophy of Emotion*, pp. 237–259, Oxford: Oxford University Press.

Church, J. (2003) Depression, depth, and the imagination, in Philips, J. & Morley, J. (eds.) *Imagination and Its Pathologies*, Cambridge, MA: MIT Press.

Clark, A. (1997) *Being There: Putting Brain, Body and World Together Again*, Cambridge, MA: MIT Press.

Clark, D.A. & Beck, A.T. (1989) Cognitive theory and therapy of anxiety and depression, in Kendall, P.C. & Watson, D. (eds.) *Anxiety and Depression: Distinctive and Overlapping Features*, pp. 379–411, San Diego, CA: Academic Press.

Clarke, D.M. & Kissane, D.W. (2002) Demoralization: Its phenomenology and importance, *Australian and New Zealand Journal of Psychiatry*, **36**, pp. 733–742.

Clark, H. (2008) *Depression and Narrative: Telling the Dark*, Albany, NY: SUNY Press.

Cocude, M., Charlot, V. & Michel, D. (1997) Latency and duration of visual mental images in normal and depressed subjects, *Journal of Mental Imagery*, **21** (1–2), pp. 127–142.

Cole-King, A. & Lepping, P. (2010) Suicide mitigation: Time for a more realistic approach, *British Journal of General Practice*, **60**, pp. 3–4.

Colombetti, G. (2007) Enactive appraisal, *Phenomenology and the Cognitive Sciences*, **6**, pp. 527–546.

Colombetti, G. & Thompson, E. (2008) The feeling body: Toward an enactive approach to emotion, in Overton, W.F., Mueller, U. & Newman, J. (eds.) *Body in Mind, Mind in Body: Developmental Perspectives on Embodiment and Consciousness*, pp. 45–68, New York: Lawrence Erlbaum Associates.

Colombetti, G. & Ratcliffe, M. (2012) Bodily feeling in depersonalization: A phenomenological account, *Emotion Review*, **4** (2), pp. 145–150.

Condon, W.S. (1979) Neonatal entrainment and enculturation, in Bullowa, M. (ed.) *Before Speech*, pp. 131–148, Cambridge: Cambridge University Press.

Craig, A.D. (2002) How do you feel? Interoception: The sense of the physiological condition of the body, *Nature Reviews Neuroscience*, **3** (8), pp. 655–666.

Craig, A.D. (2008) Interoception and emotion: A neuroanatomical perspective, in Lewis, M., Haviland-Jones, J.M. & Feldman Barrett, L. (eds.) *Handbook of Emotion*, pp. 272–290, New York: Guilford Press.

Craig, A.D. (2009) How do you feel — now? The anterior insula and human awareness, *Nature Reviews Neuroscience*, **10** (1), pp. 59–70.

Critchley, S. & Schürmann, R. (2008) *On Heidegger's Being and Time*, Levine, S. (ed.), London: Routledge.

Csordas, T.J. (2008) Intersubjectivity and intercorporeality, *Subjectivity*, **22**, pp. 110–121.

Csordas, T.J. (in press) Cultural phenomenology of psychiatric illness, in Kirmayer, L., Lemelson, R. & Cummings, C. (eds.) *Revisioning Psychiatry: Cultural Phenomenology, Critical Neuroscience, and Global Mental Health*, Cambridge: Cambridge University Press.

Csukly, G., Czobor, P., Szily, E., Takács, B. & Simon, L. (2009) Facial expression recognition in depressed subjects: The impact of intensity level and arousal dimension, *Journal of Nervous and Mental Disease*, **197**, pp. 98–103.

Custance, J. (1952) *Wisdom, Madness and Folly: The Philosophy of a Lunatic*, New York: Pellegrini and Cudahy.

Cutting, J. (2002) *The Living, the Dead, and the Never-alive*, Haywards Heath: Forest Publishing Company.

Damasio, A.R. (1994) *Descartes' Error: Emotion, Reason, and the Human Brain*, New York: Putnam.

Damasio, A.R. (1999) *The Feeling of What Happens: Body and Emotion in the Making of Consciousness*, New York: Harcourt Brace.

Damasio, A.R. (2010) *Self Comes to Mind: Constructing the Conscious Brain*, New York: Random House.

Daniels, J.K., Coupland, N.J., Hegadoren, K.M., Rowe, B.H., Densmore, M., Neufeld, R.W. & Lanius, R.A. (2012) Neural and behavioral correlates of peritraumatic dissociation in an acutely traumatized sample, *Journal of Clinical Psychiatry*, **73** (4), pp. 420–426.

Darwin, C. (1872/1998) *The Expression of the Emotions in Man and Animals*, Ekman, P. (ed.), Oxford: Oxford University Press.

Davidson, P.W. (1966) Depersonalization phenomena in 214 adult psychiatric in-patients, *Psychiatric Quarterly*, **40** (1–4). pp. 702–722.

Davidson, R.J., Jackson, D.C., et al. (2000) Emotion, plasticity, context, and regulation: Perspectives from affective neuroscience, *Psychological Bulletin*, **126** (6), pp. 890–909.

Davis, M. & Whalen, P.J. (2001) The amygdala: Vigilance and emotion, *Molecular Psychiatry*, **6**, pp. 13–34.

Deigh, J. (2010) Concepts of emotions in modern philosophy and psychology, in Goldie, P. (ed.) *The Oxford Handbook of Philosophy of Emotion*, pp. 17–40, Oxford: Oxford University Press.

Dennett, D.C. (1988) Précis of the intentional stance, *Behavioral and Brain Sciences*, **11**, pp. 495–505.

Denton, D. (2006) *The Primordial Emotions: The Dawning of Consciousness*, New York: Oxford University Press.

de Sousa, R. (1987) *The Rationality of Emotions*, Cambridge, MA: MIT Press.

de Sousa, R. (2006) Restoring emotion's bad rep: The moral randomness of norms, *European Journal of Analytic Philosophy*, **2** (1), pp. 27–45.

de Sousa, R. (2007) *Why Think? Evolution and the Rational Mind*, Oxford: Oxford University Press.

de Sousa, R. (2010) The mind's Bermuda Triangle: Philosophy of emotions and empirical science, in Goldie, P. (ed.) *The Oxford Handbook of Philosophy of Emotions*, pp. 93–117, Oxford: Oxford University Press.

de Sousa, R. (2011) *Emotional Truth*, Oxford: Oxford University Press.

Di Simplicio, M., Norbury, R., *et al.* (2011) Short-term antidepressant administration reduces negative self-referential processing in the medial prefrontal cortex in subjects at risk for depression, *Molecular Psychiatry*, **17** (5).

Döring, S. (2007) Seeing what to do: Affective perception and rational motivation, *Dialectica*, **61** (3), pp. 363–394.

Dozier, M., Chase Stovall, K. & Albus, K.E. (2008) Attachment and psychopathology in adulthood, in Cassidy, J. & Shaver, P. (eds.) *Handbook of Attachment*, 2nd ed., pp. 718–744, New York: Guilford Press.

D'Sa, C. & Duman, R. (2002) Antidepressants and neuroplasticity, *Bipolar Disorders*, **4** (3), pp. 183–194.

Duranti. A. (2010) Husserl, intersubjectivity, and anthropology, *Anthropological Theory*, **10** (1–2), pp. 16–35.

Dutta, R., Greene, T., Addington, J., McKenzie, K., Phillips, M. & Murray, R.M. (2007) Biological, life-course, and cross-cultural studies all point toward the value of dimensional and developmental ratings in the classification of psychosis, *Schizophrenia Bulletin*, **33** (4), pp. 868–876.

Edelman, G.M. & Tononi, G. (2000) *Consciousness: How Matter Becomes Imagination*, London: Allen Lane.

Ehrenreich, B. (2009) *Smile or Die: How Positive Thinking Fooled America and the World*, London: Granta Books.

Ehrsson, H. (2007) The experimental induction of out-of-body experiences, *Science*, **317** (5841), p. 1048.

Eisenberger, N.I., Liebermann, M.D. & Williams, K.D. (2003) Does rejection hurt? An fMRI study of social exclusion, *Science*, **203**, pp. 290–292.

Ellenberger, H.F. (1958) A clinical introduction to psychiatric phenomenology and existential analysis, in May, R., Angel, E. & Ellenberger, H.F. (eds.) *Existence: A New Dimension in Psychiatry and Psychology*, pp. 92–124, New York: Basic Books.

Elliott, C. (2003) *Better than Well: American Medicine Meets the American Dream*, New York: Norton.

Elster, J. (1984) *Ulysses and the Sirens: Studies in Rationality and Irrationality*, Cambridge: Cambridge University Press, in collaboration with Maison des Sciences de l'Homme, Paris.

Enoch, M.D. & Trethowan, W.H. (1991) *Uncommon Psychiatric Syndromes*, Oxford: Butterworth-Heinemann.

Erk, S., Martin, S. & Walter, H. (2005) Emotional context during encoding of neutral items modulates brain activation not only during encoding but also during recognition, *NeuroImage*, **26**, pp. 829–838.

Erk, S., Mikschl, A., Stier, S., Ciaramidaro, A., Gapp, V., Weber, B. & Walter, H. (2010) Acute and sustained effects of cognitive emotion regulation in major depression, *Journal of Neuroscience*, **30** (47), pp. 15726–15734.

Escobar, J., Gomez, J. & Tuason, V.D. (1983) Depressive phenomenology in North and Southamerican patients, *American Journal of Psychiatry*, **140**, pp. 147–151.

Ey, H., Bernard, P. & Brisset, C. (1960) *Manuel de Psychiatrie*, Paris: Masson.

Ferreira, B. (2002) *Stimmung bei Heidegger: Das Phänomen der Stimmung im Kontext von Heideggers Existenzialanalyse des Daseins*, Dordrecht: Kluwer Academic Publishers.

Fincham, B., Langer, S., Scourfield, J. & Shiner, M. (2011) *Understanding Suicide: A Sociological Autopsy*, Basingstoke: Palgrave Macmillan.

Fingerhut, J. (2012) The body and the experience of presence, in Fingerhut, J. & Marienberg, S. (eds.) *Feelings of Being Alive — Gefuehle des Lebendigseins*, pp. 167–199, Berlin: de Gruyter.

Fonagy, P., Leigh, T., Steele, M., Steele, H., Kennedy, R., Mattoon, G., Target, M. & Gerber, A. (1996) The relationship of attachment status, psychiatric classification, and response to psychotherapy, *Journal of Consulting and Clinincal Psychology*, **4**, pp. 22–31.

Frankfurt, H. (1971) Freedom of the will and the concept of a person, *Journal of Philosophy*, **68**, pp. 5–20.

Frankfurt, H. (2006) *Taking Ourselves Seriously & Getting it Right*, Stanford, CA: Stanford University Press.

Freeman, L. (2011) Reconsidering relational autonomy: A feminist approach to selfhood and the other in the thinking of Martin Heidegger, *Inquiry*, **54** (4), pp. 361–383.

Freud, S. (1957) Mourning and melancholia, in *The Standard Edition of the Complete Psychological Works of Sigmund Freud*, vol. 14, London: Hogarth.

Freud, S. (1967) *Trauer und Melancholie*, Frankfurt: Fischer.

Frijda, N.H. (1986) *The Emotions*, Cambridge: Cambridge University Press.

Frijda, N. (1993a) Moods, emotion episodes, and emotions, in Lewis, M. & Haviland, J.M. (eds.) *Handbook of Emotions*, pp. 381–404, New York: Guilford Press.

Frijda, N. (1993b) The place of appraisal in emotion, *Cognition & Emotion*, 7, pp. 357–387.

Frijda, N. (2001) The self and emotions, in Bosma, H.A. & Kunnen, E.S. (eds.) *Itentity and Emotion: Development Through Self-Organization*, pp. 39–57, Cambridge: Cambridge University Press.

Frijda, N. (2009) Emotion experience and its varieties, *Emotion Review*, 1 (3), pp. 264–271.

Frijda, N., Sjoberg, L., *et al.* (1989) Emotion and cognition, in McConkey, K.M. & Bennett, A.F. (eds.) *Cognition in Individual and Social Contexts: Proceedings of the 24th International Congress of Psychology of the International Union of Psychological Science*, vol. 3, pp. 325–406, Amsterdam: North-Holland.

Friston, K. (2005) A theory of cortical responses, *Philosophical Transactions of the Royal Society of London, B: Biological Sciences*, **360** (1456), pp. 815–836.

Friston, K. (2010) The free-energy principle: A unified brain theory?, *Nature Reviews Neuroscience*, **11** (2), pp. 127–138.

Froese, T. & Fuchs, T. (2012) The extended body: A case study in the neurophenomenology of social interaction, *Phenomenology and the Cognitive Sciences*, **11**, pp. 205–236.

Fuchs, T. (2000) *Psychopathologie von Leib und Raum: Phänomenologisch-empirische Untersuchungen zu depressiven und paranoiden Erkrankungen*, Darmstadt: Steinkopff.

Fuchs, T. (2001) Melancholia as desynchronization: Towards a psychopathology of interpersonal time, *Psychopathology*, **34**, pp. 179–186.

Fuchs, T. (2002a) *Zeit-Diagnosen: Philosophisch-psychiatrische Essays*, Kusterdingen: Die Graue Edition.

Fuchs, T. (2002b) The phenomenology of shame, guilt and the body in body dysmorphic disorder and depression, *Journal of Phenomenological Psychology*, **33**, pp. 223–243.

Fuchs, T. (2002c) The challenge of neuroscience: Psychiatry and phenomenology today, *Psychopathology*, **35**, pp. 319–326.

Fuchs, T. (2003) The phenomenology of shame, guilt and the body in body dysmorphic disorder and depression, *Journal of Phenomenological Psychology*, **33**, pp. 223–243.

Fuchs, T. (2005a) Corporealized and disembodied minds: A phenomenological view of the body in melancholia and schizophrenia, *Philosophy, Psychiatry, & Psychology*, **12**, pp. 95–107.

Fuchs, T. (2005b) Implicit and explicit temporality, *Philosophy, Psychiatry, & Psychology*, **12**, pp. 195–198.

Fuchs, T. (2007) The temporal structure of intentionality and its disturbance in schizophrenia, *Psychopathology*, **40**, pp. 229–235.

Fuchs, T. (2010) Phenomenology and psychopathology, in Gallagher, S. & Schmicking, D. (eds.) *Handbook of Phenomenology and the Cognitive Sciences*, pp. 547–573, Dordrecht: Springer.

Fuchs, T. (2011) The brain — a mediating organ, *Journal of Consciousness Studies*, **18** (7–8), pp. 196–221.

Fuchs, T. (2012) The feeling of being alive: Organic foundations of self-awareness, in Fingerhut, J. & Marienberg, S. (eds.) *Feelings of Being Alive*, Berlin/New York: De Gruyter.

Fuchs, T. (2013a) Temporality and psychopathology, *Phenomenology and the Cognitive Sciences*, **12**, pp. 75–104.

Fuchs, T. (2013b) The phenomenology of affectivity, in Fulford, B., Davies, M., Graham, G., Sadler, J. & Stanghellini, G. (eds.) *The Oxford Handbook of Philosophy and Psychiatry*, pp. 612–631, Oxford: Oxford University Press.

Fuchs, E., Czéh, B., *et al.* (2004) Alterations of neuroplasticity in depression: The hippocampus and beyond, *European Neuropsychopharmacology*, **14**, pp. 481–490.

Fuchs, T. & De Jaegher, H. (2009) Enactive intersubjectivity: Participatory sense-making and mutual incorporation, *Phenomenology and the Cognitive Sciences*, **8**, pp. 465–486.

Fukunishi, I., Nakagawa, T., Nakamura, H. & Ogawa, J. (1993) A comparison of Type A behaviour pattern, hostility and Typus Melancholicus in Japanese and American students: Effects of defensiveness, *International Journal of Social Psychiatry*, **39** (1), pp. 58–63.

Gallagher, S. (2000) Philosophical conceptions of the self: Implications for cognitive science, *Trends in Cognitive Science*, **4** (1), pp. 14–21.

Gallagher, S. (2005) *How the Body Shapes the Mind*, Oxford: Oxford University Press.

Gallagher, S. (2007) The natural philosophy of agency, *Philosophy Compass*, **2** (2), pp. 347–357.

Gallagher, S. (2011) Introduction, in Gallagher, S. (ed.) *The Oxford Handbook of the Self*, pp. 1–29, New York: Oxford University Press.

Gebsattel, E. von (1954) *Prolegomena einer medizinischen Anthropologie*, Berlin: Springer.

George, C., Kaplan, N. & Main, M. (1984/1985/1996) *The Adult Attachment Interview*, unpublished manuscript: University of California, Berkeley.

George, C. & West, M. (2001) The development and preliminary validation of a new measure of adult attachment: The adult attachment projective, *Attachment and Human Development*, pp. 30–61.

George, C. & West, M. (2012) *The Adult Attachment Projective Picture System*, New York: Guilford Press.

Ghaemi, S.N. (2008) Why antidepressants are not antidepressants: Step-BD, STAR*D, and the return of neurotic depression, *Bipolar Disorders*, **10**, pp. 957–968.

Giddens, A. (1991) *Modernity and Self-Identity: Self and Society in the Late Modern Age*, Cambridge: Polity.

Gillath, O., Bunge, S.A., Shaver, P.R., Wendelken, C. & Mikulincer, M. (2005) Attachment-style differences in the ability to suppress negative thoughts: Exploring the neural correlates, *NeuroImage*, **28**, pp. 835–847.

Gilman, C. Perkins (1935) *The Living of Charlotte Perkins Gilman: An Autobiography*, Madison, WI: University of Wisconsin Press.

Glannon, W. (2002) Depression as a mind–body problem, *Philosophy, Psychiatry, & Psychology*, **9**, pp. 243–254.

Glaser, B.G. (1978) *Theoretical Sensitivity: Advances in the Methodology of Grounded Theory*, Mill Valley, CA: Sociology Press.

Glaser, B.G. (1992) *Basics of Grounded Theory Analysis: Emergence vs. Forcing*, Mill Valley, CA: Sociology Press.

Glaser, B.G. (2005) *Grounded Theory Perspective III: Theoretical Coding*, Mill Valley, CA: Sociology Press.

Glaser, B.G. & Strauss, A.L. (1967) *The Discovery of Grounded Theory: Strategies for Qualitative Research*, New York: Aldine.

Goel, V., Gold, B., *et al.* (1998) Neuroanatomical correlates of human reasoning, *Journal of Cognitive Neuroscience*, **10** (3), pp. 293–302.

Goldie, P. (2000) *The Emotions: A Philosophical Exploration*, Oxford: Oxford University Press.

Goldie, P. (2009) Getting feeling into emotional experience in the right way, *Emotion Review*, **1**, pp. 232–239.

Goldie, P. (ed.) (2010) *The Oxford Handbook of Philosophy of Emotion*, Oxford: Oxford University Press.

Gordon, R.M. (1987) *The Structure of Emotions: Investigations in Cognitive Philosophy*, Cambridge: Cambridge University Press.

Gotlib, I.H., Krasnoperova, E., Yue, D.N. & Joormann, J. (2004) Attentional biases for negative interpersonal stimuli in clinical depression, *Journal of Abnormal Psychology*, **113**, pp. 121–135.

Graham, G. (2010) *The Disordered Mind*, London and New York: Routledge.

Grandjean, D. & Scherer, K.R. (2008) Unpacking the cognitive architecture of emotion processes, *Emotion*, **8** (3), pp. 341–351.

Griesinger, W. (1867) *Die Pathologie und Therapie der psychischen Krankheiten*, 2nd ed., Stuttgart: Krabbe.

Griffiths, P.E. (2004) Towards a 'Machiavellian' theory of emotional appraisal, in Cruse, P. & Evans, D. (eds.) *Emotion, Evolution and Rationality*, pp. 89–105, Oxford: Oxford University Press.

Griffiths, P.E. & Scarantino, A. (2009) Emotions in the wild: The situated perspective on emotion, in Robbins, P. & Aydede, M. (eds.) *The Cambridge Handbook of Situated Cognition*, pp. 437–453, Cambridge: Cambridge University Press.

Grinberg, L. (1964) On two kinds of guilt: Their relation with normal and pathological aspects of mourning, *International Journal of Psychoanalysis*, **45** (2–3), pp. 366–371.

Gross, G., Huber, G., Klosterkotten, J. & Linz, M. (2008) *Bonn Scale for the Assessment of Basic Symptoms*, Aachen: Shaker Verlag.

Gunderson, J. (1984) *Borderline Personality Disorder*, Washington, DC: American Psychiatric Press.

Gunderson, J. & Philips, K.A. (1991) A current view of the interface between borderline personality disorder and depression, *American Journal of Psychiatry*, **148** (8), pp. 967–975.

Gureje, O., Simon, G.E. & Üstün, T.B. (1997) Somatization in cross-cultural perspective: A world health organization study in primary care, *American Journal of Psychiatry*, **154**, pp. 989–995.

Haar, M. (1992) Attunement and thinking, in Dreyfus, H. & Hall, H. (eds.) *Heidegger: A Critical Reader*, Cambridge: Blackwell.

Hamilton, M. (ed.) (1984) *Fish's Schizophrenia*, 3rd ed., Bristol: Wright.

Handest, P. & Parnas, J. (2005) Clinical characteristics of first-admitted patients with ICD-10 schizotypal disorder, *British Journal of Psychiatry*, **187**, s49–s54.

Harkavy Friedman, J. & Asnis, G. (1989a) Assessment of suicidal behavior: A new instrument, *Psychiatric Annals*, **19**, pp. 382–387.

Harkavy Friedman, J. & Asnis, G. (1989b) Correction, *Psychiatric Annals*, **19**, p. 438.

Harmer, C. (2008) Serotonin and emotional processing: Does it help explain antidepressant drug action?, *Neuropharmacology*, **55** (6), pp. 1023–1028.

Harmer, C., Goodwin, G., *et al.* (2009) Why do antidepressants take so long to work? A cognitive neuropsychological model of antidepressant drug action, *British Journal of Psychiatry*, **195** (2), p. 102.

Harris, C., Sharman, S.J., Barnier, A.J. & Moulds, M. (2010) Mood and retrieval-induced forgetting of positive and negative autobiographical memories, *Applied Cognitive Psychology*, **24**, pp. 399–413.

Harris, E.C. & Barraclough, B. (1997) Suicide as an outcome for mental disorders: A meta-analysis, *British Journal of Psychiatry*, **170**, pp. 205–228.

Harrison, N.A., Brydon, L., Walker, C., Gray, M.A., Steptoe, A. & Critchley, H.D. (2009) Inflammation causes mood changes through alterations in subgenual cingulate activity and mesolimbic connectivity, *Biological Psychiatry*, **66**, pp. 407–414.

Hatfield, E., Cacioppo, J. & Rapson, R.L. (1994) *Emotional Contagion*, New York: Cambridge University Press.

Hatzimoysis, A. (2005) Emotional feelings and intentionalism, in Hatzimoysis, A. (ed.) *Philosophy and the Emotions*, pp. 105–112, Cambridge: Cambridge University Press.

Haug, E., Lien, L., Raballo, A., Bratlien, L., Oie, M., Parnas, J., Andreasen, O., Melle, I. & Moller, P. (2012) Self-disorders and early differential diagnosis in first episode psychosis, *Journal of Nervous and Mental Disease*, **200**, pp. 632–636.

Hawton, K. & van Heeringen, K. (eds.) (2000) *The International Handbook of Suicide and Attempted Suicide*, Chichester: Wiley.

Healy, D. (2004) *Let them Eat Prozac: The Unhealthy Relationship between the Pharmaceutical Industry and Depression*, New York: New York University Press.

Heidegger, M. (1927/1962) *Being and Time*, Macquarrie, J. & Robinson, E. (trans.), Oxford: Blackwell.

Heidegger, M. (1929–30/1995) *Basic Concepts of Metaphysics: World — Finitude — Solitude*, McNeil, W. & Walker, N. (trans.), Bloomington, IN: Indiana University Press.

Heidegger, M. (1977) Letter on humanism, in Krell, D.F. (ed.) *Basic Writings*, pp. 239–276, New York: Harper & Row.

Heidegger, M. (1983) *Die Grundbegriffe der Metaphysik: Welt, Endlichkeit, Einsamkeit*, GA 29–30, Frankfurt am Main: Vittorio Klostermann.

Heidegger, M. (1986) *Sein und Zeit*, 6th ed., Tübingen: Max Niemeyer Verlag.

Heidegger, M. (2001) *Zollikon Seminars: Protocols–Conversations–Letters*, Boss, M. (ed.), Mayr, F. & Askay, R. (trans.), Evanston, IL: Northwestern University Press. (Original work published 1987.)

Helm, B.W. (2001) *Emotional Reason: Deliberation, Motivation, and the Nature of Value*, Cambridge: Cambridge University Press.

Helm, B.W. (2002) Felt evaluations: A theory of pleasures and pains, *American Philosophical Quarterly*, **39**, pp. 13–30.

Hilton, S. & Elder, G.H. (2007) Time, self and the curiously abstract concept of agency, *Sociological Theory*, **25** (2), pp. 170–191.

Hollan, D. (2008) Being there: On the imaginative aspects of understanding others and being understood, *Ethos*, **36** (4), pp. 475–489.

Hollan, D. & Throop, J. (2008) Whatever happened to empathy?: Introduction, *Ethos*, **36** (4), pp. 385–401.

Holmes, E.A., Lang, T.J., Moulds, M.L. & M, S.A. (2008) Prospective and positive mental imagery deficits in dysphoria, *Behaviour Research and Therapy*, **46**, pp. 976–981.

Holzman, P.S., Shenton, M.E. & Solovay, M.R. (1986) Quality of thought disorder in differential diagnosis, *Schizophrenia Bulletin*, **12** (3), pp. 360–371.

Horwitz, A. & Wakefield, J. (2007) *The Loss of Sadness: How Psychiatry Transformed Normal Sorrow into Depressive Disorder*, Oxford: Oxford University Press.

Hsu, M., Bhatt, M., Adolphs, R., Tranel, D. & Camerer, C.F. (2005) Neural systems responding to degrees of uncertainty in human decision-making, *Science*, **310** (5754), pp. 1680–1683.

Hume, D. (1777/1975) *Enquiries Concerning Human Understanding and Concerning the Principles of Morals*, Oxford: Clarendon Press.

Hume, D. (1978) *A Treatise of Human Nature*, Selby-Bigge, L.A. (ed.), Oxford: Clarendon Press.

Hume, D. (1779/2008) *Dialogues Concerning Natural Religion*, Gaskin, J.C.A. (ed.), Oxford: Oxford Paperback.

Hunter, E.C.M., Sierra, M. & David, A.S. (2004) The epidemiology of depersonalisation and derealisation: A systematic review, *Social Psychiatry and Psychiatric Epidemiology*, **39** (1), pp. 9–18.

Humpston, C. (2011) *Triphase*, (unpublished poem).

Hurley, S.L. (1998) *Consciousness in Action*, Cambridge, MA: Harvard University Press.

Hürlimann, F., Kupferschmid, S. & Simon, A.E. (2012) Cannabis-induced depersonalization disorder in adolescence, *Neuropsychobiology*, **65** (3), pp. 141–146.

Husserl, E. (1931/1962) *Ideas: General Introduction to a Pure Phenomenology*, New York: Macmillan.

Husserl, E. (1948/1997) *Experience and Judgement*, Evanston, IL: Northwestern University Press.

Husserl, E. (1950/1999) *Cartesian Meditations*, Dordrecht: Kluwer.

Husserl, E. (1973) *Zur Phänomenologie der Intersubjektivität*, III: 1929–1935, *Husserliana*, Vol. XV, Kern, I. (ed.), Den Haag: M. Nijhoff.

Husserl, E. (1989) *Ideas Pertaining to a Pure Phenomenology and to a Phenomenological Philosophy: Second Book*, Rojcewicz, R. & Schuwer, A. (trans.), Dordrecht: Kluwer.

Hutto, D. (2005) Knowing *what*? Radical versus conservative enactivism, *Phenomenology and the Cognitive Sciences*, **4**, pp. 389–405.

Ivarsson, T., Granqvist, P., Gillberg, C. & Broberg, A.G. (2010) Attachment states of mind in adolescents with Obsessive-Compulsive Disorder and/or depressive disorders: A controlled study, *European Child & Adolescent Psychiatry*, **19**, pp. 845–853.

Jack, D. (1991) *Silencing the Self: Women and Depression*, Cambridge, MA: Harvard University Press.

Jackson, M. (ed.) (1996) *Things as They Are: New Directions in Phenomenological Anthropology*, Bloomington, IN: Indiana University Press.

Jacobs, K.A. (2011, December) *Experience of Inability in Mental Disorder — Changes of Caring in Depression*, oral presentation at the '*animal emotionale* II' project workshop 'Existential Feelings and Psychopathology', Osnabrück, Germany.

Jacobs, K.A., Stephan, A., Paskaleva, A. & Wilutzky, W. (forthcoming) Existential and atmospheric feelings in depressive comportment, *Philosophy, Psychiatry, & Psychology*.

James, W. (1884) What is an emotion?, *Mind*, **9** (34), pp. 188–205.

James, W. (1898) *Principles of Psychology*, Cambridge, MA: Harvard University Press.

Jamison, K.R. (1995) *An Unquiet Mind*, New York: Vintage Books.

Jaspers, K. (1946/1963) *General Psychopathology*, Hoenig, J. & Hamilton, M.W. (trans.), Chicago, IL: University of Chicago Press.

Jaspers, K. (1997) *General Psychopathology*, Hoenig, J.J. & Hamilton, M.W. (trans.), Baltimore, MD: Johns Hopkins University Press. Originally published (1959) *Allgemeine Psychopathologie*, 7th ed., Berlin: Springer.

Jenkins, J.H. (in press) Psychic and social sinew: Life conditions of trauma among youths in New Mexico, *Medical Anthropology Quarterly*, **27**.

Johnson, H.K. (1935) The symptom of loss of feeling — a gestalt interpretation, *American Journal of Psychiatry*, **91**, pp. 1327–1341.

Joorman, J., Teachman, B.A. & Gotlib, I.H. (2009) Sadder and less accurate? False memory for negative material in depression, *Journal of Abnormal Psychology*, **118** (2), pp. 412–417.

Joseph, A.B. (1986) Cotard's syndrome with coexistent Capgras' syndrome, syndrome of subjective doubles, and palinopsia, *Journal of Clinical Psychiatry*, **47**, pp. 605–606.

Kane, S. (2001) 4.48 Psychosis, *Complete Plays*, pp. 203–246, London: Methuen Drama.

Kant, I. (1855) *Critique of Pure Reason*, Meiklejohn, J.M.D. (trans.), London: Henry G. Bohn.

Kapfhammer, H.-P. (2006) Somatic symptoms in depression, *Dialogues in Clinical Neuroscience*, **8**, pp. 227–239.

Kaplan, B. (ed.) (1964) *The Inner World of Mental Illness*, New York: Harper and Row.

Karp, D.A. (1996) *Speaking of Sadness: Depression, Disconnection, and the Meanings of Illness*, Oxford: Oxford University Press.

Katz, J. & Csordas, T. (eds.) (2003) Phenomenology and ethnography. Theme issue, *Ethnography*, **4** (3).

Kean, C. (2011) Battling with the life instinct: The paradox of the self and suicidal behavior in psychosis, *Schizophrenia Bulletin*, **37** (1), pp. 4–7.

Kempf, L., Hussain, N. & Potash, J.B. (2005) Mood disorder with psychotic features, schizoaffective disorder, and schizophrenia with mood features; trouble at the border, *International Review of Psychiatry*, **17**, pp. 9–19.

Kendell, R. & Jablensky, A. (2003) Distinguishing between the validity and utility of psychiatric diagnoses, *American Journal of Psychiatry*, **160**, pp. 4–12.

Kendler, K.S. (1991) Mood-incongruent psychotic affective illness, *Archives of General Psychiatry*, **48** (4), pp. 362–369.

Kenny, A. (2003) *Action, Emotion and Will*, New York: Routledge.

Kernberg, O. (1975) *Borderline Conditions and Pathological Narcissism*, New York: Jason Aronson.

Kimura, B. (1992) *Écrits de psychopathologie phénoménologique*, Bouderlique, J. (trans. to French), Paris: Presses Universitaires de France.

Kimura, B. (1995) *Zwischen Mensch und Mensch. Strukturen japanischer Subjektivität*, (Hito to Hito no Aida, 1972), Darmstadt: Wissenschaftliche Buchgesellschaft.

Kimura, B. (2000) *L'Entre. Une approche phénoménologique de la schizophrénie*, Vincent, C. (trans. to French), Grenoble: Éditions Jérôme Millon.

Kirmayer, L.J. (2001) Cultural variations in the clinical presentation of depression and anxiety: Implications for diagnosis and treatment, *Journal of Clinical Psychiatry*, **62** (Suppl. 13), pp. 22–28.

Kirmayer, L. (2008) Empathy and alterity in cultural psychiatry, *Ethos*, **36** (4), pp. 457–474.

Kirmayer, L.J. & Groleau, D. (2001) Affective disorders in cultural context, *Psychiatric Clinics of North America*, **24**, pp. 465–478.

Kirsch, I. (2009a) *The Emperor's New Drugs: Exploding the Antidepressant Myth*, London: The Bodley Head.

Kirsch, I. (2009b) Special Articles Antidepressants and the placebo response, *Epidemiologia e psichiatria sociale*, **18** (4), p. 318.

Kirsch, I., Deacon, B.J., Huedo-Medina, T.B., Scoboria, A., Moore, T.J. & Johnson, B.T. (2008) Initial severity and antidepressant benefits: A meta-analysis of data submitted to the Food and Drug Administration, *PLoS Medicine*, **5** (2), e45.

Kissane, D.W. & Clarke, D.M. (2001) Demoralization syndrome — a relevant psychiatric diagnosis for palliative care, *Journal of Palliative Care*, **17**, pp. 12–21.

Kitanaka, J. (2012) *Depression in Japan: Psychiatric Cures for a Society in Distress*, Princeton, NJ: Princeton University Press.

Klein, D.N. (2010) Chronic depression: Diagnosis and classification, *Current Directions in Psychological Science*, **19**, pp. 96–100.

Klein, D.N., Arnow, B.A., Barkin, J.L., Dowling, F., Kocsis, J.H., Leon, A.C., Manber, R., Rothbaum, B.O., Trivedi, M.H. & Wisniewski, S.R. (2009) Early adversity in chronic depression: Clinical correlates and response to pharmacotherapy, *Depression and Anxiety*, **26**, pp. 701–710.

Kleinman, A. (1988a) *Rethinking Psychiatry: From Cultural Category to Personal Experience*, New York: The Free Press.

Kleinman, A. (1988b) *The Illness Narratives*, New York: Basic Books.

Kleinman, A. & Good, B. (1985) *Culture and Depression*, Berkeley, CA: University of California Press.

Koehler, K. (1979) First rank symptoms of schizophrenia: Questions concerning clinical boundaries, *British Journal of Psychiatry*, **134**, pp. 236–248.

Koenigs, M., Young, L., Adolphs, R., Tranel, D., Cushman, F., Hauser, M. & Damasio, A. (2007) Damage to the prefrontal cortex increases utilitarian moral judgements, *Nature*, **446** (7138), pp. 908–911.

Koenigs, M. & Grafman, J. (2009) The functional neuroanatomy of depression: Distinct roles for ventromedial and dorsolateral prefrontal cortex, *Behavioural Brain Research*, **201** (2), p. 239.

Kraepelin, E. (1913) *Psychiatrie*, 8th ed., Leipzig: J.A. Barth.

Kramer, P. (1994) *Listening to Prozac*, London: Fourth Estate.

Kramer, P. (2005) *Against Depression*, New York: Viking Press.

Kraus, A. (1977) *Sozialverhalten und Psychose Manisch-Depressiver: Eine existenz- und rollenanalytische Untersuchung*, Stuttgart: Ferdinand Enke Verlag.

Kraus, A. (1991) Der melancholische Wahn in identitätstheoretischer Sicht, in Blankenburg, W. (ed.) *Wahn und Perpektivität (Forum der Psychiatrie)*, pp. 68–80, Stuttgart: Ferdinand Enke Verlag.

Kraus, A. (2002) Melancholie: Eine Art von Depersonalisation?, in Fuchs, T. & Mundt, C. (eds.) *Affekt und affektive Störungen*, pp. 169–186, Paderborn: Schöningh.

Kraus, A. (2008) Melancholic depersonalisation, *Comprendre*, **16–17–18**, pp. 243–248.

Kring, A.M., Kerr, S.L., Smith, D.A. & Neale, J.M. (1993) Flat affect in schizophrenia does not reflect diminished subjective experience of emotion, *Journal of Abnormal Psychology*, **102**, pp. 507–517.

Kring, A.M., Kerr, S.L. & Earnst, K.S. (1999) Schizophrenics show facial reactions to emotional facial expressions, *Psychophysiology*, **35**, pp. 186–192.

Krishnadas, R. & Cavanagh, J. (2012) Depression: An inflammatory illness?, *Journal of Neurology, Neurosurgery and Psychiatry*, **83**, pp. 495–502.

Kronmüller, K.-T., Backenstrass, M., Kocherscheidt, K., Hunt, A., Unger, J., Fiedler, P. & Mundt, C. (2002) Typus Melancholicus personality type and the five-factor model of personality, *Psychopathology*, **35**, pp. 327–334.

Kuiper, P.C. (1991) *Seelenfinsternis. Die Depression eines Psychiaters*, Frankfurt: Fischer.

Kumazaki, T. (2011) What is a 'mood-congruent' delusion? History and conceptual problems, *History of Psychiatry*, **22**, pp. 315–332.

Kunzendorf, R.G., Deno, S., Flynn, H., Rosa, N., Shedlack, J., Burns, J. & Georges, M. (2010) Depression, unlike normal sadness, is associated with a 'flatter' self-perception and a 'flatter' phenomenal world, *Imagination, Cognition and Personality*, **30** (4), pp. 447–461.

Lambert, M.V. & Sierra, M. (2002) The spectrum of organic depersonalization: A review plus four new cases, *The Journal of Neuropsychiatry and Clinical Neurosciences*, pp. 141–154.

Lambie, J.A. & Marcel, A.J. (2002) Consciousness and the varieties of emotion experience: A theoretical framework, *Psychological Review*, **109**, pp. 219–259.

Laing, R.D. (1965) *The Divided Self*, New York: Penguin.

Lake, R. (2008) Hypothesis: Grandiosity and guilt cause paranoia; paranoid schizophrenia is a psychotic mood disorder; a review, *Schizophrenia Bulletin*, **34** (6), pp. 1151–1162.

Landis, C. (1964) *Varieties of Psychopathological Experience*, New York: Holt, Rinehart and Winston.

Lang, J. (1938) The other side of auditory hallucinations, *American Journal of Psychiatry*, **94**, pp. 1089–1097.

Laureys, S. & Tononi, G. (2008) *The Neurology of Consciousness: Cognitive Neuroscience and Neuropathology*, Waltham, MA: Academic Press.

Law, I. (2009) Motivation, depression and character, in Broome, M.R. & Bortolotti, L. (eds.) *Psychiatry as Cognitive Neuroscience: Philosophical Perspectives*, pp. 351–364, Oxford: Oxford University Press.

Leder, D. (1990) *The Absent Body*, Chicago, IL: University of Chicago Press.

Ledoux, J.E. (2012) Rethinking the emotional brain, *Neuron*, **73** (4), pp. 653–676.

Lee, D.T.S., Kleinman, J. & Kleinman, A. (2007) Rethinking depression: An ethnographic study of the experiences of depression among Chinese, *Harvard Review of Psychiatry*, **15**, pp. 1–8.

Lee, W.E., Kwok, C.H.T., Hunter, E.C.M., Richards, M. & David, A.S. (2010) Prevalence and childhood antecedents of depersonalization syndrome in a UK birth cohort, *Social Psychiatry and Psychiatric Epidemiology*, **47** (2), pp. 253–261.

Levy, K.N., Meehan, K.B., Kelly, K.M., Reynoso, J.S., Weber, M., Clarkin, J.F. & Kernberg, O.F. (2006) Change in attachment patterns and reflective function in a randomized control trial of transference-focused psychotherapy for borderline personality disorder, *Journal of Consulting & Clinical Psychology*, **74**, pp. 1027–1040.

Linger, D. (2010) What is it like to be someone else?, *Ethos*, **38** (2), pp. 205–229.

Little, M., Jordens, C., Paul, K., Montgomery, K. & Philipson, B. (1998) Liminality: A major category of the experience of cancer illness, *Social Science & Medicine*, **47** (10), pp. 1485–1494.

Lindholm, C. (2007) An anthropology of emotion, in Casey, C. & Edgerton, R.B. (eds.) *A Companion to Psychological Anthropology: Modernity and Psychocultural Change*, pp. 30–47, Oxford: Blackwell.

Llinás, R.R. (2002) *I of the Vortex: From Neurons to Self*, Cambridge, MA: MIT Press.

Lloyd, D. (2011) Is 'cognitive science' an oxymoran?, *Philosophy, Psychiatry, & Psychology*, **18**, pp. 283–286.

Lutz, C. & White, G.M. (1986) The anthropology of emotions, *Annual Review of Anthropology*, **15**, pp. 405–436.

MacIntyre, A. (1999) *Dependent Rational Animals: Why Human Beings Need the Virtues*, London: Duckworth.

Main, M. & Goldwyn, R. (1985–1996) *Adult Attachment Classification System*, unpublished manuscript: University of California, Department of Psychology, Berkeley.

Maj, M. (2012) When does depression become a mental disorder, in Kendler, K.S. & Parnas, J. (eds.) *Philosophical Issues in Psychiatry II: Nosology*, pp. 221–228, Oxford: Oxford University Press.

Marotta, J.J. & Behrmann, M. (2004) Patient Schn: Has Goldstein and Gelb's case withstood the test of time?, *Neuropsychologia*, **42**, pp. 633–638.

Mathew, R.J., Wilson, W.H., Chiu, N.Y., Turkington, T.G., Degrado, T.R. & Coleman, R.E. (1999) Regional cerebral blood flow and depersonalization after tetrahydrocannabinol administration, *Acta Psychiatrica Scandinavica*, **100** (1), pp. 67–75.

Matthews, A. & MacLeod, C. (2005) Cognitive vulnerability to emotional disorders, *Annual Review of Clinical Psychology*, **1**, pp. 167–195.

Matussek, P. (1987) Studies in delusional perception, in Cutting, J. & Shepherd, M. (eds.) *The Clinical Roots of the Schizophrenia Concept*, pp. 89–103, Cambridge: Cambridge University Press.

Mayberg, H.S. (2003a) Modulating dysfunctional limbic-cortical circuits in depression: Towards development of brain-based algorithms for diagnosis and optimised treatment, *British Medical Bulletin*, **65**, pp. 193–207.

Mayberg, H.S. (2003b) Positron emission tomography imaging in depression: A neural systems perspective, *Neuroimaging Clinics of North America*, **13**, pp. 805–815.

Mayberg, H.S., Liotti, M., Branna, S.K., McGinnis, S., Mahurin, R.K., Jerabek, P.A., Silva, J.A., Tekell, J.L., Martin, C.C., Lancaster, J.L. & Fox, P.T. (1999) Reciprocal limbic-cortical function and negative mood: Converging PET findings in depression and normal sadness, *American Journal of Psychiatry*, **156**, pp. 675–682.

Mayberg, H.S., Lozano, A.M., Voon, V., McNeely, H.E., Seminowicz, D., Hamani, C., Schwalb, J.M. & Kennedy, S.H. (2005) Deep brain stimulation for treatment-resistant depression, *Neuron*, **45**, pp. 651–660.

Mayer-Gross, W. (1935) On depersonalization, *British Journal of Medical Psychology*, **15**, pp. 103–122.

Mayer-Gross, W., Slater E. & Roth, M. (1954) *Clinical Psychiatry*, London: Cassell and Company.

McCabe, C., Mishor, Z., *et al.* (2011) SSRI administration reduces resting state functional connectivity in dorso-medial prefrontal cortex, *Molecular Psychiatry*, **16** (6), pp. 592–594.

McGlashan, T. (1982) Aphanisis: The syndrome of pseudo-depression in chronic schizophrenia, *Schizophrenia Bulletin*, **8** (1), pp. 118–134.

Mead, G.H. (1934) *Mind, Self, and Society*, Chicago, IL: Chicago University Press.

Medford, N. (2012) Emotion and the unreal self: Depersonalization disorder and de-affectualization, *Emotion Review*, **4** (2), pp. 139–144.

Medford, N. & Critchley, H.D. (2010) Conjoint activity of anterior insular and anterior cingulate cortex: Awareness and response, *Brain Structure & Function*, **214** (5–6), pp. 535–549.

Mellor, C.S. (1970) First rank symptoms of schizophrenia, *British Journal of Psychiatry*, **117**, pp. 15–23.

Merker, B. (2007) Consciousness without a cerebral cortex: A challenge for neuroscience and medicine, *Behavioral and Brain Sciences*, **30** (1), pp. 63–81.

Merleau-Ponty, M. (1942/1963) *The Structure of Behavior*, Fisher, A. (trans.), Pittsburgh, PA: Duquesne University Press.

Merleau-Ponty, M. (1945/1962) *Phenomenology of Perception*, Smith, C. (trans.), New York: Routledge.

Merleau-Ponty, M. (1962) *Phenomenology of Perception*, Smith, C. (trans.), London: Routledge.

Metzinger, T. (1999) *Subjekt und Selbstmodell: die Perspektivität phänomenalen Bewusstseins vor dem Hintergrund einer naturalistischen Theorie mentaler Repräsentation*, Paderborn: mentis.

Metzinger, T. (2003) *Being No One: The Self-Model Theory of Subjectivity*, Cambridge, MA: MIT Press.

Mezzich, J. & Raab, E. (1980) Depressive symptomatology across the Americas, *Archives of General Psychiatry*, **37**, pp. 818–823.

Michal, M., Sann, U., Niebecker, M., Lazanowsky, C., Kernhof, K., Aurich, S. & Berrios, G.E. (2004) The measurement of the depersonalisation-derealisation-syndrome with the German version of the Cambridge Depersonalisation Scale (CDS), *Psychotherapie, Psychosomatik, medizinische Psychologie*, **54** (9–10), pp. 367–374.

Michal, M., Röder, C.H., Mayer, J., Lengler, U. & Krakow, K. (2005) Spontaneous dissociation during functional MRI experiments, *Journal of Psychiatric Research*, **41** (1–2), pp. 69–73.

Michal, M., Beutel, M.E., Jordan, J., Zimmermann, M., Wolters, S. & Heidenreich, T. (2007) Depersonalization, mindfulness, and childhood trauma, *Journal of Nervous and Mental Disease*, **195** (8), pp. 693–696.

Michal, M., Wiltink, J., Subic-Wrana, C., Zwerenz, R., Tuin, I., Lichy, M. & Beutel, M.E. (2009) Prevalence, correlates, and predictors of depersonalization experiences in the German general population, *Journal of Nervous and Mental Disease*, **197** (7), pp. 499–506.

Miller, A.H., Maletic, V. & Raison, C.L. (2009) Inflammation and its discontents: the role of cytokines in the pathophysiology of major depression, *Biological Psychiatry*, **65**, pp. 732–741.

Minkowski, E. (1927) *La schizophénie*, Paris: Payot.

Minkowski, E. (1933/1970) *Lived Time*, Evanston, IL: Northwestern University Press.

Molina Castillo, J.J., Martínez De La Iglesia, J., Albert Colomer, C., Berrios, G., Sierra, M. & Luque Luque, R. (2006) Cross-cultural adaptation and validation of the Cambridge Depersonalisation Scale, *Actas Espanolas De Psiquiatria*, **34** (3), pp. 185–192.

Moran, R. (2001) *Authority and Estrangement: An Essay on Self-Knowledge*, Princeton, NJ: Princeton University Press.

Mori, M. (1970) The uncanny valley, *Energy*, **7** (4), pp. 33–35.

Morrison, A.P. & Haddock, G. (1997) Self-focused attention in schizophrenic patients with and without auditory hallucinations and normal subjects: A comparative study, *Personality and Individual Differences*, **23** (6), pp. 937–941.

Mula, M., Pini, S. & Cassano, G.B. (2007) The neurobiology and clinical significance of depersonalization in mood and anxiety disorders: A critical reappraisal, *Journal of Affective Disorders*, **99** (1–3), pp. 91–99.

Mula, M., Pini, S., Calugi, S., Preve, M., Masini, M., Giovannini, I. & Cassano, G.B. (2010) Distinguishing affective depersonalization from anhedonia in major depression and bipolar disorder, *Comprehensive Psychiatry*, **51** (2), pp. 187–192.

Müller, N., Schwarz, M.J., Dehning, S., Douhe, A., Cerovecki, A., Goldstein-Müller, B., Spellmann, I., Hetzel, G., Maino, K., Kleindienst, N., Möller, H.-J., Arolt, V. & Riedel, M. (2006) The cyclooxygenase-2 inhibitor Celecoxib has therapeutic effects in major depression: Results of a double-blind, randomized, placebo controlled, add-on pilot study to Roboxetine, *Molecular Psychiatry*, **11**, pp. 680–684.

Mundt, C., Backenstrass, M., Kronmiller, K.T., Fiedler, P., Kraus, A. & Stanghellini, G. (1997) Personality and endogenous/major depression: An empirical approach to Typus Melancholicus: 2. Validation of Typus Melancholicus core-properties by personality inventory scales, *Psychopathology*, **30** (3), pp. 130–139.

Murray, L. (2009) *Killing the Black Dog*, New York: Farrar, Straus and Giroux.

Nagel, T. (1986) *The View from Nowhere*, Oxford: Oxford University Press.

Nakanishi, T., Isobe, F. & Ogawa, Y. (1993) Chronic depression of monopolar, endogenous type: With special reference to the premorbid personality, 'Typus Melancholicus', *Japanese Journal of Psychiatry & Neurology*, **47** (3), pp. 495–504.

National Collaborating Centre for Mental Health (2010) *Depression in Adults with a Chronic Physical Health Problem: The NICE Guideline on Treatment and Management*, London: RCPsych Publications.

N'Diaye, K., Sander, D. & Vuilleumier, P. (2009) Self-relevance processing in the human amygdala: Gaze direction, facial expression, and emotion intensity, *Emotion*, **9** (6), p. 798.

Nelson, B., Thompson, A. & Yung, A. (2012) Basic self-disturbance predicts psychosis onset in the ultra high risk for psychosis ('prodromal') population, *Schizophrenia Bulletin*, **38** (6), pp. 1277–1287.

Niedenthal, P.M. (2007) Embodying emotion, *Science*, **316**, pp. 1002–1005.

Noë, A. (2004) *Action in Perception*, Cambridge, MA: MIT Press.

Northoff, G. (2007) Psychopathology and pathophysiology of the self in depression — neuropsychiatric hypothesis, *Journal of Affective Disorders*, **104** (1–3), pp. 1–14.

Northoff, G. & Panksepp, J. (2008) The trans-species concept of self and the sub-cortical-cortical midline system, *Trends in Cognitive Sciences*, **12** (7), pp. 259–264.

Nussbaum, M. (1990) *Love's Knowledge*, Oxford: Oxford University Press.

Nussbaum, M. (2001) *Upheavals of Thought: The Intelligence of Emotions*, Cambridge: Cambridge University Press.

Ochsner, K.N., Bunge, S.A., *et al.* (2002) Rethinking feelings: An fMRI study of the cognitive regulation of emotion, *Journal of Cognitive Neuroscience*, **14** (8), pp. 1215–1229.

O'Connor, T. (1995) Agent causation, in O'Connor, T. (ed.) *Agents, Causes, Events: Essays on Indeterminism and Free Will*, New York: Oxford University Press.

Osaka, N., Osaka, M., Morishita, M., Kondo, H. & Fukuyama, H. (2004) A word expressing affective pain activates the anterior cingulate in the human brain: An fMRI study, *Behavioral Brain Research*, **153**, pp. 123–127.

Pacherie, E. (2008) The phenomenology of action: A conceptual framework, *Cognition*, **107**, pp. 179–217.

Pacherie, E. (2011) Self-agency, in Gallagher, S. (ed.) *The Oxford Handbook of the Self*, pp. 442–464, New York: Oxford University Press.

Panksepp, J. (1998) *Affective Neuroscience: The Foundation of Human and Animal Emotions*, Oxford: Oxford University Press.

Panksepp, J. (2012) What is an emotional feeling? Lessons about affective origins from cross-species neuroscience, *Motivation and Emotion*, **36** (1), pp. 4–15.

Panksepp, J. & Northoff, G. (2009) The trans-species core SELF: The emergence of active cultural and neuro-ecological agents through self-related processing within subcortical-cortical midline networks, *Consciousness and Cognition*, **18** (1), pp. 193–215.

Panksepp, J. & Biven, L. (2012) *The Archaeology of the Mind: Neuroevolutionary Origins of Human Emotions*, New York: W.W. Norton & Company.

Parnas, J. (2012) A sea of distress, in Kendler, K.S. & Parnas, J. (eds.) *Philosophical Issues in Psychiatry II: Nosology*, pp. 229–233, Oxford: Oxford University Press.

Parnas, J., Handest, P., Saebye, D. & Jansson, L. (2003) Anomalies of subjective experience in schizophrenia and psychotic bipolar illness, *Acta Psychiatrica Scandinavica*, **108** (2), pp. 126–133.

Parnas, J., Moller, P., Kircher, T., Thalbitzer, J., Jansson, L., Handest, P. & Zahavi, D. (2005) EASE: Examination of Anomalous Self-Experience, *Psychopathology*, **38**, pp. 236–258.

Parnas, J. & Sass, L. (2011) The structure of self consciousness in schizophrenia, in Gallagher, S. (ed.) *The Oxford Handbook of the Self*, pp. 521–546, New York: Oxford University Press.

Paskaleva, A. (2011) *A Phenomenological Assessment of Depression Narratives*, Masters thesis, Osnabrück: PICS 2011, vol. 03, [Online], http://ikw.uni-osnabrueck.de/en/system/files/03-2011.pdf

Pasolini, P.P. (1964) Una disperata vitalità, in Pasolini, P.P., *Poesia in forma rosa*, pp. 114–135, Milan: Garzanti Editore.

Paykel, E.S., Myers, J.K. & Lindenthal, J.J. (1974) Suicidal feelings in the general population: A prevalence study, *British Journal of Psychiatry*, **124**, pp. 460–469.

Pazzagli, A. & Rossi Monti, M. (2000) Dysphoria and aloneness in borderline personality disorder, *Psychopathology*, **33** (4), pp. 220–226.

Persad, S.M. & Polivy, J. (1993) Differences between depressed and non-depressed individuals in the recognition of and response to facial emotional cues, *Journal of Abnormal Psychology*, **102**, pp. 358–368.

Petrilowitsch, N. (1956) Zur Psychopathologie und Klinik der Entfremdungs-depression, *Archiv für Psychiatrie und Zeitschrift für die gesamte Neurologie*, **194**, pp. 289–301.

Pfeiffer, W. (1984) Transkulturelle Aspekte der Depression, *Nervenheilkunde*, **3**, pp. 14–17.

Piguet, C., Dayer, A., Kosel, M., Desseilles, M., Vuilleumier, P. & Bertschy, G. (2010) Phenomenology of racing and crowded thoughts in mood disorders: A theoretical reappraisal, *Journal of Affective Disorders*, **121**, pp. 189–198.

Plath, S. (1966) *The Bell Jar*, London: Faber and Faber.

Ploghaus, A., Tracey, I., Gati, J.S., Clare, S., Menon, R.S. & Matthews, P.M. (1999) Dissociating pain from its anticipation in the human brain, *Science*, **284**, pp. 1979–1981.

Posner, M.I. & Raichle, M.E. (1994) *Images of the Mind*, New York: Freeman.

Pringle, A., Browning, M., *et al.* (2011) A cognitive neuropsychological model of antidepressant drug action, *Progress in Neuro-Psychopharmacology and Biological Psychiatry*, **35** (7), pp. 1586–1592.

Prinz, J.J. (2004) *Gut Reactions: A Perceptual Theory of Emotion*, New York: Oxford University Press.

Pugmire, D. (2005) *Sound Sentiment: Integrity in the Emotions*, Oxford: Oxford University Press.

Raballo, A. & Nelson, B. (2010) Unworlding, perplexity and disorders of transpassibility: Between the experiential and the existential side of schizophrenic vulnerability, *Psychopathology*, **43**, pp. 250–251.

Raballo, A., Saebye, D. & Parnas, J. (2011) Looking at the schizophrenia spectrum through the prism of self-disorders: An empirical study, *Schizophrenia Bulletin*, **37** (2), pp. 244–251.

Radden, J. (1996) *Divided Minds and Successive Selves: Ethical Issues in Disorders of Identity and Personality*, Cambridge, MA: MIT Press.

Radden, J. (ed.) (2000) *The Nature of Melancholy: From Aristotle to Kristeva*, Oxford: Oxford University Press.

Radden, J. (2003) Is this Dame Melancholy? Equating today's depression and past melancholia, *Philosophy, Psychiatry, & Psychology*, **10**, pp. 37–52.

Radden, J. (2007) Defining persecutory paranoia, in Chung, M., Fulford, B. & Graham, G. (eds.) *Reconceiving Schizophrenia*, pp. 255–273, New York: Oxford University Press.

Radden, J. (2009) *Moody Minds Distempered: Essays on Melancholy and Depression*, Oxford: Oxford University Press.

Radden, J. (2010) Multiple selves, in Gallagher, S. (ed.) *The Oxford Handbook of the Self*, pp. 547–570, New York: Oxford University Press.

Radovic, F. & Radovic, S. (2002) Feelings of unreality: A conceptual and phenomenological analysis of the language of depersonalization, *Philosophy, Psychiatry, & Psychology*, **9** (3), pp. 271–279.

Raison, C.L., Capuron, L. & Miller, A.H. (2006) Cytokines sing the blues: Inflammation and the pathogenesis of depression, *Trends in Immunology*, **27**, pp. 24–31.

Ratcliffe, M. (2005) The feeling of being, *Journal of Consciousness Studies*, **12** (8–10), pp. 43–60.

Ratcliffe, M. (2006) Phenomenology, neuroscience, and intersubjectivity, in Dreyfus, H.L. & Wrathall, M.A. (eds.) *A Companion to Phenomenology and Existentialism*, London: Blackwell.

Ratcliffe, M. (2008a) *Feelings of Being: Phenomenology, Psychiatry and the Sense of Reality*, Oxford: Oxford University Press.

Ratcliffe, M. (2008b) Touch and situatedness, *International Journal of Philosophical Studies*, **16** (3), pp. 299–322.

Ratcliffe, M. (2009a) Belonging to the world through the feeling body, *Philosophy, Psychiatry, & Psychology*, **16** (2), pp. 205–211.

Ratcliffe, M. (2009b) Understanding existential changes in psychiatric illness: The indispensability of phenomenology, in Broome, M. & Bortolotti, L. (eds.) *Psychiatry as Cognitive Neuroscience: Philosophical Perspectives*, Oxford: Oxford University Press.

Ratcliffe, M. (2009c) Existential feeling and psychopathology, *Philosophy, Psychiatry, & Psychology*, **16** (2), pp. 179–194.

Ratcliffe, M. (2010a) The phenomenology of mood and the meaning of life, in Goldie, P. (ed.) *The Oxford Handbook of Philosophy of Emotion*, pp. 349–371, Oxford: Oxford University Press.

Ratcliffe, M. (2010b) Depression, guilt, and emotional depth, *Inquiry*, **53** (6), pp. 602–626.

Ratcliffe, M. (2010c) Binary oppositions in psychiatry: For or against?, *Philosophy, Psychiatry & Psychology*, **17**, pp. 233–239.

Ratcliffe, M. (2010d) The phenomenology and neurobiology of moods and emotions, in Schmicking, D. & Gallagher, S. (eds.) *Handbook of Phenomenology and Cognitive Science*, pp. 123–140, Berlin: Springer.

Ratcliffe, M. (2012a) Varieties of temporal experience in depression, *Journal of Medicine and Philosophy*, **37** (2), pp. 114–138.

Ratcliffe, M. (2012b) Phenomenology as a form of empathy, *Inquiry*, **55** (5), pp. 473–495.

Ratcliffe, M. (2012c) What is touch?, *Australasian Journal of Philosophy*, **90** (3), pp. 413–432.

Ratcliffe, M. (2012d) The phenomenology of existential feeling, in Fingerhut, J. & Marienberg, S. (eds.) *Feelings of Being Alive — Gefuehle des Lebendigseins*, pp. 23–53, Berlin: de Gruyter.

Ratcliffe, M. (2013) Phenomenology, naturalism and the sense of reality, *Royal Institute of Philosophy*, Suppl. **72**, pp. 67–88..

Ratcliffe, M. (2013a) What is it to lose hope?, *Phenomenology and the Cognitive Sciences*, **4** (4), pp. 597–614.

Ratcliffe, M. (2013b) Depression and the phenomenology of free will, in Fulford, K.W.M., Davies, M., Gipps, R.G.T., Graham, G., Sadler, J.Z., Stanghellini, G. & Thornton, T. (eds.) *Oxford Handbook of Philosophy and Psychiatry*, pp. 574–591, Oxford: Oxford University Press.

Ratcliffe, M. & Broome, M. (2012) Existential phenomenology, psychiatric illness and the death of possibilities, in Crowell, S. (ed.) *Cambridge Companion to Existentialism*, pp. 361–382, Cambridge: Cambridge University Press.

Ravitz, P., Maunder, R., Hunter, J., Sthankiya, B. & Lancee, W. (2010) Adult attachment measures: A 25-year review, *Journal of Psychosomatic Research*, **69**, pp. 419–432.

Reddy, V. (2008) *How Infants Know Minds*, Cambridge, MA: Harvard University Press.

Reed, G.F. & Sedman, G. (1964) Personality and depersonalization under sensory deprivation conditions, *Perceptual and Motor Skills*, **18** (2), pp. 659–660.

Ressler, K. & Nemeroff, C. (2001) Role of serotonergic and noradrenergic systems in the pathophysiology of depression and anxiety disorders, *Anxiety*, **12** (S1), pp. 2–19.

Reutens, S., Nielsen, O. & Sachdev, P. (2010) Depersonalization disorder, *Current Opinion in Psychiatry*, **3**.

Rhodes, J. & Gipps, R.G.T. (2008) Delusions, certainty, and the background, *Philosophy, Psychiatry, & Psychology*, **15**, pp. 295–310.

Ricoeur, P. (1950/1966) *Freedom and Nature: The Voluntary and the Involuntary*, Kohák, E.V. (trans.), Evanston, IL: Northwestern University Press.

Ricoeur, P. (1960) *Philosophie de la volonté II: L'homme faillible*, Paris: Aubier.

Ricoeur, P. (1992) *Oneself as Another*, Chicago, IL: University of Chicago Press.

Roberts, R.C. (2003) *Emotions: An Essay in Aid of Moral Psychology*, Cambridge: Cambridge University Press.

Robinson, J. (2005) *Deeper than Reason: Emotion and its Role in Literature, Music, and Art*, Oxford: Oxford University Press.

Röder, C.H., Michal, M., Overbeck, G., van De Ven, V.G. & Linden, D.E.J. (2007) Pain response in depersonalization: A functional imaging study using hypnosis in healthy subjects, *Psychotherapy and Psychosomatics*, **76** (2), pp. 115–121.

Roozendaal, B., McEwen, B., *et al.* (2009) Stress, memory and the amygdala, *Nature Reviews Neuroscience*, **10** (6), pp. 423–433.

Rorty, A.O. (ed.) (1980) *Explaining Emotions*, Berkeley, CA: University of California Press.

Rosenstein, D.S. & Horowitz, H.A. (1996) Adolescent attachment and psychopathology, *Journal of Consulting & Clinical Psychology*, pp. 244–253.

Rosfort, R. & Stanghellini, G. (2009) The person in between moods and affects, *Philosophy, Psychiatry, & Psychology*, **13** (3), pp. 251–266.

Rowe, D. (1978) *The Experience of Depression*, Chichester: John Wiley & Sons.

Rümke, H. & Neeleman, J. (1942/1990) The nuclear symptom of schizophrenia and the praecox feeling, *History of Psychiatry*, **1** (3), pp. 331–341.

Ryle, G. (2009) *The Concept of Mind*, London: Penguin Classics.

Sacco, G. & Ruggieri, V. (1997) Mental imagery and symptom patterns, *Imagination, Cognition and Personality*, **17**, pp. 313–321.

Sachs, A. (2007) A memoir of schizophrenia, *Time Magazine* (August 27), [Online], http://www.time.com/time/arts/article/0,8599,1656592,00.html, see more at http://triplehelixblog.com/2013/04/the-trials-of-schizophrenia/#sthash.Ve2ZVxkB.dpuf

Sadler, J.Z. (2004) Diagnosis/antidiagnosis, in Radden, J. (ed.) *The Philosophy of Psychiatry: A Companion*, Oxford: Oxford University Press.

Saks, E. (2007) *The Center Cannot Hold*, New York: Hyperion.

Saleptsi, E., Bichescu, D., Rockstroh, B., Neuner, F., Schauer, M., Studer, K., Hoffmann, K. & Elbert, T. (2004) Negative and positive childhood experiences across developmental periods in psychiatric patients with different diagnoses — an explorative study, *BMC Psychiatry*, pp. 4–40.

Sander, D., Grafman, J., *et al.* (2003) The human amygdala: An evolved system for relevance detection, *Reviews in the Neurosciences*, **14** (4), pp. 303–316.

Sander, D., Grandjean, D. & Scherer, K.R. (2005) A systems approach to appraisal mechanisms in emotion, *Neural Networks*, **18**, pp. 317–352.

Sander, D., Grandjean, D., *et al.* (2007) Interaction effects of perceived gaze direction and dynamic facial expression: Evidence for appraisal theories of emotion, *European Journal of Cognitive Psychology*, **19** (3), pp. 470–480.

Sartre, J.-P. (1939/1971) *Sketch for a Theory of the Emotions*, Mairet, P. (trans.), London: Methuen & Co Ltd.

Sartre, J.-P. (1939/1994) *Sketch for a Theory of the Emotions*, London: Routledge.

Sartre, J-.P. (1943/2003) *Being and Nothingness*, London: Routledge.

Sartre, J.P. (1989) *Being and Nothingness*, Barnes, H.E. (trans.), London: Routledge.

Sass, L.A. (1992) *Madness and Modernism: Insanity in the Light of Modern Art, Literature, and Thought*, New York: Basic Books.

Sass, L. (1994) *The Paradoxes of Delusion: Wittgenstein, Schreber, and the Schizophrenic Mind*, Ithaca, NY: Cornell University Press.

Sass, L. (2003) 'Negative symptoms,' schizophrenia, and the self, *International Journal of Psychological Theory*, **3** (2), pp. 153–180.

Sass, L. (2004a) Schizophrenia: A disturbance of the thematic field, in Embree, L. (ed.) *Gurwitch's Relevancy for the Cognitive Sciences*, pp. 59–78, Dordrecht: Springer.

Sass, L. (2004b) Affectivity in schizophrenia: A phenomenological view, *Journal of Consciousness Studies*, **11** (10–11), pp. 127–147.

Sass, L. (2007) Contradictions of emotion in schizophrenia, *Cognition and Emotion*, **21** (2), pp. 351–390.

Sass, L. (2013) Delusions and double bookkeeping, in Fuchs, T. & Stanghellini, G. (eds.) *One Century of Karl Jaspers' General Psychopathology*, pp. 95–106, Oxford: Oxford University Press.

Sass, L. & Parnas, J. (2003) Schizophrenia, consciousness, and the self, *Schizophrenia Bulletin*, **29** (3), pp. 427–444.

Sass, L. & Parnas, J. (2007) Explaining schizophrenia: The relevance of phenomenology, in Chung, M., Fulford, W. & Graham, G. (eds.) *Reconceiving Schizophrenia*, pp. 63–96, Oxford: Oxford University Press.

Sass, L., Parnas, J. & Zahavi, D. (2011) Phenomenological psychopathology and schizophrenia: Contemporary approaches and misunderstandings, *Philosophy, Psychiatry, & Psychology*, **18**, pp. 1–23.

Sass, L. & Pienkos, E. (2013) Delusions: The phenomenological approach, in Fulford, W., Davies, M., Graham, G., Sadler, J. & Stanghellini, G. (eds.) *Oxford Handbook of Philosophy and Psychiatry*, pp. 632–657, Oxford: Oxford University Press.

Sato, T., Sakado, K. & Sato, S. (1992) Differences between two questionnaires for assessment of Typus Melancholicus, Zerssen's F-list and Kasahara's Scale: The validity and relationship to DSM-III-R personality disorders, *Psychiatry and Clinical Neurosciences*, **46** (3), pp. 603–608.

Sato, T., Sakado, K. & Sato, S. (1993) Typus Melancholicus measured by a questionnaire in unipolar depressive patients: Age- and sex-distribution, and relationship to clinical characteristics of depression, *Psychiatry and Clinical Neurosciences*, **47** (1), pp. 1–11.

Sauer, H., Richter, P. & Sass, H. (1989) Zur prämorbiden Persönlichkeit von Patienten mit schizoaffektiven Psychosen, in Marneros, A. (ed.) *Schizoaffektive Psychosen*, pp. 109–118, Berlin: Springer.

Scarry, E. (1985) *The Body in Pain: The Making and Unmaking of the World*, Oxford: Oxford University Press.

Schechtman, M. (2011) The narrative self, in Gallagher, S. (ed.) *The Oxford Handbook of the Self*, pp. 394–416, New York: Oxford University Press.

Scheler, M. (1916/1966) *Der Formalismus in der Ethik und die materiale Wertethik*, Gesammelte Werke, Band 2, Bern: Francke Verlag.

Scherer, K. (2005) What are emotions? And how can they be measured?, *Social Science Information*, **44**, pp. 695–729.

Scherer, K.R., Schorr, A. & Johnstone, T. (eds.) (2001) *Appraisal Processes in Emotion: Theory, Methods, Research*, Oxford: Oxford University Press.

Scherer, K.R. & Brosch, T. (2009) Culture-specific appraisal biases contribute to emotion dispositions, *European Journal of Personality*, **23**, pp. 265–288.

Schmidt, G. (1987) A review of the German literature on delusion between 1914 and 1939, in Cutting, J. & Shepherd, M. (eds.) *The Clinical Roots of the Schizophrenia Concept*, pp. 104–133, Cambridge: Cambridge University Press.

Schmitz, H. (1989) *Leib und Gefühl. Materialien zu einer philosophischen Therapeutik*, Paderborn: Junfermann.

Schneider, K. (1920) Die Schichtung des emotionalen Lebens und der Aufbau der Depressionszustände, *Zeitschrift für die gesamte Neurologie und Psychiatrie*, **59**, pp. 281–286.

Schneider, K. (1959) *Clinical Psychopathology*, New York: Grune & Stratton.

Sechehaye, M. (1962) *Autobiography of a Schizophrenic Girl*, New York: Penguin.

Seligman, M.E.P. (1975) *Helplessness: On Depression, Development and Death*, San Francisco, CA: Freeman and Co.

Seth, A. (2009) Explanatory correlates of consciousness: Theoretical and computational challenges, *Cognitive Computation*, **1** (1), pp. 50–63.

Seth, A., Suzuki, K. & Critchley, H.D. (2012) An interoceptive predictive coding model of conscious presence, *Frontiers in Psychology*, **2** (January), pp. 1–16.

Shaw, F. (1997) *Out of Me*, London: Penguin.

Sheets-Johnstone, M. (1999) Emotion and movement: A beginning empirical-phenomenological analysis of their relationship, *Journal of Consciousness Studies*, **6** (11–12), pp. 259–277.

Sheline, Y., Wang, P., *et al.* (1996) Hippocampal atrophy in recurrent major depression, *Proceedings of the National Academy of Sciences*, **93** (9), p. 3908.

Shneidman, E.S. (1996) *The Suicidal Mind*, Oxford: Oxford University Press.

Sierra, M. (2009) *Depersonalization: A New Look at a Neglected Syndrome*, Oxford: Oxford University Press.

Sierra, M. & Berrios, G.E. (1997) Depersonalization: A conceptual history, *History of Psychiatry*, **8** (30), pp. 213–229.

Sierra, M. & Berrios, G.E. (2000) The Cambridge Depersonalisation Scale: A new instrument for the measurement of depersonalisation, *Psychiatry Research*, **93** (2), pp. 153–164.

Sierra, M. & Berrios, G.E. (2001) The phenomenological stability of depersonalization: Comparing the old with the new, *Journal of Nervous and Mental Disease*, **189**, pp. 629–636.

Sierra, M., Baker, D., Medford, N. & David, A.S. (2005) Unpacking the depersonalization syndrome: An exploratory factor analysis on the Cambridge Depersonalization Scale, *Psychological Medicine*, **35**, pp. 1523–1532.

Sierra, M., Gomez, J., Molina, J.J., Luque, R., Muñoz, J.F. & David, A.S. (2006) Depersonalization in psychiatric patients: A transcultural study, *Journal of Nervous and Mental Disease*, **194** (5), pp. 356–361.

Sierra, M. & David, A.S. (2010) Depersonalization: A selective impairment of self-awareness, *Consciousness and Cognition*, **20** (1), pp. 99–108.

Sierra-Siegert, M. & David, A.S. (2007) Depersonalization and individualism: The effect of culture on symptom profiles in panic disorder, *Journal of Nervous and Mental Disease*, **195** (12), pp. 989–995.

Silber, E., Rey, A.C., Savard, R. & Post, R.M. (1980) Thought disorder and affective inaccessibility in depression, *Journal of Clinical Psychiatry*, **41** (5), pp. 161–165.

Simeon, D., Guralnik, O., Schmeidler, J., Sirof, B. & Knutelska, M. (2001) The role of childhood interpersonal trauma in depersonalization disorder, *American Journal of Psychiatry*, **158** (7), pp. 1027–1027.

Simeon, D., Knutelska, M., Nelson, D. & Guralnik, O. (2003) Feeling unreal: A depersonalization disorder update of 117 cases, *Journal of Clinical Psychiatry*, **64** (9), pp. 990–997.

Simeon, D., Kozin, D.S., Segal, K., Lerch, B., Dujour, R. & Giesbrecht, T. (2008) De-constructing depersonalization: Further evidence for symptom clusters, *Psychiatry Research*, **157** (1–3), pp. 303–306.

Slaby, J. (2008) Affective intentionality and the feeling body, *Phenomenology and the Cognitive Sciences*, 7, pp. 429–444.

Slaby, J. (2010) The other side of existence: Heidegger on boredom, in Flach, S., Margulies, D.S. & Söffner, J. (eds.) *Habitus in Habitat II — Other Sides of Cognition*, pp. 101–120, Bern: Peter Lang.

Slaby, J. (2012) Affective self-construal and the sense of ability, *Emotion Review*, **4** (2), pp. 151–156.

Slaby, J. & Stephan, A. (2008) Affective intentionality and self-consciousness, *Consciousness and Cognition*, **17**, pp. 506–513.

Smith, J. (1999) *Where the Roots Reach for Water*, New York: North Point Press.

Solomon, A. (2001) *The Noonday Demon: An Anatomy of Depression*, London: Chatto & Windus.

Solomon, R.C. (1976) *The Passions: Emotions and the Meaning of Life*, New York: Doubleday.

Solomon, R.C. (1988) On emotions as judgements, *American Philosophical Quarterly*, **25**, pp. 183–191.

Solomon, R.C. (1989) Emotions, philosophy, and the self, in Kaplan, B. Cirillo, L. & Wapner, S. (eds.) *Emotions in Ideal Human Development*, pp. 135–149, Hillsdale, NJ: Lawrence Erlbaum Associates.

Solomon, R.C. (1993) *The Passions: Emotions and the Meaning of Life*, Indianapolis, IN: Hackett.

Solomon, R.C. (2007) *True To Our Feelings: What our Emotions Are Really Telling Us*, Oxford: Oxford University Press.

Solovay, H.K., Shenton, M.E., Gasperetti, C., Coleman, M., Kestnbaum, E., Carpenter, J.T. & Holzman, P.S. (1986) Scoring manual for the Thought Disorder Index, *Schizophrenia Bulletin*, **12**, pp. 483–496.

Spiegel, D., Loewenstein, R.J., Lewis-Fernández, R., Sar, V., Simeon, D., Vermetten, E. & Dell, P.F. (2011) Dissociative disorders in DSM-5, *Depression and Anxiety*, **28** (9), pp. 824–852.

Spitzer, R.L., Gibbon, M., Skodol, A.E., Williams, J.B.W. & First, M.B. (eds.) (2002) *DSM-IV-TR Casebook: A Learning Companion to the Diagnostic and Statistical Manual of Mental Disorders, Fourth Edition, Text Revision*, Arlington, VA: American Psychiatric Publishing.

Stanghellini, G. (2000) The doublets of anger, *Psychopathology*, **33** (4), pp. 155–158.

Stanghellini, G. (2004) *Disembodied Spirits and Deanimatied Bodies: The Psychopathology of Common Sense*, Oxford: Oxford University Press.

Stanghellini, G. & Bertelli, M. (2006) Assessing the social behaviour of unipolar depressives: The criteria for Typus Melancholicus, *Psychopathology*, **39** (4), pp. 179–186.

Stanghellini, G., Bertelli, M. & Raballo, A. (2006) Typus Melancholicus: personality structure and the characteristic of major unipolar depressive episode, *Journal of Affective Disorders*, **93** (1–3), pp. 159–167.

Stanghellini, G. & Rosfort, R. (2013) *Emotions and Personhood: Exploring Fragility — Making Sense of Vulnerability*, Oxford: Oxford University Press.

Starker, S. & Singer, J.L. (1975) Daydreaming and symptom patterns of psychiatric patients: A factor-analytic study, *Journal of Abnormal Psychology*, **84**, pp. 567–570.

Stern, D.N. (1985) *The Interpersonal World of the Infant: A View from Psychoanalysis and Developmental Psychology*, New York: Basic Books.

Stern, D.N. (2010) *Forms of Vitality: Exploring Dynamic Experience in Psychology, the Arts, Psychotherapy, and Development*, New York: Oxford University Press.

Steward, H. (2009) Animal agency, *Inquiry*, **52** (3), pp. 217–231.

Stocker, M. (1983) Psychic feelings, their importance and irreducibility, *Australasian Journal of Philosophy*, **61**, pp. 5–26.

Stocker, M. (1996) with Hegeman, E., *Valuing Emotions*, Cambridge: Cambridge University Press.

Stoerring, G. (1987) Perplexity, in Cutting, J. & Shepherd, M. (eds.) *The Clinical Roots of the Schizophrenia Concept*, pp. 79–82, Cambridge: Cambridge University Press.

Strasser, S. (1956/1977) *Phenomenology of Feeling: An Essay on the Phenomena of the Heart*, Wood, R.E. (trans.), Pittsburgh, PA: Duquesne University Press.

Straus, E.W. (1958) Aesthesiology and hallucinations, in May, R., Angel, E. & Ellenberger, H.F. (eds.) *Existence: A New Dimension in Psychiatry and Psychology*, pp. 139–169, New York: Basic Books.

Stuart, S. (2002) A radical notion of embeddedness: A logically necessary precondition for agency and self-awareness, *Metaphilosophy*, **33** (1/2), pp. 98–109.

Styron, W. (2001) *Darkness Visible*, London: Vintage.

Sullivan, H.S. (1953) *The Interpersonal Theory of Psychiatry*, New York: W.W. Norton and Company.

Svenaeus, F. (2000) *The Hermeneutics of Medicine and the Phenomenology of Health: Steps Towards a Philosophy of Medical Practice*, Dordrecht: Kluwer Academic Publishers.

Svenaeus, F. (2007) Do antidepressants affect the self? A phenomenological approach, *Medicine, Health Care and Philosophy*, **10** (2), pp. 153–166.

Svenaeus, F. (2008) *Tabletter för känsliga själar: Den antidepressiva revolutionen*, Nora: Nya Doxa.

Svenaeus, F. (2009) The ethics of self-change: Becoming oneself by way of antidepressants or psychotherapy?, *Medicine, Health Care and Philosophy*, **12** (2), pp. 169–178.

Tatossian, A. (1997) *La Phenomenologie des Psychoses, L'Art du Comprendre*, Paris: Le Cercle Hermeneutique.

Tavris, C. (1989) *Anger: The Misunderstood Emotion*, revised ed., New York: Simon and Schuster.

Taylor, D. (2008) Psychoanalytic and psychodynamic therapies for depression: The evidence base, *Advances in Psychiatric Treatment*, **14**, pp. 401–413.

Taylor, M.A. (1992) Are schizophrenia and affective disorders related? A selective literature review, *The American Journal of Psychiatry*, **149** (1), pp. 22–32.

Taylor, M.A. & Abrams, R. (1973) The phenomenology of mania: A new look at some old patients, *Archives of General Psychiatry*, **29** (4), pp. 520–522.

Taylor, M.A. & Heiser, J.F. (1971) Phenomenology: An alternative approach to diagnosis of mental disease, *Comprehensive Psychiatry*, **12**, pp. 480–486.

Teasdale, J.D., Moore, R.G., Pope, M., Williams, S. & Segal, Z.V. (2002) Metacognitive awareness and prevention of relapse in depression: Empirical evidence, *Journal of Consulting and Clinical Psychology*, **70**, pp. 275–287.

Tellenbach, H. (1961/1976) *Melancholie. Problemgeschichte, Endogenität, Typologie, Pathogenese, Klinik*, dritte, erweiterte Auflage, Heidelberg: Springer Verlag.

Tellenbach, H. (1980) *Melancholy: History of the Problem, Endogeneity, Typology, Pathogenesis, Clinical Considerations*, Pittsburgh, PA: Duquesne University Press.

Thompson, E. (2007) *Mind in Life: Biology, Phenomenology, and the Sciences of Mind*, Cambridge, MA: Harvard University Press.

Thompson, T. (1995) *The Beast: A Reckoning with Depression*, New York: Putnam.

Thorsrud, H. (2009) *Ancient Scepticism*, Stocksfield: Acumen.

Tölle, R. (1987) Persönlichkeit und Melancholie, *Nervenarzt*, **58**, pp. 327–339.

Tsuang, M.T. & Simpson, J.C. (1984) Schizoaffective disorder: Concept and reality, *Schizophrenia Bulletin*, **10** (1), pp. 14–25.

Undurraga, J. & Baldessarini, R.J. (2012) Randomized, placebo-controlled trials of antidepressants for acute major depression: Thirty-year meta-analytic review, *Neuropsychopharmacology*, **37**, pp. 851–864.

Urfer, A. (2001) Phenomenology and psychopathology of schizophrenia: The views of Eugene Minkowski, *Philosophy, Psychiatry, & Psychology*, **8** (4), pp. 279–289.

van Os, J. (2009) A salience dysregulation syndrome, *British Journal of Psychiatry*, **194**, pp. 101–103.

van Os, J. (2012) Introduction: The extended psychosis phenotype — relationships with schizophrenia and with ultrahigh risk status for psychosis, *Schizophrenia Bulletin*, **38** (2), pp. 227–330.

Van Wingen, G.A., von Eljndhoven, P., Cemers, H.R., Tendolkar, I., *et al.* (2010) Neural state and trait bases of mood-incongruent memory formation and retrieval in first-episode major depression, *Journal of Psychiatric Research*, **44**, pp. 527–534.

Varga, S. (2012) Depersonalization and the sense of realness, *Philosophy, Psychiatry, and Psychology*, **19**, pp. 103–113.

Varela, F., Thompson, E. & Rosch, E. (eds.) (1991) *The Embodied Mind*, Cambridge, MA: MIT Press.

Verster, J.C. (2008) The alcohol hangover — a puzzling phenomenon, *Alcohol & Alcoholism*, **43**, pp. 124–126.

Videbech, P. & Ravnkilde, B. (2004) Hippocampal volume and depression: A meta-analysis of MRI studies, *American Journal of Psychiatry*, **161** (11), pp. 1957–1966.

Vogeley, K. & Gallagher, S. (2011) Self in the brain, in Gallagher, S. (ed.) *The Oxford Handbook of the Self*, pp. 111–136, New York: Oxford University Press.

Vogt, B.A. (2005) Pain and emotion: Interactions in subregions of the cingulate gyrus, *Nature Reviews Neuroscience*, **6**, pp. 533–544.

Vogt, K. (2010) *Stanford Encyclopaedia of Philosophy*, [Online], http://plato.stanford.edu/entries/ skepticism-ancient/ [26 Jan 2012].

von Gebsattel, E. (1937) Zur Frage der Depersonalisation, *Nervenarzt*, **10** (169–178), pp. 248–257.

von Zerssen, D. & Possl, J. (1990) The premorbid personality of patients with different subtypes of an affective illness: Statistical analysis of blind assignment of case history data to clinical diagnoses, *Journal of Affective Disorders*, **18** (1), pp. 39–50.

von Zerssen, D., Tauscher, R. & Possl, J. (1994) The relationship of premorbid personality to subtypes of an affective illness: A replication study by means of an operationalized procedure for the diagnosis of personality structures, *Journal of Affective Disorders*, **32** (1), pp. 61–72.

von Zerssen, D., Asukai, N., Tsuda, H., Ono, Y., Kizaki, Y. & Cho, Y. (1997) Personality traits of Japanese patients in remission from an episode of primary unipolar depression, *Journal of Affective Disorders*, **44** (2), pp. 145–152.

Vuilleumier, P., Armony, J.L., Driver, J. & Dolan, R.J. (2003) Distinct spatial frequency sensitivities for processing faces and emotional expressions, *Nature Neuroscience*, **6** (6), pp. 624–631.

Walter, H. (1998) Emergence and the cognitive neuroscience of psychiatry, *Z Naturforsch*, **53c**, pp. 723–737.

Walter, H., Berger, M. & Schnell, K. (2009a) Neuropsychotherapy: Conceptual, empirical and neuroethical issues, *European Archives of Psychiatry and Clinical Neuroscience*, **259**, pp. 173–182.

Walter, H., Kalckreuth, A., Schardt, D., Stephan, A., Goschke, T. & Erk, S. (2009b) The temporal dynamics of voluntary emotion regulation: Immediate and delayed neural aftereffects, *PLoS ONE*, **4** (8), e6726.

Walter, H. & Michal, M. (in press) Depersonalization disorder, emotion regulation and existential feelings, in Mishara, A., Corlett, P., Fletcher, P. & Schwartz, M. (eds.) *Phenomenological Neuropsychiatry: How Patient Experience Bridges Clinic with Clinical Neuroscience*, Berlin/New York: Springer.

Weber, M. (1904/1949) Objectivity in social science and social policy, in Shils, E.A. & Finch, H.A. (eds.) *The Methodology of the Social Sciences*, pp. 49–112, New York: Free Press.

Wehr, T.A. & Goodwin, F.K. (1983) Biological rhythms in manic-depressive illness, in Wehr, T.A. & Goodwin, F.K. (eds.) *Circadian Rhythms in Psychiatry*, pp. 129–184, Pacific Grove, CA: Boxwood.

Westen, D., Moses, M.J., Silk, K.R., Lohr, N.E., Cohen, R. & Segal H. (1992) Quality of depressive experience in borderline personality disorder: When depression is not just depression, *Journal of Personality Disorder*, **6** (4), pp. 382–393.

Westen, D., Nakash, O., Thomas, C. & Bradley, R. (2006) Clinical assessment of attachment patterns and personality disorder in adolescents and adults, *Journal of Consulting and Clinical Psychology*, **74**, pp. 1065–1085.

Westlund, A. (2009) Rethinking relational autonomy, *Hypatia*, **24** (4), pp. 26–49.

WHO (1993) *The ICD-10 Classification of Mental and Behavioural Disorders: Diagnostic Criteria for Research*, Geneva: World Health Organization.

WHO (2007) *International Statistical Classification of Diseases and Related Health Problems*, 10th ed., Geneva: WHO.

Wiersma, J.E., van Schaik, D.J., Blom, M.B., Bakker, L., van Oppen, P. & Beekman, A.T. (2009) Treatment for chronic depression: Cognitive behavioral analysis system of psychotherapy (CBASP), *Tijdschr Psychiatr*, pp. 727–736.

Wiggins, O.P. & Schwartz, M.A. (1991) Research into personality disorders: The alternatives of dimensions and ideal types, *Journal of Personality Disorders*, **5** (1), pp. 69–81.

Williams, J.M.G. (2001) *Suicide and Attempted Suicide: Understanding the Cry of Pain*, London: Penguin.

Wilutzky, W., Walter, S. & Stephan, A. (2011) Situierte Affektivität, in Slaby, J., Stephan, A., Walter, H. & Walter, S. (eds.) *Affektive Intentionalität: Beiträge zur welterschließenden Funktion der Emotionen*, pp. 283–320, Paderborn: mentis.

Wing, J.K., Cooper, J.E. & Sartorius, N. (1974) *Measurement and Classification of Psychiatric Symptoms: An Instruction Manual for the PSE and Catego Program*, Cambridge: Cambridge University Press.

Wittgenstein, L. (1969) *On Certainty*, Anscombe, G.E.M. & von Wright, G.H. (eds.), Oxford: Basil Blackwell.

Wolf, S. (1990) *Freedom Within Reason*, Oxford: Oxford University Press.

Wolpert, D.M. & Ghahramani, Z. (2000) Computational principles of movement neuroscience, *Nature Neuroscience*, **3** (Suppl. November), pp. 1212–1217.

Woolf, V. (1930/2002) *On Being Ill*, Ashfield, MA: Paris Press.

World Health Organization (1992) *The ICD-10 Classification of Mental and Behavioural Disorders: Clinical Descriptions and Diagnostic Guidelines*, Geneva: World Health Organization.

Wright, S., Young, A.W. & Hellawell, D.J. (1993) Sequential Cotard and Capgras delusions, *British Journal of Clinical Psychology*, **32**, pp. 345–349.

Wyllie, M. (2005) Lived time and psychopathology, *Philosophy, Psychiatry, & Psychology*, **12**, pp. 173–185.

Young, A.W., Leafhead, K.M. & Szulecka, T.K. (1994) The Capgras and Cotard delusions, *Psychopathology*, **27**, pp. 226–231.

Young, I.M. (2005) *On Female Body Experience*, Oxford: Oxford University Press.

Zahavi, D. (2005) *Subjectivity and Selfhood*, Cambridge, MA: MIT Press.

Zahavi, D. (2011) Unity of consciousess and the problem of self, in Gallagher, S. (ed.) *The Oxford Handbook of the Self*, Oxford: Oxford University Press.

Zanarini, M.C. & Frankenburg, F.R. (1997) Pathways to the development of borderline personality disorder, *Journal of Personality Disorders*, **11** (1), pp. 93–104.

Zanarini, M.C., Frankenburg, F.R., Hennen, J. & Silk, K.R. (2003) The longitudinal course of borderline psychopathology: 6 year prospective follow up of the phenomenology of borderline personality disorder, *American Journal of Psychiatry*, **160**, pp. 274–283.

Zobel, I., Werden, D., Linster, H., Dykierek, P., Drieling, T., Berger, M. & Schramm, E. (2010) Theory of mind deficits in chronically depressed patients, *Depression and Anxiety*, pp. 821–888.

Chapter Abstracts

Benson, Gibson & Brand

Based on a qualitative study with 124 participants we explore what is in ordinary language referred to as 'suicidal feelings'. We identify four interrelated aspects of this experience, which together suggest that 'suicidal feelings' is in fact a 'feeling of being suicidal', an existential feeling. Although each experience is unique in its presentation, it is also the case that people who are suicidal tend to experience a combination of the following: 1) loss of consistency and/ or coherence in their sense of self; 2) a disruption in the reciprocal action between self and world; 3) serious depletion of their mental resources; and 4) a disturbance of embodiment. We then argue that 'the feeling of being suicidal' should be understood as a disruption in the experience of the self as an agent and that this forms the appropriate background for interpreting suicidal thoughts and intentions.

Buchheim, Viviani & Walter

Attachment is the way we relate to others. The way we attach to others is developed early in childhood, can be impaired by early traumatic life events, and is disturbed in many psychiatric disorders. Here we give a short overview about attachment patterns in psychiatric disorders with a focus on depression, and discuss two recent empirical studies of our own that have investigated attachment related brain activation using fMRI. In the first study with patients with borderline personality disorder we used a paradigm in which patients produced narratives in response to attachment pictures and measured brain activity while participants were talking. Our results are consistent with the view that BPD pathology might be correlated with traumatic attachment fear related to autobiographic abuse and loss experiences. In the second study we investigated patients with major depression undergoing therapy in a longitudinal design. In this study we used a design with individualized stimuli that were extracted from narratives produced outside of the scanner. We found that patients, as compared to healthy controls, showed differences in a pre–post comparison. The significant correlation of changes in the subgenual cingulate and medial prefrontal cortex with symptom improvement provides evidence that these regions are involved in mediating therapy related effects.

Carel

In this chapter I explore the tacit underlying sense of bodily certainty that characterizes normal everyday embodied experience. I then propose illness as one instance in which this certainty breaks down and is replaced by bodily doubt. I characterize bodily doubt as radically modifying our experience in three ways: loss of continuity, loss of transparency, and loss of faith in one's body. I then discuss the philosophical insights that arise from the experience of bodily doubt. The paper uses a Humean framework with regards to bodily certainty, treating it as a taken for granted tacit aspect of normal experience. I argue that although bodily certainty is not rationally justifiable, we are nonetheless unable to reject it. Bodily certainty is thus revealed to be part of our brute animal nature. I conclude by suggesting that the study of pathology is a philosophical method useful for illuminating tacit aspects of experience.

Csordas

Working toward a phenomenological account of depression, this chapter suggests that the relevant level of analysis is that of experiential immediacy based on intersubjectivity. The argument focuses on the experience of one boy and one girl who participated in the study Southwest Youth and the Experience of Psychiatric Treatment (SWYEPT), in which we followed the experience of adolescent psychiatric inpatients and their families over the course of a year. I emphasize the role of language as a form of disclosure and empathy in the interview setting in elaborating a set of criteria for inferring immediacy from interview data, and point to how illness experience is bound up with domains of the life-world such as relationships, religion, morality, reflexivity, identity, and treatment.

Fuchs

According to current opinion in western psychopathology, depression is regarded as a disorder of mood and affect on the one hand, and as a distortion of cognition on the other. Disturbances of bodily experience and of social relations are regarded as secondary to the primarily 'inner' and individual disorder. However, quite different concepts can be found in cultures whose members do not experience themselves as much as separate individuals but rather as parts of social communities. Disorders of mood or well-being are then conceived less as intra-psychic, but rather as bodily, interpersonal, or atmospheric processes.

On this background, the chapter describes depression as a disorder of intercorporeality and interaffectivity. After developing these phenomenological concepts, it analyses depression as a 'detunement' of the resonant body that mediates our participation in a shared affective space. Instead of expressing the self, the body is turned into a barrier to all impulses directed to the environment. This impairs particularly the patient's interaction with others, resulting in a general sense of detachment, separation, or even segregation. Moreover, the restriction of the lived body also corresponds to the triggering situations of depression, namely experiences of a disruption of social bonds. Thus, intercorporeality and interaffectivity are presented as crucial dimensions for an ecological and non-reductionist view of depression.

Gaebler, Lamke, Daniels & Walter

Describing, understanding, and explaining subjective experience in depression is a great challenge for psychopathology. Attempts to uncover neurobiological mechanisms of those experiences are in need of theoretical concepts that are able to bridge phenomenological descriptions and neurocognitive approaches, which allow us to measure indicators of those experiences in quantitative terms. Based on our own ongoing work with patients who suffer from depersonalization disorder (DPD) and describe their experience as flat and detached from self, body, and world, we introduce the idea of phenomenal depth as such a concept. Phenomenal depth is conceptualized as a dimension inherent to all experiences, describing the relatedness of one's self with one's mental processes, body, and the world. More precisely, it captures the experience of this relatedness and embeddedness of one's experiences, and it is thus a meta- or second-order experience. The psychopathology of DPD patients can be understood very generally as an instance of reduced phenomenal depth. We will argue that similar experiences in depression can also be understood as a reduction in phenomenal depth. We relate those ideas to neurocognitive studies of perception, emotion regulation, and the idea of predictive coding. Finally, we will speculate about possible neuro-biological underpinnings of the dimension of phenomenal depth.

Gerrans & Scherer

Although depression is characterized as a mood disorder it turns out that, like moods in general, it cannot be explained independently of a theory of emotion. In this chapter we outline one promising theory of emotion (Multicomponential Appraisal Theory) and show how it deals with the phenomenon of depressive mood. An important aspect of MAT is the role it assigns to peripheral information processing systems in setting up emotional responses. The operations of these systems are automatic and opaque to consciousness, but they represent information about the significance of the environment for the subject, bias cognition and behaviour, and have a characteristic phenomenology. We show how understanding the nature of peripheral appraisal provides a principled way to link neurochemistry and mood via an information processing theory of the circuitry targeted by antidepressant treatment. The discussion is organized around Matthew Ratcliffe's distinction between pre-intentional and intentional feelings and suggests that the MAT might provide a way to link phenomenological and mechanistic accounts of feeling states characteristic of depression.

Radden

This discussion is about the moods characteristic of depressive and manic states. Moods are distinguished from the emotions they often accompany, and the relationship between these less and more cognitive, and seemingly less and more intentional, states is provided preliminary clarification. Epistemic deficiencies identified here, when combined with differences of quality and quantity in the moods and motivations that beset the depression and mania sufferer, seem likely to hinder self-knowledge and self-integration. These deficiencies, it is argued, may help explain why the extreme moods found in states of depression and mania contribute to our inclination to regard these conditions as disorder.

Ratcliffe, Broome, Smith & Bowden

This chapter argues that the DSM diagnostic category 'major depression' is so permissive that it fails to distinguish the phenomenology of depression from a general 'feeling of being ill' that is associated with a range of somatic illnesses. We start by emphasizing that altered bodily experience is a conspicuous and commonplace symptom of depression. We add that the experience of somatic illness is not exclusively bodily; it can involve more pervasive experiential changes that are not dissimilar to those associated with depression. Then we consider some recent work on inflammation and depression, which suggests that the experience of depression and the 'feeling of being ill' are, in some cases at least, much the same (thus calling into question a more general distinction between psychiatric and somatic illness). However, we add that the phenomenology of depression is heterogeneous and that many cases involve additional or different symptoms. We conclude that 'major depression' is a placeholder for a range of different experiences, which are almost certainly aetiologically diverse too.

Sass & Pienkos, Part I

This chapter provides a critical survey of some subtle and often overlooked disturbances of self-experience that can occur in schizophrenia, melancholia, and mania. The goal is to better understand both similarities and differences between these conditions. We present classical and contemporary studies, mostly from the phenomenological tradition, and illustrate these with patient reports. Experiential changes in five domains of selfhood (following Parnas et al., 2005) are considered: Cognition, Self-Awareness, Bodily Experiences, Demarcation/Transitivism, and Existential Reorientation. We discuss: I. major differences involving self-experience between schizophrenia and affective disorders; II. experiences in which these conditions nevertheless resemble each other; III. suggestions on how these experiences may still differ on a more subtle, phenomenological plane. While affective patients may undergo significant changes in self-experience, their underlying sense of basic or minimal selfhood ('ipseity') remains intact. In schizophrenia, basic self is disturbed, and this may help to account for many characteristic disturbances of this disorder.

Sass & Pienkos, Part II

This chapter offers a comparative study of abnormalities in the experience of space, time, and general atmosphere in three psychiatric conditions: schizophrenia, melancholia, and mania. It is a companion piece to our previous article entitled 'Varieties of Self- Experience'; here we focus on experiences of the world rather than of the self. As before, we are especially interested in similarities but also in some subtle distinctions in the forms of subjectivity associated with these three conditions. As before, we survey phenomenologically-oriented clinical and theoretical accounts as well as patient reports. Experiences involving forms of alienation from the practical and social world and a sense of uncanniness seem to be common in both schizophrenia and affective disorders. But despite some significant similarities, changes in schizophrenic subjectivity appear to be more pervasive and profound, involving experiences of fragmentation, meaninglessness, and ineffable strangeness that are rare or absent in the affective disorders.

Slaby, Paskaleva & Stephan

We propose an action-oriented understanding of emotion. Emotions are modifications of a basic form of goal-oriented striving characteristic of human life. They are appetitive orientations: pursuits of the good, avoidances of the bad. Thus, emotions are not truly distinct from, let alone opposed to, actions — as erroneously suggested by the classical understanding of emotions as 'passions'. In this chapter, we will outline and defend this broadly enactive approach and motivate its main claims. Our proposal gains plausibility from a literature- and interview-based investigation of emotional changes characteristic of clinical depression. Much narrative evidence from patient reports points towards the conclusion that many of those changes might result from a catastrophic alteration of the basic form of goal-pursuit at the root of human emotionality. The experience of profound depression could in this respect be a kind of inverted image of non-pathological emotionality — a highly unnatural passivity, giving rise to a profound — and quite horrifying — sense of incapacity.

Stanghellini & Rosfort

Persons with borderline personality disorder are often described as affected by extreme emotional fluctuations and by the sudden emergence of uncontrollable and disproportionate emotional reactions. Borderline persons frequently experience their own self as dim and fuzzy, are deprived of a stable sense of identity and unable to be steadily involved in a given life project. We will interpret these typical features as fluctuations between a clearly normative emotion such as anger and the more diffuse and confusing background of bad moods like dysphoria. Our main focus will be on dysphoria. The intentional structure that characterizes much of human emotional experience, we shall argue, is absent in dysphoria. If we imagine emotions as fluxes of intentionality that innervate the body and connect it to the world, dysphoria is empty intentionality, so to speak, devoid of the moderating power of language and representation. Dysphoria exerts a centrifugal force which fragments the borderline person's representations of herself and of others, inducing a painful experience of incoherence and inner emptiness, a feeling of uncertainty and inauthenticity in interpersonal relationships, and an excruciating sense of futility and inanity of life. But it also entails a sense of vitality, although a disorganized, aimless, and explosive one — a desperate vitality.

Svenaeus

This chapter will explore the relationship between selfhood and depression, by focusing upon the lived body's capacity to 'resonate' with the world and thus open up an 'attuned' space of meaning. Persons will become differently tuned in different situations because they embody different patterns of resonance — what is most often referred to as different temperaments — but the self may also suffer from idiosyncrasies in mood profile that develop into deficiencies of resonance, making the person in question ill. In many cases of depression one might describe this as a being out of tune in the sense of being oversensitive to the sad, anxious, and boring tune qualities of the world. This phenomenological model allows us to describe a spectrum of various normal sensitivities which might favour certain moods over others, but also to identify pathologies, like depression, in which the body is out of tune and makes the being-in-the-world overwhelmingly unhomelike.

About Authors

Outi Benson is the Research Manager at the mental health charity SANE. Since graduating from University of London (Birkbeck College) with an MPhil in Philosophy, she has worked in the area of mental health research. Her main focus is on the subjective experience of mental health problems and how service user insights can be combined with philosophical theory and used to inform the science of psychopathology and care development. She is the chief investigator on three recent qualitative studies into suicide and self-harm.

Hannah Bowden is a PhD student in the Philosophy Department at Durham University. She works in phenomenology and philosophy of psychiatry with particular interests in the phenomenology of depression, bipolar disorder, and eating disorders.

Sarah L. Brand completed a PhD in Cognitive Psychology at UCL in 2007 and, after working as a Research Psychologist at Great Ormond Street Hospital and a Postdoctoral Researcher at Melbourne University, joined the SANE research team for a period of two years. She is now a Research Fellow at the University of Exeter Medical School, working on projects relating to health and well-being and the environment.

Matthew Broome is Senior Clinical Research Fellow in the Department of Psychiatry at the University of Oxford. Recent work has examined the prodromal phase of psychosis and the formation of delusions as well as the clinical correlates of mood dysregulation. He co-edited *Psychiatry as Cognitive Neuroscience: Philosophical Perspectives* (OUP 2009) and *The Maudsley Reader in Phenomenological Psychiatry* (CUP 2013). He is currently working on the connection between mood instability and paranoia, the relationship between autism and schizophrenia, and issues of responsibility in mental illness.

Anna Buchheim completed her diploma in Psychology at the University of Regensburg and got her PhD and venia legendi at the University of Ulm. She is now Full Professor for Clinical Psychology at the University Innsbruck, Psychoanalyst (IPA). Her research interests are attachment research, narrative approaches, psychotherapy research, psychoanalysis, and neuroimaging.

Havi Carel is Senior Lecturer in Philosophy at the University of Bristol. She is currently a British Academy Fellow, writing on a monograph for OUP on the phenomenology of illness. She is the author of *Illness* (Acumen 2008), shortlisted for the Wellcome Trust Book Prize, and of *Life and Death in Freud and Heidegger* (Rodopi 2006). She is the co-editor of *Health, Illness and Disease* (Acumen 2012), *New Takes in Film-Philosophy* (Palgrave 2010), and *What Philosophy Is* (Continuum 2004). She recently co-edited a special issue of *Philosophy* on 'Phenomenology and Naturalism' (CUP 2013). In 2009–11 Havi led an AHRC-funded project on the concepts of health, illness, and disease, and in 2011–12 she was awarded a Leverhulme Fellowship.

Thomas Csordas received his PhD in Anthropology from Duke University in 1980, and is currently Professor of Anthropology at UCSD, where he is also Founding Director of the Global Health Minor. He has served as co-editor of *Ethos* (1996–2001) and as President of the Society for the Anthropology of Religion (1998–2002). His research interests include anthropological theory, comparative religion, medical and psychological anthropology, cultural phenomenology and embodiment, globalization and social change, and language and culture. Recent publications include *Body/Meaning/Healing* (Palgrave 2002); and (edited) *Transnational Transcendence: Essays on Religion and Globalization* (University of California Press 2009).

Judith Daniels is a Postdoctoral Fellow in the Division of Mind and Brain Research at the Charité - Universitätsmedizin Berlin. She also completed postdoctoral fellowships in the Department of Neuropsychiatry at the University of Western Ontario and in the Department of Child and Adolescent Psychiatry at the University Medical Center Eppendorf. Her research focuses on altered experiencing of self and others during chronic depersonalization and acute dissociation, bottom-up processes as the basis of pathological emotion regulation, variability in complex trauma sequelae such as complex PTSD, and interdependencies between alteration of the resting-state and the functional processing of emotions and self.

Thomas Fuchs is Karl Jaspers Professor of Philosophy and Psychiatry, and Head of the Phenomenology Section at the Psychiatric Department, University of Heidelberg. He is Coordinator of the European Research Project 'TESIS' (Towards an Embodied Science of Intersubjectivity, www.tesis-itn.eu). His main research areas are in phenomenological psychology, psychopathology, and theory of neuroscience.

Michael Gaebler is a doctoral student in the Division of Mind and Brain Research at the Department for Psychiatry and Psychotherapy of the Charité - Universitätsmedizin Berlin. He completed a Dual-Masters in 'Brain and Mind Sciences' at the Ecole Normale Supérieure in Paris and University College London. After having focused on language from several perspectives, he is now interested in explicitly non-verbal, affective mental processes and in bridging phenomenology in philosophy and psychiatry by means of neuroimaging.

Philip Gerrans is Professor in the Philosophy Department at the University of Adelaide. His main research interest is the use of psychological disorder to study the mind. He has written on developmental disorders (autism and Williams syndrome), cognitive neuropsychiatry, and, more recently, on moral psychopathologies (such as psychopathology) and the emotions.

Susanne Gibson studied philosophy at Cardiff University and has teaching and research expertise in medical ethics. She joined the research team at SANE in 2010 , where she has been able to continue to use her training in philosophy to explore the real world, this time working on a programme of qualitative research into first-person experiences of suicide.

Jan-Peter Lamke is a doctoral student in the Division of Mind and Brain Research at the Department for Psychiatry and Psychotherapy at the Charité - Universitätsmedizin Berlin. He completed a Masters in Neuroscience at the University of Bremen. He is interested in the interplay between task and rest in emotional and self-related processing and in linking psychiatric research to current debates in the philosophy of mind.

Asena Paskaleva is a PhD student at the Institute of Cognitive Science at the University of Osnabrück, Germany. She works on narratives of depression within the *animal emotionale* research group.

Elizabeth Pienkos is an advanced doctoral student in Clinical Psychology at the Graduate School of Applied and Professional Psychology, Rutgers University. She is interested in the phenomenology of schizophrenia and other psychoses and in applying phenomenology to clinical practice.

Jennifer Radden is Professor of Philosophy Emerita at the University of Massachusetts Boston and Ethics Consultant at McLean Hospital. She received her graduate training at Oxford, and has published extensively on mental health concepts, the history of medicine, and ethical and policy aspects of psychiatric theory and practice. Her recent books include edited collections *The Nature of Melancholy* (2000) and *Oxford Companion to the Philosophy of Psychiatry* (2004), and monographs *Moody Minds Distempered: Essays on Melancholy and Depression* (2009), *The Virtuous Psychiatrist: Character Ethics in Psychiatric Practice*, co-authored with Dr John Sadler (2010), and *On Delusion* (2011).

Matthew Ratcliffe is Professor of Philosophy at Durham University. Most of his recent work addresses issues in phenomenology, philosophy of psychology, and philosophy of psychiatry. He is author of *Rethinking Commonsense Psychology: A Critique of Folk Psychology, Theory of Mind and Simulation* (Palgrave 2007) and *Feelings of Being: Phenomenology, Psychiatry and the Sense of Reality* (OUP 2008). Topics he is currently working on include empathy, the phenomenology of depression, and the nature of auditory verbal hallucinations.

René Rosfort studied philosophy and theology in Copenhagen and Florence, and in 2008 he received his PhD in Ethics and Philosophy from the Centre for Subjectivity Research, University of Copenhagen. He is currently working as a Postdoctoral Fellow at the Søren Kierkegaard Research Centre, University of Copenhagen, on a project concerning Kierkegaard, psychopathology, and naturalism.

Louis A. Sass is Distinguished Professor in the Department of Clinical Psychology at Rutgers University. He is the author of many articles on phenomenological psychopathology, as well as of *Madness and Modernism: Insanity in the Light of Modern Art, Literature, and*

Thought and *The Paradoxes of Delusion: Wittgenstein, Schreber, and the Schizophrenic Mind*.

Klaus Scherer is Professor Emeritus at the University of Geneva. His major research interest is in the further theoretical development and empirical test of his Component Process Model of Emotion (CPM), specifically the modelling of appraisal-driven processes of motor expression and physiological reaction patterns, as well as the reflection of these processes in subjective experience. Other major research foci consist of the study of the expression of affect in voice and speech and applied emotion research.

Jan Slaby is Assistant Professor in Philosophy of Mind at Freie Universität Berlin. He is a researcher in the interdisciplinary cluster 'Languages of Emotion', funded within the German Excellence Initiative until 2014. He obtained his PhD in Philosophy and Cognitive Science at the University of Osnabrück in 2006 with a thesis on affective intentionality. He is the co-initiator of the 'critical neuroscience' initiative (www.critical-neuroscience.org) that engages with methodological, social, and institutional issues surrounding the booming human neurosciences.

Benedict Smith is currently Teaching Fellow in the Department of Philosophy at Durham University. His recent research has focused on topics in moral philosophy such as the nature of motivation, trust, the role of character in moral action, and the nature of values in psychiatry. He is author of *Particularism and the Space of Moral Reasons* (Palgrave Macmillan 2011).

Giovanni Stanghellini is Professor of Dynamic Psychology and Psychopathology at 'G. d'Annunzio' University (Chieti, Italy), and Profesor Adjuncto at 'D. Portales' University (Santiago, Chile). He has written extensively on the philosophical foundations of psychopathology, especially from a phenomenological and anthropological viewpoint. He is co-editor of the series *International Perspectives in Philosophy and Psychiatry*. His books, all published by OUP, include *Emotions and Personhood* (with R. Rosfort, 2013), *One Hundred Years of Karl Jaspers' General Psychopathology* (edited with T. Fuchs, 2013), and *The Oxford Handbook of Philosophy of Psychiatry* (edited with K. Fulford *et al.*, 2013).

Achim Stephan is Professor for Philosophy of Cognition at the Institute of Cognitive Science at the University of Osnabrück. Recently, he was a member of two research groups at the Center for Interdisciplinary Research (Bielefeld) on 'Emotions as Bio-Cultural Processes' and on 'Embodied Communication in Humans and Machines'. He was the speaker of two research groups on *animal emotionale* funded from 2005–09 and from 2009–13 by the Volkswagen foundation within the research initiative 'Key Issues in the Humanities'. Together with Matthew Ratcliffe he directed the bi-national research project 'Emotional Experience in Depression — a philosophical study', funded by both the German DFG and the British AHRC.

Fredrik Svenaeus is Professor of Philosophy at the Centre for Studies in Practical Knowledge, Södertörn University, Sweden. His main research areas are philosophy of medicine, bioethics, medical humanities, and philosophical anthropology. He has published a number of articles and books on these subjects, most often from a phenomenological viewpoint. Two recent examples are: 'The Relevance of Heidegger's Philosophy of Technology for Biomedical Ethics' (*Theoretical Medicine and Bioethics* 2013); 'Anorexia Nervosa and the Body Uncanny: A Phenomenological Approach' (*Philosophy, Psychiatry, & Psychology*, 2013).

Roberto Viviani completed his medical and specialist training in psychiatry, and then took his PhD at Cambridge University. He works on developing and applying neuroimaging methods to the investigation of psychiatric illness. His area of expertise covers neuroimaging data in novel modalities, such as perfusion imaging, and their application to the investigation of genetic polymorphisms relevant for psychopharmacology and affect regulation.

Henrik Walter is Full Professor for Psychiatry, Psychiatric Neuroscience and Neurophilosophy at the Charité - Universitätsmedizin Berlin. He graduated in medicine and philosophy from the Justus-Liebig-University in Giessen, holds a PhD in philosophy, and is board certified in psychiatry and pychotherapy as well as in neurology. His research focuses on cognitive neuroscience in psychiatry, philosophy of mind, and neuroethics, ranging from executive function, emotion and motivation, interaction of emotion and cognition to social cognition, volition, and imaging genetics.

Index